Politics and Sociology

Pierre Bourdieu

Politics and Sociology

General Sociology, Volume 5

Lectures at the Collège de France (1985–1986)

Edited by Patrick Champagne and Julien Duval,
with the collaboration of Franck Poupeau
and Marie-Christine Rivière

Translated by Peter Collier

polity

First published in French in *Sociologie générale. Volume 2. Cours au Collège de France* (1983–1986) © Éditions Raisons d'Agir/Éditions du Seuil, 2016

This English edition © Polity Press, 2023

Polity Press
65 Bridge Street
Cambridge CB2 1UR, UK

Polity Press
111 River Street
Hoboken, NJ 07030, USA

All rights reserved. Except for the quotation of short passages for the purpose of criticism and review, no part of this publication may be reproduced, stored in a retrieval system or transmitted, in any form or by any means, electronic, mechanical, photocopying, recording or otherwise, without the prior permission of the publisher.

ISBN-13: 9781509526727 hardback

A catalogue record for this book is available from the British Library.

Library of Congress Control Number: 2023932268

Typeset in 10.5 on 12 pt Times NR MT Pro
by Cheshire Typesetting Ltd, Cuddington, Cheshire
Printed and bound in Great Britain by CPI Group (UK) Ltd, Croydon

The publisher has used its best endeavours to ensure that the URLs for external websites referred to in this book are correct and active at the time of going to press. However, the publisher has no responsibility for the websites and can make no guarantee that a site will remain live or that the content is or will remain appropriate.

Every effort has been made to trace all copyright holders, but if any have been overlooked the publisher will be pleased to include any necessary credits in any subsequent reprint or edition.

For further information on Polity, visit our website:
politybooks.com

Contents

Editorial Note	viii
Acknowledgements	x

Lecture of 17 April 1986   **1**
First session (lecture): recapitulation – Symbolic capital
– Cognition and misrecognition – Symbolic power as
fetish – Socialisation through social structures – A political
phenomenology of experience – Nostalgia for a lost paradise –
From *doxa* to orthodoxy – Returning to symbolic power
Second session (seminar): biography and social trajectory (1)
– The problem of the unity of the self – The unity of the self
across different spaces – The name as foundation of the socially
constituted individual – Curriculum vitae, *cursus honorum*,
criminal record, school reports

Lecture of 24 April 1986   **28**
First session (lecture): the *fidēs*, a historical realisation of
symbolic capital – An ethnology of the unconscious – The
examples of ethnicity and the designer label – The habitus as
determination and as sensitivity
Second session (seminar): biography and social trajectory (2)
– Importing a literary break – Establishing consistency – The
space of biographical discourse – From the life story to the
analysis of trajectories

vi   *Contents*

Lecture of 15 May 1986   **58**
First session (lecture): a dispositional solution – The
independence of the habitus from the present – Prediction,
protention and projection – Changing the habitus – Power – The
petit-bourgeois relation to culture
Second session (seminar): *To the Lighthouse* (1) – Fields as traps
– A man-child – Men, oblates of the social world

Lecture of 22 May 1986   **86**
First session (lecture): summary of previous lectures – Socialised
individual and abstract individual – Habitus and the principle
of choice – Mental structures and objective structures – The
magical match of the body with the world – The false problem
of responsibility – Coincidence of positions and dispositions –
Amor fati
Second session (seminar): *To the Lighthouse* (2) – Incorporating
the political – Paternal power and the verdict effect – The
somatisation of social crises – *Metamorphosis* and the founding
experience of primordial power

Lecture of 29 May 1986   **114**
First session (lecture): the division of labour in the production of
representations – A theory of action – The conditions of rational
decision – The problem as such does not exist – Deliberation as
accident – A broader rationalism – Alternatives and logic of the
field
Second session (seminar): the field of power (1) – The field
of power and differentiation of the fields – The emergence of
universes 'as such' – Power over capital – Power and its
legitimisation

Lecture of 5 June 1986   **140**
First session (lecture): eternal false problems – The alternative of
mechanism and purposiveness, and the conditions of rationality
– Scientific oppositions and political oppositions – The practical
mastery of structures – Imposing the right point of view
Second session (seminar): the field of power (2) – The example
of the 'capacities' – Educational system, *numerus clausus* and
social reproduction – The search for stable forms of capital –
The strategies of reproduction according to species of capital
– Sociodicy and ideology

Contents

Lecture of 12 June 1986   **170**

First session (lecture): the space of positions and the space of standpoints – The representation of the social world at stake – A collective construction – A cognitive struggle – Making the implicit explicit – The specificity of the scientific field
Second session (seminar): the field of power (3) – Boundaries of the fields and right of entry – The example of the literary field – Flow of capital and variations in the exchange rate – Establishing a new mode of reproduction – Maxwell's demon

Lecture of 19 June 1986   **197**

Practical struggles and struggles among theoreticians – The struggles of the professional explicators – Science of science and relativism – Science as a social field – A rationalist relativism – The vulnerability of social science – The Gerschenkron effect – The problem of the existence of social classes – 'Class': a well-constructed fiction – Constructed classes and infra-representational classes – The constructivist phase

Situating the Later Volumes of *General Sociology* in the Work of Pierre Bourdieu   **225**

Summary of Lectures of 1985–86   **243**

Notes   248
Index   281

Editorial Note

This book forms part of the ongoing publication of Pierre Bourdieu's lectures at the Collège de France. A few months after his final lecture in this institute in March 2001 Bourdieu had published under the title of *Science of Science and Reflexivity*[1] a condensed version of the last year of his course (2000–1). After his death, *On the State* was published in 2012, followed by *Manet: A Symbolic Revolution* in 2013, corresponding to the lectures that he gave in 1989–92 and 1998–2000 respectively.[2] The publication of the 'General Sociology' lectures that he gave during the first five years of his teaching at the Collège de France, between April 1982 and June 1986, was then started. A first volume appeared in 2015, collecting the lectures given during the 1981–82 and 1982–83 academic years.[3] The second French volume collects the three following academic years. This English translation presents the third of those years, 1985–86, with its eight two-hour lectures.

This edition of 'General Sociology' follows the editorial options defined at the moment of publication of the lectures on the State, which aim to reconcile faithfulness with readability.[4] The published text represents a transcription of the lectures as they were given. In the great majority of cases, the transcription used in the present publication relies on recordings. However, for some of the lectures the recordings could not be found and the text published here is based on the literal transcriptions that Bernard Convert made for his personal use. He kindly sent them to us and we are very grateful to him. Finally, in one case (part of the lecture for 7 March 1985, in *Principles of Vision: General Sociology, Volume 4*), lacking any recording or transcription, Bourdieu's argument has been reconstructed using the only material available: Bernard Convert's notes from the lecture.

As in the previous volumes, the passage from the spoken to the written word has required some minor rewriting, which scrupulously

Editorial Note ix

respects the approach applied by Bourdieu himself when he revised his own lectures and seminars: making stylistic corrections and emending oral infelicities (repetitions and linguistic tics, etc.). On one or two exceptional occasions only, we have curtailed the development of an argument, when the state of the recordings did not allow us to reproduce it in a satisfactory manner. The words or passages that were ambiguous or inaudible or that reflected a momentary interruption in the recording have been signalled thus [. . .] when it was impossible to recover them, and have been placed between brackets when their accuracy could not be guaranteed.

Acknowledgements

The editors would like to thank Bruno Auerbach, Amélie and Louise Bourdieu, Pascal Durand, Johan Heilbron, Remi Lenoir, Amín Perez, Jocelyne Pichot and Louis Pinto for their collaboration. They particularly wish to thank Bernard Convert and Thibaut Izard for their continual and often essential help.

Lecture of 17 April 1986

First session (lecture): recapitulation – Symbolic capital – Cognition and misrecognition – Symbolic power as fetish – Socialisation through social structures – A political phenomenology of experience – Nostalgia for a lost paradise – From doxa *to orthodoxy – Returning to symbolic power*
Second session (seminar): biography and social trajectory (1) – The problem of the unity of the self – The unity of the self across different spaces – The name as foundation of the socially constituted individual – Curriculum vitae, cursus honorum, *criminal record, school reports*

First session (lecture): recapitulation

I shall start by reminding you of the general direction of my lecture course, which I shall continue today as it enters what I think will be its last stage. I had developed a series of analyses in which I set out the notion of the habitus in relation to the notion of the field. In the first set of lectures, a few years ago, I spelled out the theoretical presumptions that underlie the notion of the habitus, and the reasons why I introduced this notion instead of the purposive or mechanist philosophies normally used to account for any action. Then I went on to describe what I understood by the notion of the field, making a distinction between two procedures: after a first approach that you might call physicalist, consisting in analysing the field as a field of forces, I proceeded last year to analyse the field in terms of a field of struggles. While moving between the two, I considered the relation between the habitus and the field: the field of forces becomes a field of struggles when it is composed of social agents endowed with categories of perception and appreciation, and perceiving this field as a site of conflict.

Lecture of 17 April 1986

I showed that the structure of the field as a field of forces is defined through the structure of the distribution of capital: what makes the structure of a field is the distribution of the elements that constitute the field, which I name species of capital. I analysed the different forms of capital, with the different advantages they offer as tools for the struggle in a field. At that point I announced a further study of the interplay of forces within what I call the field of power – the space where these different forces, different species of capital and their diverse advantages come into conflict. I continued (in my course of lectures last year) with a sociology of the perception of the social world, through an analysis of the social agents' arguments about the social world. I indicated that we need to distinguish between a field of forces and a field of struggles in the social world, for the social world is not simply a site where forces are felt. Social agents are not simply particles entering a field of forces: they are endowed with faculties of perception and appreciation, which means that their representation of the world they inhabit, and which subjects them to its forces, helps to define their actions in this world. Their representation of the social world depends on the one hand on their position in this world, and on the other hand on the categories of perception and appreciation they have acquired during their previous experience of the world which constitutes their habitus.

This sociology of perception led on to an analysis of the interplay of symbolic powers and an analysis of the social world as the site of a struggle for the legitimate vision of the world, which I called the *nomos*, in the original sense of the word (the law), but also in the sense of the principle of vision and division; this struggle is a fight for the legitimate principle of vision and division, or indeed for the legitimate principle of distribution. In my last lecture, I attempted to restate this analysis in a sort of history of representations of our knowledge of the social world. In so doing, I reminded you that, in order to conceive this perception of the social world in these terms – not simply as an act of cognition but as an inextricably cognitive and political act – we had to integrate approaches that are normally incompatible. What we might call a Kantian or neo-Kantian approach insists on the fact that the world is apprehended through universal cognitive structures. I showed that we could trace the genealogy of these cognitive structures, and then that these cognitive structures existed in an objectified state in the form of structured and structuring symbolic systems, such as language and culture and so on. I then underlined the fact that, in our differentiated societies, these structuring and structured systems are produced by the efforts of specialists, such as religious or intellectual agents. Consequently what we might call – to conflate two notions

Lecture of 17 April 1986 3

that philosophical tradition finds conflictual – a 'sociology of symbolic forms'[1] depends on a sociology of the specialised fields of production, of which the religious field is one typical example.

Symbolic capital

Having set out the argument that I wish to pursue today, I would like now to try to tease out the logic of the symbolic struggle. Symbolic struggles enjoy a certain independence from struggles oriented towards material gains. They have their own specific logic, whether in the case of the everyday symbolic struggles among ordinary agents, which have been particularly well described by the sociological traditions of inter-actionism or ethnomethodology, or in the case of struggles between professionals, such as those that take place within specialised fields (such as the religious, intellectual or artistic fields).

These symbolic struggles are politico-cognitive struggles: they have cognitive repercussions that engender political consequences. Here the social agents confronting each other are unequally armed for the struggle, since the specific weapon used in these struggles is what I call symbolic capital, a notion that I must now try to explain in detail. When in a previous lecture I analysed the different species of capital, I withheld the notion of symbolic capital, insofar as the logic of my procedure prevented me from introducing it, because I was exploring a physicalist position and I had not yet introduced the relation of agents to their capital. Yet it seems to me that symbolic capital exists, in a way, in the relation between any form of capital and the social agents who apprehend it, whether according to the categories of perception imposed by the form of capital considered, or according to the categories of perception organised or imposed by the structure of the field in which this capital functions.

I would like to give a more concrete form to what I have just expressed in very abstract terms. Basically, symbolic capital is economic, cultural or social capital when the latter are perceived through categories of perception that are suitable, that is, appropriate to the social conditions of production and operation of the particular species of capital. For example – to adopt Bertrand Russell's famous argument – we cannot exclude the fact that pure physical force may itself exercise a form of symbolic imposition when it is perceived not simply as brute force but as a function of categories of perception and appreciation that treat force as the manifestation of legitimacy, as a power implying the affirmation of its own recognition.[2] What is true of physical

4 *Lecture of 17 April 1986*

violence – which can, then, when it is noted and recognised, be transformed into symbolic violence – is also true of a purely economic force when it is perceived through the appropriate categories of perception. We see this when economic capital, according to the philosophy of the *self-made man* for instance, is recognised as symbolic power, as a worldly sign of election by other-worldly forces. In some Puritan philosophies, economic capital itself may be constituted in some ways through the agents' perception of it as symbolic power. This is even truer of cultural capital, which, as I explained at length in my earlier lectures, is incorporated, and to some extent written into, the seemingly innermost memories and dispositions of the habitus. Cultural capital is particularly predisposed to function as symbolic capital, as charisma or gift, insofar as it lends itself both to cognition and misrecognition.

Cognition and misrecognition

[I should explain briefly that] this notion of cognition and misrecognition is important for understanding the specific status of symbolic capital. Symbolic capital is a force that affects all those who, in order to perceive it, adopt those categories of perception which grant it that status; symbolic capital, then, enjoys a sort of circularity. It is based on an act of cognition by the person who feels its force, and this act of cognition entails recognition; in recognising any symbolic capital as such, I am accepting the categories of perception through which it demands to be perceived. This kind of circularity is at the heart of the problem of legitimacy. I must have said this already over the last few years: there is no power that does not demand to be perceived according to its own norms of perception. If when reflecting on power we resort to the purposive logic of propaganda or of conspiracy theory, as do for example the so-called 'critical' philosophers of the Frankfurt school,[3] we tend to think that power uses a kind of intentionally engineered process to impose its own representation of itself.

In fact what I find important in understanding the effects of symbolic domination is that the symbolic effects I am referring to are in a way constitutive, and come to fruition without any intention of symbolic imposition or propaganda. There is in the very logic of the different forms of power an inherent tendency to impose their own categories of perception and in this way to be both recognised and misrecognised, that is, to have the truth of their force misrecognised. And the definition of symbolic power that I have to offer is a definition of legitimacy. In the light of this logic, legitimacy is a force of recognition based on

Lecture of 17 April 1986 5

misrecognition. A symbolic power is a power that is recognised insofar as it is not recognised as power. It becomes recognised insofar as it prevents us from recognising the arbitrariness at the source of its efficacy. I must emphasise that this kind of misrecognition, this twisted and tortured cognition, can thus be obtained without any deceitful intention. I even think that the most subtle forms of domination operate beyond any domineering intention on the part of the dominant; which will lead me in due course to reconsider the case of paternalism, a particularly subtle form of domination whereby the dominant impose the categories of their own perception beyond any perverse intention to dominate or deceive. In a sense we might even say that the most subtle forms of domination are those where the deceiver is also deceived, and in fact what I am in the process of describing under the name of symbolic capital is what Weber called 'charisma' (*khárisma*, 'grace'),[4] the kind of grace, in every sense of the term, that accompanies power: the grace, beauty and charm of power is something that power exerts *ex ipso*, by virtue of its very existence, independently of any intention to justify. And yet such intentions to justify are not entirely absent. They may come to reinforce the specific effects of power.

Moreover, in saying that symbolic power supposes, in those affected by it, not only knowledge but an act of cognition and misrecognition, we come to share certain concerns of contemporary philosophy. Philosophers have discovered power in recent years and have on occasion come close to the kind of analyses that I am offering here, but with simplifications and mutilations that I believe I need to analyse briefly to avoid giving you the impression that I am just repeating their arguments. As I am sure you know, there have been discussions of the 'site' of power, questioning whether power comes from above or below, and, in a kind of reversal whose social (but not intellectual) logic is understandable, some philosophers have been led to say that power comes from below,[5] that there is a kind of love for power, that, in a way, the dominated create their own domination through a sort of perverse submission to the charm of power. As you can see, these analyses are apparently quite close to what I have been saying. But at the same time they are very different. Firstly, questioning the 'site' of power is extremely naive. If you have followed the analyses of the notion of field that I have expounded, or the analyses of the relations between the notion of capital and the notion of field, you will have understood that asking where the source of power is located – or, which comes to the same thing, where the source of any change or subversion of power might be situated – is extremely naive, insofar as it is the structure of the field as such which is the site of power. Asking what constitutes the power of the artist who multiplies the value of a work by adding his signature – or the power of the dress designer whose original label multiplies the value of a creation[6] – is to gloss over the question of the source within which the power manipulated by the holder of power is produced. The question of power is on the one hand a question of the social conditions of the production of power, and on the other hand a question of the social conditions of manipulation by a person or group of the power they have accumulated. That is one consideration.

Symbolic power as fetish

Secondly, symbolic power, as I have defined it, as a specific effect of any species of power when it is recognised, since it is produced by an act of recognition, obviously supposes some contribution of those affected by it: there is no symbolic power without the complicity, collaboration or contribution of those who suffer it. To speak of symbolic power, then, is to give the traditional notion of fetishism a more rigorous sense. Symbolic power, like the fetish, is the product of the subjective projection of a subjective act of cognition, recognition and misrecognition, which experiences the power produced through this projection as something objective. In a moment I shall turn to a very fine analysis by Benveniste of the notion of *fidēs*, where we see quite clearly this shift from the subjective to the objective. In fact, in its simplest definition, the true sense of fetishism lies in the act of the creator worshipping his own creation – this is the Pygmalion effect. The creator's worship of his own creation is based on his ignorance of his own contribution to producing the effects that he experiences. We should not understand this effect of fetishism too naively, if we are to avoid falling back upon the kind of philosophy that, in seeking the site of power, runs the risk of seeming to be answering the question of who is responsible for the power.

I think that one of the great difficulties for social science is that questions of truth ('What are the facts in this case. . .?') are most often translated into questions of responsibility. One of the great sources of error in the social sciences is the tendency to wonder: 'Who is at fault here?' Is the person responsible for power the guilty dominator? Might the poor old dominated not be contributing to their own domination, which would be a way of exonerating the dominant? The question 'Who is at fault?', which subtends these debates on the sites of power, begs the simple question of how the specific form of power

Lecture of 17 April 1986

that is symbolic power, which can only operate through a cognitive relation between dominant and dominated, actually functions. It is not through some kind of perversion that the dominated concede to power – whether its force is physical, economic or cultural – through a recognition that reinforces the primary power with a secondary power conferred by legitimacy; it is rather because, as I said just now, the categories of perception that the dominated apply to the dominant power thus constituted as symbolic power are the product of the very exercise of these powers.

I refer you to the example of the patterns of perception of works of art, or, more generally, the objects of aesthetic judgement as they are constituted in the shape of pairs of adjectives. (I have used this example often, and I apologise to those of you who know what I am going to say, but I do sometimes take different routes that pass through the same point.) Barthes, in his last writings on music, observed that most judgements of taste are adjectives;[7] I think that we might even say they are exclamations, like [the Polynesian] *mana*! or [the Sioux's] *wakanda*! Ethnologists have noted that the very general concepts which we find many societies use to record the extraordinary, the *mana*, the formidable, are adjectives that function as exclamations, as cries of admiration. Lévi-Strauss, commenting on Marcel Mauss's famous text ['Sketch for a General Theory of Magic'], says that these judgements resemble a man's admiring wolf whistle in the presence of a beautiful girl.[8] Exclamations of admiration, often expressed as adjectives, appear to be typical products of symbolic capital, while they do in fact also produce symbolic capital. I don't want to take this too far, but it is not the beautiful girl who produces the wolf whistle, it is the wolf whistle that produces the beautiful girl, given the fact that to constitute the beautiful girl as a beautiful girl, you need to have the categories of perception which enable you to constitute her as a beautiful girl. The universes producing the categories of perception (such as 'slim', 'fat'/ 'light', 'fine' / 'heavy') are producing at once the beautiful girl and the admiration produced by her relation to the categories used in perceiving her.

This symbolic effect is linked, not to some kind of violent intention, but to a sort of constitutive violence inherent in the functioning of certain fields, where the fundamental social relations are crystallised into adjectives. For instance, the contrast between the rare and the common, so powerful in judgements of taste (and particularly in questions of taste concerning scholarly art), is a clear transposition of the basic contrast between what is exclusive (what in fact or in law is reserved for a few) and whatever is common, vulgar and widely

8 *Lecture of 17 April 1986*

available. The mental structures used by social agents to perceive the social world are largely a product of the incorporation of the social structures that they apply to it: this circularity lies behind the symbolic reinforcement of the effects exercised by the different forms of capital, and lies behind their recognition. We can see how the symbolic effect of capital is in a way exercised automatically, independently of any intention by the dominant, and the complicity granted by the dominated to the principle of domination over them is not the evidence of betrayal, cowardice or abandonment that certain post-'68-ish analyses see in it; it is in reality a structural effect that depends on the fact that the structures of perception which we apply to the social world are to a great extent the product of the incorporation of the structures of the social world itself.

If (following Mauss's very fine comment) fetishism shows how 'society always pays itself with the false coin of its dreams',[9] if we are always more or less fetishist in our perception of the social world, if (in fetishist fashion) we accept tokens in place of gold coin (which is what fetishism is), if we agree to bow down to the images that we have ourselves graven, it is not from a sort of abandonment, giving in to the effect of individual liberty, yielding to individual choice and responsibility, but from a sort of structural domination whereby, because we belong to social fields, we tend to incorporate and internalise the structures of their worlds, leading us to apply to these worlds the categories of perception that suit them best.

Socialisation through social structures

In fact all power pursues this effect of circularity. I said at the start that all power has an interest in imposing its own categories of perception. I think that this simple argument should enable us to understand what is behind all the aesthetics of power. The powers harbour a transhistorical aesthetic. The equestrian statue, for instance, is no historical accident; it is the manifestation of the intention of all power to show itself off in the most favourable light possible. Similarly, the choice of the frontal view that we find in Byzantine mosaics and in a host of other social representations is a kind of strategy of self-presentation that suits power and the powerful insofar as it imposes respect on others and keeps them at a distance; the frontal aspect solicits a reverence associated with distance (the object represented requires to be observed from in front, and from below). In most cases the imposition of the right perception, of the right viewing position, which is written into the very intention of symbolic domination, has no need of explicit expression. It is obtained through the very logic of the effect of inculcation inherent in all social existence. I have not said it (because I have so insisted on it in my previous lectures. . .), but what is assumed throughout my analysis is that any social order through its very existence exercises an effect of inculcation, an effect of education. We tend to associate education with an explicit pedagogic action, but there is a form of socialisation that is exercised through the very functioning of the social world, and I think that the most powerful forms of education are those that operate through the social structure itself.

There is a kind of structural education. I showed it at work in Kabyle society: the social space being structured, the initiation into space, into movement within a house or a village, is itself an initiation into the structures according to which the social space is structured. We could show the same thing occurring in childhood games: there are structures immanent in these games, and what is learned through the rules of the game are also [social] structures, for instance the division of labour between the sexes, or a structure of domination in archaic society.[10] What Sartre called the 'inertia violence' of social structures[11] has a pedagogic impact, so that the structures of perception that come to be applied to perceiving the actions through which the social structure is revealed tend to adapt themselves automatically to suit these social structures. Thus – and this I believe is the most striking paradox that emerges from these analyses – the social world tends to be perceived as being self-evident, taken for granted.

A political phenomenology of experience

I shall now develop this point a little further in an attempt to break with this kind of guilt-ridden philosophy that sees power arising from below, and also with certain post-phenomenological representations of the experience of the social world as a world that is 'taken for granted'. These representations, which have been developed by ethnomethodology in particular, tend in a way to depoliticise, or at least to negate the political dimension of this perception. (That was not well expressed – I shall now explain differently what I am trying to say.) If I wanted to draw parallels in a scholarly fashion, I would say that those who, like Foucault in certain writings,[12] insist on the fact that the dominated are complicit in their own domination, and that we consequently need to look for power almost everywhere, instead of only in the sites conventionally designated for us to seek it out, politicise too much, and

10   *Lecture of 17 April 1986*

ultimately develop a philosophy of domination that I find rather naive. Conversely, those who, like some American 'sociologists' who are in fact ethnomethodologists, have extrapolated Husserl's and Schütz's phenomenological analyses of the experience of the ordinary world and who insist on the fact that our primary experience of the social world is a feeling that it goes without saying, depoliticise too much, in that they ignore the social and historical conditions that enable us to see these experiences as self-evident. Formulating things in this way allows me to situate the debate, because my own argument does not arise out of nowhere, but, like all scientific argument, from within a space of positions, and a part of its value lies in its ability to overcome contradictory positions. I am explaining these contradictions to help you understand them, but also because my argument might seem too obvious, if you did not bear in mind the problems that it is addressing and the difficulties that it attempts to overcome.

I shall now return to my exposition: the phenomenologists, and especially Schütz, have taken it upon themselves to elaborate the primary, spontaneous – or lived, as we might say – experience of the social world as we encounter it in our everyday lives. For our fundamental experience is that the world appears to be self-evident, or *taken for granted*. This is no more than a development of Husserl's celebrated analysis, according to which perceptual experience, as opposed to experience through imagination or memory, for instance, is an experience whose modality – whose belief status, if you like – is a modality of *doxa*.[13] Consequently, any perception implies adhesion or belief, or in Husserl's words, 'a thesis of existence',[14] although this thesis of existence is not posited as such: you have to be a phenomenologist to realise that perception implies a tacit thesis of existence, a non-thetic thesis. The role of phenomenology is to render explicit these implicit presumptions of ordinary experience. The ethnomethodologists develop these analyses and describe the conditions in which this experience of the world is manifested as self-evident. But their aim is to describe an experience, and for them social science has no object other than to describe methodically our actual experience of the social world. It is in a way a systematised account of the verbal accounts that agents give of their experience of the social world. Its relation to our ordinary experience of the world is one of continuity (rather than fracture).

This is not my vision at all: I think that science should analyse both this primary experience of the world and the social conditions that make it possible, the conditions in which it comes to pass, all of which presuppose breaking with primary experience and establishing what are the objective conditions, say, which produce social structures and

Lecture of 17 April 1986

categories of perception, and which foster the interplay between objective structures and cognitive structures. We should then look away from experience as we live it if we want to fully understand it; it is not enough to describe experience in its own terms, we need to establish the conditions of its actual production and operation. If we remain within a phenomenological or ethnomethodological perspective, we set ourselves the task of describing this experience through insisting on this kind of originary relation to the world as a relation that is doxic and self-evident. I would simply like to add that there are social conditions which make this experience possible. Which means that this experience is not universal: there are situations in which the world ceases to be self-evident or taken for granted. To understand both how we experience the world as self-evident, and how we experience crises of confidence in critical situations when the world totters and ceases to be self-evident, we need to understand the social conditions that make this experience possible, that is, the conditions controlling the harmonious interplay between the structures of perception and the objective structures, and the conditions of discord that cause this harmony to fail.

Consequently, if we return to the analysis of power, the social world reveals itself as self-evident on a much wider scale than a politicised representation of the social world might lead us to believe. If the analysis I have to offer is right, we can understand how even those of the dominated who suffer the most brutal structural constraints in the social fields can perceive as natural this world which our interpretation would reveal to be revolting and shocking to our own categories of perception. My analysis therefore takes into account the paradox that what some perceive as scandalous is perceived by others as natural, and not scandalous. This is because what are the most revolting social conditions from the point of view of, for instance, the categories of perception of a French intellectual in the 1980s can be perceived as natural and self-evident by people whose categories of perception of these conditions are the product of precisely those conditions. To take an example which is helpful because topical: the facts that feminist denunciations have retrospectively made appear intolerable and impossible to countenance may continue to function as self-evident, as going-without-saying, for women who still have their categories of perception attuned to these conditions. Symbolic revolutions, of which I have given examples over the last few years,[15] are revolutions in categories of perception which tend to provoke a disjunction between the objective structures and the categories within which they are produced. This disjunction is extremely painful because the harmony

12 *Lecture of 17 April 1986*

between social structures and mental structures is a source of great satisfaction.

Nostalgia for a lost paradise

I shall take this argument a little further: it is basically quite simple (I think that you are all able to extrapolate from it), but its consequences are complex. This is because, as so often in sociology, it touches on what is most profound in our relation to the social world, on elementary, originary social investments, so that we may very well understand the analysis in the abstract without really comprehending it, and fall at the first hurdle into the traps that my analyses have just exposed.

The charm of pre-capitalist societies, which all ethnologists note in their logbooks, is to a considerable extent the product of what I have just mentioned. If pre-capitalist societies, like peasant societies, exercise such fascination on agrarian imaginations or conservative thinking, it is because they procure the experience of happiness that the obvious provides. There is some fine analysis by Hegel of pre-Abrahamic life,[16] that is, life in a self-evident world, where people may experience the at once cognitive and political happiness that consists in knowing the world as it requires to be known, being at home in the world like a fish in water, without feeling the weight of social constraints and structures, submitting, in fact, to the world as it is, in what you might call a passive, dominated, submissive and alienated manner, yet at the same time untroubled by any submission, domination or alienation, insofar as they are wedded to the world, so to speak. The nuptial metaphor is no accident: in a way, they marry the world, they join bodies, which is easy enough to understand if we realise that the structures of the world have in truth become bodily structures. One of the functions of the concept of the habitus is to remind us that the structures of the social world become bodies, and when the body is structured along the lines of the structures of the world, there is a kind of body-to-body relation, an infra-conceptual, infra-thetic, infra-conscious communication which is a form of the experience of happiness, the happiness of the self-evident that goes without saying.

There is a very fine passage in *Pleasures and Days* where Proust describes the experience of a little village where we know when the baker is going to open his shutters, where we can identify every sound, where everything is predicted in advance, everything is structured. This experience of being profoundly related to the world, as described by

Lecture of 17 April 1986 13

phenomenology and ethnomethodology, exercises a kind of charm and I think that it forms one of the deepest foundations of political nostalgia. Think of all that nostalgia for a return to our origins, of those who after May 1968 sought a return to more natural worlds,[17] with contradictory consequences, because this nostalgia for return may as well be fascist as leftist (which shows how these things need to be analysed in depth if we want to find our way, or not lose our way and meet people we would not like to cross paths with [*laughter*]). I think that this nostalgia for a lost paradise (in the notion of paradise there is the absence of a break between the subject and the world), for an originary, infra-conscious harmony between the subject and the world, is one of the profoundest of the social fantasies that obviously haunt agricultural or agrarian ideologies, but perhaps most other ideologies too.

With this analysis, I have wanted to say that this sort of immersion of the subject in the world may be found in places where we didn't expect to find it. It is not so surprising to find it in agricultural villages or primitive societies, but we can also find that a Renault factory is home to forms of experiencing the world as self-evident and creating the effect that I have described just now, resulting from the fact that the structures of perception constituting the world are at least in part constituted by the world that they constitute. By the same token, doxic experience is a fundamentally political experience.

From *doxa* to orthodoxy

My argument in fact entails comparing two things that we do not normally consider together, for simple reasons. In fact, as I often remark (not to talk up my own analyses, but rather to stimulate a form of intellectual imagination), one of the difficulties in social science, along the lines I have been suggesting, is that positions which are intellectually compatible may be difficult to render compatible in sociological terms: there are things that we have trouble considering together because they are far distant or even contradictory in the space of possible thoughts. This is the case for two things that I have just been comparing: a reflection on the doxic experience of the world according to Husserl, and a reflection on the notion of orthodoxy (and I don't mean simply comparing the word 'orthodoxy' with the notion of *doxa*). What makes comparing these two analyses difficult is that basically, for historical reasons, the phenomenological tradition tends to exclude political reflection, and political reflection tends to exclude the phenomenological

14 *Lecture of 17 April 1986*

type of reflection. Which means that we have problems trying to make a sort of political phenomenology of the founding political experience of the world, seen as depoliticised. This is what I have been driving at.

Following the completely depoliticised logic of the ethnomethodologists and saying that the world appears as self-evident is to forget that this is a political fact, and saying it without elaborating the social conditions that generate this harmony between the subjects of the experience and the objects which render the experience possible prevents us from seeing both the generality and the extent of this experience and its limits. Ultimately, this forbids us raising the question of the social conditions that render the experience possible (for this would obviously raise the question of its limitations: if you say 'conditions rendering possible', you are implicitly saying that if these conditions are not met, the experience no longer exists). To raise the question of the social conditions rendering doxic experience possible is to raise the political question of the conditions in which this doxic experience may be rent or fractured in order to allow a critical perception of the social world.

All this may be summed up in the opposition between *doxa*, orthodoxy and heresy. Doxic experience is the experience of the world as taken for granted, and I think that, in every social subject's experience, a very considerable part is left to the things that go without saying. Simply, the proportion that is taken for granted varies according to collective and individual histories: the zone of what is left to the taken-for-granted is not always as important as the zone of what is not taken for granted, as an object of discussion which may lead us back to the *doxa* – but a *doxa* to which we can choose to return is no longer a *doxa*, it is an orthodoxy, it is a righteous or a right-wing *doxa*, it is an elective *doxa*. I mentioned in passing the nostalgia for return: the return to the lost paradise of the *doxa* is a conservative ideology. Orthodoxy is different from *doxa* by all the distance between the precomposed or pre-reflexive and the reflexive, conscious and composed, so that we cannot think of orthodoxy without thinking of heterodoxy. Orthodoxy is heterodoxy overcome, and is therefore no longer a *doxa*. In the celebrated words of an Arab philosopher, 'tradition is a choice that is unaware of choosing'.[18] The most consummate tradition is no longer perceived as tradition, it becomes traditionalism. A tradition that you choose as a tradition does not procure the inexhaustible charm of tradition in the first degree, insofar as that ever existed, which is another question.

I shall finish with this point. *Doxa* and orthodoxy are separated by an act of constitution calling into question the object at issue, estab-

Lecture of 17 April 1986   15

lishing it as possessing the possibility of being otherwise, and as soon as what was taken for granted is thought to possess the possibility of being otherwise, two possibilities are confronted, a space of possibilities opens up and each and every position is situated in a space of oppositions. In fact, we have passed from the *doxa* as immediate, pre-reflexive belief to opinion as explicit standpoint, explicitly situated in a space of compossible and alternative opinions.

Returning to symbolic power

This has taken me away from my initial proposition, which I shall briefly summarise. Symbolic power is a form of power that is exercised with the complicity of those who suffer it. In this sense, it is a form of fetishism. But this complicity is never a consciously accorded or subjectively extorted recognition; it is a structural complicity that depends in a way on the fact that the structures producing the capital concerned tend to be reproduced in the structures of perception that come to perceive the capital. This kind of structural harmony linked to the effect of socialisation exercised by absolutely any form of power explains the experience of power recognised but misrecognised as power, and explains the kind of fetishism whereby social agents grant a bonus to power, that is, a recognition of power, the most absolute recognition being doxic, where the power is not even recognised as power. It is known, since there is an act of cognition, but this act of cognition is deficient because it is not perceived as a choice; it is an act of adherence, which does not perceive itself as such but as something different. What the notion of symbolic power wants to compensate for, then, is not a structural mystification (the word 'mystification' is very dangerous because it immediately makes us think of very Frankfurt School-type critical notions[19]), but a sort of structural symbolic alienation.

I shall stop there. In the second session I shall follow my tradition and move beyond the structured and somewhat closed argument where I aim for a long-term, overall (even total, or slightly totalitarian for some tastes) coherence. I shall offer instead, as I have in previous years, some improvisations on shorter topics over a timescale of one or two sessions, on diverse subjects, generally linked either closely or loosely to the overall lecture course, but still independent. I'd like to remind you that, as in the past, you are very welcome to pass me any written questions during the break or at the end of a lecture, and I'll try to answer them the following week.

16   *Lecture of 17 April 1986*

Second session (seminar): biography and social trajectory (1)

In this second session I shall discuss a technique which, for some time now, has often been used by ethnologists and sociologists: the technique of the life story.[20] The talk I want to give you could be called: 'The biographical illusion'. If I were a follower of fashion, I would say that I am going to deconstruct[21] the notion of biography. In the alternative terminology that I have been using for years now,[22] I would say that a biography or a life story is a preconstructed notion, that is, a common-sense notion which has come to take its place in common scientific parlance, having infiltrated science without passing border controls. These preliminary checks are basic to scientific practice, which must start by submitting to criticism these theories, whether popular or academic, which become part of received theory – these *folk theories*, as ethnomethodologists call them. But in this particular case – and here lies the divergence from certain fashionable uses of deconstructionism – the work of deconstruction is not an end in itself. One danger of the deconstructionist fashion, in fact, is that it happily leads to a sort of nihilism: people play with deconstruction for the sheer pleasure of deconstructing, and, in general, they stop half way through [. . .] the deconstruction does not go all the way, and it produces no scientific effects. My work, on the other hand, will analyse the notion of biography or life story to try to see what scientific approach it substitutes, and therefore what we could replace it with. In fact I might give my talk the title: 'Biography and trajectory as preconstructed and constructed objects'.

I could start by invoking the modern novel, especially the *nouveau roman*, which to a certain extent may be read as a reflection on the impossibility of the life story. As so often happens, the artistic field and the literary field are in advance of the scientific field: they subject to their scrutiny things that the scientific field accepts as taken for granted. Whereas the literary field constantly calls into question the idea of narration, of 'narrativity' as a continuous or linear discourse, the sociologists or ethnologists continue, without entertaining a moment's doubt, to write a continuous discursive narrative. Today it is true that this sort of reflexive scrutiny of discourse is starting to be practised in the social sciences, but with a considerable delay. There is nothing artily unscientific in the desire to exploit this literary experience in an attempt to achieve scientific results.

I shall start by quoting a passage from the latest book by Robbe-Grillet, which is a strange book: it is a kind of autobiography written by someone who attacks the whole possibility of autobiography. His book is still in its way a naive biography, as all its enemies and all the enemies of the nouveau roman have remarked. But he is obliged to ask himself a certain number of questions; his book is a naive biography within which the question of biographical naivety is raised. Writing about what he himself has just narrated, he writes:

> This is all real, that is, fragmentary, elusive, insignificant and even so accidental and spontaneous that each event at any moment appears to be gratuitous, and ultimately all existence appears bereft of any unifying significance. The emergence of the modern novel is linked to precisely this discovery: reality is discontinuous, formed of unique, single elements juxtaposed without reason, and all the more difficult to grasp for constantly intruding unexpectedly, irrelevantly and arbitrarily.[23]

I find this text interesting, not so much for its argument, but for its central sentence 'each event . . . unifying significance') which raises the age-old question of the unity of the self over a period of historical time. Obviously we could find the same problem in Proust, but also in Joyce or Virginia Woolf. The whole tradition of the modern novel discusses the question of the possibility of a life story in the light of the fact that a life is something so discontinuous: does the novelist not produce an artefact by the simple fact of making a story out of something that does not have the structure of a story?

The question raised is that of the correspondence between the structure of life, which is discontinuous, disorganised and has neither head nor tail (it is all 'sound and fury',[24] etc.), and the structure of the narrative, which is linear (this is Saussure's formula: language is linear, it unfolds through time, it is vectorial, it goes in one single direction, it is therefore coherent, it tends to be organised in the service of an end which is at once a term and a *telos*[25]). In other words, is there not the effect of an imposition of structure in the simple fact of adopting the simple technique of storytelling?

You know that there came a time when some novelists used a tape recorder to write their novels: they recorded themselves, and then recomposed the text. The sociologist or ethnologist who uses a tape recorder to record his enquiry and who then transcribes the recorded narrative is responding to a positivist definition of science: what could be less interventionist than using a simple recording? But we might reflect on the simple verb *to record* or 'to register', for the word invokes 'records', which are things that we register because they are remarkable (like 'world records', among others). We tend to record only remarkable

18   *Lecture of 17 April 1986*

performances, and that is what I want to try to analyse: what is a life? When we speak of a 'life story', is it really a life that we are discussing? Does a life have a history, and in what sense? In the sense of *Geschichte* (lived history) or *Historie* (historical enquiry)?[26] Is it a story fabricated by the teller? A history as it unfolds? And moreover, does the fact of being the historiographer of someone else's life not imply an action on the part of the writer?

The problem of the unity of the self

This question of the unity of the self, of the self as a whole, is an old philosophical question that goes back to Hume. I want to quickly recall the history of the problem because it seems to me to underpin the apparently more positive, historical and sociographic enquiry that I shall go on to develop. Hume said, more or less, that ultimately we cannot find any proof of the existence of the self (Condillac said roughly the same thing): try as we might, all we can find are successive sensations and impressions; for instance, impressions of hot or cold, light or shade, love or hate.[27] Ultimately the self would be reducible to this rhapsody of sensations, to this series of impressions with neither head nor tail.

In a way, the philosophy of Virginia Woolf is very close to this. Modern novelists took note of this kind of empiricist philosophy of lived experience and stopped describing a character as a totalised person with a unifying, creative principle. Their ambition is the opposite of that of the seventeenth-century moralists,[28] who sought to unite all the disparate and disjointed things into a unity that they established, but only because it was pre-established: 'character', in the old definition, is a sort of divine imprint that creates a unity from the sensible diversity that our intuition encounters; characters act and do all sorts of things, but they have a unity, their attitudes are marked with the imprint of a unity that the moralist grasps and then establishes in a word (such as 'the misanthropist',[29] for instance).

We know how Kant replied to this attack by the empiricist tradition on the possibility of this unity.[30] Translated into our own social terms, he argues that unity is to be found in the subject of the action [. . .], in the self as unifying principle of this diversity. Retranslated into a more scientific turn of phrase, we might wish to ask whether there exists an active principle that might be irreducible to the series of positive perceptions. Kant at least distinguished the direction in which we might seek: is there an active unifying principle that surmounts, so to speak,

Lecture of 17 April 1986   19

the disjointed sensations in a sort of ambition to construct a life as a unity?

Following another logical thread, we might also examine those situations that prefigure a crisis, and call into question the unity of an existence or a life as a whole. This is the problem of conversion, which was much debated in the nineteenth century and could be very interesting. I should say in passing that the question of the habitus is among other things an attempt to reply to these questions: the habitus is a unifying principle and motive force which is historical and a product of history, but it is also at the same time an active, constituent part of history at every moment. I am mentioning this problem of the unity of the self merely to remind you of it, but there is in the United States a very lively tradition of moral philosophy that raises it more concretely (concerning economic issues like credit or insurance policies, for instance). They discuss, for example, whether taking out an insurance policy today to guarantee cover of the cost of care in the case of dementia in later life has a sense: is the self who has become insane the same as the one who had taken out the policy insuring against dementia? These academic questions are not as absurd as they seem because, here again, they force us to confront issues and call into question what was taken for granted. We might make another observation of the same type: when we punish a criminal with a twenty-year sentence, we are presuming that he will be the same in twenty years' time; but are the person who earned the punishment and the person who will suffer it the same person? It is not self-evident, and if we followed through all the implications, we might discover all sorts of contradictions both in the theories of those who support these penalties and in the theories of those who contest this kind of punishment. The question of the unity of the self over a period of time is a difficult one, and I shall show that society does reach a certain conclusion on the issue.

The unity of the self across different spaces

If the unity of the self over a period of time is problematic, it is the same across different spaces. The question is less often discussed, but it is important. One contemporary tradition of analytic philosophy approaches it from the angle of Leibniz's theory of possible spaces,[31] and raises the issue of whether it is possible to generalise propositions to apply to all possible spaces. This problem, which may seem once again to be an academic problem, can be retranslated into the language of sociology: what is it that makes a person who operates across different

20   *Lecture of 17 April 1986*

social spaces the same person? This is a problem that confronts the sociologist: for instance, faced with an inspector of finance who teaches at Sciences Po, what code should we apply?[32] Should we classify this person as an inspector of finance and director of the cabinet of the minister of finance, or as a professor at Sciences Po? Or should we create a sort of multiple identity? Likewise, how do we classify the multiple properties of a professor at the Collège de France who writes for *Le Monde* and who is, for instance, a member of the management committee of the Centre Pompidou?[33]

What is it finally that creates unity in such multiple characters? We would say that it is the individual, that is, the biological individual, whose body is the bearer of these different significations: it is the same biological individual who has these different properties and who exists in these different spaces. But as a sociologist developing a theory of fields, I remind you that what exists from a sociological point of view is not the biological individual, it is what I call the 'agent', that is, the biological individual as a bearer of properties that generate effects in a field; in a sense, the biological individual pure and simple, bereft of properties, has no existence in a field. He is an intruder, 'a fish out of water', that is, someone who enters a game without having any of the properties needed by a player; as far as the game is concerned it is as if he does not exist, he is not an agent. We could devote a whole study to the intruder and intrusion, the blunderer and his blunders. In painting, we have the example of Le Douanier Rousseau, that is, the naive painter, who wants to play the game but has no knowledge of the rules and becomes a kind of painter-object. He is a painter as seen and named by others, but he is not really the subject of what he does, he is not an agent.[34]

So what we are going to say is that the same individual will be several agents: according to the field in which he intervenes, he will be different. In the light of traditional logic, we would talk of his 'role', a word that I abhor because it supposes the idea of developing a text that is already written, the idea of something explicit and precomposed. My argument [developed in other lectures], that the agent will act in a given field through the relation arising between a habitus – and a certain number of properties associated with this habitus – and a field, has nothing to do with playing a part: what is set in motion is a generative machine. The same person can produce very different effects in different fields. Just as the unity of the person over a period of time is problematic, so the problem of the unity of the person across different spaces arises, since the same habitus will produce different or even contradictory results in the different fields. People who see the habitus as a sort of

Lecture of 17 April 1986   21

little machine, a little programme set up once for all time, forget that the habitus is always in relation with a field and that the same habitus can produce contradictory effects – even in the same field, when this has changed.

In this context I like to give the example of the bishops: the bishops, with their aristocratic origins, who before the war were the incarnation of religious conservatism, are today the incarnation of religious progressivism:[35] the same social origin produces effects which are intelligible in each of the two different states of the space, but which have an opposing significance. Similarly, the same habitus borne by the same biological individual (for instance a banker who is an art collector) may be progressive and avant-gardist in the artistic space at one and the same time, but in the economic field innovative in different ways, or conservative. In short, the same habitus can engender apparently contradictory results. The problem of the unity of the 'social person' (the term being understood in contradistinction to the individual) is raised.

The name as foundation of the socially constituted individual

Now, drawing on the resources available in several different traditions, I would like to show how the social world tends to resolve these problems. How does the social world tend to establish identity in a lasting way? I should say in passing that I shall indulge in a reflection touching on the notion of identity. (I think that if I were to be asked to consider the notion of identity, I would be as embarrassed as the rest of you; one of the intellectual strategies that I employ in this kind of case consists in approaching big topics from an angle that renders them manageable.) Through this reflection on biography, it is a reflection on identity that I shall be attempting to sketch out, while knowing full well that it is partial, imperfect and incomplete.[36]

The social world tends to prejudge identity – and to demand it. And yet this phrase, like all those that have 'the social world' or 'society' as their subject, has no sense (if we use them nonetheless, it is because they are telegraphic and economic). Let us rather say that, among the expectations written into the social fields, there is the expectation of consistency (*constant sibi*, as they said in Latin), of self-consistency, faithfulness to oneself, through time and across space. One technique that the social world tends to use to produce this consistency is the effect of nomination, which I analysed in another context last year. This is the effect of the proper name. Here I shall just refer briefly to

22   *Lecture of 17 April 1986*

a tradition of philosophical reflection on the proper name that can be retranslated into sociological terms. In fact, through nomination the social world tends to ensure that kind of consistency of the nominal that is one of the traps laid to catch the sociologist. I have denounced it several times here: one error constantly committed by historians and sociologists – whenever the latter go in for history – is to believe that the consistency of names guarantees the consistency of things. For example, they feel authorised by the fact that we can speak of 'professors' in the nineteenth as well as the twentieth century to make statistical comparisons over time, but while the word may have stayed the same the thing might have changed. My criticism of statistical categories and narratives is founded on a criticism of the consistency of the nominal [. . .] which we should see both as an obstacle to scientific knowledge and as a social effect [. . .] (this [i.e. the fact that it is both an obstacle to knowledge and a social effect] is what I was saying at the outset about deconstruction). Recognising preconstructions is a scientific act on two accounts: in overcoming an obstacle and in contributing to scientific knowledge.

Kripke offers a theory of the proper name[37] that diverges from Russell's, which I have already mentioned,[38] but is interesting for the problem at issue. Kripke qualifies proper names as 'rigid designators': they are words that designate the same object in all possible universes, in which they differ from common nouns. The most obvious example is the notion of a group, which designates different things in mathematics, sculpture or sociology. Most common nouns designate different things when we change spaces, whereas the characteristic of the proper name is always to rigidly designate the same thing in all possible spaces. This is important for the questions I have raised: the art-collecting banker is always designated by the same name, as is the finance-inspecting professor from Sciences Po. The proper name is a sort of labelling that ensures the consistency of the nominal beyond all possible fragmentation of the self.

In a book entitled *Semantic Analysis*, another linguist, Ziff, adds something very interesting – in passing, because he is obviously not a sociologist. He agrees with Kripke that 'the proper name is a fixed point in a turning world':[39] the proper name has a kind of consistency amid a world of change. But Ziff adds that the specific manner of assigning proper names to individuals involves rites of baptism (it is always good to see linguists practise sociology, especially when it is correct. . .). The rites of baptism stand for the adequate, necessary and specific manner of assigning proper names to individuals. The rites of baptism are the form par excellence of what I call 'rites of institution' (rather than 'rites

Lecture of 17 April 1986

of passage'):[40] they are rites through which groups assign a socially defined identity to individuals, a socially defined essence, in a way. We see that the proper name is a kind of social birth certificate. It is no accident if in all societies bestowing a name is accompanied by ritual.

I have shown in the case of the Kabyle (and since then, many scholars have found it in other societies) that, in a society where people are called 'So-and-so, son of So-and-so', the attribution of a name and first name is a site of struggle and conflict, because to take possession of a name is not only to assume a fixed, accredited identity but also to inhabit a symbolic space and be clothed with more or less authority.[41] The name is a kind of capital. It is part of someone's symbolic capital. When we say of someone in our society that they have a great name, or of an artist that he has made his name, we are referring to a dimension of their symbolic capital. Similarly, in a society like Kabyle society, having a first name identical to that of a prestigious grandfather is tantamount to appropriating the grandfather's capital, and there may be a struggle between brothers who are sons of the same grandfather to give their sons, the grandsons, the first name of the honourable grandfather. In my book *The Logic of Practice* I have analysed these problems of succession, that is, the struggle to appropriate symbolic capital. This is a case where it is clear to see that symbolic capital is not insignificant; it is something that may trigger conflict, even though it seems undefinable. But in order to fight for a first name, you need to possess the corresponding categories of perception: you need in fact to attribute value to the first name, that is, to base your system for constructing social reality on divisions according to names. In societies where division according to names is not structured in the same way, people will not fight over first names. This is evidence to support what I was arguing just now [in the lecture].

Names, then, are rigid designators that ensure consistency over time: Mr X, from the time he was at primary school up to the moment when he enters the Académie Française, remains the same person, and we don't doubt for a moment that the man admitted to the Académie today is the same little schoolboy. It is the role of the biographer to affirm this continuity. Obviously there is a whole composition here; if, like André Chamson (whose biography you might reread),[42] the subject of the biography attended school in a little country village, we'll say: 'It's marvellous, the school has fulfilled its liberating mission and led him from the humblest origins to the highest peaks' – we will construct that cognitive identity and use it as the foundation for a whole theory. With the simple act of giving the same proper name, the biographer already takes on board a complete theoretical construction,

24 *Lecture of 17 April 1986*

and the most exemplary biographies are obituaries. I have often used obituaries as an object of study in analysing values, which has rudely shocked my colleagues.[43] When I take the professors as my object of study (as I have done for all the social categories I have looked at), the obituaries are extremely interesting, because they relate to a life that is over. We might remember some of Sartre's remarks, or Malraux's phrase,[44] 'Death transforms life into destiny' [. . .]: the idea of a life as a whole is affirmed precisely at the moment when it comes to an end, and the obituary is a kind of totalising statement that tries to organise into a unifying discourse the objective unity of an exemplary existence, since only people who deserve them get obituaries (but that is another story. . .). [. . .]

Proper names, as the 'rigid designators' that Kripke calls them, guarantee the identity of the individual in all possible worlds, that is, across time and, in the moment, across space. The proper name follows the individual across all possible spaces, and therefore across all possible life stories. We think of those modern novels where the same character leads several lives, but always under the same name. Some science-fiction novels are very interesting from this point of view, since they can be quite scholarly in their structure and refer to philosophical theories like the one I am exploring here, the theory of possible worlds. The modern novel constructs the individual living in several worlds, a functioning but fictitious individual, composed of discontinuous phases marked by changes in most of his properties. You might speak of the same character at different stages. It started with *Sentimental Education*, where thirty years separate the first presentation of the character from his final appearance: a fictional unity is affirmed against the fragmentation of these different states.[45]

The descriptions of each individual are valid not only for each of the stages, but also through the different stages and the different possible worlds, and it is the proper name that ensures this identity. Here I refer to an analysis of the use of the proper name in Proust by Eugène Nicole,[46] which observes that Proust makes unusually frequent use of the proper name preceded by the definite article: 'the Buckingham Palace Swann', 'the former Albertine', 'the rubber-clad, rainy-day Albertine'; he precedes the name with the definite article, which accentuates the fragmentation and dispersal of the person, as if the proper name were the only unifying factor. Eugène Nicole writes that the proper name preceded by the definite article manifests the 'sudden revelation of a fragmented, plural subject'. Through this usage expressing both unity (as produced by the universal designator – 'Albertine' is always Albertine) and diversity (recalled by the article), Proust frac-

Lecture of 17 April 1986 25

tures the universal designator: he reminds us that this universal designator designates as universal something that is nonetheless particular; the constant Albertine hides the rainy-day Albertines and the sunny-day Albertines. In fact, this simple linguistic usage raises the problem that I wanted to discuss today.

Curriculum vitae, *cursus honorum*, criminal record, school reports

The proper name, being socially constituted and taking the form of the socially known, recognised and acknowledged baptismal name, is one of the foundations of the socially constituted individual, who takes on the guise of different agents according to the fields (cf. the example of the art-collecting banker). With the proper name, then, we have the first stage of the composition of an identity. There is a second stage of composition – which carries on from the first – with all the institutions that tend to ensure consistency by drawing up an inventory of the properties belonging to a socially constituted individual. The paradigms are the curriculum vitae, the criminal record and the *cursus honorum*,[47] or the biographies in biographical dictionaries. The people who consult *Who's Who* as a basis for statistical data should no doubt think about the criteria governing the properties selected by *Who's Who*: why are some properties chosen and others not? I reflected along these lines when considering the family photograph albums that I worked on in depth some years ago: a family album being a place of family consensus, there are some photos that you won't find there. Similarly, there are events and things that cannot be recorded in a curriculum vitae because a curriculum vitae is an official biography, obeying criteria pertinent to the social space concerned.

The social world disposes of all sorts of institutions that totalise and unify the agent, institutions that are coded, codified and have their own specific logic. It is as a function of social criteria, then, that social identity is defined. The identity card, as an elementary form of curriculum vitae, contains a certain number of minimal properties, which may well be open to debate. For instance, in the papers that you have to fill in at present to become a citizen of the United States, there are questions that scandalise some Americans: should you put 'Black', 'Chicano', 'Mexican', etc.? [These designations reflect] a whole precomposed taxonomy, which gives an implicit definition of identity. Finally, there is a precomposition of national identity given through the taxonomies used to register people. At the level of the census, it is the same: what are the properties selected as constituting your identity according to

26   *Lecture of 17 April 1986*

the questions asked in the census?[48] For instance, in France, they don't ask for your religion; in the States, they do.

I believe that these questions are extremely important because they show us that there is an idea of identity in force in any given social world, and this identity is guaranteed by the proper name and by certain categories of census information which assign and channel the determining properties. I remind you of the analysis that I conducted in the past, which may have seemed abstract at the time,[49] according to which the *census*, which is both the census and the task of the *censor* in ancient Rome, designates the identity to be used as the basis for allocating tax liability. It is a classification providing a judicial basis for defining your tax band, that is, your commercial value from the point of view of the State. The *censor*, as author of the *census*, or today the holder of the statistical authority of the State (like INSEE), has properties different from those of the sociologist. I remind you of the rather abstract analysis[50] that I conducted in *Homo Academicus*, when I constructed the identity of a professor and created a code into which I introduced a series of properties, some already codified (like 'Agrégé of the University'), others not (like 'has written more than twenty-five books translated into foreign languages'). I was acting as a *censor*, but without any force of law: we do not allocate taxation or university careers on the basis of the number of books translated into foreign languages (which is perhaps a pity . . .[*laughter*]); the act has no validity. Whereas if it were performed by a statistician from INSEE, it might be recorded on identity cards or used as a basis for calculating income tax, benefits, perks, exemptions or sanctions, etc.

To return [to my main argument]: identity as defined by the curriculum vitae, the *cursus honorum* and the criminal record supposes consistency of the self. The criminal record, or the school grades that follow a pupil all their life, reply unreservedly to the question: 'Is this the same individual?' The idea of a conversion, or a radical break, is to a certain extent excluded: your acts pursue you. There is then in these institutions a whole philosophy of the consistency of the self, and the construction of this consistent self functions according to the criteria of pertinence of any given society: it depends on what that society is interested in, that is, on the properties that are efficacious and active, all others being excluded (for instance, educational qualifications will be considered insofar as they may be a basis for predicting behaviour).

To recapitulate, and to introduce [. . .] the next stage of my analysis. Our life, our existence, which when seen as an objective truth presented by the novel or by lived experience appears to be something incoherent, inconsistent and fragmentary, is established as a unitary whole

Lecture of 17 April 1986

by the social world through the rites of institution sanctioned by the allocation of names, nominations and then institutions such as the curriculum vitae, which is a kind of extension of the proper name. A curriculum vitae in fact records the different acts of nomination associated with the original nomination: 'He was appointed *agrégé*, assistant, professor, etc., in such and such a year.' These successive acts of nomination are in a way a development of that original nomination whereby a proper name was assigned to the individual. The social world, then, tends to postulate the consistency of the nominal and to introduce a consistency that is not necessarily that of lived experience.

Now we might raise the following question: is the biographer or the interviewer who asks someone to record their life story on tape committing an act of construction? If they are, what is the [aim?] of this act? Are they hoping to record an official life story at that moment, a *curriculum*? If that is the case, they need to know that is what they are doing. Or are they hoping to capture the image of a fragmentary life that the novelist reproduces? And what part is played, in this act of reconstruction, by the representation that the interviewee might have of the different acts and social situations that are being used to create his identity: a trial or an exam, for instance, the typical situations that generate an official identity; or, in other cases, situations, also socially constituted, where we produce our own identity – self-advertisement, autobiography or apologia, the sort of discourse where we project what we claim to be our true nature, etc. In other words, is the act of recording innocent if it is situated in a space of acts of recording that is already codified, whose representation by the recorder himself is confused and whose interviewees also have confused representations varying markedly according to their milieu, as they situate themselves in relation to this space, whether they realise it or not?

Next time – now that I have exposed the implicit presuppositions of the act of recording and constituting an identity – I shall try to show how we might construct the notion of the trajectory of a life in a completely different way.

Lecture of 24 April 1986

First session (lecture): the fidēs, *a historical realisation of symbolic capital – An ethnology of the unconscious – The examples of ethnicity and the designer label – The habitus as determination and as sensitivity Second session (seminar): biography and social trajectory (2) – Importing a literary break – Establishing consistency – The space of biographical discourse – From the life story to the analysis of trajectories*

First session (lecture): the *fidēs*, a historical realisation of symbolic capital

In my last lecture, I drew attention to the fact that what I call symbolic power or symbolic capital is a relationship, a cognitive relationship. It is in fact a power that is established in a relation between an agent, or more precisely a habitus, and an ensemble of properties available in a given society. This relationship, I would suggest, is constituted reciprocally; on the one hand, through the properties perceived; on the other hand, by the categories established to perceive them. As in all relationships, you can emphasise one term or the other to produce contradictory theories, objectivist or subjectivist, and those of you who have followed my teaching for a length of time[1] will know that one of the central aims of my research is to overcome the spurious antagonism between objectivism and subjectivism that I believe prevents us from understanding social facts in their full complexity.

The better to understand this notion of symbolic capital – this kind of subjective phenomenon functioning as if it were objective, this sort of relation between an agent and objective reality tending to pass as an objective something that is the product of an act performed by the agent, this *noesis* (to borrow a Greek term from Husserl) which becomes *noema*[2] and which is perceived as the product of its own product, in short, this fetishism, since that is what it really is – I propose to refer to Benveniste's analysis of the word *fidēs* in his *Dictionary of Indo-European Concepts and Society*. We could say that the notion of *fidēs*, as described by Benveniste in an analysis that is at once linguistic and anthropological, is a kind of historical realisation of what I call 'symbolic capital'. I shall therefore use this analysis to go on to show the dangers of what we might call ethnologism, that is, the act of transporting uncritically into complex and differentiated societies notions borrowed from pre-capitalist societies. I shall use the notion of *fidēs* [in this lecture] in two ways: first to help us reflect on the notion of symbolic power and then later as an opportunity to warn you of the kind of imports that are often rather surreptitiously smuggled in by semi-educated anthropologists; these ethnological borrowings allow for some clever effects (I am thinking for example of certain historians or sociologists), but scientifically speaking, they are counter-effects.

The most modern sense and the most straightforward translation of the notion of *fidēs* would be a subjectivist one: *fidēs* can be translated as 'faith', 'confidence' or 'fidelity', words which invoke a subjective relation to an institution or a person. Benveniste tries to show that this subjectivist sense conceals a more ancient, objectivist sense: in which case *fidēs* can be translated as 'faith' or 'confidence' but as 'credit' or 'credibility', that is, something that belongs to the object or person considered rather than to the subject considering.

To briefly summarise Benveniste's argument:[3] he ties the notion of *fidēs* to its lexicological origins. He relates *fidēs* to *peitho, peíthomaï*, the Greek verb meaning 'to obey'. (In passing: the whole problem of symbolic power is a problem of obedience. One of the questions I am trying to answer through my reflection is something not at all self-evident: why we obey, or what it is to obey an order. Or, conversely, what it is that renders an order liable to be obeyed.) *Fidēs*, then, relates to *peitho*, which means, in the active form, 'to persuade', and in the reflexive form,[4] *peíthomaï*, 'to obey'.[5] Other words from the same family are: *pístis*, which means 'trust' and 'faith' (this is the subjective sense), and *piostós*, 'faithful'. Then Benveniste moves on to the objectivist sense in the phrase '*fidēs est mihi apud aliquem*'. The literal translation of this phrase is the starting point for his analysis: 'it is the other who puts his trust in me and it is at my disposal' (rather than 'I trust him').[6]

(A short parenthesis for those of you who have made or are making the effort to translate from the Latin – and the same is true for Greek: we realise that what are often taught as idiomatic or eccentric expressions to be learnt by heart to avoid misinterpreting them are in fact

30 *Lecture of 24 April 1986*

nearly always anthropological realities, different modes of thinking from ours. If we taught Latin the way we teach ethnology, people might understand Latin better, but obviously that would remove much of the charm of the notion of humanity which, supposing a sort of eternity, is incompatible with the idea of anthropologisation.)

Fidēs is something that we deposit in someone, but it is a deposit whose nature as a deposit is in a way forgotten. Benveniste then discusses another primitive source, the notion of *kred*.[7] He says that *credere*, 'to believe', 'obey', 'trust', is to 'place one's *kred* in a person', deposit *kred* in them (which gives us our word 'credit'), this kind of bizarre substance that enables someone to affect me, to make me trust them. It is because I credit him that I trust him. It is because I have credited him with something that I have forgotten that I am trusting him.

(I am taking my time over the analysis of *fidēs*, firstly because this is the beginning [of this course of lectures], and beginnings are always difficult, but also because we need to operate a sort of conversion of thinking that is extremely difficult. I myself, when I went through this analysis while preparing the lecture, found it difficult because, to enter into the spirit of the analysis, we need in a way to change our habitual perspectives and modes of thinking. But the philological hesitation is, I believe, useful in making us work through this *metanoia* [conversion], this change of posture represented by the ethnological approach, in gradual stages. To appreciate Benveniste's analysis, we need to proceed slowly: if we swallow it like a pre-packaged take-away – it is unfortunately part of the nature of education to serve up take-aways, often without giving any idea of the process that went into their making – it appears easy; we will swallow it whole and make a note saying 'Benveniste wrote that *fidēs* is an objective property, that of giving *kred*', but we won't have understood it at all.)

Fidēs is confidence, and we need to unite the two senses of the word, the subjective and the objective sense: '*Fidēs* designates the confidence which the speaker *inspires* in his interlocutor, and which he enjoys with him.'[8] It is therefore a guarantee to which he can have recourse. By the same token, we can follow Benveniste in identifying *fidēs* with *potestas* (a term that we may translate as 'potency'). *Fidēs* is potency; having somebody's *fidēs* is being the person in whom they have deposited their *kred*, and it is having power over them. You see the switch that has occurred: the *fidēs* is no longer the confidence I place in somebody, but the authority I have over somebody who trusts me. This means that this authority is a 'protection for somebody who submits to it, an exchange for, and to the extent of, his submission'.[9] This kind of very subtle relationship is, in the majority of primitive societies, the basis

Lecture of 24 April 1986 31

of work relations and dominant power relations. For example, it is in many societies the relation between the landowner and his sharecropper. In our own societies, it is the relation of male domination (I shall return to this today and again later, for I think that we find the whole problem of relations between the sexes looming up behind this kind of structure). Relations of the *fidēs* type then have a dual sense (taking the word sense as both meaning and direction): they are relations of authority which entail both domination and protection; they are relations of authority that only work with the complicity of the person they are imposed on. And they can always be described in two ways, favourable or unfavourable, which is moreover another obstacle to their comprehension.

Among the obstacles to describing such extremely complex relations, apart from feeling impelled by some objective or subjective bias, there is the desire to make a stand, that is, to be for or against. This is, as I think you have understood, one of the elementary obstacles to sociological analysis. What I mean is not that we shouldn't have our opinions on the social world, but that primitive opinion (of the type: 'I'm for', 'I'm against', 'This paternalism is disgusting' or 'This enchanting relationship is amazing') is a major obstacle to an analysis, because it divides, or rather (because it would be too good if it did actually 'divide'. . .) it grasps only one face of a reality that is essentially ambiguous, double, twofold. The structural ambiguity of the notion of *potestas* or *fidēs* may be inferred from the fact that it is a relation of domination which is at the same time a relation of protection. It is a relation which, from the point of view of the dominant, may then be perceived as a power, a right or a sort of possession, and which from the point of view of the dominated may be perceived as obedience, but also as security, as insurance for the future. In fact we could say that in the majority of primitive societies, relations of the *fidēs* type were the only kinds of insurance and assurance in all senses of the term. In particular, for the most needy, the fact of having deposited their *kred* with a good guarantor, a man of his word and a man of money (the two things often going together), was the only guarantee against future poverty, famine or other calamity. It is obedience, then, but also insurance for the future.

To continue with Benveniste's analysis. *Fidēs*, that sort of subjectivity constituted as objectivity, is the fact of placing one's confidence in somebody, as when we say: 'He has my confidence' (there we are in the subjective, I think). 'I have confidence in him' signifies: 'He has my confidence', 'He possesses something that I have given him.' It is then a quality belonging to a being who attracts confidence, and it functions

32 *Lecture of 24 April 1986*

as a form of protective authority over the person who trusts in him. To show you why this analysis, which I am taking my time over, is not as simple as all that: *fidēs* is what Weber called charisma (you may well have been thinking of this already, particularly since I drew the parallel last time). For those of you who did not know it (but in fact nobody knows it, although it is there in Weber to be read), I want to point out that, when he discusses the notion of charisma, Weber says in a brief parenthesis: 'It is the same thing as *mana*.'[10] When we know what *mana* meant in Durkheim's thought, this simple parenthesis is a powerful riposte to those who take pleasure in setting Weber against Durkheim, for instance. Charisma is a power of the same type as *mana* or *baraka*, that is, something that is deposited in people, a property possessed by agents (or also by institutions or agents acting on behalf of an institution). Properties of the *mana* type are properties belonging to a person. They seem written into their bodies, their charm (*charisma* is a word from the same family as 'charm'), their presence, their way of being, their deportment. They inspire confidence and seem therefore to project an objective condition, whereas they are the product of a subjective act.

In another stage of his argument Benveniste says that one of the recipients of the *kred* was the champion.[11] In Homeric struggles, the champion was the person who fought in the name of the whole group and became, as in our societies, not only the spokesman for the group, but their liegeman [a person initially entirely devoted to God, and by extension to a cause or a party], the hero acting in the name of the group. This divine or human champion is the one to whom they entrust the *kred*, leaving him in exchange the duty to bestow on those who have supported him the benefits won through his exploits. This makes us think of some modern forms of politics: the champion is the person whose *supporters* we are, whom we back, in whom we place our confidence and whom we attempt to help. The acclamation and, more generally, all sorts of other kinds of expression of our emotional enthusiasm have, I believe, a social significance: they reveal a contract of delegation. To be the *supporter*, to back and to applaud, is much more than to 'give moral encouragement', it is to grant the *kred* to those who excel. We tend to understand this either too well or not at all, which generally comes to the same thing: how is it that acclamation pushes people to surpass themselves and creates an almost psychosomatic effect? One of the problems that I want to approach is the mystery of symbolic power: it acts on bodies and it exerts magical effects. It can cure, but on occasions it can kill; it can lead people to surpass themselves, and it can create desire, fury or fear, partly because it acts

Lecture of 24 April 1986   33

directly on the body. To understand how it acts on the body, I should explain how its relation to the habitus is involved. What I said in very abstract terms last time – that symbolic power only works on agents endowed with structures compatible with the structures involved in its composition – will then take on a very concrete aspect through these analyses. The analysis of acclamation is a first indication of this meaning.

At this point, listening to what I have been saying, you may once again have thought of Weber's analysis of charisma: the charismatic chief brings the benefits of the exploits and miracles that he accomplishes in the name of a group, and he is able to continue on condition that he bestows happiness on those who trust him; he is condemned to perform miracles, he has to prove his charisma through his exploits and through the happiness, *baraka*, blessings and *mana* that he spreads around him. It is no accident if we speak of the 'radiance' of a character and if representations of royalty, for example, are very often solar. They are not a metaphor, in the dull sense of our modern minds, but something very real: charisma is an outpouring of blessings, happiness, strength and the like. The person who holds, or more precisely, concentrates the *kred* is the holder of a kind of magical force. Here I continue to follow Benveniste's analysis. . .

(I should make it clear that for me ethnology is also a way of authenticating things that I would not presume to say in my own name, for fear of seeming delirious to any rather positivistic minds. Anthropological analysis enables me, at any rate, to reveal the deepest foundations of the functioning of the whole social world, things that are very difficult to express because the effort to name them is on the one hand disqualified by the fact that they are often expressed by amateurs, semi-educated scholars, media-loving ethnologists or popular reviews, and, on the other hand, discredited in advance by the positivist readings that are unfortunately dominant in the social sciences. To say that there is a magical communication between the spectators and players of a sport is either a trendy analysis in *Le Nouvel Observateur* or something very risky and bizarre. This is one of the reasons why I am using anthropological analysis to boost my credibility. In so doing I am working with *kred* myself, while discussing *kred*. . . I am saying this, firstly to help my bid for *kred* succeed, but also because it provides protection.)

The hypothesis underlying the idea of charisma and *fidēs* (as fully discussed in Benveniste's book) is that each social agent is the bearer of a sort of miniature capital of magical force, and under certain conditions they can place it in a superior being who operates a kind of

34 *Lecture of 24 April 1986*

concentration of magical capital: the small bearers of magical capital will concentrate their capital in the person of a champion, a hero. If you reread Lévi-Strauss's celebrated analyses of the sorcerer and his magic,[12] you will see that they are a particular case, a partial image of what I have been saying, using Benveniste's arguments. This comment is slightly unflattering for Lévi-Strauss, but I don't say it for the fun of it: his analysis is one of the most widely known in the social sciences; it is one of those things which, since they circulate easily at a superficial level, enable us to dispense with in-depth analysis and which are, I think, one of the sources of what I called 'ethnologism' at the start of this lecture, which in my opinion has an extremely sinister influence on the social sciences, especially among historians.

To conclude with Benveniste. The *kred*, which in some cases is materialised and given (it is given to the champion before the combat), is then 'some kind of "pledge", or "stake", something material but which also involves personal feeling, a notion invested with a magic power which all men possess and which may be placed in a superior being'.[13] To sum up this analysis: the *kred* is a pledge and something that commits you; to place your *kred* in somebody is to give them your engagement, to give them a hold over you, but by giving them something. We can say that the *kred* is a fetish: the relation that I have just described at length seems to me to be a relation of fetishism whereby I help to generate a power that acts upon me. It is not an individual operation between a singular agent and another agent, or between a singular agent and an institution, but a collective operation, the fetish effect being facilitated by the fact that the person credited with charisma receives this credit from a considerable number of people: there is a sort of transcendence of the collective over and above the relation to each individual act of credit.

An ethnology of the unconscious

This analysis was important in explaining what for me seems implied by the notion of symbolic capital, even by the most desacralised forms of symbolic capital, like the authority of a gendarme or a professor, but more generally in all forms of institutionalised authority, including sacerdotal authority. This means making another adjustment to Weber's analysis: Weber is right to contrast priesthood and prophecy,[14] but – and he says it himself[15] – the sacerdotal charisma possesses an institutional charisma, whose function is based on its manifest delegation. That said, it is important to bear in mind that, even in the

Lecture of 24 April 1986

most routine and banal or, in a word, the most bureaucratic forms of charisma, quasi-magical mechanisms (in the sense of a long-distance action on the body) intervene and, I have to say straight away, one of the questions posed by symbolic power is how it comes to pass that someone can act on bodies at a distance and produce emotions at a distance. How is it that some people are able to provoke somatic phenomena through a simple verbal action? How is it that a proclamation by the Pope can galvanise all the world's Christians?

This analysis of *fidēs* was important to defamiliarise (one of the functions of ethnology), by returning to the sources in a way, returning to the original social experiences that we needed to rediscover. At the same time, it indicates a form of realism. For substances, as I never tire of repeating, are the enemy of science. The notion of *kred*, in fact, is the common notion of power. Most of our enquiries into power deploy typically realist questions which tend to ask: 'Where does the power lie?' It would suffice to study the first-degree discourse of the press, which from time to time asks: 'Where does power lie today?', 'Who are the powerful?' Many seemingly scientific enquiries are of the same type: *Who Governs?* is the well-known title of a book by Dahl on power in the United States.[16] You might also think of the *Who's Who?* directory and its notion of 'who' is 'who', it being understood that the 'who' are the powerful. The very idea of power is a realist idea and implies a search for a sort of object located in certain places in the social world. Yet, as I have said [in the previous lecture], analyses of the type 'power comes from below' are naive, firstly because they situate power down below, but above all because they raise the question of power in terms of a location.

The analysis of *kred* is also important as part of a psychoanalysis of the scientific mind. What Benveniste has to offer is an ethnology of our unconscious where power is concerned. We think through language, which is why I believe that the philosophy of language, when intelligently conducted, is a valid instrument of sociological enquiry. Unfortunately, as all philosophers, particularly many analytic philosophers, despise things social, they stop at the point where things become interesting, often in fact because they would not know how to go further (it is not at all easy to go further, as I shall show you in a moment in the case of the proper name). Language is interesting in the sense that we deposit ourselves in it, our implicit philosophy of the social world becomes crystallised in it. The theory of the *kred* is a 'folk theory', as the ethnologists say; it is a popular theory of power. If you want to know what your theory of power is (or your theory of friendship or love), look at the language you use! This is what Benveniste

36 *Lecture of 24 April 1986*

teaches us, and ethnology makes its own kind of contribution to a psychoanalysis of the scientific mind.

The spontaneous theory of power ensnares us because it tricks us into seeing power as substance: it transforms a system of relations into a substance, even if this substance is indefinable. All the ethnologists have said it: the quality that all these substances like power (*mana*, *baraka*, etc.) have in common is that they are indefinable. They are interjections, exclamations, cries of admiration, etc. They are realities difficult to capture in words, but which are nonetheless very real. To escape from this realist vision of power or symbolic capital, we need in a way to shift our ground and reconstitute the system of relations within which the process described by Benveniste functions.

What are the social conditions enabling these processes whereby an agent becomes the subject of an object he has constructed as a fetish? The sense of my analysis is the following: we cannot understand symbolic capital or its symbolic effects without having recourse to what I call the *illusio*. Since it was quite some time ago that I discussed it in a lecture,[17] I shall remind you of the essentials. The *illusio* names the fundamental relation between a habitus and a field, the fundamental relation between on the one hand a socialised agent who, through their original experience of the social world, has acquired categories of perception and appreciation, and on the other hand a structured space. This relation, which I call the *illusio*, is a sort of immediate adherence of the agent to the world as given, which I mentioned last time under the heading of the notion of *doxa*, but with something extra: the *illusio* is indeed an immediate adherence to the proposals of the social world, to the *nomos* or the fundamental law of the social world, to the rules of the game (which are not constituted as rules), but at the same time it is connected with an investment in the game, and we could translate *illusio* by 'interest' or by 'investment'. The *illusio* is what makes us experience the game as worth being played.

I have made a detour via the *illusio* because symbolic power is a special case of the *illusio*: its function is based on *illusio*, it is a dimension of *illusio*. For a symbolic power to operate, we need an agent to have been established as the central bank for the deposit of symbolic capital; but for such an agent to be so established (established for instance as an 'author' in a literary field or a star couturier in the field of high fashion[18]), the field must exist as such. Marcel Mauss, who is, I believe, my only real precursor in the notion of field, noted it very well in his 'Essay on Magic':[19] for a magician to become the holder of a real power to act on people's bodies, a space must have been created where people believe in magic, where there are magical acts

Lecture of 24 April 1986 37

and objects, rivalry over magic, struggles between sorcerers for the true power of magic, and so on. In any case, for the concentration of capital to be possible, a field of production of capital must exist. The magical cosmos must exist for the magician, and his magical effect, to be possible. It is therefore not simply the relation of a believer to the object of belief, a one-to-one person-to-person relation, that we have to consider – it is a space in its entirety.

In his famous 'Essay on Magic', which changes its meaning entirely when read in the way that I suggest, Mauss refutes in succession all attempts to situate the principle of magic in a particular site.[20] He does with magical power exactly what I have done briefly with power in our societies. He says: 'You are looking for magical power, you are going to look for it in the sorcerer, or in objects, but you will not find it, because it is in the field itself.' It is the same with power: you can hunt for it in businessmen, bishops, bosses, the 'top hundred families' or the 'hundred most powerful men', but you won't find it. What we need to find is what makes the powerful powerful; how, for instance, the belief that produces the great artist as a holder of the power of creation is itself created.

The examples of ethnicity and the designer label

The analysis of *fidēs* was important insofar as it gives us a close-up view of the substantialist, realist error. The reduction of *fidēs* to a personal, one-to-one relation leads us to forget the social conditions producing the relation: for this relation to become possible, a whole universe, a whole cosmos, has to be established. I may sound very abstract, especially with my use of Greek and Latin terms, but I am thinking of extremely concrete things, and this survey of the foundations, although it may not plumb the most profound metaphysical depths, is extremely important for a proper understanding of even some very trivial things.

I am thinking for instance of the notion of ethnicity. It is a serious problem: Why, in most societies, are certain ethnic groups devalued? Why, in most societies, are certain groups stigmatised? Conversely, why does belonging to certain groups, such as those with a certain skin colour or a certain bodily *hexis*, confer a kind of capital? We can find historical reasons, but if we raise this kind of question seriously we do in fact raise all the questions that I raised this morning and in the previous lecture. I am not going to perform the exercise, but if you develop what I have said about the notion of 'race' (I place the word in inverted commas: I mean ethnicity), you will see that we can describe the notion

38   *Lecture of 24 April 1986*

of ethnicity as a form of symbolic capital, positive or (in the case of the stigmatised) negative, and I believe that my double critique of *fidēs* as substance and of the notion of *fidēs* as simple projection will take on its full meaning.

Let us take for instance Sartre's famous analysis in *Anti-Semite and Jew* of the racist's relation to the race that is stigmatised.[21] As always, Sartre adopts a radically subjectivist position that is partly true, or rather (since truth may not be halved) neither true nor false. He adopts the subjective side of the *fidēs* relation: he considers that it is the racist who creates the stigma, which then becomes the accumulation of a series of acts of consciousness through which the subjects establish a property that exists only in and through their gaze. This amounts to saying: 'Change your gaze and you will make the ethnic difference disappear.' This position can lead, as subjectivism often does, to a form of spontaneist voluntarism, which envisages political action as a sort of appeal for conversion: 'Be good, stop being racist, drop your racist gaze and the accursed race will disappear.' But in fact, to make the racist gaze disappear, you would have to make the racist more or less disappear. Just remember everything that I was saying earlier about the notion of *fidēs* – you could replace *fidēs* with 'the sacred', it works the same way: does the sacred produce acts of consecration or is it produced by such acts? This is an eternal problem, and Otto's book on the sacred,[22] for example, focuses on this alternative (I could develop this at length). The racist gaze is a product of social circumstances. To account for the experience of the sacred, the *kred* and the *fidēs*, the experience of the accursed or chosen race, you need to take into consideration not only a subjective and constituent relation that is fetishist in the naive sense, but also the construction of the space that renders the fetish possible.

This is true also in the case of art. I say this rather sarcastically because of a phrase from Walter Benjamin: as soon as we see research likely to result in some progress, people hurry to diminish it by finding a predecessor. This is no bad thing, but reactions like 'It was there in Gramsci already', 'It was there in Benjamin already' prevent us from seeing what is new, and its importance as something new, as progress (in other words, such reactions are a defence mechanism). Benjamin's famous sentence on the fetishism of the author, or, I forget the exact details, the proper name in art,[23] raises the question that I have been discussing this morning. Although the proper name, or the author, is a fetish, it is not the result of a fetishist act performed by an individual believer, nor even by a group of believers; it takes the whole structure of the artistic field to be mobilised to produce the fetish of the proper

Lecture of 24 April 1986 39

name. You only need a historical overview of the birth of the artistic field to see that it took five or six centuries of collective work to construct little by little, in dribs and drabs, the fetishism of the author in the modern sense of the term, which was not really established before the 1880s, the process having started in the Quattrocento through successive innovations (the signature of the painter, etc.).[24]

The idea that we can reduce an author (I am putting this clumsily, but it is a difficult problem) to being the product of an act of subjective oblation, whereby I abdicate my constructive freedom by forgetting the constructive power that I have exercised and by suffering in bad faith a power that I myself have produced (a Sartrean analysis of bad faith would come in useful here[25]) is a very naive argument. Collective bad faith is in fact not the sum of individual acts of bad faith. It is of another order, and Mauss's magnificent statement, which I quoted last time, that 'society always pays itself with the false coin of its dreams',[26] reminds us that fetishism, as concentration of symbolic capital, is not the result of many little individual calculations whereby the subject abdicates its freedom to constitute dominant figures as dominant. We see in passing that the Sartrean tradition and those who say that 'power comes from below' share the idea that in the last analysis social agents are responsible for creating the power that acts upon them, which is true, but not at all in the sense intended by the philosophers of the subject. I find it hard to express these very difficult things . . . I think that you have already understood, but I am persuaded that, in a moment's time, you and I will all make mistakes that confound the analysis I have just made, for, however obvious, it does at the same time oppose all the deepest tendencies of our thinking.

Collective bad faith is not the sum of individual acts of bad faith. The institutionalisation of symbolic power turns it into a sort of substance, an omnipresent, impalpable reality like *mana* or *baraka*, something which is everywhere but which under certain conditions some people can mobilise because they are recognised as worthy of mobilising this social energy, which is everywhere and nowhere. To understand the miracle of the designer label (I take this example because it is doubtless the most extraordinary) – wherein a stylist, by the simple act of writing his signature on an object, multiplies its value a thousand times – we can't just invoke the relation between a mystified, self-mystifying client (suffering bad faith) and the object; we need to reconstitute the whole universe which produces the client as well as the object. We need to reconstitute the social conditions of the production of a space capable of producing something so formidable, incredible and implausible that it convinces the client to sign a cheque for several hundred dollars for

40 *Lecture of 24 April 1986*

something that, without the label, would be worth a hundred times less. Often we only half understand this kind of mystery of the social world.

I may well be giving you the impression that I am confusing things that are very different, but I think that the problem of ethnicity is of the same order: objects that are stigmatised and execrated (in the negative form of the sacred) function according to the same logic as sacred, consecrated objects. To account for the phenomenon of negative symbolic power, associated for example with ethnic identity, it is not enough to grasp a relation that could be explained by an act of conscious awareness. I did myself last time drop a hint that sociology, as a force of revelation dissipating misunderstanding, might have a critical virtue able to help neutralise some of the effects of social mechanisms; this was an attack of intellectual utopianism (but since this is not one of my habitual vices, the temptation to transgress must have been very powerful), which is understandable: for an intellectual the idea that they may be of some use, however limited, is their reason for living. The illusion that acquiring knowledge or raising consciousness may dissipate misunderstanding comes from the fact that we reduce social relations deriving from a structure to being direct social relations between the fetish and the subject worshipping it.

The habitus as determination and as sensitivity

I shall now try to proceed a little faster. What I want to show, finally, is that the social condition enabling this kind of fetishist relation, which lies at the heart of the very existence of the social world, is the relation between, on the one hand, the habitus as a system of principles of perception of the social world and, on the other hand, the social space. If the habitus is produced through the incorporation of social structures and becomes inserted in a social space that is the source of its own structures, the question of the source of action arises in a very strange fashion. In fact, since the habitus is produced by the structures of the field, we could as easily say that the field determines the habitus as we could that the habitus determines the practices. We could also say that the agents are 'self-determining', if we take the expression in its literal sense: the agents are only determined insofar as there exists in them a principle through which the virtual determinations of the field can operate. For instance, the specific determinations that the field exerts on somebody who is sensitive to the game of art will have no effect on somebody who is not. The paradox of the particular form that social determinations take is that they need the collaboration (rather than the 'complicity', an awful word that has no meaning other than a moral connotation) of those who suffer these determinations.

Next time, I shall take Virginia Woolf's book, *To the Lighthouse*, to try to show how a fundamental difference between men and women, linked to the division of labour between the sexes, is that the women, due to the very logic of the process of socialisation, are less disposed than the men to be taken in by the social *illusio*: they are less taken in by social games, which, depending on the viewpoint we adopt, either privilege them or victimise them. In the same way we could say that the dominated are less taken in by the social games of culture. The social games of culture leave them cold, which is one way for them to exclude themselves when these are the dominant games, where you need to 'belong': the worst way to be excluded is to be excluded in such a way that you exclude yourself, and the worst way of excluding yourself is to be uninterested in the game.

Thus it seems to me that what is generated in this relation between a field and a habitus structured according to the structures of the field is the *illusio*. The habitus is determined, or it determines the world to determine it, in this relation. There are determinations that only affect those people who are determined to perceive them (others will not even perceive them) and, having perceived them, are sensitive to their effects. There is then a sensitivity to the injunctions of a space which is the product of a particular relation between a habitus and a field. In place of the simplistic notion of 'stimulus-reaction' we substitute the notion of the habitus, with its very different definition of the relation between social agents and the world. The stimulus which determines and triggers action, which causes somebody to act or not to act, is the product of a relation between two historical products: a field which is itself a product of history (as the field of painting today is the cumulative product of a whole series of artistic revolutions) and the habitus which, as the incorporation of the structures of this field, is also a product of history. It is in this relation that there arises a determination which seems spontaneous, but which in fact, as it passes through the cognitive structures of the habitus, passes through a whole historical process.

Here we need to analyse some very concrete things. We say for instance: 'People are sensitive to. . .', or we wonder about differences in sensitivity to disorder (M. Chirac was talking about order and disorder yesterday evening[27]). When you are a sociologist, you know in advance who is more attentive to this or to that: there is a kind of elective, selective attentiveness – or deafness. We might say that one of the dimensions of the habitus is a differential sensitivity to what is universally proposed; for example, order and disorder. If, as François Boivin has done,[28] you study the current evolution of the differential appeal of religious and lay educational establishments, you will be obliged to take into account the differential sensitivity of families according to their habitus – that is, their positions in the social world, their history, etc. – to order and disorder in educational establishments, and the crucial factor will appear to be that, other things being equal, the probability of sending your children to a private school is linked to a stronger sensitivity to this kind of disorder.

Another example: the research on fertility that I conducted some years ago.[29] The details are too complicated to be repeated here (that said, you can find them anywhere, they have become common knowledge), but we were able to show that an important factor in the differential fertility of different families was a differential sensitivity to security or insecurity: it all looks as if the social agents, following the most unconscious impulses of the habitus (rather than rational calculations for the future), register an ensemble of very different factors (the risk of war, the threat of crisis, the value of the franc, family benefits, health-care provision, etc.) which help to create a context of security or insecurity. It is this sensitivity to security (which, again, is a reciprocally determined relationship) that is the true determining source of choices in fertility. In the same way, choosing to become a bishop or a teacher depends on issues of security.

I am rather embarrassed to say that I'm afraid you may be losing the drift of the argument, which is most important (I shall try to make things clearer next time). I shall attempt to sum it up in a few sentences. To understand the phenomena that I have been describing, which show how people can be affected by a very strange symbolic type of power, we need to take into account the fundamental relation between social agents and the social worlds they inhabit, which is a relation of investment, of *illusio*, which, although it may be an illusion for somebody observing the game from the outside, is not experienced as illusory at all by those on the inside – for them there is nothing more serious. To understand the phenomena of symbolic power, we need to look at our foundational relationship with the social world, involving the very depths of the body, whereby we are in a way domesticated and appropriated (in both the active and the passive senses) by the social world that we ourselves appropriate. It is this fundamental relation, which involves the totality of the field rather than being constituted in small stages in a personal relation between an individual x and an individual y, that is the source of all the effects of symbolic power.

Lecture of 24 April 1986 43

Next time, I shall attempt to develop this obscure relation between an agent and the social world, taking the example of the relations between the sexes and using Virginia Woolf to help me say what I would not otherwise venture to say.

Second session (seminar): biography and social trajectory (2)

I would like to reply briefly to a question [that I received during the break]: 'Can the analysis that you presented this morning be applied to the symbolic capital acquired in everyday life by a banal commercial brand like *Pampers*, *La vache qui rit* or *Omo*?' I think it can, even if, within the overall class of symbolic power, things are specific, forms are nuanced and the social conditions of their possibility various. This is a big problem for advertisers: the symbolic capitals that they fabricate are fictions which we know to be fictions (the word 'fiction' says it plainly: it is something that is forged or fabricated),[30] whereas our more established illusions, that is, social illusions, tend to seem to be customs dating from 'time immemorial' – they benefit from a sort of amnesia regarding their genesis. I think that the work of the advertisers consists in mimicking, with greater or lesser success, our great social illusions. Hence the role of tradition. It is no accident if, when a business is taken over, the name of the brand is an issue that has to be negotiated: the symbolic capital of a firm exists, and it is very strongly linked to its historical tradition.[31] When they say 'Business founded in 1832', this is of course a guarantee of honourable reputation, reliability and consistency, but there is also an effect of tradition. We could trace the link between tradition and nobility, as well as other important things (but I cannot develop them here).

I shall switch from one subject to another. There are days when I am happy to change subjects, and others where I would prefer to continue with the same. Today is one of those days when I would be rather tempted to continue, to try to pursue some of the many routes that I have barely sketched out, but I shall in fact return to the biographical illusion and what I was saying last time about the usage of the life story as method.

I remind you briefly of the major themes. The notion of a life story is based on unconscious presumptions that, as in any institution, function independently of the researchers. If it enjoys a certain social success among sociologists, it is because it is a vehicle for an enormous social unconscious, which is in fact the collective unconscious. To comment briefly on this collective unconscious: to speak of a life

44 *Lecture of 24 April 1986*

story means establishing a life as a story, as a history, which answers to a socially constituted and approved temptation – a life may be the object of a narrative that has a sense (that is, both a meaning and an orientation), a linear narrative that has a beginning and an end, 'an end of story'. There is a kind of soft Hegelianism behind the theory of the story of a life and a life as history: the biographer is situated at the end of the story, and he tells the story while knowing how it ends. What Bergson called the 'retrospective illusion'[32] is thus one of the classic illusions of the biographer. It is the illusion of the person who knows the end and who says 'already', 'from then on. . .', 'from that moment', or 'From his early childhood, he had a talent for music.' He endows the whole story with a kind of purposiveness. Similarly, people may say spontaneously in interviews: 'I have always loved music. . .'. Formulae such as 'from the beginning' cover an implicit philosophy that views life as a story unfolding, and all the metaphors used to speak of a life are dynamic metaphors: the 'course', the 'curriculum', the 'pathway', the 'route' understood as 'road travelled', like a journey, with the stages covered (*opus operatum*) or the distance still to come.

The famous title of Maupassant's first novel, *A Life* (1883), is interesting because it draws on both senses of the word 'life': at once what is narrated (the history, the *Geschichte*) and the narrative of the history (the *Historie*). The life story implies the postulate that it is a coherent story: 'I am going to narrate in a coherent, chronological fashion.' For instance, in a book whose author I forget, *Flaubert's Parrot*,[33] the second chapter, 'Chronology', is a sort of ordered biography of Flaubert. So we identify chronological order with a kind of logical order. If you look at biographies written in the form of interviews (we don't have a word for it in French, which is a nuisance; the English do, 'life story', which is more helpful), you will see straight away that the person telling their life story gets events in the wrong order: they lose the thread, mix things up, tell things backwards. Sociologists are often rather rigid (for several reasons: they don't dispose of much time for the interview, they don't want to have to listen to the interview hundreds of times, and then there is the microphone, and the tape that is bound to run out [*laughter*]), so they put the biographic subject back on track ('Look, you were talking about 1924, let's go back to there, etc.') and replace him in chronological time.

In short, behind this very simple notion of a life story, there is a philosophy of collective history and a philosophy of individual history, which, being implicit, will be constantly at work. The effort to make it explicit, as I am doing here, is neither a luxury nor an epistemological

Lecture of 24 April 1986 45

point of honour for a researcher trying to look smart; it is simply the minimal condition for knowing what we are doing, which is simply, as I so often say, the Saussurean definition of epistemology.[34]

Importing a literary break

There is, firstly, a theory of life as a story and then a theory of that story being a coherent, linear and chronological discourse. As soon as you proceed chronologically you are going to implicitly suppose that B comes after A (it was bound to do so. . .) or that A will be the cause of B. You will create relations, and your respondents will not contradict you, because of a kind of anthropological point of honour (I think that there are anthropological invariants): everyone wishes to give meaning to their lives . . . they cannot tell you their life story like a Faulkner narrative. They get mixed up all the time, but despite everything they restore some order, they select, they emphasise some things and hide others, they create links and relations, they make sense. They establish relations where causes determine effects, relations where events have final causes. Overall, the narrative will be coherent, and it is no accident: the interests of the biographical writer and the biographical subject coincide, the biographical writer also wants a reasonably coherent package. This philosophy of the story as history does not disturb him, we had to wait for Faulkner to say that: life is perhaps the story of a madman. Subject and writer of biography are complicit. The interest of Faulkner, in *The Sound and the Fury* in particular, is to remind us that this definition of life as an orderly story is arbitrary. 'The sound and the fury' is borrowed from a famous tirade from the end of *Macbeth*: 'Life's . . . a tale told by an idiot, full of sound and fury, signifying nothing.'[35]

One small thing: what is most surprising is that sociologists who are not always uneducated can read the nouveau roman without their practice being affected. Given the fact that social scientists have been raised to shun literature and are constantly being told 'What you are doing is not science', or 'In fact, it is very well written, and therefore it is not science', they are obliged to defend themselves. What I am saying here is typical of research in the sociology of science. In particular, what Lepenies says of Buffon illustrates this very well: the famous Buffon, who was celebrated for his style, was in short scientifically undermined because he wrote too well.[36] There are also studies of Kant: I don't know whether they discover purposive intention, but at all events they note that he wrote very badly and that this was one way

46   *Lecture of 24 April 1986*

for him to break with social discourse and affirm a sort of scientificity or theoreticism independent of literature.

We need to remember that the social sciences are latecomers to the scientific world and that in the field of disciplines they hold the lowest rank in the hierarchy of the sciences and also in the hierarchy of the humanities. Thus defined by a double negative, they have a perpetual problem of identity, and writing is not an insignificant question. Therefore it is dangerous for them to look up references to Éditions de Minuit for a critique of biography; you need a rich symbolic capital to be able to do so [*laughter*[37]]. Consequently, we lead a kind of intellectual double life: we are very interested in the nouveau roman, but we continue to design biographies as if nothing had changed. This is a very general problem: I think that, for historical reasons, the artistic and literary fields have made all sorts of discoveries that are important for the social sciences, and may even be ahead of them in the theory of temporality or in the example that I am going to take today.

Another obstacle that hinders the assimilation by sociology of such conquests is that they are very often imported by the least serious specialists in the social sciences, who degrade the profession and who are in fact really 'men of letters' (in the pejorative sense of the term). It's the same with imports from ethnology: if just now I took so many precautions before making some legitimate borrowings, it is because I could cite the name of fifteen people, mostly French in fact (since France has specialised in these random raids on neighbouring disciplines), who have mishandled these imports. Importing them is difficult for all these reasons. I think that what I am doing here could be made more widely available. I know quite a few people who have something really important to say, but since they don't use the appropriate language and don't want to establish the problem of language as needing research (because it is a 'literary' thing – [not intrinsically, but because of the form that] literature has taken since the nineteenth century), they can be silenced by the current state of the languages available, by the type of language that is allocated to them, or by the dominant definition of language at a certain moment. I could go on, but the parenthesis would last too long, useful perhaps for some of you, but not for others.

Literature is a terrain where the break with this somewhat Hegelian definition of biography has happened, and on two levels at once: with the idea of the story as a linear, oriented narrative and at the same time with the idea of a life as something to narrate, a story or history. Insofar as many novels tell a story that is the story of a life (that of the author or a character), we could not liquidate the theory of the story in the sense of a discourse without considering whether to liquidate the

Lecture of 24 April 1986 47

theory of a life as discourse. Faulkner, Virginia Woolf, Joyce and then the nouveau roman have put the question, and the phrase by Robbe-Grillet that I quoted for you last time is an attack on the idea of a life as discourse which targets both the level of the narrated and the level of the mode of narration: 'This is all real, that is, fragmentary, elusive, insignificant and even so accidental and spontaneous that each event at any moment appears to be gratuitous, and ultimately all existence appears bereft of any unifying significance.'[38] Robbe-Grillet, then, passes from an attack on a unifying, totalising discourse, on the novel as totalisation, to an attack on the idea that life itself is totalisable or unifiable. His conclusion is that life is absurd, and bereft of sense and coherence.

We are not obliged to reach the same conclusion, and in any case I don't think that we can answer the question within the limited frame of sociology. But as sociologists we are obliged to respond to the two-pronged interrogation: firstly, is a narrative a coherent order, and secondly, is existence coherent? If, when we grasp its reality, life is found to be disorder, why should we put it in order, and if on the contrary life tends to reveal an order, what are the social principles generating that order? How does the social world go about giving life the appearance of a narrative and making all the socially approved forms of life stories coherent? The examples that I gave [in the last lecture]: the identity card, the curriculum vitae, the official biography and the biographical notices in *Who's Who?* are coherent, oriented and homogeneous affairs. All lives are different, yet they are always shown following the same pattern: there is a trajectory, that is, a cursus, a linear, oriented trajectory, marked out in stages (such as studies and examinations). How does the social world instil order, and why that particular order?

Establishing consistency

I gave you one of the principal determinants of this sort of biographical totalisation-unification: the proper name. The proper name is important, because for logicians it is a kind of acid test, or cross to bear: they don't know what to do with it, since it raises so many questions. It may sound arrogant to say so, but it seems to me to be a typical case where sociology, drawing on the findings of philosophers of language, can solve a problem of logic that is a problem of socio-logic, of sociology. I am saying this rather arrogantly, but I shall not write it down (when you come to read what I am working on now,[39] you will be able to verify that I will not be saying what I am saying here now). But I think

48   *Lecture of 24 April 1986*

that it is useful to say it, not in order to blow my own trumpet, but in order to bear in mind that certain problems of logic may well be sociological problems, and that if they can be solved in sociological terms, it is because they were in fact really sociological. This does not mean that the logical work by the logicians is useless, far from it, and I can say in all sincerity and modesty that without the work of the logicians I would not have even thought of the question, and consequently I would not have found the elements necessary for proceeding with these sociological problematics.

The proper name for Kripke is a rigid designator, which I referred to last time. It is a way of designating a person in such a way that they will continue to bear this designation through time and across social spaces (it is I who am adding 'across social spaces', but this is in fact implied in some of the logicians' analyses). Take the example of Marcel Dassault:[40] as an agent, he is at once a member of parliament, an aircraft constructor and president of several industrial concerns (which already amounts to several identities – for one man, that is already quite a lot), film producer, newspaper director and no doubt other things that I forget. . . What makes the unity of Marcel Dassault? It is the expression 'Marcel Dassault', and then the body of Marcel Dassault, the biological individual, but the biological individual only as socially established by the act of nomination.

What was said by Ziff, as a linguist, is important: nomination is a baptismal rite that endows a biological individual with a name for life, a name that establishes them, once for all time, as the bearer of an identity. The original baptismal nomination will become a foundation for all the later nominations; all of which (such as 'I appoint you president', 'I appoint you minister' or 'agrégé' or 'professor') appear to apply to the biological individual, but in reality affect the social person, that is, the biological individual as socially established, the social personage irreducible to one or other of their moments in time or any one of their states in one of the fields. For instance, to take a more concrete example of the problem: when M. Dassault needed to use his economic power as a press magnate, he signed a cheque. But the signature is once again a socially established property, it is a sign. . . You have the signature, what it signals, and the proper name. What is signalled, if you think about it, is something different again.

(Those of you who are not familiar with sociological manners must be saying to yourselves: 'But he is retailing trivial anecdotes, things we all know about. . .'. The problem is that knowing them so well, we no longer really know them. It is not easy to think at one and the same time of proper names, signs of identity and signatures, because

Lecture of 24 April 1986

the social conditions under which we think of these different things are too diverse; they are different fields and, if the logicians refuse to get involved – I am ready to bet that ten centuries of logic will never produce the relation between the proper name and the signature – it is because these fields are constitutions. I have always said that a field is a constitution, a *nomos* which, without explicitly affirming it, forbids you from thinking certain things in the space of that field. And yet there are so many things that we can only think by leaping over the barriers between fields.)

The inaugural nomination through which an individual receives a proper name is one of those rites of institution where you are told: 'This is what you are' (and implicitly always: 'This is all you are'). Rites of institution are an affirmation of a socially recognised nature associated with a limit; 'You are a man' means: 'You are not a woman', 'Take care not to be effeminate' – there are a good deal of negative aspects, and conversely, for 'You are a woman.' This inaugural act of nomination transforms the biological individual into a social personage who will be independent of passing time. In fact, what remains constant from birth until death is the proper name and what goes with it, that is, all the successive acts of attribution by which this sort of propertyless being, the proper name, becomes associated with properties, to such an extent that it ends up becoming almost the substance of all these accidents, that is, of all the properties that somebody can accrue in the course of a life.

Analyses of the proper name thus almost all agree in saying that the proper name, unlike the common noun, cannot be developed: it implies nothing, contains no information, it merely designates and indicates. It is often compared to the deictics ('here', 'there') which point out but give no information. I think that if this is the case, it is precisely because the proper name, as the product of a rite of institution, is a kind of constitution, a thesis with no content, like all acts of institution of the masculine/feminine type, rites of passage such as circumcision, where an arbitrary frontier of a quasi-magical type is drawn. The proper name carries no information: what it refers to (and here what I said in my last lecture about Proust and Albertine remains true) remains an anecdotal rhapsody, a 'tale told by an idiot' as Faulkner saw it, a series of things 'signifying nothing' that are not totalisable or cumulative, such as 'the former Albertine', 'the rubber-clad, rainy-day Albertine'.[41] In other words, it is a fragmentary and plural subject, its only consistency being this sort of consistency of the nominal instituted by the proper name through a sort of founding abstraction. The proper name is a kind of decision to blot out everything the post-Faulknerian

50 *Lecture of 24 April 1986*

novelist, say (it is more difficult in literature than in painting to find the breaks), tried to grasp, that kind of fragmentary subject with its differential sensitivity, impossible to totalise or unify.

It will act as the basis of what we call our ID, the civic status that is in legal terms the ensemble of those properties attached to a person, which have juridical effect under civil law. These properties will be nationality (which itself entails juridical effects: it implies obligations, duties, prohibitions, etc.), gender, age and profession. These properties, known as 'certificates' ('birth certificate', 'certificate of baptism', 'marriage certificate', etc.), which are described as registrations ('We hereby register. . .'), are in fact institutions that while apparently registering do actually institute. They are performatives that constitute a person as masculine, as French, and this transhistorical identity that the social world constitutes will provide the basis for a whole series of juridical certificates allocating the social categories (as I analysed them last year) through which society says what a person is. They are a series of acts of attribution associated with the proper name functioning as substance. Because of this, the proper name does not contain information, and yet the social world manages to [get round?] the kind of vacuum linked to the arbitrariness of the act of institution by giving a kind of official description of a social essence, established by the initial act of institution, that transcends the fluctuations of history.

In other words, the social institution delivers a series of certificates (which certify that the person concerned has such and such a property) of capacity or incapacity, all based on the postulate which lay at the heart of the attribution of the proper name: the consistency of the nominal beyond time and across space. I constantly denounce this postulate in my scientific research, but if historians and sociologists succumb to this illusion of the consistency of the nominal, it is precisely because the whole social order is founded on this effort to establish realities that escape time, to constitute what the English call *responsible* people, that is, people you can count on at any time. The postulate of consistency is linked to the existence of a social world affirming its permanence through its very existence. (This would merit a long debate, but I shall just insert a parenthesis, no doubt understandable only by professionals: I think that, to give meaning to his work, the sociologist or ethnologist postulates a sort of minimal functionalism, that is, that a social order tends to ensure its own perpetuation, its own eternalisation.)

I think that the great majority of social acts, particularly rituals, and especially the category of rituals that I call 'rites of institution', serve the purpose of establishing consistency. In a universe in flux, individuals are biological, they are mortal, even kings die, and this is one of

Lecture of 24 April 1986   51

society's great problems. To be able to say 'The king is dead, long live the king' (as shown in Kantorowicz's splendid book) the king has to have two bodies, a real body that dies and another that survives. This sort of principle of consistency is, I believe, a condition of the existence of societies (which does not mean that societies don't change). This postulate of consistency is in a way specified in the case of individuals by the assignation of lasting identities. The famous individual of 'methodological individualism' is a product constructed by the social world in hundreds of different ways, but among others in the ways that I have just indicated.

There is then the individual and all the properties that we assume to be constant, such as the property of being the head of a family. If we think about it, this property [of the father as head of the family] is very variable: the rights associated with being the father of three children, for instance, disappear when one of the children reaches the age of eighteen. The property of father as head of the family, however, is constituted once for all time, like the properties of a son, mother or wife, all properties that are constituted as constant, in general by acts of institution that are also acts of eternalisation. These consistent properties are associated with the most consistent of the constant properties, which is the person socially constituted through the proper name. There you are, I think that I have more or less finished the critical analysis of the notion of the proper name. I don't want to go on about it any further.

The space of biographical discourse

This critique of the presuppositions of the notion of a life story, and with it the practice of recording somebody's life story, has the aim of trying to understand what is happening when you record a life story, that is, what you do without realising it. [Thus you may hope to understand] the social conditions of production of the artefact that a life story is. For everything can always be retrieved by science. We can, for instance, always make a secondary statistical analysis of a disastrous statistical survey, as long as we rethink the social conditions of the construction of the sample and the categories of analysis. Similarly, we can make a scientific analysis of the stupidest biography (while often deploring many of its features), as long as we bear in mind as far as possible the social conditions of production of that artefact, the biography. Of course, a life story is a method which is not one. We should throw it overboard; it was smuggled into science, like so

52   *Lecture of 24 April 1986*

many common-sense notions (good sociologists do us all a favour by throwing overboard all sorts of jetsam and false concepts, and they are obliged to forge scholarly words to get round the common words bundled up in philosophies that haven't been analysed). That said, if people continue to produce them, it may happen that life stories become usable, as long as we admit that they are artefacts.

We also need to know the social laws governing the particular exchange that is the recording of a life story. It is not trivial to recall that the exchanges which establish scientific information are social exchanges (not many sociologists know this, although today it is becoming commoner; fifteen years ago, I assure you, there weren't so many). An enquiry, being a social relationship, is itself subject to social laws, especially the laws of production of discourse: a habitus, that of the biographical subject, is faced with a market and is therefore subject to the specific sanctions of the market. These sanctions depend on the representation that the biographical subject has of the biographer, of his representation of the idea of a life story. These representations also depend on how he pictures the situation and how he thinks of it by analogy with situations that he may have seen on television, where a politician or a writer is being interviewed. Even a good sociologist will be making use of these images, without realising it. The problem for the sociologist is to get people to speak and to say things that they would not say without the sociologist. If the sociologist has to intervene as a writer, he'll say that he is writing a 'biography' (rather than a 'life story') and he will not guarantee anonymity (because it would no longer be interesting for the writer – this brings us back to the proper name. . .). He does all this in a semi-conscious way, like an ordinary social agent who might, for the sheer pleasure of getting someone to speak, 'worm' some information out of them, as we might say. [. . .]

In fact, an enquiry is situated between an official police-style investigation (and very often sociologists' enquiries resemble subtle detective operations, appearing to expect obedience) at one extreme, and at the other extreme a confession where you forget yourself, where you let yourself go and you chat to a friend. These are the possible states of the market. Then there are the people who tell their own life: Annie Ernaux's story, *La Place*,[42] or Proust. It is not often that I offer definitions, but I can give a definition of biography. The biography covers all forms of public and therefore official presentation (as soon as there is publication, there is officialisation) of a private representation of somebody's life, public or private. A biography is a manifestation, it's a public show, it's a visible display for everybody's eyes. Because it is published, everybody can read it, whence the problems it causes: 'What if my father reads this biography? And if my mother reads it? And if my neighbours or the people I mention read it?' Sociologists face this problem all the time: should they indicate the proper name of the interviewee, or make them anonymous?

A biography is a public, and therefore official, presentation of a private image of a public or private life, but what I deliver is not my life, it's my representation of my life, it's my vision of my life. Now this is socially regulated: as you know from what I said earlier, it is something that the social world doesn't allow to be done any old how. To be the biographer of a king, you have to show your credentials; Marin wrote a very fine article on a historiographer who presented his candidature to Louis XIV and who tried to convince him that his viewpoint was the right one.[43] The social world controls people's viewpoints, and in particular the viewpoint of the subject on his own self. To abandon the right to write your biography to the first person who asks would, as you remember Faulkner said, result in 'a tale told by an idiot'. What the social world wants is not people who are going to tell their story to passers-by in the street, but *curriculi vitae* and *cursi honorum*, things organised in due form, that is, in the form of a form (as in English, an official form), which means subject to legal formalities and formal sanctions, since literary form is a formal form like any other. It is a euphemisation (I have made these analyses in the past).

Whether recorded by sociologists or others, the biographies that you are likely to come across will establish a place of possible discourses that will vary in very important ways, and not only according to the social origin of the enquiry, but to a much more pertinent degree according to the relation between the habitus of the biographical subject and the situation of the biographer, that is, according to the degree of censorship and its form, and therefore the degree of euphemisation and codification. Given the social conditions of production of the most likely biographies, everything leads us to believe that there is a strong likelihood of obtaining life stories designed as histories, and therefore as artefacts. In other words, we will have biographies that are, to different degrees, official; it is important to know this so as not to take statements of official ID for confidential information. This is one thing.

From the life story to the analysis of trajectories

We may wonder whether the criticism I have made disqualifies any study of human life considered as a process unfolding in time? I think not. It is obvious that in sociology we cannot avoid taking human existence into account as a cumulative experience involving a memory. The notion of a habitus is itself an acknowledgement of that reality. As I was saying just now, history is in action at every instant, through the habitus which is in a way the form it takes in the present moment; we could say, briefly, that the habitus is what mobilises history at a given moment in time. To understand this habitus in a non-substantialist, non-realist manner, we have to study it at its genesis, that is, relate it to the constitutive process whose product it is; and understanding it in its genesis means understanding the trajectory of which it is the outcome.

The change in word [i.e., the substitution of 'trajectory' for 'life story'] is important. Why say 'trajectory'? Because in so doing we think straight away of a space: we cannot think of a trajectory without thinking of the space within which it operates. Whereas the paradox of people who speak of life stories (you will see to what extent effects that have an unconscious impact are terrible) is that they manage to think of a life story as if it unfolded outside all space. That is tantamount to describing a journey without saying which countries are travelled through. This is what it is all about. Saying 'trajectory' is saying 'movement in a space' – the social space.

If you want to understand, for instance, why Flaubert is Flaubert, you have to know the events of Flaubert's life. But if you are Sartre,[44] you will do everything backwards and you will tell the story of a life before finding out about the universe in which this life story unfolds. You will say: Flaubert was born into a family of provincial notables, his father was a doctor in Rouen, he saw corpses in the courtyard when he was a child, he had an attack of epilepsy, etc. You will then have a chronological history (and then, in the second volume, you will say: 'Well, yes, but at the time there was the bourgeoisie'). You will tell of Flaubert's entry into the *lycée*, but at the time what was there beside the *lycées*? Were there colleges? The *lycée* is one point among others. If we place the *lycée* in a space, we start to understand what it meant to enter the *lycée* rather than entering a Jesuit college (in fact, this does have a connection with the dad who's a doctor, and not much of a believer, etc.). In other words, we have to situate each of the bifurcations of the story that ordinary biographies record in terms of a curriculum vitae, in the context of its relation to other possibilities. (On the subject of bifurcations, Virginia Woolf's anti-history is interesting because, as all the commentators have remarked, she makes the crises disappear entirely. I think that we don't even notice the death of the heroine in *To the Lighthouse*: we change chapters and we notice that the central character has disappeared, whereas in an ordinary biography, 'The

Lecture of 24 April 1986   55

Death of Mrs Ramsay' would be a complete story). Even such crucial events have no sense outside of a space.

I shall use a metaphor to help you understand. [With ordinary life stories] it is usually as if you were describing a trip on the underground without knowing the tube map: you describe your passage through a space that you don't understand, without knowing what it means to pass from one station to another because you don't know how these points are situated in relation to each other. You don't have the network of all possible routes that is represented on the tube map. For instance, to understand what it means for Flaubert to leave one review in order to write for another, you need to know the space of the reviews. In the 1950s, leaving *Esprit* to go and write for *Les Temps Modernes* was a very important move (it was in fact very unlikely – and would have been even more so in the opposite direction). There is a hierarchy among reviews. There is a space for placement and a space for movement, and to understand the movements, you need to understand the placements, in the double sense of financial invest-ment and placing in a space. In the 1950s, *Les Temps Modernes* was a much better investment than *Esprit*, and, consequently, moving from *Les Temps Modernes* to *Esprit* was really counter-productive; it was a dead end or a failure. The event is very interesting when it does happen: the writer passing from *Les Temps Modernes* to *Esprit* has no sense of placement; so we need to look at their social origins, and we shall no doubt find that he's a provincial lad who has no notion of the games played in Paris [*laughter*], whose plans are miscalculated and whose strategies backfire, against his best intentions. We cannot understand such changes unless we understand the space in which they operate.

Here I want to underline the interest of my analysis: you could easily talk for an hour on the notion of biography without thinking of the simple questions that I have been raising. You could refer to the choice of a bishop who, after studying at the École Normale in the 1930s, converted to Catholicism, joined the Sillon movement,[45] then became head of the scouts in France. It is easy enough to recount, but it has no meaning. And you might write: 'From then on he turned towards a progressive Catholicism, which we see now in the fact that he is Archbishop of Saint-Denis'; but then we have explained nothing at all, because we have made the link between the starting point which we don't understand and the finishing point which finds us equally ignorant. To know what they mean, you need to have (and have analysed) the two spaces, and they obviously change. A trajectory is in fact a movement in a space that changes, even if, of course, it

56 *Lecture of 24 April 1986*

is not changing all the time, and not at the same speed all the time, and even if we need to distinguish major from minor changes. (In passing, let me say that the notion of generation is yet another of those catastrophic common-sense notions smuggled into sociology. It is a biological type of notion and everybody has been through the process of wondering when a generation starts – how to break and divide it? Enough said.)

In fact you need to know the space in order to understand the shifts of position, their significance and their importance, which are connected. The moves imply values: since the space is oriented, there are moves upwards, and others downwards[46] which are failures, regressions, collapses or even fiascos. The construction of these spaces is then a necessary preliminary to any biography. This is a complete reversal of the apparently scientific approach adopted by so many people, including those, like Sartre, who think they are writing social history. Sartre in fact continues to implicitly accept the most naive philosophy of history as if it were history itself. To be rather wicked, I might say that the notion of an 'original project'[47] is obviously the ideology of the professional biographer: it is what enables him to say things like: 'From then on' or 'From that moment. . .'. That said, their approach has one advantage, because it is founded on a philosophy of the subject and of liberty. What makes the philosophers more interesting than the historians and the literary historians is that they commit their blunders openly, which does lead them to make some progress. (This is not a simple joke at their expense: historians seem always to be more scientific than the sociologists, for example, simply because their blunders are scientific and secret, with no hint of shame. . ..) There is great virtue in triumphal errors. God knows that Sartre made some, and his 'original project' is one of them.

I shall finish now. This substantiation of the notion of biography shows up the difference between social ageing and biological ageing. It is of course self-evident that there is no social ageing without biological ageing. Any displacement in social space takes time. As Bergson said, you have to 'wait until the sugar melts'.[48] Similarly, you have to take time to construct a career, and as I have shown several times in my research,[49] social differences often translate into temporal differences. Moving through social space takes time and is therefore accompanied by biological ageing. Because of this, we tend to confuse biological ageing and social ageing, which are rather like the two faces of the same coin. But if you have been paying attention to what I am saying, you will understand that social ageing has nothing to do with biological ageing. To give you an idea: a social existence, a socially constituted biography, a curriculum vitae, are a series of unavoidable crossroads we are all confronted with; at each crossroad we age socially, insofar as potentials die at each of them, and we could count a social age by the number of branches on the tree of potentials that have died.

Lecture of 15 May 1986

First session (lecture): a dispositional solution – The independence of the habitus from the present – Prediction, protention and projection – Changing the habitus – Power – The petit-bourgeois relation to culture Second session (seminar): To the Lighthouse *(1) – Fields as traps – A man-child – Men, oblates of the social world*

First session (lecture): a dispositional solution

Today I would like to continue to analyse the relation between the habitus and the field that I have set out, to try to show the nature of that relationship. In fact nowadays people tend to use the notion of the habitus rather mechanically, reducing it to the traditional form that it took in Aristotle, the scholastic tradition and others,[1] whereas I think that we need to restore its full implications. In my analyses today I shall aim to show that resorting to this model, far from being a mere historical gesture, enables us to avoid all sorts of false problems in the social sciences, and in philosophy too. Basically, one of the questions that the notion of the habitus aims to solve is the one put by Wittgenstein: 'What does it mean to follow a rule?'[2] If this query by Wittgenstein has given rise to an immense philosophical literature, it has inspired sociologists and anthropologists less, although they are confronted with the problem directly. I believe that the notion of habitus represents one possible solution to the question 'What do I call a rule?' – in my opinion the only good solution, which is sometimes named by philosophers the 'dispositional solution', an expression associated with the name of Gilbert Ryle. I shall return to this.

To say that the habitus is the source of our practices, and that action is determined by the relation of a habitus to a field, is to say that the

Lecture of 15 May 1986   59

habitus determines its action, which should disturb those who see in the notion of habitus a determinist concept. The habitus determines what it is in a situation that determines it. As a system of dispositions and patterns of perception and appreciation, it establishes the social significance of the situation, it endows it with sense. The habitus selects from within the situation the features that are pertinent from its point of view (the habitus is in fact a socially situated and durable point of view). In a way, it establishes the event or the situation as a significant event, and it is this significant event that motivates its reaction to the situation. It is, then, the relation between the habitus and the field that establishes the social world as the site for things to be done (as when we say: 'That's what needed to be done', 'He did what had to be done', 'It was the only thing you could do', etc.) or not to be done, the site for emergencies, objective imperatives or, in Weber's terms, objective potentials.

In this light – remembering what I said previously some time ago[3] – the idea that the source of action resides in the very obscure relation between the habitus and the field enables us to avoid the alternative that social scientists and action theorists fall into when they set mechanical determination of action following a stimulus/reaction pattern in opposition to calculated, rational and conscious action (Weber, who is one of the rare sociologists to have thought about what the determining sources of an action can be, calls the stimulus/reaction pattern 'merely reactive behaviour', *bloss Reaktion*).[4]

The notion of the habitus echoes the logic that Ryle sometimes calls 'dispositional' in *The Concept of Mind*, where he elaborates its philosophical definition. To explain what he means by a 'dispositional reaction', Ryle writes: 'I shall shortly argue that to explain an act as done from a certain motive is not analogous to saying that the glass broke because the stone hit it, but to the quite different type of statement that the glass broke, when the stone hit it, because the glass was brittle.'[5]

In other words, to understand a reaction, we need to know the durable dispositions of the agent producing that reaction: these durable dispositions may be in a way solicited by an accidental cause (in this particular case, the stone), but the veritable source of the reaction lies in the durable dispositions of the agent in question. This is what I was saying last time when I drew on the notion of sensibility or sensitivity ('sensitivity to disorder', 'sensitivity to order', 'sensitivity to security', etc.): this sensibility – this kind of factor that sociologists constantly invoke in order to explain, for instance, the phenomena of delinquency – is a permanent, differential property of socialised individuals, written into their habitus. [. . .]

60 *Lecture of 15 May 1986*

I have mentioned the alternative of conscious action and mechanist reaction in which sociology is traditionally trapped. In anthropology (as I showed some time ago),[6] Lévi-Strauss avoided this alternative by playing on the ambiguity of the word 'rule', which may refer to a transcendental rule, that is, a norm explicitly stated, socially established and possibly guaranteed by the law (in this case the rule becomes a juridical rule, accompanied by sanctions), or to a rule immanent in the game, that is, something regular. Lévi-Strauss (as I have shown in discussing his preface to *The Elementary Structures of Kinship*) appears to evade this alternative through a kind of permanent play on both senses of the word. The rule of kinship can in fact be treated as an explicit, consciously enunciated form, dictated by some agency (difficult to define in this particular case, since in general there is no judicial system in those societies where people talk of rules of kinship – but we can always hypothesise. . .), and it is true that anthropological enquiries show us that all societies have a form of marriage that they prefer.

During the structuralist years, the rule for kinship could also be understood as a 'model', the word 'model' being fashionable, and the structuralists played with the physicalist connotations of the notion of model to say that, in their matrimonial behaviour (at the time people did not talk of 'matrimonial strategies'), social agents set in motion unconscious models that are inscribed in the structure of the brain, or who knows where (there are some very strange things in Lévi-Strauss's writing on this subject). Ultimately, the dual meaning of the word 'rule' and the alternative of the norm and the physical model represent another form of the alternative of the conscious and the unconscious, of the action as mechanist reaction and the action as explicit, rational and conscious project.

The independence of the habitus from the present

It is this set of alternatives that we need to reject in order to account for something which is very strange when you come to think of it, but which imposes itself as obvious once you do take it into account: the fact that social agents are never reducible to the contemporary state of their practices, that what they do or what they think is never completely intelligible in the momentary instant of synchrony, in the immediate present. Yet it is this sort of instantaneous agent who is set up as the behaviourist model or the model of conscious calculation: the calculating subject, *homo oeconomicus calculans*, taking command of the universe of pertinent variants in order to determine the rational action and make the right choice at the right moment, acting, as we say, when fully informed of the facts. As I have said on a previous occasion,[7] there is no fundamental difference between an action fully informed of the facts and an action determined by the facts; basically, it comes to the same thing. This is why, as happens so often in the social sciences, the two opposing positions encourage each other and the scientific debates continue to infinity. (There are a whole lot of social mechanisms that support this indefinite reproduction of false problems, starting – as I always say – with the education system, which loves to take false problems and turn them into three-part essays.)

For social agents are never reducible to a present moment: they are history incorporated. To show this, I shall take an example that will provide an introduction to what I shall be saying in the second session: the celebrated example of the digressions in Virginia Woolf. [. . .] I think that we understand Virginia Woolf's novels better if we see them as a series of bubbles that the linear disposition of writing forces her to develop successively, but which are contemporaneous. In *To the Lighthouse* we are in this way inside Mr Ramsay's mind for a few seconds, then we move into Mrs Ramsay's mind: so we have a sort of speech bubble, as in a cartoon,[8] where a series of thoughts has been developed, while at the same time, there was another thought bubble. The second bubble was contemporaneous with the first, but in the novel they follow on, and since we are in the habit of reading things that are written successively and which happen successively, we read as successive things that are actually contemporaneous. This is why we have trouble understanding this kind of novel and see a rejection of realism and verisimilitude in something that is in fact much more faithful to reality than the classic Balzacian unfolding of the order of narrative. These Woolfean digressions are very interesting. (I am tending to use novels to say things that, since I am not a psychologist, I am not qualified to say, but that I feel psychologists do not really say: you take your pickings where you find them. . ..)

In his magnificent book, *Mimesis*, Auerbach offers a very fine and much lauded commentary entitled 'The Brown Stocking'.[9] It deals with a passage from *To the Lighthouse*. This novel is about a planned trip to a lighthouse and about Mrs Ramsay, who is knitting a stocking for the lighthouse keeper's little boy. She tries it on her son, who is waiting impatiently to go out and who is furious with his father, who has said that it is going to rain and that they can't make the trip (these details are important because of what I am going to tell you in a moment). Around something as insignificant as a stocking, a whole series of thoughts occurs in different characters, in particular those of

62   *Lecture of 15 May 1986*

Mrs Ramsay concerning the father's words, the little boy's chagrin, her vision of the social world with the poor and the orphans needing help. All this is developed in a great 'speech bubble'.

More generally, in Virginia Woolf, insignificant events trigger a series of representations that constantly drift away from the present time and the people present, and move through the layers of time. And the plurality of minds, the plurality of agents endowed with a habitus, find expression in multiple time scales. These apparently contemporaneous agents (they are in the same room and can talk to each other) are at the same time separate from each other, their thoughts developing in different social times in their different histories, whose generating principle is their habitus. Basically it is because they have different histories that they have different temporal representations, that they inhabit different time scales. This analysis – which is no doubt not very original as literary criticism, but which becomes more original if we apply it to the everyday social world – is very close to what Heidegger says in the second part of *Being and Time* on the subject of public and private time. The public 'temporality' that people follow when they want to 'be on time', to meet others at an agreed time and an agreed place, this time that we agree to observe (making a date means coming to an agreement about our private time scales, it means placing our private time scales in parenthesis in order to agree to coincide synchronically with public time), this public, socially constituted time, this calendar time,[10] which is a very important historical conquest (calendars have not always existed – the first were mostly made by the church in an attempt to synchronise their festivals), masks our private times, our private experiences of the present as constituted by our habitus, which are themselves constituted in time.

This leads us to say that this habitus, which is often seen as a kind of iron cage in which the agents are enclosed, is also something that represents freedom from the present. For instance, in *To the Lighthouse* we have, as I have said, a kind of series of bubbles, then it is time for the family meal – a moment when, in the logic of the novel, all the bubbles ought to converge for everyone to be synchronised. Each in their own corner has been turning their own history into a little story, and now they are coming together simultaneously for the time of the meal, which, in a private house, is a public moment. This is the moment when the heroine of the novel enacts her official role as 'the lady of the house', so to speak, dominating the scene. And the domineering mistress tells the time and says 'You will be on time', and the people are on time, they synchronise their clocks. Then the bubbles start to function again.

Lecture of 15 May 1986   63

Depending on your mood, you may find what I am saying gratuitous or slightly bizarre, but it is an important key for understanding what the habitus is really doing in its relationship with a social world. The representations of the social world or the field where they act that agents conjure up are linked to the immediate moment of action [. . .] only through the mediation of the habitus, which is independent of the present moment. The mind's representations enjoy a sort of temporal independence from the present, and from the external stimulus that has triggered them. This independence of the habitus from the present is the foundation of what we need to know in order to understand the reaction of an agent and the nature of the stimulus that makes them act. In Ryle's example, the stone is not enough; you need to know how brittle the glass is. Similarly, a political event is not itself enough; you need to know the socially constituted, differential sensitivity of the different agents to order, disorder and crisis, etc. External reality does of course exist, but this is only a starting point, for the *stimuli* come somewhere between the pretext for or occasion of the practice and its trigger; they are not at all, as one might have thought, determining (in the mechanist sense of the term). The analogy of a spring is perhaps more accurate than Ryle's example: the event unleashes springs that pre-exist it; if we know the habitus, we can get to know the springs which will properly enable us to predict how a person will react to an event.

(In passing, we might contrast Virginia Woolf with Proust.[11] Proust, who is always credited with a very complex theory of temporality, is ultimately much more simplistic than Virginia Woolf. I shall not develop this – since I have already done my literary stint, you would find me over the top – but, basically, Proust has psychologised the notion of habitus. He did say some very interesting things, but not in the places where we usually look for them. And it is not in the places that he thought he was being profound that he really was. It seems to me that he was much more of a sociologist than a psychologist, and that his best theories are sociological rather than psychological;[12] which is quite the opposite of what people usually say about him, when they follow a kind of Bergsonian scenario involving the madeleine cake, etc.[13])

The habitus, then, is a sort of incorporated structure which orients our perceptions. Here I believe that the notion of habitus calls for an important remark. I was saying the other day that symbolic capital is established through a cognitive relationship,[14] while explaining that 'cognition' is not to be reduced, as we usually think, to intellectual knowledge. Given the alternative of reaction and consciousness, we do in fact automatically lean towards consciousness: we think for instance

64 *Lecture of 15 May 1986*

that the relation to cultural capital which establishes the latter as symbolic capital is a cognitive, intellectual, conscious and thetic relation, implying a position conscious of that relation. In fact the implications of knowledge can be of a different order from those that we normally associate with 'cognition' or 'knowledge'. By linking the term to an intellectualist and cognitive philosophy, we forget that there are modes of knowledge which are practical, infra-conceptual, infra-thetic (neither explicit nor explicitly constituted) and, basically, corporeal.

This knowledge that the habitus practises, so to speak, is quasi-corporeal and calls for metaphors taken from dance and sport, practices where the agents do what has to be done in the mode of gymnastics, not the mode of algebra. I remind you here of an important argument that I have often rehearsed: the structuralist error, in particular in the case of myth and ritual, lies in describing as an algebra rituals that are a gymnastics. It is not because there is a logic of ritual, and because we are able to construct systems of oppositions ([just as I argued earlier] on the theories of kinship), that this gymnastics should be either, as Lévi-Strauss suggests, a system of unconscious mathematical models buried within the dualism of the brain (I am barely making this up), or a system of consciously posited norms. In fact the habitus is precisely that mode of practical knowledge (thinking always of the metaphor of a feel for the game) able to master a situation at a level below any conscious awareness and yet without being a mechanist reaction.

In the relation between a habitus and a field there arises what we may call a 'feel for the game', a feel for the logic of the game ('logic' being understood in the practical sense of: 'How does it work?', 'What is going to happen?', 'What will turn up?', 'Which way will he pass the ball?', 'Where will he place the ball?', and so forth). This practical feel for the game is a form of knowledge, which translates into anticipation, for there is such a thing as a practical prediction (the word 'prediction' is yet another of those intellectualist words). On the subject of science, Cavaillès said quite rightly that 'to predict something is not to foresee it':[15] scientific prediction is not an intuitive anticipation; it is a construction, a theoretical hypothesis. But in practical life, to predict is to foresee. Cavaillès is clearly right in scientific terms, but in practical terms, to predict is to foresee.

Prediction, protention and projection

Now I would like to expand upon this last point a little, taking the distinction between protention and projection made famous by Husserl.[16]

This distinction has never been much explored, while people have reflected more on the complementary distinction between retention and memory. To explain, briefly, Husserl insists on the fact that perceiving the present is always perceiving something beyond the actual, immediate present. There is a sort of halo of non-presentness surrounding the immediate present, surrounding what he calls the 'directly perceived'. He speaks of pre-perceptive anticipations and of retentions, which are not posited as future. This pre-perceptive anticipation, or protention, is not a projection. It is a future which is not posited as such, but which is part of the present, which is virtually present. Husserl takes the example of the part of the table which you do not see because the legs are hidden (this is how philosophers work, they always take slightly bizarre examples): that part which you don't see is to-be-perceived, it is forth-coming; if you walk round the table you will see it, and it will offer itself up to be perceived, although you do not perceive it now. It is a sort of future-to-come that is present in the present. In the same way, retention is not a memory, but something which has been actualised, something which you have presentified at one instant t and which, now that you are looking at something else, has become in-actual and de-presentified. This analysis, which may seem purely formal, is I believe crucial. It is the foundation of a genuine sociological theory of temporality, insofar as 'to temporalise oneself' is to pass from one thing to another ... (I am not trying to achieve a philosophical effect and it would be better to express that in two different ways [in a philosophical way and a more concrete way] because both ways are right, and important for understanding the issue.)

Temporalisation, the process whereby I temporalise myself, as a phenomenologist would put it, is the process whereby I take an interest in different objects successively. What was actualised in the previous moment as the centre of interest of my practice falls into the past, into retention, as my attention comes to focus on a different actuality. To act, then, is to temporalise oneself. I generate time by the simple fact of presentifying successive moments. I thus generate the subjective dimension of temporality. (Two years ago I elaborated the argument about the objective dimensions in a lecture discussing the opposition between cumulative play [as in bridge] and discontinuous play [as in roulette].[17] I mention this in case you want to make the connection, but I shall not develop it here, it would lead me to lose the whole thread of the current argument.)

This analysis of temporality seems to me to be important for understanding our practical relation to the world, through the practical logic of anticipation implied in the relation between the habitus and the

66 *Lecture of 15 May 1986*

field. Having a feel for the game means having a practical mastery of the logic of the game (we should place the word 'logic' in inverted commas, for it is not a question of logical logic, but of a practical logic which is in any case not entirely logical and is not conceived as such by the agent who masters it in practice). The feel for the game is a practical mastery of the logic of the game, that is, a mastery of the objective potential of the game, of what the game 'is big with', as Leibniz would say.[18] To have a feel for the game is to understand immediately what is happening and to anticipate in practice what is going to happen, not in the mode of prediction but in the mode of protention: what is going to happen is inscribed in the present as a virtual present. It is not a projection, it is a 'goes-without-saying', like the apple that is inherent in the tree (even if it is not there, it is as if it were already there).

This is very important for understanding behaviour such as the panic behaviour that Sartre has attempted to analyse,[19] or the behaviour of emotional shock or fear, where in fact I act in relation to the future as if it were already there. As with the famous statement: 'I've had it', or 'I'm dead and buried': since I am saying it, I can't have gone under yet. I believe that this is evidence of the ontological status of protention, which is not a projection, since a projection is a contingent future; it may or may not come to pass. The future of the action is not a contingent future, but a present future, which is already there.

As I have often said, the practical mastery of a field is a feel for placement, that is, a feel for the place where you need to place yourself, where you should place your actions, where you should invest, and which can operate on the level of 'it goes without saying'. According to this logic, the knowledge I am talking about is no kind of intellectual, theoretical knowledge. To give you an idea of the intellectualist form of the theory of perception, we might quote a sentence by Alain which is highly typical: 'Perception is the beginnings of a science',[20] which is to say that perception is basically a cognitive behaviour of the same type as scientific procedure, but simply less perfect, less good. It is true that perception leads us to make hypotheses, and validate, invalidate or correct them, but Alain's formula is false: in fact *it all comes to pass as if* we were making hypotheses; we constantly anticipate – we cannot understand what we are doing by referring only to the immediate present, any more than to the immediate past. As I was saying just now, we have to involve more than the present in order to understand what is going through the minds of the characters in Virginia Woolf's novel. Similarly, to understand what a tennis player is doing, we have to take into account much more than the immediate present, this 'much more' being generated in the relation between a well-formed habitus which has a feel both for the game in the present and for the future of the game. It would be the same for a financial specialist, or for a well-informed intellectual who knows how to select the right investment terrain to place his next scientific article: I think that even very different terrains all obey this same logic.

As I have often said, the fact that these are practical, infra-conscious strategies is extremely important: it shows that the strategies are not conscious strategies, and that successful strategies do not have to be constituted as strategies. People of high social origins, for example, are innocent (I am repeating myself, but my analysis is well justified): since they feel perfectly at home in the field, they feel no constraint and do not even have to calculate the right path to take.

Changing the habitus

In its relation to the field, the habitus anticipates, and it is through these anticipations that it changes. This is obvious and is implicit in the use that I have always made of this notion. But I am obliged to remind you that the habitus is not a kind of intelligible fate or character, fixed once for all time. It is a system of dispositions, which are strong but restrictive (there are limits to what you can do with a given habitus), and yet open, in particular to experience, which acts like a sort of scientific experiment: I constantly experiment, and sometimes it succeeds, sometimes it doesn't. If it succeeds, if it 'works out', the habitus is strengthened, we remain within the order of the unconscious. The better it works, the less we need to resort to the anticipations of the conscious mind and formulate them as hypotheses. But if on the other hand it doesn't work out, there may be a crisis. The crisis is the mismatch between the logic anticipated practically by the habitus and the objective logic of the game, between subjective time and objective time. Faced with a crisis and a mismatch, we may have reflexive considerations or a moment of conscious awareness, for instance, which can lead us to substitute conscious strategies for our unconscious ones, since social subjects are obviously not doomed to stay stuck in a fixed habitus. As when we are driving, we are mostly on automatic pilot, but from time to time we see a red light and have to put on the brakes.

There are also other obvious things, but I should perhaps have said them more clearly in order to avoid the crasser type of criticism: if Leibniz said that 'in three quarters of our actions we are empirics'[21] (which means: in three quarters of our actions we are our habitus), there remains a quarter of our actions which correspond precisely to

68 *Lecture of 15 May 1986*

situations where the habitus is wrong-footed (which I find a pertinent metaphor). In these cases, practical, corporeal expectations are disappointed, and this mismatch and the resulting critical shock engender reflection, changing the nature of the motivation of the action, which calls for the habitus to consider change (things are in fact much more complicated, but I don't have the wherewithal to say more about it here). In other words, here again we are dealing with very paradoxical structures which our habitual structures of thinking (such as cause and effect) prevent us from noticing. We could say that it is the structure of the habitus that again engenders the events likely to change the structure of the habitus. It is in fact as a function of the structures of my thinking that I shall find something shocking. We all know this, but it needs to be taken on board: something that one person will find shocking another will find banal, and something that will be a major event for a habitus, asking questions of it and calling on it to change, will still be generated through the structures of the habitus. In other words, it is still the habitus (as I said just now at the beginning of the lecture, the habitus determines itself) that contributes to defining the principles and therefore the limits of its own transformation. Consequently, the habitus certainly changes, but always within certain limits.

Power

That is a first set of analyses. I would like now to show the impact of these analyses in the domain of power. I have referred on several occasions to the problems of domination, to the question of whether 'power comes from above or below', and the alternative of manipulation or submission, what Montaigne's friend La Boétie called 'voluntary servitude':[22] should domination be thought of in terms of a logic of propaganda that the powerful exercise over the dominated, as a sort of manipulation? Although individual philosophers can be very subtle, as a body they often fall for these grand alternatives [. . .] Thus when they suddenly start to discuss power (which they had never spoken of before), they fall into the alternative of domination-manipulation (see Althusser, instrumental logic, the diabolic, manipulative State, etc.) versus voluntary servitude (I am not exaggerating – and if I wanted to be cruel, I could give you chapter and verse. . .).

This alternative seems to me to be grounded in a basic error in the theory of action, in a wrong answer to Wittgenstein's question 'What does following a rule mean?' It is ultimately based on an intellectualist

Lecture of 15 May 1986 69

vision of action. In a fundamental error that is quasi-constitutive of thinkers' thought (for philosophers, but also for anthropological and sociological thinkers), or even of the status of a thinker, the thinkers project their mode of thinking into the heads of people who just think. When they think about what an agent is doing, whether it is a woman accomplishing a rite or a politician taking a decision, they tend to project their own mode of thinking, linked to social conditions of possibility which are very different from those facing the social agents, which precisely exclude accomplishing a rite or taking a decision. I habitually sum up this error with a famous formula by Marx, who says that Hegel 'takes the things of logic to be the logic of things'.[23] In other words, the thinkers put into practice the logic that they ought to construct in order to understand the practice. This is very clear in the example of the rule: agents do not act at random (otherwise there would be no social sciences. . .), there is a logic in their practices and we may presume a sort of consistency in their reactions (in fact, an agent stimulated in the same way on two different occasions reacts in the same way).

We verify this postulate of consistency by establishing regular patterns: as sociologists, we establish regular patterns; we know that where one thing increases, another may diminish (for instance, the more urban we become, the fewer children we have). But although we establish a regularity, we do not question what it signifies. Does the existence of a regular relation between a situation and an action authorise us to say that it is the rule for us to do this when we are in that situation? According to the splendid words of a linguist, Ziff, the fact that the train regularly arrives late does not authorise us to conclude that the rule is for the train to arrive late.[24] The whole Lévi-Straussian play on words that I referred to just now resides in this slippage, based on the idea that regularity supposes a rule or something like a rule, that is, the fact of acting deliberately with a view to a determined end. We always suppose that what we register is the result of a calculation or deliberation. This is a sort of intellectualist philosophy of practice. Otherwise we have the mechanist vision, and in fact both visions can coincide, as is shown by the notion of apparatus.[25] (What I am analysing at this moment is the collective unconscious of our times, it is the philosophy of history that implicitly underpins our thinking about the social world and what you see in the papers – for instance, when they say 'The prime minister has decided that. . .', 'Russia is going to. . ., etc.', 'The Communist Party demands. . .', there is a whole philosophy of the social world, a whole theory of action that we accept in an unconscious way.)

70   *Lecture of 15 May 1986*

The mechanist philosophy and its opposite, the purposive, are not as antagonistic as they seem. Both in fact suppose that the principle of action can be specified and isolated. I take the example of the notion of apparatus which – as we see from the metaphor of the apparatus – belongs to a mechanist philosophy: for those who use the notion, an apparatus can select ends, it is even what an apparatus is for; when, for instance, the 'ideological apparatuses of the State'[26] are nasty, manipulative and domineering, they are pursuing ends. We can't know how they attain those ends, but it is their role as self-regulating mechanisms to attain them. I cannot take this argument further just by improvising. I would need to see the texts, to analyse the language and its metaphors; because these arguments play so much with language, they work very well when language, as Wittgenstein said, is 'idling', when it 'goes on holiday'.[27] You just let language proceed, it is mechano-purposive.

What the notion of habitus and everything that I have been saying call into question is this intellectualist vision, and above all the alternative according to which either there is no cognition, and agents are robots who react automatically to mechanical stimuli, or they are consciously aware of everything they do, and they select their ends. Neither of these hypotheses is able to account for the most subtle, profound and I think most important aspect of power, that is, the fact that agents determine themselves to be determined. We only need to apply the argument that I was developing just now. We could say that agents determine themselves to obey or suffer even the most alienating determinations, but only if we are clear what we mean when we say 'I determine myself'.

I shall refer briefly to Sartre's well-known argument. This is not one of the old references linked to my formative years: nowadays the most subtle defenders of methodological individualism[28] (there are some, especially abroad[29]) often refer to Sartre. I saw this ten years ago and I mentioned it in a text where I attacked them in self-defence.[30] It was Sartre in fact who provided the most telling, even supremely telling, formulation of what we might call 'methodological individualism', that is, the idea that actions have at their source an individual, instantaneous a-historical subject, who decides on the spur of the moment and who even determines themself to be determined. Sartre's analyses (such as Sartre facing the mountain: the mountain is only an obstacle because I constitute it as such[31]) lead us to interpret the phenomena of domination as the effects of bad faith, and that is what I wanted to discuss: if the subject of the action is a Sartrean subject, to say: '*I* am determining *myself*' is to say that *I am* deceiving *myself*, in bad faith, that is, in a lie where the deceiver is the same person as the deceived.

Lecture of 15 May 1986

The famous analyses of the emotions are the most typical case. We need to confront two analyses: the analysis of emotion, where Sartre says that the grisly face which terrifies me is constituted as terrifying by me[32] (I place myself, in a way, in a state of panic), and his analysis of the revolutionary situation – Sartre says: 'The revolutionaries are serious, it is not because the world is revolting that they are in revolt, it is because they are in revolt that they find the world revolting.'[33] In other words, it is the 'I' that constitutes the world with its objective properties.

If we now return to the notion of habitus and everything that I was saying about 'anticipation' – and the almost bodily relation between the habitus and a future which is not a future but an already-present and already-here – we can clearly see that we are founding both the seriousness of emotion and the seriousness of action. It is true that *I* am determining *myself*: if I had a different habitus, what seems revolting to me would not seem revolting at all. But it remains the case that, constituted as I am, the world is *really* revolting. This is deadly serious. This is not something that I could change by an act of consciousness that would make me aware of the fact that I am freely freeing myself of my freedom, that I am freely alienating my power to suspend all alienation, etc. I believe that the same philosophy underpins all theories of the type that speak of 'the thrill of power' or 'power as what I use to get my kicks' (which is decidedly a metaphor for our times[34]).

I oppose these ultra-subjectivist theories with an analysis in which socially constituted social agents, endowed with durable dispositions to constitute the world in a certain fashion, confront a world that they have produced, but not in the absolute liberty of a lightning flash of lucid decision; they produce it according to incorporated rules that they never fully master, and whose effects they come to discover, for instance, through the side-effects that they suffer. I think that my analysis is important; in general, I believe that we should sometimes do things that appear gratuitous, theoretical, abstract or philosophical (words that many find pejorative) in order to deconstruct the very concrete mechanisms of our immediate experience. In the second session I shall illustrate my argument with an analysis of the relations of domination between masculine and feminine that we can find in Virginia Woolf's novel, and I believe that these rather abstract analyses [of the first session] will become very concrete.

72   *Lecture of 15 May 1986*

The petit-bourgeois relation to culture

To counter the alternative of alienation or voluntary submission, we should resume for instance the analysis of the relations between the petit bourgeois and the bourgeois in the mechanisms of access to culture. Let me briefly remind you of the analysis that I have so often elaborated,[35] for you to see how it functions in the light of what I have just been saying. The relation to culture, from the viewpoint of a petit-bourgeois habitus, is the form par excellence of what I call the *illusio*, that is, a very serious investment in something that might appear illusory to someone who sees it from the outside. There is something important that I have not yet said, but that I shall return to in a moment in the context of Virginia Woolf: the *illusio* is not illusory; a person who is caught up in the game takes the game very seriously. The notion of habitus has the function – and this is what I want to discuss today – of accounting for the extreme seriousness of an investment in games that can appear derisory when viewed from the perspective of a different habitus or of a habitus engaged in a different game.

The petit-bourgeois relation to culture is the kind of aspiration which corresponds to all the analyses [that I was developing during the first session] of aspiration, temporalisation – 'I temporalise myself' – and the future – 'I have a future', 'my future lies in culture', 'I want to rise [socially] through culture', etc. We could say that it is through this sort of anticipation that the petit bourgeois is attracted to and caught up in the game, and (I shall return to this metaphor) lets himself be taken in by the game. This desire to appropriate culture and use it for self-advancement, which is one of the principles of the acquisitive greed that often defines the petit-bourgeois relation to culture, is a kind of anticipation that is generated in an individual relationship between an individual habitus and an individual field.

Since I don't have time to develop this analysis here, I shall take one extreme case of this attitude, which I described in *Homo Academicus*, using the sub-category (of the category that I have just mentioned) constituted by the oblates of the educational system, the sons of primary-school teachers who become professors at the Sorbonne. These people experience the highest degree of the domination of culture, and we could say (if we wanted to speak in the language of the victim, which lurks behind what we normally say and makes us say so many silly things) that they are, in a way, those most victimised by the domination of culture: like Cottard[36] in *In Search of Lost Time*, they will never be truly cultivated ... In Proust, they are always slightly ridiculous, they know the etymology of the names of the nobility, but they don't

Lecture of 15 May 1986 73

have the proper deportment. These people who are at once dominated by culture and who never completely master it – since in order to master it completely you must have no need to dominate it – are the incarnation, I believe, of one of the relations of domination that we cannot describe according to the simple alternative of instrumentalisation or self-mystification. It is a sort of domination that they collaborate in, to such an extent that they may experience it as one of the great accomplishments of humanity. I shall leave it there. I shall return to it in a moment on the subject of masculine/feminine domination, where I think things will appear in a more subtle light.

Second session (seminar): *To the Lighthouse* (1)

A brief commentary on this reference, which creates a link between our two sessions this morning. Among the studies that I am signalling is, first, 'attribution theory'.[37] This interesting theory, which follows the same logic as what I was saying earlier, consists in establishing a relation between the representation that people make of the causes of an event and their ways of reacting to that event. This is not as trivial as you might think: one tradition of psychology and sociology studies the birth and evolution of conflict, from the conflict we might call 'informal' (the kind that arises between neighbours, for instance) to the conflict juridically established as a law suit. In the discussion that has been running over the last fifteen years in the United States around the process involved in the establishment of a juridical dispute (how does a dispute become a law suit?), psychologists have revealed things in the logic of *kategorein/kategoreisthai*,[38] [a Greek verb meaning] 'to attribute', but also 'to accuse publicly', that I often repeat: 'Tell me whom you accuse and I'll tell you how you'll react.' If, in Freud's famous example,[39] I say: 'Yes, it is my fault, I should not have lent you the copper kettle, etc.', or if I say: 'They are really disgusting, they gave me my copper kettle back with a hole in it', the reaction is different. Psychologists establish very clearly that the reaction to something varies according to the way that the affair has been constructed. They link the tendency to blame oneself or others with the mode of reaction, which is already interesting. But being psychologists they don't look into the social genesis of the dispositions that lead us to constitute an event one way rather than another. As a sociologist, I would immediately advance the hypothesis that the tendency to blame is not distributed at random between the sexes, the positions in the social space and people's social trajectories.

74   *Lecture of 15 May 1986*

My second set of references is to battered women.[40] Domestic violence has been the object of very interesting feminist studies, but since you have heard me expatiating at length on the *habitus determining itself*, you should find obvious things that are not so obvious for many people. We note for instance that abused women return much more often to the site of violence than counsellors and social workers suppose. This tendency of the female victims to return to be beaten up again seems largely inexplicable to social workers who, endowed with a different habitus, judge intolerable things that others may find tolerable under certain conditions. The astonishment of these counsellors finds a parallel in the astonishment of leftists faced with a certain type of submission of the dominated classes. Similarly, there are studies that show that the richer you are, the more sensitive you are to injustice. In fact, when you are compiling statistics and you ask: 'How many times have you been a victim of injustice in your life?', the rich, whom we might suppose to have been less exposed to injustice, complain as much as the poor, whom we might suppose to have been more exposed, which leads us to believe that the rich are more sensitive, since the data are calculated on the basis of this equation between sensitivity and exposure to injustice.

Now two philosophical works. Kripke[41] offers a long discussion of the problem posed by the expression 'following a rule', and offers a rigorous, if difficult and slightly tedious critique of the dispositional explanation (which is the category in which the notion of habitus is situated). If you are feeling brave enough, it is interesting to read this very rigorous critique of the notion of disposition. The article by Pascal Engel[42] is perhaps even more useful because he sums up in a very skilful and subtle way the debate over the expression 'following a rule', from Wittgenstein, Ryle and Kripke through to Davidson. He offers a theory that, if I were a philosopher, would be mine. Fundamentally it is very close to what I have been saying about the habitus. I read it only very recently and I was most pleased to find a confirmation of what I had been advocating.

Fields as traps

Now I shall move on to my analysis of Virginia Woolf and the subtle forms of domination that appear in relations between the sexes. As you will surely have noticed, I am allowing myself more freedom in these second sessions, which are in principle more of a seminar than a strictly formal lecture. What I am going to say may not have a perfectly logical rigour. This is because of the freedom I am allowing myself, but also, I think, because what I am trying to say here is rather complicated, with its infinitesimal nuances, and does not easily lend itself to translation into brutally simple and direct propositions. In fact, the example of masculine/feminine relations seems to me to be the ideal terrain for me to offer an illustration of the theory of domination[43] that I have pursued in my analysis of the relations between habitus and field. It allows me to refute the ordinary theories of domination. In particular, it seems to me that it entirely dissolves the 'instrumentalist/thrill-seeking' alternative. What I am going to present you with should make concrete what I have been obliged to say so far in a very abstract manner.

One of the reasons why domination in the relations between the sexes is misunderstood is because the sexual dimension of the domination masks the political aspect of this domination. At the same time, the interest of this form of domination is to reveal how political domination may pass through the body and what is least under control in the body, like desire and such things that people tend to discuss in very naive terms. Ultimately, using Virginia Woolf, I would like to establish that there is a social constitution of the body (I have much reflected on the word 'constitution' over the past years[44]) in its apparently deepest and most crudely biological determinations: what goes under the name of desire, *libido* and the like. The central thesis that I would like to develop, based on a reading of Virginia Woolf, is that the social world proposes games, and these games can only welcome people disposed to invest in them. It is therefore in a certain fashion, and a game objectively constituted in a compatible fashion, that the *illusio* is created as an entirely serious illusion – always the same paradox – which is an illusory relation for somebody situated outside it, but something very serious, unavoidable and insurmountable for anybody within it.

At the risk of shocking you (but supported, after all, by Sartre, who said 'Elections, booby traps'[45]), I would like to show you how the social fields function as booby traps. I was not sure whether to put it to you in those terms, but since this expresses very clearly the central idea that I want to develop today, it will make it easier for you to understand what I am going to say. The social world lays traps and these traps are so well laid that people are pleased and even delighted to make pratfalls into them. There is in the expressions 'booby trap' and 'pratfall' a kind of knowing smile: we see the game as it is (it's a trap) but we also see at the same time that there is something moving and pathetic in falling into something so blatant (what I have just said is in fact a feminine view of the masculine 'booby trap').[46] In general terms, I shall be developing the following thesis: the major masculine games, whose

76   *Lecture of 15 May 1986*

paradigm is war (but all the other masculine games, including the intellectual game, are derivative forms of this), are 'booby traps', into which fall only those who are disposed to fall. Consequently, women have the privilege of not being entrapped, but this privilege, when the games are prestigious, serious and empowering, is a privation, a mutilation (I point out for the attention of all those who argue in simple terms – 'Are we privileged or not?' – that we can have the privilege of not falling into the trap of a game that implies privilege. . .). It seems to me that the mistakes, even the political ones, of the feminist movement or the macho movement – which has no need to be organised in order to exist [*laughter*] – depend on the fact that people don't want to see the kind of contradiction enclosed in the terms 'booby trap' or 'pratfall'. This is the thesis that I shall develop in detail, in a rather dispersed order, with the help of Virginia Woolf.

A man-child

To start with, I shall tell you a story. At the start of the novel entitled *To the Lighthouse* a little boy gets ready with his mother to go and visit the lighthouse.[47] He is very excited, and is busy cutting out pictures while talking to his mother, who promises the trip to the lighthouse: 'Yes, of course, if it's fine tomorrow' (p. 5). It is the greatest day of his life, he has been thinking of it for months. And then his father comes by and declares 'it won't be fine' (p. 6). This is the paternal verdict, which destroys the little boy's dreams (I shall return later to the father/son relation which is homologous with the masculine/feminine relation). Mr Ramsay, the father, who has just made this peremptory declaration (he is a great philosopher who has theories on nature and existence, among other things), will be shown up in a quite ridiculous situation. It starts on p. 20 (it is important to indicate the pages, because we need to note the logical order of successive events). Ramsay is somebody who is so serious that, on a first reading, we fail to understand what is happening to him: we cannot imagine, given our presumptions as to what makes a man, that a man should place himself in such a ridiculous situation. We might have to conduct an enquiry to prove it, but my guess is that many of those who have read the novel will not have noticed.[48] Firstly, Mrs Ramsay hears him: 'Suddenly a loud cry, as of a sleep-walker, half-roused, something about "Stormed at with shot and shell"[49] sung out with the utmost intensity in her ear' (p. 20). And then we lose this gentleman, finding ourselves back inside the mind of his wife; then we come across him again, surprised once more, 'shouting, gesticulating:

Lecture of 15 May 1986 77

"Someone had blundered"', but by different characters, Lily Briscoe and her friend, William Bankes (p. 22). We start to realise that he has been caught in a rather ridiculous pose. Later, we find him on p. 82, and we start to discover the key to what has been happening: 'And his habit of talking aloud, or saying poetry aloud, was growing on him, she [i.e. his wife, who has also overheard the scene and who is slightly embarrassed] was afraid; for sometimes it was awkward.' He has then been in a ridiculous situation because he was reciting a war poem where he took himself for the general and had forgotten himself: he had shouted out loud and everyone had discovered him in an infantile state. A little earlier, we see his malaise when he realises he's been noticed. His wife, who understands that he has been noticed and that he is unhappy, says: 'All his vanity, all his satisfaction in his own splendour, riding fell as a thunderbolt . . . had been shattered, destroyed' (p. 36). So he was outraged and anguished. And a little later (p. 38): 'Already ashamed of that petulance, of that gesticulation of the hands when charging at the head of his troops. . .!' [*laughter*].

In the telescoping of these two scenes, as experienced by the main character, we see this man, the fearsome parent who has just stifled the dreams of his child, surprised in the act of playing a game. And what did this game consist in? He was playing at war, which is the game par excellence, as I wrote a long time ago in my study of the Kabyle.[50] War is the most extraordinary game invented to test our honour, because we gamble with our lives there. So he has been surprised playing a war game, where Virginia Woolf's procedure has led him to reveal the private key to his innermost secret, which could not be communicated in any other way: he lives his status as an intellectual as an *illusio*, he lives intellectual life as a war. Afterwards, this will be developed: he has just discovered that he has been seen playing this ridiculous game. The *illusio* is seen by somebody who is not a victim of the illusion:

> He shivered; he quivered. All his vanity, all his satisfaction in his own splendour, riding fell as a thunderbolt, fierce as a hawk at the head of his men through the valley of death [*quite like a Western*], had been shattered, destroyed. Stormed at by shot and shell, boldly we rode and well [*here we have the masculine vision: 'I shall die upright, in a hail of bullets'*], flashed through the valley of death, volleyed and thundered – straight into Lily Briscoe and William Bankes. (p. 36)

Here we have one of Virginia Woolf's typical techniques, the cinematic 'dissolve' shot: 'Straight into . . . Lily Briscoe and William Bankes!'

78   *Lecture of 15 May 1986*

What a come-down! We are in our dream world and we bump into somebody who sees us playing like a child. We could say that the whole thing is an unimportant incident (he talks to himself, he recites poetry), but the feminine gaze sees that it is something more important: it is his whole relation to his career, with his relation to other philosophers and his disciples, that is, everything that we should not see, which is revealed.

It would be too long to read out, but I refer you to pp. 40 to 42, which develop the theme of war as metaphor for the intellectual adventure or the intellectual adventure as war. I'll read you a little of it anyway. So Ramsay sees himself in the Valley of Death:[51]

> Feelings that would not have disgraced a leader who, now that the snow has begun to fall and the mountain-top is covered in mist, knows that he must lay himself down and die before morning comes, stole upon him, paling the colour of his eyes [. . .] Yet he would not die lying down; he would find some crag of rock, and there, his eyes fixed on the storm, trying to the end to pierce the darkness, he would die standing. [*This is already the intellectual metaphor*] Surely the leader of a forlorn hope may ask himself that, and answer, without treachery to the expedition behind him, 'One perhaps'. One in a generation [*Here he is wondering: will I be famous in a generation to come?*]. Is he to be blamed if he is not that one? [*He is wondering whether he is the first, if he will continue to be famous, as the leading philosopher*] . . . provided he has toiled honestly, given to the best of his power, till he has no more left to give? And his fame lasts how long? It is permissible even for a dying hero to think before he dies how men will speak of him hereafter. (pp. 41–2)

And it continues. He will meet his death as a 'fine figure of a soldier', 'leader of the doomed expedition', and afterwards, even if I have not followed the exact order of the novel, he will rush up to his wife, who has surprised him, to seek her sympathy – he has fallen into the 'booby trap', he has suffered greatly and he is asking for the 'warrior's rest'. He goes to seek the sympathy of the person who has seen through his *illusio*, that is, at once the vanity and the reality of suffering. He will say to her 'Life is terribly hard.' He will be forgiven for acting like a child. It is a magnificent description, a very fine passage.

I am embarrassed to have read all that out, but I am speaking metaphorically of things that are very real. What is said in metaphorical terms, I think, is this: Mr Ramsay is a man-child, he plays like a child and this war game is only one manifestation of what he is doing all the time. You could meditate on this maxim: the difference between a man and a woman is that the man is a child when he tries to act the man, whereas the woman is a child (we talk of a 'woman-child') when she acts like a child. I'm not sure whether I am making myself clear: the social games where men fall into the trap, the games of manliness, the games of war and conflict ('I shall die standing'), the masculine *illusio,* are a man's game, a game worthy of a man and recognised as worthy of a Man (with a capital M), a man as opposed to a woman: these games worthy of a man are children's games, but, since they are games that people call men's games, we don't notice that they are games for child-men, and we wouldn't say: 'He's a child-man.' In fact what this analysis makes us realise is that the dominant person, in this particular case the person acting the masculine role, enters into a sort of alienation which is the condition of his privilege. The games of *libido dominandi* are reserved for him because he has this property – of being trained to play these games.

Men, oblates of the social world

Here the start of the novel becomes interesting. The very beginning, where we see the little boy cutting out pictures, is followed by a passage where the mother describes her little boy. She sees through his superficial personality as a small child the man that he will become, and she predicts that he will be a diplomat[52] (p. 6). Then she says: 'Indeed, she had the whole of the other sex under her protection' [this is her protective side, which we shall discover later], 'for reasons she could not explain' (p. 8) [. . .]. 'She could not explain': it is her feminine habitus that is constituted like this; her role is to be a protector, that is, to have that kind of respect for the child within the man, which is never so well revealed as when he acts like a man. 'She had the whole of the other sex under her protection; for reasons she could not explain. . .': the habitus is the site of reasons that we cannot explain.

We find this again a little later, on the subject of her son: 'for there was in all their [the women's] minds a mute questioning of deference and chivalry, of the Bank of England and the Indian Empire, of ringed fingers and lace, though to them all there was something in this of the essence of beauty, which called out the manliness in their girlish hearts. . .' (p. 9).

There is a description – I shan't inflict it on you, you can read it – of the effects of the specifically feminine socialisation that is one of the

80   *Lecture of 15 May 1986*

conditions, not for the non-participation of women in the game, since the game is recognised as a masculine game, but for the special indulgence that women grant this game... I think that for the important social games (the Bank of England, diplomacy, the senior civil service, etc.) to function, they have to be constituted as masculine, that is, to function as traps for men constituted after a certain fashion. But they also need to be constituted as masculine in the eyes of the women who exclude themselves from them but recognise them, and desire to enter by proxy. 'By proxy', that is, through the son – since it is a fantasy that she weaves around her son – and also through her husband, who is the legitimate repository of the vicarious aspiration to master the games, but games which can only be mastered by proxy, through the mediation of a man. This kind of division of the structure of representations, of the habitus, is the condition for the functioning of the mechanism (here we see how a mechanism of domination is only possible if it encounters matching dispositions). In this sense, we could say that 'power comes from below', but that doesn't make sense: it needs the habitus, and obscure determining forces... I shan't repeat myself.

The dominant person, in this particular case Mr Ramsay, is a victim of his domination: he has placed himself in a ridiculous position, he has played at being a 'general', he is suffering, he has been rude, he has been most disagreeable, which makes him unhappy, and what is more, as a victim of his privilege he comes to beg for sympathy, which he obtains, since the 'warrior's rest' is part of the traditional definition of the division of labour between the sexes. In fact (if you think of what I was saying [at the end of the first session today] about the petite bourgeoisie), Marx's famous axiom, 'The dominant is dominated by his domination', which is one of the sayings that Marxists have always forgotten and never properly exploited, now takes on its full meaning. We can see, in this particular case, how we cannot understand the dominant if we don't understand that in certain cases they suffer in addition from being dominant, and that it even sometimes happens that they throw themselves at the feet of the dominated. If you pick up the analogy that I described rather badly at the end [of the first session] because I didn't have much time left, you will see that there are many mechanisms of the same type. Men, as victims par excellence of the *illusio*, and being dedicated to it from childhood, are the oblates of the social world, and the more so the higher we rise in the social hierarchy. Just as the humble primary school teacher is the oblate of the university system, so more generally the social world dedicates its male children very early on to its great careers and grand ambitions (which is the difference, I believe, between men and women).

Lecture of 15 May 1986 81

What I call rites of institution,[53] which are generally called 'rites of passage', are in my opinion reducible 90 per cent of the time to acts of nomination where people are told: 'You are a man', which implies, 'You can and you must participate in the masculine games', 'You can and you must be a warrior', 'You must be virile', which means 'You must assert your rights in virile games', 'You must assert yourself in virile games.'[54] The rites of institution, then, are rites that install in the established heritage (following the general law of inheritance) a propensity to invest in the heritage. This is one of the problems of succession in princely families. You would think that it is always pleasant to receive an inheritance, but you are forgetting the fear of the ungrateful heir, that is, the heir who does not want to inherit, and who, not wanting to inherit, repudiates the testament. This is one of the themes of Flaubert's *Sentimental Education*.[55] The ungrateful heir refuses to be the beneficiary of the heritage. He doesn't do what should be done by a loyal heir. It's the son of the king making a fuss about becoming a king.

In the division of labour between the sexes, it is the men who inherit social seriousness. It is they who must play the serious social games, seriously ('to play seriously' is an old philosophical reference:[56] *spoudaïos paizein*; *paizein* is 'to play', 'act the child' – *païs* is 'the child', and *spoudaïos* is 'seriously'). They must participate seriously in the games that the social world decrees to be serious. They must be appropriately socialised and invest in the stakes that are proposed by the different fields. Producing this kind of invested habitus is therefore a determining factor, and one aspect of socialisation in all societies consists in getting the boys to internalise the social, that is, masculine, stakes which are the monopoly of men, and which men may have only if they are 'real men', 'really men'.

(I think that a serious error has been made in discussions of rites of passage: they have always been described as rites designed to mark the passage from childhood to the adult age. This is the theory of Van Gennep, which is nothing more than a scientific translation of our spontaneous representation of the social world. In fact, what this passage disguises is the fact that the rites of institution apply only to boys, and what matters is the fact that they distinguish between those boys who are worthy of rites of institution and those who are not. The rites of passage, then, are rites of discrimination – an exemplary rite of this type being circumcision – which, through a social, statutory and sanctioned difference, separate the men who are really men from the non-men. Their most important function is thus hidden by a superficial function. This parenthesis is intended to relate my argument to a previous analysis of mine, that some of you already know.)

82 *Lecture of 15 May 1986*

The problem with rites of institution is how to get the children to participate in the puerile game of virility, 'virility' being taken in all the senses of the term, both sexual and social. I think that I shall develop this later on: the notion of potency, which can apply to the social as well as the sexual terrain, is a determining link in the chain connecting the social mechanisms of domination to the socially established forms of sexual domination. In general, if we follow Virginia Woolf's thinking, a man is that sort of overgrown child who gets caught up in all the games socially designated as serious, and takes all these games seriously.

To take an example from the Kabyle, who are quite simply at the extreme limit of our European societies, their affirmation of the opposition between masculine and feminine is particularly striking and clear-cut: for the Kabyle, economics in the sense that we understand it – that is, economics based on calculation, where you have to repay what you have borrowed (and by a fixed date) – is a job for the women. The women, who are not burdened with virility, indifference to calculation, nobility, dignity, honour and points of honour, etc., may allow themselves to be sordid enough to say: 'You will repay me. . .'. If you think about it, this division of labour does still exist in our societies,[57] in much more subtle forms: 'You will tell him. . .' [*laughter*], etc. The Kabyle are not at all ignorant of economics in the modern sense of the term, with its calculations and interest and so on, but this economics, repressed by the men, may be admitted by the women, who by definition lack dignity, or enjoy it only by proxy. I am drawing on specific surveys: they have their point of honour where their husbands are concerned, insofar as they must protect the honour of their husbands. The Kabyle are thus a 'larger copy' (Plato always used this metaphor of the 'larger copy'[58]) of the way we value honour: if you look at the chapter I wrote on the structures of mythical thinking in *The Logic of Practice*,[59] you will find a psychoanalysis of the unconscious, of your and our unconscious, and of the deep, socially constructed structures of the masculine/feminine opposition in our societies, with all its connotations, like the wet and the dry, for instance.

In this example we see again that privilege brings the privilege to suffer stress. Men earn the right to be censored: they earn a kind of right-and-duty to reject economics, dignity and points of honour, they earn the right-and-duty to risk their lives, to be killed for a yes or a no, they earn the right-and-duty to take on all the risks implied in the grand idea of dignity that has been inculcated in them, on pain of being found 'girlish'. We see that right and privilege imply a formidable stress: on the economic plane, they cannot have the privilege of women, which

Lecture of 15 May 1986 83

is being free to speak simply, with no historical baggage. The division of labour in marriages,[60] for instance, follows this logic: the women are entrusted with the job of saying what the men may not say; they incarnate the realist dimension in the division of labour, the reality principle, whereas the men represent the principle of social pleasure that supposes formidable censorship and formidable self-repression. The women, insofar as they are irresponsible, commit only themselves, and can always be disavowed, especially if they are old. The women then, in all simplicity, can assume the unmentionable roles that the men must divest themselves of in order to accede to the status of real men.

I could go on, but, because you might be thinking that I am making some of this up, I shall read you a passage from Kant's *Anthropology*:

But just as it does not belong to women to go to war, so women cannot personally defend their rights and pursue civil affairs for themselves, but only by means of a representative ['*women cannot*', *is obviously normative, it is not a positive description; it pronounces a rule in the sense, not of regularity, but of a norm*]. And this legal immaturity with respect to public transactions makes women all the more powerful in respect to domestic welfare, because here the *right of the weaker* enters in, which the male sex by its nature already feels called on to respect and defend. But to *make* oneself [*in the case of women*] immature, degrading as it may be, is nevertheless very comfortable [*which is not wrong: the dominant always have a very clear view of the interests of the dominated*], and naturally it has not escaped leaders who know how to use this docility of the masses (because they hardly know how to unite on their own). . .

Here, you see, we have moved from the women to the dominated. The analogy of gender is very important to our thinking of politics; we need to think of politics in terms of gender to be able to think of gender in terms of politics – this is what I wanted to say today. As in Virginia Woolf, a cinematic 'fade in – fade out' takes us from woman to the masses. The 'masses', like woman, cannot think, they do not synthesise, and they do not ordinarily enjoy any *a priori* synthetic unity. [*Bourdieu continues the quotation from Kant:*]

it has not escaped leaders who know how to use this docility of the masses (because they hardly know how to unite on their own) and to represent the danger of making use of one's *own* understanding

84 *Lecture of 15 May 1986*

without the guidance of another as very great, even lethal. Heads of state call themselves *fathers of the country*, because they understand better how to make their *subjects* happy than the subjects understand; but the people are condemned to permanent immaturity with regard to their own best interest.[61]

This is stated here in raw, brutal terms, but in fact one of the major contemporary debates among political philosophers and jurists in the United States is over what they call 'paternalism',[62] in a sense which is different from the sense it is given in France. It is the problem of knowing under what conditions and to what extent those who govern can bestow happiness on their subjects regardless of their views: is it legitimate (these are philosophical and ethical discussions of the highest order), in the name of a superior specific competence and a better knowledge of causes and reasons, to contradict the dominated in a way by imposing things on them that are in their best interest? These debates start out from very concrete problems – relatively marginal issues like drugs or suicide – and are then generalised to take in the whole gamut of political problems. The idea of creating the happiness of the dominated regardless of their views, which can be found as far back as Plato, and which is constantly present in political debate, is in my opinion closely linked to the representation of the division of labour according to a model whose paradigm is the division of labour between the sexes, that is, a model of irresponsibility and responsibility, of resignation and proxy. For any of you who think that I have strayed into rather distant abstractions, I would remind you that even today, as I have ascertained in my surveys, the 'don't know' or 'no answer' responses come more often from women than men.[63] Similarly, when you question couples leaving a museum, it is an uphill task to get the wife to reply without her saying: 'But my husband knows more about it. . .'.[64] These structures are not anthropological structures at all, in the sense given by the Laboratory of Social Anthropology.[65]

It seems to me that if you have made the connection between what I was saying at the start of the lecture and what I am saying now, you should be able to formulate the conclusions to this exercise yourselves. The famous theme of power as desire, a chic reversal of the ordinary vision according to which power resides on high, does have something to tell us. In fact, from this theory of the division of labour between the sexes leading to a vicarious kind of relation to power for women, being dominated in the division of labour between the sexes, we can devise a sort of political theory of desire and ask whether we might not investigate the source of all forms of masculine desire in the will to power,

Lecture of 15 May 1986   85

with relations between the sexes being conceived after the model of wars, battles and hunting (we can think of many such metaphors. . .), and on the feminine side, investigate desire as desire for elective submission, but by proxy. [. . .]

These things are difficult to say in polite terms, at any rate polite in my eyes, because I myself have interiorised other, somewhat archaic values, like those I have described; so it is not easy for me to discuss these things in simple terms. I shall therefore say only one thing, and I shall try next time to reflect more accurately on the words that I should use: we need to reflect on notions of charisma and charm, asking ourselves whether masculine charisma and charm (which sound trivial but are not as trivial as all that if we look at them hard enough) might not have some links with the charms of power, and whether the beauty susceptible of attracting desire or lust might not be a specific form of the perception of power, through eyes socially conditioned to love power.

Lecture of 22 May 1986

First session (lecture): summary of previous lectures – Socialised individual and abstract individual – Habitus and the principle of choice – Mental structures and objective structures – The magical match of the body with the world – The false problem of responsibility – Coincidence of positions and dispositions – Amor fati
Second session (seminar): To the Lighthouse *(2) – Incorporating the political – Paternal power and the verdict effect – The somatisation of social crises –* Metamorphosis *and the founding experience of primordial power*

First session (lecture): summary of previous lectures

I have here a question that I hesitate to reply to immediately ... Nonetheless, I prefer to dispel the ambiguity immediately in a few words: 'In the last lecture you said: "The masses are feminine", and you added: "of course!" The question is the following: what does this femininity of the masses consist of (your exact sentence was: "The masses are feminine, of course")?' I think that there is a terrible misunderstanding here. And yet I am more or less certain to have said at the time that I was not speaking in my own name, but expressing our collective representation. I remember having said in my commentary on Kant's text, following the logic of my argument, that 'the masses are feminine, of course'. It was therefore not a statement that I was making on my behalf, it was not a normative, but a constative utterance. That said, the misunderstanding is interesting. I have constantly analysed this in my previous lectures: it is down to the fact that one cannot observe and record anything in the social world without laying oneself open to people taking it as a norm. Since we habitually speak

Lecture of 22 May 1986

of the social world only to say what it should be, when sociologists do their job and try to say what it is, they run the risk of people thinking they are saying what it should be – or should not be, which comes to the same thing. This is, then, a typical misunderstanding that I wanted to point out straight away; unfortunately, it must happen much more often than I realise.

I shall continue to pursue the arguments that I was developing last time, but since I have more or less reached the half-way stage of these lectures, I would like to remind you of the general drift of my thesis, so that you do not lose your bearings. I try in my analyses to give each hourly unit a logical unity, but I also try to link these logical units into a temporal sequence, and I have tried to link these lectures into a sequence over five successive years. Of course I realise that most of you will not have followed the whole set of lectures, and even those who have followed all of them must have lost their way from time to time, even in the course of a single year. It is because I believe that the essence of what I intend to say will only take shape over the course of the whole series, that I sometimes wish to recapitulate.

A rapid summary: I tried last year to describe and analyse our perception of the social world; I tried to set out a sociology of the perception of the social world, to show how the social world is perceived as a function of the categories which compose the agents' habitus. Following on from this, I have tried this year to analyse the fundamental relation between the habitus and the field, to show what it consists of. I started with an analysis of symbolic capital as being something engendered in the relation between a habitus and a particular type of field. It was in this context that I referred to Benveniste's analysis of the notion of *fidēs*:[1] I showed that symbolic capital, or symbolic power, is a cognitive connection established in a relationship within a field. The experience of capital as symbolic capital, the experience for instance of physical force or economic power as symbolic power, is a particular case of the fundamental phenomenon which in my opinion characterises our relation to the social world and which I call *illusio*, that is, a relation of founding adherence to the social world, the kind of doxic relation that is generated in the relation between a habitus socialised in conformity with the structure of a field and the field in which it is engaged.

I took in passing, rather hastily, the example of the notion of ethnicity. I pointed out – although you will certainly have forgotten, because I did it so quickly – that in analysing symbolic capital one thing that I was bearing in mind was the issue we commonly handle under the title of racism, the problem of telling what ethnicity is, since it is a property that exists essentially through its perception by others. I believe that

88   *Lecture of 22 May 1986*

the analyses that I made last time apply to this particular case in a particularly pertinent manner. If the notion of the ethnic, or race – which is the most usual expression of the thing – exists through its perception by social agents, this does not mean that it is a subjective creation that could be transformed with the wave of a magic wand, with an ethnic conversion determined by some moral sermon of whatever order.

One function of the analysis of the habitus that I made the other day is precisely to show that the *illusio*, the kind of fundamental adherence through which the agents find themselves implicated in the social game, is in no way an arbitrary contractual relationship, which agents might choose deliberately to join and to leave: it is a sort of very fundamental linkage in which the body in particular is profoundly implicated. This is easy to understand if you bear in mind the definition of the habitus that I keep repeating: the habitus is society embodied and, when I have the habitus of the social order in which I am lodged, I embody this social order which in a way speaks directly to my body, through for instance sentiment, fear, intimidation, desire and so forth. (This brings us to what I was arguing last time in the seminar on the subject of Virginia Woolf and which I shall perhaps return to in a moment.)

The founding relation to the social world, then, is not the relation of a cognitive subject to an object of cognition. That is where I left off. Ultimately, one of the functions of the notion of habitus is to break with this subjective vision, this philosophy of a subject, in the sense of a transcendental subject that constitutes what it perceives in terms of universal categories. The habitus constitutes what it perceives, but as a function of categories that are themselves historically established. They are the product of the social world that they apply to and they are very deeply incorporated, in such a way that the relation between the subject and the social world is of the order of what certain philosophers who have broken with the philosophy of the subject – Heidegger, for instance – have described as the relation between on the one hand *Dasein* – a word used to avoid speaking of the 'subject' – the human being that we are, the existing, the being, the habitus, and on the other hand the world, which is what we call 'being'. Ultimately, I think that, after following my argumentation through, we can appropriate some classic analyses. We would find the same thing in the later Merleau-Ponty:[2] the relation between what is commonly called the subject and the world is not a cognitive relationship in which the subject, as an autonomous principle, might conceive and constitute reality, but an obscure, infra-conceptual kind of relationship, which is far from being conceptualised (and which moreover is altered through the simple fact of conceptualisation, which makes it difficult to make an adequate

Lecture of 22 May 1986 89

analysis of this experience), a profound, body-to-body relationship. This is why I think that the metaphors taken from sport which I often use[3] are most adequate: sport is, if I may say so, the terrain where we best feel this sort of immediate, pre-reflexive, non-thetic experience linking the 'subject' with a universe that is always socially established.

This fundamental, obscure, ontological relationship, then, is not reducible to what philosophers of the subject make of it: the most radical, exemplary and logical paradigm and form – to the point of absurdity – is Sartre's theory of a free subject freely establishing the social world, and, by the same token, confronted with the problem of whether the world is serious. I mentioned this last time: do I find the world revolting because I am a rebel or am I a rebel because the world is objectively revolting? This is developed at the beginning of the last part of *Being and Nothingness*,[4] and it is a scholarly version of the old question: do I love her because she is pretty or is she pretty because I love her? This question, which is one of the questions that set philosophers against one another, has no sense in the problematic as I pose it. (If I were English or American, I would speak of a 'do-I-love-her-because-she-is-pretty? *fallacy*', and all the textbooks would immediately quote it as the '*Bourdieu fallacy*' [*laughter*]. But I think it is important sometimes to coin phrases of this kind because they are striking, they stick in the mind and then become defence mechanisms against the speechifiers who waffle on about this kind of alternative; one of the functions of sociology is to provide defence mechanisms against wrong thinking; which is why I have made this little digression.) The faintly ridiculous alternative between subjectivism and objectivism, which I deliberately present in derisory guise but which is very serious and mobilises the most powerful philosophical energies, disappears as soon as we take seriously the notion of habitus; that is, the relation between society embodied and society objectified. This relationship, in which we are held at every moment, makes us feel at home in the social world because we are ourselves one of the states of the social world.

I have repeated this many times, but it is worth repeating once more: the individual/society alternative that we all have in mind, perhaps because it springs to mind spontaneously, but also because it is reinforced by the academic world (it is a classic topic, a *pons asinorum*: everyone has had to write an essay on this type of alternative in some form or other), must be abandoned in favour of the idea that society exists in a bodily as well as an objective state. More exactly, the institution is instituted in two ways, in things and in bodies,[5] and (I am repeating myself, but I need to, because this is absolutely crucial) this existence in two forms means that when we relate to the social world it

90 *Lecture of 22 May 1986*

is in a way the social communicating with itself. What makes this sort of experience understandable is the character of the cognitive relation, which is at once immediate, obscure and very profound, rather than a cognitive relation in the sense that we usually mean, that is, a conscious one. We must then bear in mind the need for this ontological cognitive relationship which unites the social agents with the world in which they act, in order to avoid the whole series of errors which I have denounced all through these last lectures and which are all founded on the principle of the illusion of the subject and the intellectualist illusion that it fosters.

In particular, the question that I have asked about power – 'Does power come from on high or from down below?' – is a variant of the question: 'Do I love her because she is pretty or is she pretty because I love her?' Power should be thought of as symbolic power: it can only operate as long as it is not recognised as power and violence, but recognised by an act of cognition which is not the act of intellectual cognition that would be undertaken by a free subject asking himself whether he should recognise it or not, but the act of a sort of socialised body which recognises in a kind of corporeal way. To take an example that everyone will understand: 'Power intimidates', means that the body recognises power, sometimes in spite of the conscious mind, and the body can be found revolting by a consciousness that does not master it. I have used the example of intimidation, but I could just as easily have said: 'Power attracts desire.' I did not, because it is fashionable[6] and ultimately becomes one of the representations that are subjectivist and idealist (and also biologist and naturalist). If power attracts desire according to the logic that I am following, it is because desire is one of the modalities of the relation between the socialised body and the objectified institution. In other words, this particular *libido* is always constituted in a social logic: there is no non-socialised *libido*. This does not mean that there is no libido in the state of a pre-socialised drive, as presented by psychoanalysis, but it only appears and breaks through into social existence in a socialised form, and this desire for power is accomplished in a relation between a certain habitus and a certain power. A type of power desirable for some is not desirable for others, insofar as desire is a form of the relation between a habitus and a specific field in which the power is effective and manifest.

Socialised individual and abstract individual

I have obviously already suggested it, but I would like in passing to develop in a rapid parenthesis the implications of what I have just said

Lecture of 22 May 1986

about the notion of the individual. They are things that I have said several times (I do happen to repeat myself, like today, albeit usually on purpose, I hope. . .), but I want to say it again because the individual is back in fashion. (I shall return to this in a moment: unfortunately passing fashions are a feature of the social sciences, which incidentally proves that they have not yet attained a decisive autonomy. They are present in the natural sciences too, but in the social sciences the fashions are more brutal and simple; orchestrated as they are by the weekly press, they are more widely known.) Since the individual has been back in fashion for a few years now,[7] I feel obliged to make this remark and unravel the implications that you will certainly have unravelled for yourselves: why use the notion of habitus, and how to situate it rapidly in relation to the notion of the individual?

In this respect, the habitus could be characterised as the real individual as opposed to the abstract individual. The biological individual is an incontrovertible fact. Social science must accept it as such, but what it takes as its object of study is not the biological individual, who concerns the biologist, it is the socialised individual, who is the incorporation of the social world. In this respect it is different from the biological individual but also from the abstract, universal individual, as seen by the economist, for example. This abstract, universal individual, reduced to its ability to make a rational calculation of the best use of certain properties that are independent of it, does not correspond to anything scientifically real. This applies to the economic individual and the legal individual: law and economics deal with the same abstract, universal individual, a sort of man without qualities supposedly invariant in time – as we argued last week. Ultimately, there is no difference between the economist's abstract individuals and the lawyer's individuals without qualities, who are therefore equal and interchangeable, whereas the habitus reintroduces real subjects with all their history, whose traces they have incorporated, and all their own incorporated properties. As I have reminded you several times, the habitus for the scholastics was, in a manner of speaking, a person's capital, their properties (this is one of the implications of the notion of habitus that comes from the verb *habeo*, 'to have'[8]), which is what makes the difference between biological individuals, insofar as it is the incorporated trace of a particular history. Cultural capital, for instance, as I have argued in one of my previous lectures,[9] is one of these incorporated properties. This is a point that I wished to make in passing.

Proponents of what is nowadays called 'methodological individualism' oppose the individual to the totality.[10] They basically say: 'We

92 *Lecture of 22 May 1986*

present the individual in opposition to totalitarian kinds of thinking, such as Durkheimian or Marxist, which ignore the individual in favour of the whole.' In fact, this is absolutely ridiculous: the opposition is not between individual and totality at all, but between the abstract, formal individual without properties, and the individual constructed in accordance with reality – which does not mean concretely – that is, the individual endowed with all their properties. I shall not develop this further, because it does not fit in with the logic of my argument today, but I felt I had to point it out, so as not to seem out of touch, and to provide some elements of an answer to those who may sometimes wonder about the connection between what I have to say and what others say that I say.

Habitus and the principle of choice

The crux of what I wanted to say was that the relation between habitus and field is exercised below the level of consciousness and below the threshold of free choice, in the sense given by the kind of intellectualist theory that you find in Descartes and all the Cartesians, where they posit, for instance, a process of cognition examining the terms of a given alternative, followed by a deliberate process of selecting between the different possible ways of achieving the goal. The 'choices' of the habitus . . . I always place the word 'choice' between quotation marks, not in order to say that people don't choose, but to say that they don't choose in the way we think they choose. It is obvious that a player who has a feel for the game chooses (you only have to note the difference between a good and a bad player to see that the good player chooses), but he does not choose in the sense that intellectualist theory says he chooses; he does not choose in an act of free cognition, freely executed. The question of freedom, which is sometimes put to me, can therefore be seen as largely a question of the definition of freedom. If we understand freedom as making and fulfilling an explicit choice between possibilities that have been technically calculated, then it is true that we are very rarely free. If it is true that this is the definition of freedom, we are determined in 99 per cent of our actions.

In fact I think the question is wrongly put: the objective choices that social agents make are choices of which they are not the subjects in the sense of a theory of the subject, insofar as the motive behind these choices is not mastered by the person who makes them: the motive behind these choices is a habitus that does in fact choose between different possibilities, but which is not itself chosen in the moment of

Lecture of 22 May 1986 93

choosing. I think that this is the heart of the matter: since the habitus is not chosen in the moment of choosing, it can do things for me in the moment of choosing that I would not choose myself if I were choosing in the sense of the traditional intellectualist theory – see the example of the analysis of indignation that I made earlier.

The seriousness and gravity of the investments and choices of the habitus – 'The world is revolting because I find it revolting' – depend on the fact that I do not choose the principles of the choice. This is something that happens 'within me without me', as the philosophical tradition would have it: there is a sort of historical Id, the habitus, which chooses for me, and at the same time makes the kind of gravity that Sartre tries desperately to expel from the world as he construes it disappear. You may remember Sartre's analysis of the serious;[11] ultimately Sartre never manages to distinguish between what he calls the serious turn of mind, that is, bad faith, and seriousness. In fact the theory of the habitus is there to take account of the fact that our primary relation with the world is one of seriousness and gravity. To say that I take the world seriously means that when I feel fear, for example, what terrifies me seems inscribed in the objective world; I do not perceive myself as constituting the terrifying through my free abandonment, my free abdication of the freedom to constitute the world as not terrifying.

Why is this the case? Because the motivating principle, which is partly subjective in the agent, who although no longer a subject helps to construct the world as terrifying, is not constituted in the moment of executing the constitutive action. Which means that the agent can, for instance, constitute as terrifying something that somebody differently disposed would not constitute as terrifying. These things are extremely simple, and yet at the same time extremely complicated, and I think that it is important to compare Sartre's theory of the emotions with his theory of revolution – the logic is exactly the same – to understand what is at stake in the notion of habitus. The habitus, being an individual, incorporated history, constituted in a bodily state, entertains with the objective world an opaque relation, which is immediately accessible neither to the reflexive gaze, nor to exhortations of the awakening of consciousness and reason, etc.

If you think back on the question of racism,[12] Sartre is interesting once again, because he always gives the most radical, and therefore the most interesting, form of the subjectivist thesis. Philosophers find it chic to say that Heidegger is a truly profound philosopher and Sartre only a second-rate disciple (people in France tends to say it all the more, because they don't read German and have never read Heidegger

94   *Lecture of 22 May 1986*

in the original text, which they flippantly admit), but I think that Sartre is extremely interesting because he offers an absolutely exceptional, highly coherent and ultra-logical motive force. Indeed, Merleau-Ponty saw it in his book entitled *Les Aventures de la dialectique*,[13] where we could find, if we needed to, the philosophical grounding of what I am telling you. Sartre gives a highly coherent form to this subjectivist theory, and on the problem of racism he develops a theory which is perfectly consonant with his theory of the emotions and his theory of revolution: the despised race exists only in the eyes of the racist, it is constituted by the gaze of the racist. What he forgets is that this racist gaze is not self-constructed. It is not a subject: it is already constituted and we could say that racism is a passive synthesis, a synthesis without a subject. Yet for all this, the subject in action is not passive – although usually, when you make the subject disappear, it is to make the construction disappear. The paradox of the habitus is to be a cognitive disposition that constructs without forasmuch being a subject. (All this is difficult because I think it confounds your false alternatives, which is why I have trouble expressing it, and this will be the case for all the rest of these closing lectures of my course, which ultimately bring to a close the kind of synthesis that I have been developing over a number of years; this is the point where the different threads that I have been spinning become sorted and woven together. This is therefore the moment when I am most satisfied with what I am saying, and at the same time no doubt the least satisfied, because I think that in many cases I must at once overthrow alternatives and argue in their terms, because they continue to exist in your minds and also in mine.)

The habitus then is that sort of non-subject which acts as we think a subject normally acts: it is a non-subject that constructs, constitutes and makes the world, but it is not itself made, it is already made to make the world in a certain fashion. This time, I think that I have more or less covered the essential ground.

Mental structures and objective structures

Having thus described the habitus/field relation as an infra-conscious body-to-body relation, we may now better understand the effects of symbolic power, which are some of the most mysterious effects in the social world and thus some of the most difficult mysteries facing social science. You know Lévi-Strauss's famous essay on 'The Sorcerer and his Magic'.[14] It is a very Maussian text,[15] in the tradition of all the great anthropologists who had an insight into this very mysterious kind of

Lecture of 22 May 1986   95

power that in certain circumstances the social world, acting through one agent or another, could exercise over other agents at a distance through a quasi-magical kind of action. Symbolic action is a magical action: saying 'Rise up' to somebody and getting them to rise up is extraordinary, it is a denial of the laws of physics (in physics, you could not say 'Rise up!' to a stone). There is then something miraculous in symbolic action and, ultimately, this is the miracle that those who ask 'Where does power come from? From on high? From below?' want to explain. They tend to say 'He rises because somebody in power makes him rise' or 'He rises because he wants to rise.' (I am simplifying the alternatives, but if after the lecture you go and read the works of some writers whom I won't mention by name, to avoid seeming to show off, you will see that my simplistic alternatives give the substance of the scientifically constituted, and even in fact not always constituted, alternatives, because, if they were constructed in the explicit and therefore somewhat simplistic form that I use to formulate them, they would often disappear as such.)

Symbolic power is a sort of action at one remove that a certain number of philosophers have described. Austin, whom I would willingly call a social scientist and willingly appropriate, has reflected on the problem: how does it come about that in some circumstances words cause action or produce effects?[16] I think that, in order to understand this specific efficacy of the symbolic – of the word, the order or the slogan – we need to bear in mind our philosophy of the institution existing as much in bodies as in things. Given the match established between social structures and mental structures, between institutional positions and personal dispositions, this sort of magical, spontaneous adhesion of agents' dispositions to their positions leads agents to do whatever the situation or the position requires. It is then because social structures become what you might call corporeal postures that the exercise of symbolic power is possible. For instance, if intimidation is accompanied by physical changes, it is to a considerable extent because the body has been the repository of a whole series of political imperatives which have come to compose a bodily *hexis*.

I shall not develop this further, but the division of labour between the sexes, for example, can be found in some form in every society – once again, it is particularly visible in Kabyle society and in the majority of primitive societies – through a quasi-explicit apprenticeship of the differential bodily behaviour of the two sexes: the army is one of the places in our society which perpetuates the explicit teaching of the bodily postures considered legitimate: 'Attention!', 'Eyes front!' – staring straight ahead, adopting a virile posture of confrontation,

96 *Lecture of 22 May 1986*

standing erect, etc. The notion of face and facing, which is extremely important, is linked to honour: facing forward is to face up to people, it is to not turn your back on them (to show your back is an offence – I could easily develop this further); it is also to stand upright, and the order to 'Stand upright!' – you are going to think that I am playing with words, but I assure you that this is no joke – has something to do with civil rights, with the law. I could demonstrate this, but it would involve a vast digression which would entirely confuse the issue – so I merely mention it for the moment, and I shall develop it later.

So the body is a repository of political injunctions – the injunctions concerning the difference between the sexes are fundamentally political – which can then be reactivated and become as it were the springs – to use the metaphor again – that can set symbolic power in motion. In other words, if symbolic power is able to act, it is because the social-ised body is the repository of a quantity of small, socially constructed springs that may be triggered in certain circumstances. The 'Attention!' command, for example, finds its exemplary trigger in military bravado – and if there is no war, it will never be triggered. That is a caricatural example, but there are in each one of us incorporated social injunctions that may, or may not, be used, but whose existence we must suppose in order to understand how magic actions – like intimidation, or the desire for power – are able to inspire such extraordinary feats of obedi-ence (if you think about it: why should we obey?).

The magical match of the body with the world

I think we may now understand, as I have already suggested, that obedience is an act of belief. Not so much in the sense: 'I believe that I have to obey', but rather 'I obey before I wonder whether I have to obey or not, because obedience goes without saying, and in a way, the socialised body has responded to the injunction that was addressed to it.' I believe that this representation of the body as a sort of repository or hoard of the virtual actions that can be asked of it, through a certain relation between it as a socialised body and a given social space, is extremely important, if we want to avoid having to choose between the alternatives of objectivism and subjectivism. (It is sometimes impor-tant to repeat things in several different ways to be sure of mastering them completely . . .)

This analysis could become very complicated, and, although I am not sure I can handle it as an improvisation, there is a very famous analysis by Hegel of our relation to the body as he conceived it, breaking with the Cartesian and Kantian dualist vision of our relation to the body that nearly all of us have internalised because it has been developed by the Judeo-Christian tradition. Hegel wants to show that our relation to the body should not be conceived according to the traditional model of a relation between a kind of *angelus rector*,[17] or soul, and a machine, but as a kind of magical relation, and he uses the metaphor of magic.[18] Finally, he takes the examples of the virtuoso and the acrobat, and shows how in their cases the relation between intention and execution is a kind of magical relation, and that ultimately the body is something we act on magically; it is unfortunately the only such thing: it is enough for us to will it, for it to move in the direction that we want it to, as long as it is well trained. He calls this a 'dextrous habit', which is what the habitus is: the habitus creates precisely its magical relation between the subject and their body.

The mismatch between intention and practice, between intuition and practice which results in failure or clumsiness, is rather rare, because the body immediately does what we ask of it. This magical relation is the product of a certain type of socialisation, a certain type of exercise, and it is in a way the reward for a successful socialisation. I think that we should broaden out this analysis of the relation between the social world and the body: when the socialisation is successful, when the work of incorporation of the fundamental social injunctions ('Stand upright!', 'Be a man!', 'Look me in the eyes!', or, on the contrary, 'Bow down!', 'Stay where you are!', etc.) is successful, the relation between the legitimate repositories of the social order, the people authorised to act magically upon others – that is, the powerful, the men, the elders – is of the type that Hegel describes between the subject and his body. It is an absolutely magical relationship, where an order triggers an injunction, making the question of who is the subject of the obedience meaningless.

The false problem of responsibility

I would like to develop this point a little: one of the great obstacles to investigating the problem of the causality of power is that the problem is constantly couched in terms of responsibility. We ask: 'Who is responsible for power? Is it the dominant or the dominated?' In fact, saying that power comes from below means saying that it is the fault of the dominated: 'They are dominated because they like it', 'They are dominated because they let it happen.' When we face the question of responsibility, we respond with the logic of the thriller: *is fecit cui*

98   *Lecture of 22 May 1986*

prodest ['The criminal is the person who profits from the crime']. In the example of the relations between the sexes, since the dominant profit from the relation of domination, we suppose that they are responsible; or, inversely, we say that the person responsible is the person who suffers, and that they should have rebelled. This is a very real problem: remember the debates over the Jews and the concentration camps. I am talking about absolutely concrete aspects of fundamental issues. The kind of analysis that I am developing abandons this moralisation of the question and eliminates the need to look for sources. Ultimately the function of the model that I am promoting is to reject the naive search for responsibility, in favour of adopting the habitus–field relationship, which, as I have been saying, is not self-aware, which renders the search for who acts and who doesn't act in this relationship meaningless: the two parties to the relationship act by experiencing it as necessary ('It's what you have to do', 'He did what he had to do', etc.).

Thus this analysis seems to me to be necessary to give us a fair understanding of the problem of power and prevent us from making the kind of subjective response which ultimately tends to make the dominated responsible for the domination they suffer (which is an important effect of the subjectivist vision). We could project what I have been saying on to the case of values: are values forged and constructed by social subjects, or are they discovered as pre-existing? The question is meaningless: values are constructed through relationships. It is because I am constituted in a certain way that I recognise a value as a value, that it appears not to be created by me, but to exist in reality. The same analysis applies to the sacred: is the sacred made up from acts of consecration or is it the sacred that generates the acts of consecration? These are real debates – Otto's book on the sacred turns on this alternative.[19] In fact my response remains the same: to a habitus disposed to be prepared to find sacred those things that are designated as sacred in the field they inhabit, the sacred appears, not as something that they constitute as sacred and that they could constitute as non-sacred through a simple change of mind ('Cry freedom!', *Aufklärung*, etc.), but as something that really is sacred, something fascinating and terrifying, something that makes your hair stand on end, that reduces you to tears.

Coincidence of positions and dispositions

Another important phenomenon that I believe corresponds to the same scenario: the relation between agents and their positions. This is

Lecture of 22 May 1986 99

a real problem facing sociologists, if for example they try to explain the behaviour of a small-minded official, a high-handed administrator or a doctor enrolled in a trade union: should they explain their practices through the position held by the agent, the corresponding interests and potential actions written into the position he holds, or through the dispositions inherent in the agent who holds the position? In every case – and as I have said several times, this is the most common case – where there is coincidence and concordance between the position and the dispositions of the person who holds it, the question becomes meaningless: one of the ruses of social logic that the sociologist will discover is to place in a position agents who are, so to speak, made for the job, such that they don't need explicit instructions not to do anything outside the remit of the position (a vital consideration), and would not dream of doing so.

Sometimes we may dream, for there is a kind of utopia of despair: 'What would happen if we had an anarchist as President of the Republic?' In fact, it never happens! [*laughter*] The idea that someone may do something impossible in terms of the definition of the position is impossible, except for some rare historical accident. It is more complicated than it seems . . . It does happen that people are, as we say, 'ill at ease' – in fact this means 'uncomfortable in their position': they do not have the dispositions normally foreseen for the position and they distort and disrupt the position. There is a kind of struggle between the dispositions and the position: normally the position is the winner (we say: 'He adapted well'), but sometimes people may transform the position in such a way as to make it conform to their dispositions – and this is an important factor for change in the social world.[20]

The case of the perfectly accomplished socialisation that I have described is an extreme case: it is never perfectly attained, even in so-called traditional societies where the model is less ill-adapted. This kind of relation of, so to speak, spontaneous comprehension between the post and its incumbent, between the position and the agents' dispositions, makes for a contented official, well-adapted to his functions [. . .] and praised by everyone; one who, being in an important position, feels important, acts important and embodies the importance of his functions, etc. This scenario is I think a clear enough illustration of the theory of the relation between the habitus and the field that I am promoting, and we see that the alternative introduced when we ask whether the cause is the position or the individual is precisely what all the social mechanisms tend to eliminate; they aim in a way to do away with this alternative, to make the separate subject and function disappear.

100   *Lecture of 22 May 1986*

I think that this type of analysis can provide a foundation for Weber's analysis of the civil servant, which is quite admirable, but is not, I believe, given an anthropological grounding. A successful civil servant disappears behind his function. This is what Weber says: the successful civil servant is a 'they', he never responds as a person. It is the opposition between the prophet who responds in the first person and the priest who, as a servant of his church, always responds in the third person: he is the delegate of an institution, he does not work miracles, he is not the subject of his actions, he is always impersonal – he is the function itself. An official who tells you 'Regulations are regulations' – for instance because you have tried to avoid paying a parking fine by saying: 'Come on now, just between ourselves, look, I have three children, etc.' – is doing no more than pronouncing the definition of his function in functional terms, which is, 'I am only a regulation', 'I am not an "I"', 'I am a function'; the good official is identical with his function. This is very important for instance when we discuss justice and judges: a major problem in law is the passage from what Weber calls *Kadijustiz*,[21] that is, a justice where the judge is able to have personal opinions, to a justice where the judge is the code of law (or in any case where we are led to believe this, because in fact it never actually happens without some influence of the habitus). The civil servant who functions effectively is one in whom the distinction between the person and his function finally loses its sense.

We see this in particular in the area of speech, and the problem of the spokesperson is extremely important. For instance, we might well imagine a spokesperson losing their self-control and speaking in their own name. The problem has been raised in recent years by the left-wing protest groups whose emotive and spontaneous behaviour has exposed the functional impersonality of the spokesperson. The spokesperson must speak in order to say only what they have been mandated to say, they speak only to express what their function would say if it could speak: it is not the person who speaks, it is a position. Given this, it is important to note that the spokesperson has become an embodiment of the censorship inherent in the function that they perform. This is extremely important because the fact that the censorship is embodied, once again, is the best guarantee against a loose cannon. If the self-control were conscious, if at every moment, following a logic of freely willed action, they had to say to themselves 'Careful, should I be talking today or not?', 'Should I let myself go or not?', 'Do I choose to follow the pleasure principle or the reality principle?', 'Should I optimise or maximise?', it would be catastrophic for the institution, which would finally break down. Whereas, with embodied censorship, taking as our model for prediction the intuition that we have of the habitus – its general attitude, its norms of deportment and behaviour: 'Is he standing straight?', 'Is his hair cut short enough?', etc. – we have a much safer predictive model because these are indices of socialisation undergone, and therefore of the degree to which discipline has been incorporated; the more fully embodied, the better the discipline. We could discuss this opposition between discipline and incorporated censorship.

Amor fati

In fact, one of the important things that I want to use these analyses to say is that, in the extreme case of the perfect match of dispositions and positions, the relation of the habitus to the position, that is, to the field – since the position can only be defined within a field – is a relation of *amor fati*. It is the love of destiny: I love my position, I love my profession and I do everything demanded by my profession; and even more, I feel absolutely free. But we should never forget that, although I may say that I have done things of my own free will, in fact it is not I who have done them. This is why the problem of freedom is so complicated. The notion of the habitus says that I am formidably free: nobody is more free than somebody who fulfils their habitus, they live their life as being totally free; except for the fact that they have not produced their own habitus.

They may feel free to alienate themselves: there are some habitus that are made with a need for more discipline. I don't know if you saw on television the other day (for those who have no experience of the social world as it is today, television does sometimes – however rarely – provide some contact with the social world): there were interviews at 10.30 in the evening with a certain number of people (I'm afraid you will think that I am overstepping the marks of my brief, but there would be a lot to say about the kind of informal interviews practised by journalists; they are at once useful and terribly dangerous because it is an illegal practice of sociology [*laughter*]; they do absolutely monstrous things from a scientific point of view – in the best of cases; I shan't mention the run-of-the-mill ones. . .). In this broadcast, a fairly old chap, a foundry worker, said: 'The best years of my life were the years I spent on my national service', while also saying: 'I had bad luck, I did five years, I was called up three times.' It is like the paradox of women victims of domestic violence that I mentioned last time: how can a sane and normal human being say that the best years of their life were

102 *Lecture of 22 May 1986*

those? It is quite simply because there are some habitus that find their freedom in necessity, because they are constituted like that, you see.

I find it rather simple to couch the problem of freedom in terms of: 'Am I free or not?' Philosophers often say that sociologists are simplistic, but perhaps the philosophers should revise their definition of the problems. I shall finish, then, with a passage from Marx, probably his least Marxist text. It has been passed to me by a friend; it is from *The Ethnological Notebooks of Karl Marx*, published in 1972. These writings are quite astonishing. Marx says:

> Customary law is not obeyed, as enacted law is obeyed. When it obtains over small areas and in small natural groups, the penal sanctions on which it depends are partly opinion, partly superstition, but to a far greater extent an instinct almost as blind and sometimes unconscious as that which produces some of the movements of our bodies. The actual constraint which is required to secure conformity with usage is inconceivably small.[22]

If the action of socialisation, that is, the incorporation of the social, is successful, people can proceed to act with minimal disciplinary intervention. All it needs is a flick of the finger here and there: people are trained to walk in line, so they walk in line, with, from time to time, a slight wobble to the left and a slight wobble to the right . . . I think that this relation between the habitus and the field is absolutely crucial to our understanding of why the social world functions, why it is not mad and why in fact it works quite well with the minimum of fuss, when you might think that all the circumstances concur to make people quit this kind of submission to order. I think we may say that the order is not perfect enough for us not to be surprised that people find it so perfect, and the notion of habitus is a key to understanding this. I'll stop there.

Second session (seminar): *To the Lighthouse* (2)

Luckily what I have to say now follows on from what I was just trying to say. This is good because, since I have a strong feeling that I have not really managed to say what I wanted to say, I shall perhaps, if not compensate for this, at least finish what I was saying just now.

In fact, as you can quite clearly see, the particular case of sexual domination is no doubt the most useful for the mode of analysis that I am proposing. I think that the majority of the analyses that we see discussing this masculine/feminine relationship are guilty of gross naivety, partly because they fall prey to the alternatives arising from the fact that the problem is formulated in terms of a search for the responsibility of one or the other party. In this particular case, the paradox, as I tried to show last time, is that privilege can also be a trap, which does not mean that it is not still a privilege. Among the games on offer in the social world – and this is perhaps the heart of what I was saying last time – some are more gratifying, more vital and more profitable than others, and because of the differential socialisation that most societies impose on people according to their gender, the men and the women do not participate in social games in the same way, and in particular in the most profitable games. By the same token, we can describe the socially constituted distance of the women from the dominant games as an exclusion – there is a perfect analogy with the petit bourgeois – and *a fortiori*, quite simply with the dominated, where the exclusion implies a privation. But this privation, as we see in the ambiguity of the female gaze that scrutinises the infantile male, can also be considered as a relative privilege, insofar as participating in the game implies exchanging blows, taking risks, making sacrifices and suffering disappointment.

So the phenomenon can only be understood as an effect of the obscure relation of *illusio* between the player and the game, which posits the game as something formidably serious, even if the game is only serious for somebody endowed with a habitus positing the game as being worth playing. The *illusio* is paradoxically at once illusory and supremely serious because, in the eyes of the most masculine players, the stakes are the highest possible, they are risking their lives. The most serious games only exist as serious for those who have been constituted to take them seriously.

Another analogy is the differential relation to culture: depending on their social class, social agents are differently socialised, and because of this, unequally liable to consider cultural games as vital. We could make another connection with the opposition between artists and the bourgeoisie as it was defined for the whole of the nineteenth century. What makes the artists structurally homologous to the women is the fact that we never know whether their rejection of the dominant games, that is, the games of power, is the effect of an elective exclusion or an exclusion imposed. This is something that Sartre, who felt it very strongly himself, saw in the case of Flaubert:[23] Is the artists' rejection of bourgeois games imposed or chosen? Am I rejecting the bourgeois games merely because I am excluded from them? Do I say that I don't want glory, power and honours because I couldn't have them in any case, or is my rejection of them genuine? (cf. Sartre's *The Family Idiot*). It seems to me that this ambiguous relation between the artist and the

104   *Lecture of 22 May 1986*

games of power makes us think of the relation of women to the games of power, and I think that this homology of relationship explains the alliance, which is very important for our understanding of the history of literature, between bourgeois women and the artists, through the salon – I shall not develop this topic, which I have discussed on several occasions.[24] The example of gender domination is then the illustration par excellence of the analyses that I was proposing just now: it is a case where we see clearly that the *illusio* becomes corporeal and that a serious attempt to adhere to the dominant can translate into somatic experiences that we might call desire, intimidation or whatever. In other words, the analysis of the relation of gender domination as a somatised political relation enables us to understand – without resorting to alternative explanations such as psychoanalytic ones, but without necessarily excluding them – a certain number of the fundamental phenomena of the relations between the sexes.

Incorporating the political

What I am trying to say this morning is that the political is always somatised: the experiences of power profoundly transform the body, and socialisation makes us incorporate political standpoints in the form of corporeal dispositions. This was the sense of 'Stand upright!' Because of the sort of somatisation of the political that socialisation produces, sexual experience itself tends to be thought of politically. Ethnologists speak traditionally of the sexual division of labour: in many societies, the principal division of labour is the division of labour between the sexes (men perform certain tasks, women others); this division of labour according to gender is fundamental in these societies and becomes a fundamental principle of division, *principium divisionis*, a principle of classification of the world, it becomes the principle of division of all things.

I believe that I have shown this in the case of the Kabyle mythical system:[25] the division of labour between the sexes, between the masculine and the feminine, is a principle common to all the fundamental oppositions of the mythical or mythico-ritual system, from whose base we can derive all the other oppositions between the wet and the dry, east and west, the sun and the moon, etc. In other words, the mythical divisions are anchored in the principal political division of these societies, that is, in the division of labour between the sexes, so that the objective principle of division becomes the subjective principle of division, that is, the principle of vision of the objective divisions,

Lecture of 22 May 1986   105

and also the principle of vision of the division of sexual procedures (which is not the gendered division of labour) or of the division of labour in the sexual act. We need only think of the crucial role that the above/below opposition plays in most of the mythical systems and in our language, and in particular in the language of politics – it is a fundamental opposition: to submit, to bow down, to bend the knee, to bend over or to overcome, to come out on top, etc. These metaphors are political metaphors but they also structure our perception of the sexual relation, not only in its ideological representation but also in its bodily aspects. In other words, the experience of sex as an act, and also more generally the experience of sexual relations, tends to be thought politically because it is thought in terms of principles of division which are themselves political divisions. The relation between the sexes is quite generally thought in terms of the dominant and the dominated. It seems to me that the vision of the relations between the sexes which is expressed in the very masculine metaphor of conquest and war is a generalised projection of the fact that the universal principle of construction has at its source a political opposition that is sexual.

In societies like our own, which are differentiated, and differentiated according to principles other than that of the gendered division of labour, the principle of the gendered division of labour remains one of the principles of division of the world, and of private mythical systems (for instance, in poetry, poets being those who preserve myth, acting as private mythologists). In these societies, where there are no longer any collective mythologies, the principles of opposition between the masculine and the feminine remain very active in our thinking in the private sphere but also in the political sphere. This means that the sexual experience, which is lived politically (and charged with unconscious drives that are not merely political), becomes one of the principles of construction of the political sphere, one of the principles through which we interpret the political world. This is a case where we might quote Wittgenstein: it is enough to give play to our ordinary language, to give rein to the ensemble of metaphors enclosed within language (I took the example of 'above/below', 'to bow down', but you could also take the metaphors of domination, strength and weakness, etc.), to see the interplay of the sexual and the political in political thought, that is, the contamination of politics by a politico-sexual structuring of sexual experience.

Behind this remark, which seems like a rather ordinary intuition, I think that we can detect a better understanding of the phenomena of charisma or charm that I mentioned last time, and we can perhaps raise the question, as I did then, of the charm of power. Weber investigated the problem of charisma, but it was not his style to question, in the

106 *Lecture of 22 May 1986*

notion of charisma, the connotations of charm and seduction. It was not the right historical moment for Weber to be able to think like that. But I think that it is fair enough to speak of the charm of power.

In a series of seminars, some professors from the Collège de France have elaborated this notion of the charm or the beauty of power.[26] It became apparent that, in situations very different in place and time (ancient Japan, Assyria, Babylon, ancient Egypt, etc.), the notion of power – masculine, of course – was often surrounded with a set of connotations that always evoked the brilliant, the luminous and the dazzling, what stands out like a figure against a ground, what is ultimately distinct and distinguished, what enlightens. Faced with this specific kind of seduction by the brilliant, Georges Duby said, with great caution, that in the case of the medieval civilisations which he studied, you might wonder whether the courtly love of young pretenders for the wife of the prince was not a sort of vicarious love for the prince himself,[27] without necessarily relating to some repressed homosexuality, because very often (at least as I see it) this kind of social sexuality is much more general, more all-embracing and ultimately more abstract, while remaining very corporeal. It does not involve sexuality in the ordinary sense at all, which is in any case, we should remember, a nineteenth-century invention.[28] In fact sexuality only became thought of as an autonomous practical and technical operation, independent of the social and political constructions that normally accompany it, quite recently, in particular through psychoanalysis and its repercussions. It is extremely important to know this in order to avoid misunderstandings. Ethnologists have constantly pointed this out, but it has not yet filtered through to the public at large.

The charm of power, then, is connected with the sort of experience of wonder that individuals socially conditioned to recognise a certain type of power feel in the presence of power. It is an experience that we might call erotic, as long as we bear in mind what I have just said, that the erotic is not composed as such at all. It is an 'erotic' situation in the sense that I used just now when speaking of a 'love of destiny': the love of power is the love of a social destiny, composed as such, for people composed in such a way as to experience and discover it. That is more or less what I wanted to say.

Paternal power and the verdict effect

I want to return for a moment to the parallel that Virginia Woolf establishes, in a manner that I find very subtle and almost imperceptible, between feminine submission to masculine power as a desire for power and infantile submission to paternal power. As I have already explained, the very beginning of the novel shows a young child discovering the paternal verdict to be absolute and arbitrary. It is the dramatic, masculine sentence pronounced by the father which brutally cuts through (the man is constantly compared – in a very Kabyle-like comparison – to a sharp, violently penetrating knife) all the slightly confused aspirations of the child, who was hoping to go to the lighthouse, with his mother's encouragement: '"But", said his father, stopping in front of the drawing-room window, "it won't be fine"' (p. 6). This is a verdict, a sentence pronounced with authority concerning the future: it is a forecast, a prediction, a fatal judgement. The word of the father is fatal because, spoken by him, it will come true. This is the father as holder of symbolic power, the symbolic power par excellence, the primordial symbolic power; he is the father-king, the all-powerful father, in particular because he is able to tell what is true insofar as what he says will truly come to pass. This is extremely important: the father has the power to make what he says come true, because he is the one who decides.

The problem with prediction in the social sciences is shown here in its entirety: if I say that dawn will break tomorrow and I have the power to make dawn break, dawn will break. In the natural world, somebody saying that would be mad. In the social world, under certain conditions, somebody saying this might be truthful, might be telling the truth: if I am the king and I say: 'Tomorrow the Court will assemble' my speech is a *fatum*, a verdict that produces its own verification. It is a 'self-fulfilling prophecy',[29] it verifies itself, and cannot be falsified. I am not making this up; I quote Virginia Woolf: 'What he said was true. It was always true. He was incapable of untruth [*this is the limit of the powerful: they are victims of their own domination*]; never tampered with a fact; never altered a disagreeable word to suit the pleasure or convenience of any mortal being, least of all his own children, who, sprung from his own loins, should be aware from childhood that life is difficult' (p. 6).

Masculine potency (the word 'potency' has overdetermined connotations through the fact that the paradigm of sexual virility lurks behind the politicisation of the general usage of the concept), paternal power, as enshrined in the law, is a sort of absolute potency. Here we encounter the Freudian sense: it is the monopoly of the exercise of sexual potency (this in answer to a question put to me about the family) in the relatively autonomous field of the family, which in fact may by analogy be thought of as a political state system with its power,

108   *Lecture of 22 May 1986*

its ideology, its dominant and dominated, and its division of labour. The holder of paternal power has the power to pass sentence, to tell the truth, to a great extent because what he says is always true (which is one of his statutory properties and he is himself constrained by this property), and at the same time he has the power to make this truth-telling come true. We might think that his power to make truth-telling come true depends on the fact that he always tells the truth. He is bound to make people believe that he always tells the truth, that he is always truthful. The theme of the god of veracity[30] and that of the truthful father are very closely allied. If the father started to be seen as somebody who did not always tell the truth, he would lose the specific base of his power which is the symbolic power par excellence, that is, a power misrecognised as such, which is the supreme form of power, being unavoidable precisely because the idea that it is a power does not occur to people ('It's for your own good'). It is no accident that the model of paternalism is rooted in this foundational power: paternalist power aims to act only in the interest of the dominated, who need to be taught the reality of the world.

As the incarnation of the reality principle, what this power speaks of can only be real. It is the repository of the reality principle and therefore it anticipates the workings of the world. The best service that it can render is to say in advance what the world will say. It is, then, scientific: it is scientific socialism. It says: 'What I am telling you is true because it is I who am speaking and my role is to tell you what is true; and I am telling you for your own good because in any case you will discover that what I am saying is true, and it is better for you to discover it too soon than too late. My role is to teach you how to live, that is, to teach you what is true, which is that the world is difficult.' I do no more than gloss Virginia Woolf: '[. . .] least of all his own children, who, sprung from his own loins, should be aware from childhood that life is difficult'.

It is the reality principle against the pleasure principle. Under these conditions, the father cannot follow the whims of his own pleasure: a Cartesian god, or father, who is the creator of the truth of our eternal values, might amuse himself by making two plus two equal five, but it would be unliveable. His discourse must conform to the world, that is, it must be constantly confirmed by the world. For this to happen, he must announce only things that he can make happen. It is the paradigm of Jean-Christophe who orders the clouds to go in the direction that they are going.[31] Fathers who want to preserve their authority do likewise. But they may give orders to the clouds in other cases since, at least in domestic circumstances, they dispose of a certain authority. I

Lecture of 22 May 1986 109

am expressing this badly because it is difficult and because it constantly seems to sound like things we have vaguely intuited. To say it really well, I would have to work day and night at changing every word. But I want to give you an idea, that is all I can do.

In fact what we have here is a kind of primordial political experience. Within the framework of a phenomenology of the lived experience of the social world, it seems to me that this is the kind of thing that we should phenomenologise; we need to rethink the very foundations of paternal power as a paradigm of all powers. Paternal power is not only the medium through which we can think of all powers, but also the medium through which we must think them, because, given the foundational character of the experience of our relation to paternal power, the relation to the father is one of the mediations, one of the fundamental experiences, helping to constitute the repository of fundamental dispositions on which paternalistic strategies, for instance, will be able to act. Paternalism is possible because all children have had fathers and, more precisely, fathers who pass judgement, fathers who know better than their children what should be done, fathers who treat the masses as women, fathers who love their children more than they love themselves and also fathers who, for all these reasons, are profoundly intimidating: what can you say to a father except that he is right (and is always right. . .)?

Rebellion against this situation is only so dramatic because – a typical example of what I was saying just now – there is the order of the habitus that obeys and the rebellion that disobeys. I shall be saying things that are beyond my competence, but I think that if we used my analyses we could describe adolescent rebellion better than people usually do. It is a revolt, not against the father, but against obedience, against the fact that we obey, even when we don't want to. What is revolting is the fact that we obey when we want to disobey. What is revolting is the fact that our first reaction is to obey, and our habitus tends to obey, when we want to disobey. Our struggle against power is a struggle with the truth of power and the capacity of power to tell the truth, given that, for power to be really symbolically powerful, that is, misrecognised as such, it must appear to be true and therefore assume a form of realism. It is not possible for it to be a mad power. Paternal power is a realist power: 'I am acting for your own good. One day you will understand.' All this is part of the sociological definition: there is no need to look anywhere else for the source of the sociological definition of paternal potency.

What I have been trying to get across is the fact that this power, which is symbolically powerful, regal, truthful and true, quasi-divine

110 *Lecture of 22 May 1986*

and predictive (this is most important: 'I know better than you do what you are going to do, and in the end you will see that I was right, you will do what I told you to, and if you don't, you will regret it'), this power of prediction and prophecy, of acting as fate, is the symbolic power par excellence, the power to get people to freely do what has to be done, one example being intimidation which, as they say, leaves you paralysed, rooted to the spot, disarmed, disoriented and speechless ('I couldn't think of an answer'). (One reason why the sociologist is such a structurally detested social agent is that he exercises an effect of paternal verdict; he says: 'You see what is going to happen' – I won't take this further, but I think that this was important, to help us see how to self-analyse some of our own reactions.)

The somatisation of social crises

Obviously the 'Last Judgement' effect cannot succeed without the complicity of the person suffering it, but what is most terrible is that it only has its effect on believers who do not have the choice whether to believe or not: they are constituted in such a way that the question does not even occur to them. The drama of the paternal verdict is that it is not a verdict like any other: it is an absolute verdict – above all if it concerns, as *To the Lighthouse* does, a small, five-year-old child. To rebel against this verdict is to rebel against oneself, it is to throw oneself into the void, into despair, into atheism. Hegel spoke of the 'atheism of the moral world';[32] here, it would be the atheism of the family world, absolute despair. *To the Lighthouse* is the novel of absolute despair, that is, of the discovery of the wickedness of God, of the wicked God whom we must not condemn as wicked. I shall not take this further – it is not my brief to analyse the literary aspect of the novel – but I think that this is part of the strength of the primordial experience of symbolic power as a magic power par excellence.

I shall now venture way beyond the limits of my competence, but it is only in order to try to convince you of something that I believe, albeit in the order of things where proof is difficult to obtain. I was saying just now that the strength of symbolic powers is to act directly on the body and to somatise political experiences. I could cite periods of high crisis, like those that suddenly strike highly integrated pre-capitalist societies where all is in order, when they come into contact with civilisation and colonisation, and their social structures disintegrate. The misfortune and emotional shock of the crisis are then often expressed in certain individuals, particularly the elderly, in somatic guise, in terms of physical despair or disgust. One metaphor is that of vomiting: 'I spew forth this world.' We can find this in our own society. For example, among university professors who were socially very well integrated in a 'perfect' university world that was very similar to an archaic society where father/son relations are unproblematic (it was a kind of universe of simple reproduction, which gives an experience of completeness, fulfilment and beatitude!), the university crisis linked with the student movement has triggered quasi-somatic reactions of absolute despair, such as those felt in the tragedy of a world collapsing.[33] The fact that I am recounting these experiences, although I don't share the habitus that is attuned to them, proves that we can sympathise theoretically with things that we don't sense through the medium of our habitus. But in order to understand them *fully*, and in particular to understand their dramatic, emotional nature, with the phenomena of nervous breakdown and psychological crises provoked by certain crises of the social order, we must keep in mind the idea that the social order is in complicity with the hidden depths of our bodies.

Another parenthesis, before coming to another rather risky example that I want to give you: in many primitive societies, social injunctions have biological effects; there are symbolic murders (these do exist – excommunication, for instance, can be lethal). Social exclusion can provoke effects that we would consider to be somatic. This can also be observed in certain types of large modern movement, such as those regimes that we rather hastily label as 'totalitarian', those that act upon the whole person. Social universes use mechanisms whose theory they are unaware of. In other words, there is a sort of psychosomatic medicine or theory at work in a certain number of social operations, such as: discipline; organisation into small, hyper-integrated groups; sessions of self-criticism. Phenomena of exclusion (exclusion from a political party [provides the most pertinent illustration (?)] of my argument[34]) involve effects that largely overflow the control of the conscious mind. I am expressing all this rather badly, but it is to help you understand what I am referring to throughout this analysis, and to show that we are discussing an order of things which quite clearly is not controllable by the conscious mind.

Metamorphosis and the founding experience of primordial power

I turn now to my principal concern. Moving on from Virginia Woolf to Kafka's *Metamorphosis*, I shall say straight away what I have in mind: *Metamorphosis* is ultimately a metaphor for paternal potency,

112   *Lecture of 22 May 1986*

that is, a verdict, and God knows how much Kafka is interested in the problem of the verdict and also in relations with the father – I think that you have all read his *Letter to His Father*.[35] I think that we should take *Metamorphosis* as a metaphorical expression of the effect of the verdict on a child: there is a kind of somatisation of judgements like 'You are nothing but vermin', 'You are less than nothing.'[36] This somatisation is given hyperbolic expression, but I think that we can read *Metamorphosis* as a sort of symbolic expression of the property of symbolic power which is to be a magical power, which, in the case of the father/son relation, can lead to a sort of super-interiorisation of the father's discourse.

This calls for a whole socio-analysis. These are things which do not attract the psychoanalysts' attention (which is normal, it's not their job), but I would be tempted to use in-depth interviews to undertake a study similar to a psychoanalysis, a sort of anamnesis[37] of paternal discourse, with its formative paternal remarks,[38] those that have had an extraordinary effect of constitution. It is not the first things that people will say which will be significative: they need help in finding the kind of things that make us say 'That left its mark on me.' I think we would find a certain number of effects of creative nomination, that is, everything that I described last year in discussing nomination: the effects of nomination, certification and educational qualification, etc. The nomination effect may be positive (like the consecration effect) or negative (as in the case of insult or slander), and we see its supreme form, it seems to me, in this case of an incontestable power, impossible to challenge.

Another important thing is the description in Virginia Woolf's novel of the impossible situation of the mother, who could be the last resort, and who sees that the father has virtually stabbed his son to the heart, so that he does not know which saint to pray to . . . since he is faced with God the Father. Virginia Woolf was considered to be one of the great founders of feminism (American feminists are writing about three books a day on her), and she is interesting because she knows that the habitus continues to function, whatever the conscious mind may be saying. The mother is disarmed because she does not want to contribute to a drama that might prove to be even more dramatic, that is, the murder of the father. She knows that the paternal father is extremely important as the truth-teller, and that the suffering of the child comes from the fact that he has to choose between an odious truth and the death of the truth-telling prophet. She is deeply embarrassed, as we would be if we were in her place.

I believe that the paradigm of God the Father, the father as god and the father as paradigm of absolute power, is important for a true

Lecture of 22 May 1986 113

understanding of what I imply by the notion of a nomination effect. When I speak of a 'positive educational qualification' I am not saying that the diploma makes somebody intelligent, but that this certificate of intelligence can give them at least some aptitude to adopt the external signs of intelligence! [*laughter*] The same thing applies to a stigma or a condemnation ('You are dismissed', etc.). The two effects that I have just described can have absolutely terrible effects on somebody's destiny. I would like to remind you of the effect of paternal potency described by Kafka in the metaphor of the *Metamorphosis*: children take metaphors seriously, they take the words literally – 'You are nothing but vermin' becomes 'I am vermin.' The total gift of the self, the absolute *fidēs*[39] of the child in the father, is the condition of the exercise of absolute paternal power as power of creative nomination. These are words that do what they say, that have the power to endow what they say with complete existence.

We need to return to these founding experiences of primordial power in order to understand the full strength of the symbolic powers, of which the primordial power is the ultimate, and also to understand the ulterior efficacy of all the symbolic powers that are based on the leverage created by the founding power. There are some very fine passages in Freud on the professor as substitute father,[40] and here I see no difference between psychoanalysis and sociology. The professor delivers creative verdicts, he has a power of creative nomination – the Pygmalion effect. His powers of creative nomination owe a part of their efficacy to the fact that he reactivates somatised political dispositions that have been constituted in our founding relation with the ordinary, paradigmatic paternal power. For example, analyses of the kind that I am proposing are I think important in helping us to understand the neuroses related to school and the somatic effects resulting from school verdicts that psychologists and psychoanalysts often come across these days; they enable us to connect things that the division of labour between disciplines has led us to separate, since analyses of a psychoanalytic type are often driven by a kind of horror of sociology, which I shall discuss next time. Psychoanalysis and sociology are in fact discussing the same thing, so it only needs sociology to speak more clearly, as long, of course, as psychoanalysis is willing to listen [*laughter*]. I shall stop there.

Lecture of 29 May 1986

First session (lecture): the division of labour in the production of representations – A theory of action – The conditions of rational decision – The problem as such does not exist – Deliberation as accident – A broader rationalism – Alternatives and logic of the field
Second session (seminar): the field of power (1) – The field of power and differentiation of the fields – The emergence of universes 'as such' – Power over capital – Power and its legitimisation

First session (lecture): the division of labour in the production of representations

What I intend to present you with today is not so simple, and I fear in advance that I may disappoint you, and myself as well. Since I am going to situate myself at a point of debate in the social sciences where different theories of action and, more generally, of social practice are in contention, I shall have to mention a certain number of positions that I compare to my own analyses in a necessarily allusive fashion, without being able to fully explore them, having to suppose that some of you will be familiar with at least some of them. Setting my analyses up against rival theories is difficult (merely to make a rigorous presentation of the space of the theoretical possibilities in relation to which I situate my own analyses would require hours of argumentation), but it seems to me indispensable, in order to better understand and verify the analyses I have to offer. While the theories of practice and of action seem to me to be crucial issues for scientific discussion, another argument is that we cannot escape the obligatory alternatives that we find ourselves faced with as soon as we approach the problem unless we focus consciously on the theory of practice that we are using in our own scientific practice of the social sciences. For it seems to me that there is no more rigorous way of making explicit the theory of practice that we often use in a practical manner than by situating it in relation to other theories.

If I wanted to summarise the central drive of the arguments that I have developed in my previous lectures, I would say that social science has to suppose that social agents do perceive, understand and construct the social world, but through operations that, although being ordinarily understood in an intellectualist logic as acts of intellectual cognition, may remain in a state of practical, pre-reflexive, non-thetic, implicit operation, which does not imply representation in the literal sense. This theory of action and practice seems to me to be essential if we are to give an adequate account of social practices, but also to give an adequate formulation of one of the fundamental problems in social science, the problem of representation. As I have just said, our common or ordinary form of comprehension and knowledge of the social world does not imply an explicit mental representation of the object known. Remembering Leibniz's dictum according to which 'in three-fourths of our actions we are nothing but empirics',[1] we could say that in three quarters of our actions we engage a knowledge of the social world that remains in a practical state and does not imply any representation: ordinary agents, in their ordinary practice, engage in knowledge without representation.

In the light of this argument, we may wish to consider the status of people whose profession it is to produce representations. It is only if we adopt the correct theory of practice that we may correctly raise the fundamental theoretical question of the division of theoretical labour, the division of the labour of producing representations, whether they are pictorial, discursive, active or political in the broadest sense. We need to look seriously at the word 'representative' often used to designate politicians: representatives represent the groups that mandate them, they provide a representation of the alleged representations of those who mandate them. In fact, while it is in the nature of social practice to involve a kind of comprehension that does not imply representation, we see that the passage from practice to any kind of representation involves a kind of *saltus*, a qualitative leap. This is one of the reasons why it seems to me important to have a just theory of practice, and this ambition is at the heart of my argument today.

116   *Lecture of 29 May 1986*

A theory of action

I was saying last time that it is in the relation between a habitus and a field that both knowledge and motivation are born. We should look for the motor of the practice or the cause of the action (what makes people act?), not among the agents or within the field, but in the relation between a habitus and a field. Saying this is tantamount to using the metaphor of energy (which, like all metaphors, is not without danger): energy is created if the current flows between the habitus and the field. What I have tried to develop in my previous analyses are the conditions under which a habitus is composed so that it feels the injunctions of a field and gives these injunctions existence by perceiving them adequately. When the habitus is adapted to the field, energy flows, together with motivation, which is not necessarily representation, but belief, belief that it is worth the trouble, accompanied by investment and engagement in practice. We might say that it is the habitus/field relation that generates the fundamental form of 'desire' (in Spinoza's sense, and not in the restrictive sense given to it by recent philosophy[2]), which is the desire to do something, to appropriate something. Sociology recognises the existence of the *libido* that is generated in the relation between a particular habitus and a particular field: we speak of a *libido sciendi* and a *libido dominandi;*[3] there are as many *libidines* as there are fields and relations between the various habitus and fields.

It is obvious then that we can back the hypothesis that underlies the Schopenhauer-Freud tradition, that of a sort of *libido,* a fundamental impulse to persist in existence, to persevere in being, a kind of fundamental *conatus.*[4] But what matters from a sociological point of view are the different forms taken by this tendency to persevere in being. For instance, it is always within the logic of a field that what I call the strategies of reproduction are defined,[5] those strategies which have as their principle the tendency of social agents to persevere in their social being, that is, in the position that they hold within a given social space. This sort of social *conatus,* to use Spinoza's term, which is at the source of most kinds of economic behaviour in the widest sense (choosing a good school for the children, making a good investment, deciding to buy a flat instead of renting, etc.), and in particular all the strategies of reproduction, is always generated historically, in the relation between a historical habitus and a historical field.

This is important if we are to distinguish this theory of practice or action clearly from one (or perhaps the only) form of the theory of practice that is explicitly formulated today. Social science specialists paradoxically nearly always leave in an implicit state the theory of

Lecture of 29 May 1986   117

action that they necessarily mobilise (since one of the functions of social science is to give reasons for and accounts of social practices and actions). Today one of the few overtly formulated forms of a theory of action is one called 'decision theory',[6] which is an explicit, more or less codified form of the theory current in the economic tradition. This theory of rational action or calculation is in fact a paradigm that is antithetical or antinomial to the one I propose. I shall try briefly to characterise these two forms of analysis in an attempt to highlight the functions of the theory that I propose as an alternative.

The conditions of rational decision

It seems to me that one major difference lies in the fact that the theory of rational decision supposes the existence of some sort of what we might call 'desire' pre-existing the action: so the action is supposed to find its origins in an operation pre-dating the act itself. Strangely, we might find this theory as easily in the neo-marginalists[7] as in the Marxists, and one of its most typical expressions might be the famous metaphor of the architect and the bee used by Marx to characterise human action. According to this famous analysis, the difference between the architect and the bee would be a distinction between rational behaviour and instinctive action:[8] the architect draws up a plan, a preliminary model for the practical execution of the project. This philosophy of action, which I shall shortly try to show is an engineer's philosophy based on the model of technology, supposes that action is preceded by the drafting of a design, that is by a project which formulates explicit aims, in relation to which the whole of the action, and in particular the calculation of the most appropriate means, will be organised. The design most commonly takes the form of a drawing, plan, schema or diagram, to wit, a practical, visible, communicable objectification, where this preliminary objectification guarantees rational control of the coherence of the design and project, and also the compatibility of the project with the means employed.

Decision theory, then, is an intellectual's or a logician's theory, according to which a rational decision is preceded by rational deliberation. This philosophy finds its fulfilment nowadays in the mathematical analysis of the process of decision-making, or in management science, disciplines which have in common their supposition that a practical operation may be divided into separate phases. The fact that these phases correspond to different positions in the division of labour is not without importance: the division of labour, in particular bureaucratic

118   *Lecture of 29 May 1986*

labour, is based on an opposition between the phase of conception, with its planners, the executives who draft what they call the 'instructions' (or circulars or schedules), and the phase of execution by the labour force, the workers. Since this division into phases corresponds to the social division of labour, we may wonder whether the intellectualist illusion that underpins this theory of action doesn't owe part of its plausibility to the fact that it is very strongly grounded in the objective structures of the division of labour (but I shall not develop this point).

A rational decision, as defined by the partisans of this theory of action, must proceed from several successive operations. Firstly, a complete list of possible actions must be established. This is one of the conditions of rational action: you must first have examined every possibility, and every possible alternative to the choice you have to make. Secondly, since the strategy of rational deliberation leads to a rational strategy, you must study in full the consequences of the different strategies, and try to predict what costs would be incurred by each of them. Finally, you should evaluate these consequences comparatively in terms of explicit criteria of evaluation. In sum, in this perspective, for an action to be rational there has to be a premeditated design, posited as an exclusive aim, and the procedure has to be deliberately oriented towards the accomplishment of this explicitly and rigorously formulated design. A rational action, then, depends on the existence of an explicit design, the word 'explicit' being important: the rational decision starts with the linguistic formulation of the intention explicitly enunciated and objectified. You can see how opposed this is to everything that I have been saying about the sense of practice or the feel for the game as the immediate response to a problem which is not posed as a problem as such.

There is a classic objection to this vision of rational action. Even within the logical framework of the dominant paradigm, certain partisans of rational decision-making have objected that none of the three conditions is ever fulfilled in practice: it is impossible to know every possibility; knowledge of the consequences is always fragmentary; and, finally, it is impossible to have a rational knowledge of the relative values of the different consequences. Herbert Simon, who is often quoted on this subject, develops this critique in a relatively old book, *Administrative Behavior* (1947).[9] In a more recent work (1972) he moves even closer to the paradigm that I have proposed:

> The solution to a problem supposes the search for a solution in a space of alternative solutions [*but he adds:*] To have a problem implies (at least) that certain information is given to the problem

Lecture of 29 May 1986 119

solver: information about what is desired, under what conditions, by means of what tools and operations, starting with what initial information, and with access to what resources.[10]

Since this [*Bourdieu's translation of Simon into French*] is badly phrased, I shall spell it out more clearly. What seems important to me, if we expand on what Simon is saying, is that the rational decision does not start at the decisive moment of the decision: the rational decision is itself in a way preceded by, and presupposes, a whole raft of minimal preconditions, even from the point of view of the extremely abstract and reduced decision-making theory that this paradigm allows. In fact, for the problem solver to be able to solve a problem, he has to know what he wants, which is quite something. In fact he ought to know everything: he ought to know under what conditions he wants what he wants, what costs he is prepared to pay (this is enormous: the whole life history of the acting subject is at issue), which means are acceptable or unacceptable, and (this is perhaps the key question) what information and which intellectual and practical resources he wishes to engage in order to solve the problem. In short, he has to know everything that I have located in the habitus: on the pretext of correcting the abstract presumptions of the paradigm, Simon reintroduces everything that defines the antagonistic paradigm which I am proposing.

The problem as such does not exist

Simon is interesting because, basically, he does to the paradigm of rational action what Tycho Brahe[11] did to the Copernican paradigm: since he realises that such a pure and perfect model of rational action can only be constructed at the price of a fantastical abstraction, he attempts to correct the paradigm while remaining within its bounds, but he corrects it so far that he bursts those bounds. We can clearly see that, from one little adjustment to another, he finally tips over into another universe altogether. I shall now develop what is implicit in Simon's critique by very briefly reminding you of what I was saying previously, which will lead me to repeat myself, but since I shall now do it with reference to the paradigm that I have just explained, it should take on a new significance for you.

In fact Simon says that the very idea of a problem *qua* problem can only arise for an agent constituted in such a way as to find reality problematic. There is no ready-made problem as such waiting to confront a subject who would only have to take it as given and undertake

120 *Lecture of 29 May 1986*

to solve it. In this context we might take a famous saying by Marx, while giving it a very different sense: 'Men only ask questions that they can answer':[12] you need to have the theoretical and practical capacity required for the solution of a problem to make the problem exist as a problem. No problem exists as a pure problem, only practical problems exist. I would go so far as to say: are practical problems still problems? There are only practical problems, which, like the problem of a flat soufflé for a cook or a conundrum in maths for a mathematician, exist only in the relation between a habitus prepared to solve it and the difficulties that this habitus encounters. The problem, then, exists only for somebody who is socialised in such a way that on entry into the social space they flush out problems (as one flushes out grouse) that they are able to solve. The habitus flushes out problems inherent in the field. So in a way you need to have the means to overcome difficulties that present themselves as difficulties, but not as problems, since they are no sooner posited than solved: it is of the nature of the sense of practice to solve them, to overcome difficulties without constituting them as problems. Belonging to and participating in a field, which supposes an appropriate habitus (as a condition for entering the field), flushes out problems which in a way did not pre-exist it, since they are generated in the relation between the habitus and the field.

This leads the theories of rational decision-making to commit the major error that I mentioned last time, which consists in giving as the principle of an action either rational deliberation or (the only possible alternative) relying on an explicit rule. Finally, the paradigm of rational decision-making admits only two ways to determine a practice: the rational calculation that I mentioned, or relying on a rule, an express, explicit rule. The two solutions are interchangeable and are based on the same error, since we can deduce a rule from a practice without the practice having this rule as its founding principle. I have said this more than once in my previous lectures: the fact that a procedure is regular, structured and patterned, organised rather than random, does not imply that its founding principle is the structure that we can deduce through an analysis of its practices. The fundamental error in this theory of practice lies in giving as the principle of the practice the rule that had to be constructed in order to understand the practice. This is a typical, classic error in the primitive phases of a science: it consists in deducing through analysis the principle of a practice and making this principle deduced after the event the determining factor and cause of the practice.

On this point we might mention the difficulties that theoreticians and practitioners of artificial intelligence have encountered on trying to formalise the knowledge of experts. Some of you may perhaps know the problem with these expert systems, which attempt to give a rigorous, codified and therefore calculable form to practical competence: for example that of the consultant capable of making a diagnosis or the jurist capable of applying the law to a specific case[13] (it is no accident that these are the two domains where this search for the expert system has been applied). When they tried to construct such a system, they very soon realised that the practical expert systems as mastered by social agents escape codification. To coin a formula, you might say that you cannot program the sense of practice: it is impossible to enclose the consultant's sense of practice in a completely explicit program. In the logic that I am proposing, the answer to the question whether computers are intelligent is the following: they are intelligent, if you like, but with an intelligence that is not one of practical action. In obeying the paradigm of rational decision-making, instead of the paradigm that I have suggested, they are settling for programming systems that are already formalised as games (of chess, for instance) or mathematics: these function perfectly well on what is already formalised as formal. But as soon as they try to mimic the practical choices of the sense of practice, and practical intelligence, they appear deficient, which tends to show that the so-called inferior forms of intelligence are superior to the so-called superior forms of intelligence, since we are unable to enclose these 'inferior' forms within the most powerful instruments of a 'superior' intelligence.

This reference to expert systems, which would also merit a long excursus, enables us to understand that there is a kind of overflow of practice outside the set of formal rules within which we seek to enclose it. When we posit as the source of a practice a set of formal rules (such as those that compose a computer program), we can no longer regenerate even the simplest practice. If for example we cannot regenerate the practice of dialogue, it is not simply because the practice of dialogue gives rise to an infinity of possibilities, it is also because it supposes the practical recording of an infinity of non-formulaic information and generative patterns which lack the rigidity of a formal schema.

Deliberation as accident

This sheds light on the opposition between practical logic and the logic supposed by the formal systems of the theory of rational decision-making. Another difference which seems very important to me is, as I said

122 *Lecture of 29 May 1986*

last time, the fact that whereas everyday action implies making choices between alternatives, the actual principle these choices are based on is never itself chosen. We are unable to contain this principle within the fleeting moment provided by the situation or within calculations of the possibilities apparently implicated in the situation. The idea that practice has an identifiable beginning makes no sense. When we come to participate in the game, the game has already been running for some time. This is rather like what Simon was saying in the sentence that I quoted just now. In the case of a scientific problem, for instance, the whole history of the scientific field and the scholarly subject for whom the scientific problem arises are already fully present in the world of the decision. Which means that we should characterise the decision as reasonable rather than rational, for it conforms to regularities immanent in the field and not to the formal rules that we may derive from activities following the rules immanent in the field.

Another important element: these reflexive moments and determining elements of rational choice, as seen by decision theory, to wit, reflection, deliberation and premeditation, are in a way linked (this connects for instance with the whole Heideggerian theory of insertion in the world[14]) to the accidents of the immediate relation of the habitus to the field: reflection, deliberation and premeditation appear in situations of irresolution where the automatisms of practical, empirical knowledge are lacking. It is in these critical moments, that is, exceptionally and accidentally, that we fall back on rational deliberation, which does not mean that rational deliberation in these critical moments is a rational deliberation fitting the definition made by the defenders of the paradigm of rational action.

I could simply mention Sartre's sentence: 'a voluntary deliberation is always a deception',[15] but we would do better to recall some Proustian insights, such as the famous elaboration of the narrator's decision to break with Albertine.[16] Moreover, it is no accident if the decision is to break off a relationship, and it may provide another important argument to mark the difference between decision-making theory and the theory of the habitus: from the point of view of the habitus, what is natural is continuity, it is the normal insertion of the subject in the field and the universe, with the experience of constantly having to solve problems; whereas the deliberations of decision theory introduce interrogation and disappointment of expectation, then attempt to restore continuity by reformulating aims which have in fact already been established. Proust's example reads like a parody of the description of rational deliberation as presented by the theoreticians of decision-making: the narrator decides to break with Albertine and reviews in

Lecture of 29 May 1986 123

his imagination, in a quasi-hypnotic and hallucinatory fashion, every-thing that will happen, all the obviously very painful consequences of this separation (he imagines taking Albertine to the station, carrying her luggage, and so on), so much so that after all these elucubrations he decides not to break with her after all [*laughter*]. I think that this analysis is a great realist counter-attack showing our real relation to decision-making.

The ordinary experience of insertion in the world is an experience of continuity in which ends and means are given without having been posited as such; the problems are solved before they are formulated as such and regular procedures are followed without needing to be articu-lated as regulations: the experiences of crisis and deliberation are, in a way, accidents interrupting the normal course of experience.

A broader rationalism

I would therefore like to show how the analysis of action that I am proposing is opposed to the rival theory of action which supports eco-nomic theory in particular. What is at stake in this opposition is basi-cally a different definition of rationalism. Those who have defended a theory of action close to that of the habitus have often been inspired by an irrationalist logic and a rejection of the dominant rationalist model, the philosophy of the subject, the philosophy of voluntary delibera-tion, the whole Cartesian tradition of the problem of cognition and the traditional Kantian treatment of moral issues. But if we call a just defi-nition of reasonable behaviour irrationalist, this implies too narrow a definition of rationality. In other words, the irrationalists (we could cite Heidegger, for instance) ultimately agree with the rationalists of the Chicago school[17] on too narrow a definition of rationality.

The theory of practice that I am proposing through the notion of the habitus seems to me to provide the basis for a broader rationalism, where an impulsive action, a spontaneous outburst, a fit of anger, an activity designed to follow a rule, and 'instinctive' action like the activ-ity of players on the sports field can all be considered reasonable, as having an immanent reason, without making Reason their principle, as a sort of transcendental, universal faculty that the rationalist tradi-tion places at the source of practice. We might then call 'reasonable' or even 'rational' all behaviour conforming to the immanent laws of a field without necessarily being the product of a rational intention in the sense of the rationalist tradition. When we say 'Well played!', 'Well done!', or 'You did what you had to', reason, or rationality, is judged

124 *Lecture of 29 May 1986*

according to what has been done, that is, according to the practice performed and the conformity of this practice to the logic of a field, and not according to the argument that motivated the action. Making rationality depend on the condition of explicit deliberation and calculation would be giving a definition of rationality so impossible that we would have to conclude, as Kant does on the subject of moral action, that nobody has ever accomplished any rational act.[18] In short, the alternative of narrow rationalism and pure irrationalism is based, as often happens in science, on complicity in a common definition of rationality. It is because in both cases they are taking a theoretical construction as the condition for a truly rational practice, that they can either propose a definition of rational practice so extreme that no rational practice has ever been accomplished, or else argue, in the light of this ultimate observation, that no rational practice is possible.

Ultimately the key issue is the relationship between theory and practice, a theory which elucidates and makes visible, a theory that we assume should precede action for that action to be rational, and a *praxis* oriented by the habitus, involving a tacit, silent, implicit vision of what is happening in the world. The problem is posed in a particularly acute manner in the social sciences where one of the challenges is to find whether, in order to act correctly in the world, that is, in conformity with the immanent laws of the social games they are playing, social agents need an adequate theory of the social world, or whether they can make do with a sense of their position in the social world ('Where am I in the social world?'), with what Goffman calls 'the sense of one's place'.[19] Once again, it is in this apparently abstract alternative between thoughtless, random action and theoretical cognition of the objective truth of our condition that the Marxist discussion of class consciousness, for instance, is enclosed. But for class consciousness to be measurable by this standard, each agent would have to master a complete theory of the social world in order to have a full knowledge of his position in the social world.

The analysis that I am proposing takes into account the fact that agents do not act at random, but without our having to imagine that they know what they are doing. They are exercising a practical sense, which is a kind of learned ignorance, which by definition the ignorant do not know as such, but which the learned don't know either, because they are always inclined to think that only scholarly knowledge is really knowledge. When they do not find in some piece of knowledge the characteristics of scholarly knowledge – such as the explicit, the coherent and the systematic – they cry ignorance. Nicholas of Cusa's formula, which echoes a theme found in Plato,[20] is important to help

Lecture of 29 May 1986

explain those intermediate, crepuscular types of knowledge, which, although not explicit, reflexive and systematic, are sufficient to orient practice and an adequate understanding of the world.

Alternatives and logic of the field

I have been relating my analyses to the paradigm of rational cognition. But I have done this in respect of only one of the dualisms that divide these two theses. A further opposition emerges between the vision that we might call structuralist and the vision that we might call constructivist. The two pairs are almost, but not quite, completely parallel. One difficulty for science in general, and social science in particular, is that the space of possible standpoints to adopt is cleft by dualisms which divide the whole of the social field, and the whole of the scientific field within which the social field is thought. These oppositions are relatively independent of each other. They have the same properties as the oppositions within a system of myth. In a system of myth, the opposition between hot and cold is not exactly parallel to the opposition between masculine and feminine, but, when you are in the area of the hot you are more or less in the area of the masculine. Here, similarly, the opposition between the decision paradigm and the habitus paradigm, and the opposition between the construction paradigm and the structuralist paradigm, are not reducible to one another, but, if we have opted for logical calculation in the former alternative, we tend to opt for construction in the second. These alternatives, which entrap scientific discussion because they are what structures thinking in the social world, these 'epistemological couples', as Bachelard would have called them, are fictitious and must be overcome, by means of the kind of investigation into the foundations of the theory of action that I propose to undertake.

I fear I cannot evoke all the possible different alternatives (which would need a mind more vigilant and agile than mine), so I shall leave you to do all the hard work, and simply enumerate a series of oppositions that are both partly independent and yet have multiple intersections. There is first of all the opposition between objectivism and subjectivism, as well as the opposition between realism (there is an objective social world, which does exist) and idealism (the social world is my construction, there is no referent, the social world is what I think of it; it is, to transpose Schopenhauer's formula, 'my representation'[21]). Further oppositions (the first terms of my oppositions should be seen in parallel: objectivism/subjectivism, realism/idealism,

126 *Lecture of 29 May 1986*

etc.) are the oppositions between determinism and indeterminism or between determinism and liberalism. On one side of this opposition, the social world is determined, subject to laws that tend to ensure the reproduction of the social world in its given form; on the other side it is indeterminate, it is produced by the agents, it is constantly changing, it is the product of rivalries.

Another opposition is the one between scientism/centralism and spontaneism/basism, which is organised around the idea that scientific knowledge is possible, that scholars really know the world and in the light of this are in a way worthy of ruling the world. This is the myth of the philosopher king, which, from Plato to Lenin, and right up to Althusser,[22] is a recurrent myth among philosophers: the philosopher knows the world in its true state and he proceeds to break with our ordinary vision of the world; this break is a scientific break which separates the professional from the profane, and the profane are as it were deprived of the truth of the world. This scientism is connected with centralism, insofar as it is important that those who have this knowledge should govern. At the other extreme, the spontaneist vision considers that the world has no privileged place, that the social is a circle whose centre is everywhere and nowhere, and that all visions of the world are equal. We could also mention the centralism/perspectivism opposition, or even (here you will think that I am putting very different things on the same plane, but, if you think about it, there are many connections) oppose collectivism on the one hand, acknowledging the existence of collectives having a collective will and belief, to what some today call 'methodological individualism',[23] on the other hand, that is, the rejection of all collective belief, of any representation or action transcending the individual subject.

As I was saying, these different alternatives are at once independent and partly interchangeable, and it would be most interesting to conduct an empirical analysis of the way in which sociologists, for instance, in a given society at a given moment, are distributed among these different alternatives. One ought also to conduct an empirical enquiry into the way in which social agents who are not professional students of the social world are distributed among these alternatives, and measure these distributions against social properties, to see how these distributions vary according to social origins and positions held in the social world, etc. I am ready to bet that there would be very strong correlations between the standpoints adopted on these alternatives and positions held in the social world.

These alternatives are extremely strong because they have social foundations. For instance, in the case of that false opposition between 'methodological individualism' and 'collectivism', the methodological individualists orient their antagonism against collectivism. If they do this, it is because their mental structure leads them to do so, but it is also because this is a strong opposition in social reality: the opposition between socialism and liberalism is one of the major principles of opposition in social conflicts.

Since these different alternatives exist in the mind as well as in social reality, they give rise to the construction of unreal objects. Phenomena of change also follow the logic of the fields, that is, the logic of struggles, and the scientific movement appears to oscillate between one or other of these poles. In my opinion it is a mistake to describe this pendular movement in terms of fashion, as people often do; in the operation of a field, it is perfectly logical for newcomers to react against the dominant model of the previous period. If intellectual changes adopt this pendular form, if after a triumph of the objectivist position, for instance, the subjectivist position triumphs, it is because the newcomers, reacting against the objectivist position, find themselves defending the subjectivist position. This logic of the operation of the field helps to strengthen these oppositions insofar as the struggle itself, within these oppositions, also constantly helps to reinforce them and give those engaged in the field no choice but to swing from one pole to the other.

I think that one of the social mechanisms that most threatens scientific knowledge is the fact that since these epistemological pairs are incarnated in antagonistic social positions in a scientific field, they are experienced as theoretical destinies so set that it is very difficult to think in terms of a universe of thought not structured according to their opposition. This means that nothing is more difficult than to rethink these oppositions [. . .] in terms of their relation to social roots, interests and goals, in order to set our thought free, as I am trying to do today, from the structures inherently motivating our struggles, goals and profit.

(I am afraid that, come next time, I shall find that this lecture was a kind of rough draft, and I shall try to recast it for you much more elliptically, quickly and clearly. That said, I think that the offering I presented you with was partly a product of the objective difficulty of what I had to say, which was haunting me all day before I came [to give this lecture], because I had the feeling that what I wanted to say was extremely difficult. I think that I was a victim of my own great expectations [*laughter*], but there was nonetheless a relation between the subjective state that I am in and the objective difficulty of what I wanted to say [*laughter*].)

128   *Lecture of 29 May 1986*

One reason why these alternatives are so potent is that they seem to be constantly reborn. We could say, obviously cutting a few corners, that the oppositions I have noted were there in Plato already. Obviously from the point of view of a rigorous history of philosophy, you could say that is not true, that you cannot compare the opposition between [Gary] Becker and Bourdieu to the opposition between Plato's friends of the earth and friends of Ideas,[24] for they are not comparable. But on the global stage of scientific struggles and especially political struggles, where these oppositions are often reduced to relatively simple antagonisms between extremely reduced mythical contents (the totality versus the individual, etc.), I think that we are justified in making this comparison.

The fundamental problems which appear as eternal problems and which are mother's milk to the philosopher specialising in *philosophia perennis* owe their perennity to the structure of the fields, which are relatively eternal (we always find orthodoxy versus heresy, etc.). Ultimately, because of the repetitive logic of the fields, this eternalisation of problems is one of the most dangerous threats to knowledge. What I want to do today is show how by objectifying one of these antagonisms and making it explicit we could come to master it, we could [grasp (?)] both its intellectual truth and its social truth . . . I think that this sort of research is absolutely indispensable if we are to free scientific procedure from the compulsive repetition which imprisons it and which is nourished by so many different factors. For instance, in proposing forms of thought consciously elaborated to escape these alternatives, you lay yourself open in advance to being constantly considered in the light of one or other of the terms of the alternative (I can say this: it happens to me all the time. . .); they will tell you 'Yes, you are this; yes, you are that', using the logic of 'either, or'. Given the fact that these epistemological pairings are rooted in social pairings and thereby in mental structures, aggravated by the circular, enclosed nature of the intellectual world, the scientific work needed to break free of these alternatives is vulnerable to permanent misunderstanding. It seems to me, however, that the series which I have enumerated . . . I shall stop there . . . very dissatisfied! [*laughter*]

Second session (seminar): the field of power (1)

What I want to discuss today is the notion that I call 'the field of power', although I shall do so without much confidence or *certitudo sui*, for I am not perhaps in my best state of mind, so I hope that you

Lecture of 29 May 1986 129

will be indulgent.[25] This notion is something that I find very important, but that I am not very sure of. I am in the middle of the process of working on it, and one of the functions of research direction as I envisage it is to communicate 'work in progress'. That said, it is difficult to communicate when the conditions of communication are rather unfavourable, as they are here today. It would be much easier in a small seminar, with, say, fifteen people familiar enough with the logic of research to understand that research is not teaching and that the normal state of research is a somewhat fuzzy condition. Having said that in order to crave your indulgence, as the *captatio benevolentiae* of classical rhetoric would have it, I shall proceed today to present the problem and get to the heart of the details.

Why should I have invented this notion of a 'field of power' and what functions does it fulfil? My motive for turning to this notion was primarily negative, because the commonly used notion of a 'dominant class' did not satisfy me at all. Firstly, it calls on the notion of class with all its ambiguities (I shall discuss this again later on), and, on the other hand, it tends to reinforce the realist representation of power that I have denounced several times in earlier lectures. It tends to refer the fact of dominating to a population of dominant agents. In other words – as I indicated the other day – we might think that, for a sociologist, solving the problem of power would amount to answering the following question: 'Who governs? Who wields the power? Who are the people who wield the power?'[26] By speaking of the dominant classes we give the impression that there are a certain number of people who are dominant and that in describing them we would be explaining the logic of power. I dislike this substantialist logic. Even when we speak of fractions of the dominant class, we are trapped in this realist logic: we can divide a population into more or less rigorous sections, using these sections to describe the relations between these populations, relations of domination within the dominant class, but we remain trapped in a realist logic.

In speaking of the field of power, I mean to imply that power, or more precisely the different species of power, or even more precisely the different species of capital, are at once the instruments and the goals of a struggle between an ensemble of agents and institutions. In other words, the field of power has the general properties of any field: it is a place where people oppose one another, struggle and compete with one another. In this particular case, they are in competition through and for power. You might even say that they are in competition *through* a power *for* the imposition of this power as an exemplary, even unique form of power. Or again, you might say that the field of power is the

130   *Lecture of 29 May 1986*

site of a struggle for the monopoly of the legitimate possession of a determinate form of power, in relation to other powers.

You may be finding these things abstract and somewhat unreal, but this kind of construction reveals its efficacy immediately if we think of historical situations: for example, the struggles for succession within a given type of regime studied by historians, what we call the history of regimes or the comparative theory of political regimes, or again, the history of the relationship between intellectuals and the holders of economic power, or yet again (this is starting to seem rather . . .) the study of the different fractions of the dominant class at a certain moment in time, which historians today practise under the guise of prosopography. In a word, prosopography is a 'method' used by the historians of antiquity to study the elites: they study, ultimately by genealogical methods, the grand dominant families of knights or senators in ancient Greece or Rome, to try to determine how the population of the dominant was composed, what relations these people had among themselves, their degree of endogamy, their matrimonial strategies, etc. To avoid facing the theoretical questions that I am trying to raise, the historians say: 'We are doing prosopography', which means, for example, 'We are studying the genealogies of the elite in France at the end of the nineteenth or the eighteenth century.'

Although these concrete studies appear irreproachable, to my mind they are ill-formed and ill-formulated responses to the problem I am trying to pose in discussing the field of power. For it seems to me that, in any society relatively differentiated in terms of forms of power, there are struggles for power between the holders of different forms of power; and a good number of the phenomena usually dealt with as part of the history of literature or the history of art can be understood as manifestations of this rivalry between holders of different forms of power or between holders of different species of capital.

This notion of the field of power is obviously not transhistorical. One of the questions we need to ask is when does a field of power emerge, what are the conditions that produce something like a field of power, what are the conditions that make a struggle between different powers emerge? We understand straight away that, for there to be a field of power, there has to be a differentiation of the social world into different fields, which implies the emergence of different species of capital or different species of power. The comparative history of the fields of power that I hope to see emerge will therefore have to be based on a study of societies that are historically relatively differentiated, where we see oppositions emerging in a structured and permanent way,

Lecture of 29 May 1986 131

in a sort of division of the labour of domination, for example between spiritual power and temporal power.

The field of power and differentiation of the fields

What underpins this notion of a field of power is the idea that the fields of power are the end product of a process of differentiation, which we should avoid confusing with a process of stratification. Here I refer to Durkheim, who sees in the process of differentiation the main progress of the evolution of human societies. But although this process of differentiation is related to a process of stratification, it is not reducible to what we normally see in the process of stratification. To say that a society differentiates into fields is not exactly the same thing as saying that society is differentiated into social classes. I quote from Durkheim's lectures on *Pragmatism and Sociology*.[27] Reacting against what he calls Bergson's 'unitarian vitalism', Durkheim takes his inspiration from Spencer, for whom the universe is constantly moving 'from the homogeneous to the heterogeneous'. He appeals to evolution, which leads from what he calls 'the primitive undivided state' to the differentiated state characteristic of modern societies. The primitive undivided state is characterised by the fact that its diverse functions (religion, law, art, etc.) are already there, but 'in a state of confusion': the religious life, for instance, mingles ritual, morality, law, art and even the beginnings of science. Evolution progresses from this primitive undivided state to what he calls the progressive separation of all these diverse and yet originally commingled functions: 'Secular and scientific thought has moved away from religious thought; art has moved away from religious ceremonies; morality and law have moved away from ritual.'[28]

I can't do it here, but I think that it would be worthwhile making absolutely explicit one of the central keys to Durkheim's philosophy of history: Durkheim considers that this initial confusion of functions is an obstacle to the full realisation of each one of them; so it is at the expense of differentiation that each of these functions has been accomplished, and differentiation is progress. Thus, 'In the beginning, all forms of activity and all functions were gathered together, and were, in a manner of speaking, each other's prisoners. Consequently, they were obstacles for each other, each preventing the other from achieving its nature completely.'[29]

This idea can be backed up empirically. I think for instance that there are observations in Mauss's work that are inspired by the same

132   *Lecture of 29 May 1986*

philosophy of history, viewing the differentiation of the economic and the religious as an obstacle to the constitution of the economic as economic.

For instance, Mauss describes the obstacles to the rationalisation of the economy, in Weber's sense, very well; these are inherent in the fact that the fundamental economic concepts are not detached from things religious, and retain religious connotations. As Mauss says, more or less, this results in a sort of conceptual instability – a sort of instability that leads undifferentiated pre-capitalist societies to require of their social agents a kind of enormous waste of energy, linked precisely to the fact that their economic concepts are not economic; since the purification and specification corresponding to the constitution of an autonomous field are not being operated, the economic concepts are always overdetermined religiously and ethically.[30] They therefore have a sort of conceptual and practical instability which means that primitive economies (the economy of the gift, for instance, compared to the economy of exchange) are terribly costly; they are not economic because they require a waste of creative energy. If, for example, we examine the difference between paying a fee and making a gift, we see straight away that the gift implies supplementary work and a waste of energy. Mauss alludes to this.

The emergence of universes 'as such'

That said, we could develop Durkheim's analysis using the terms of a Weberian analysis that I was alluding to just now. Weber would say that the different spheres were not constituted as such, and, ultimately, the constitution of a field coincides with the constitution of a specific axiomatic. In other words, we could say, in Weber's terms (this from memory, I'm afraid I can't give you the reference, because I don't know where Weber said it, but I am fairly sure that I read it in Weber), that the emergence of a differentiated, autonomous field is manifested through the emergence of the 'as such' (*als*, in German): the economy as such, art as such, law as such.[31] In other words, with the emergence of an autonomous field, the fundamental composition of this universe, and its fundamental law, appears in an explicit, composed form. We know what game we are playing, whereas the undifferentiated pre-capitalist economies are very confused games where we never know whether we are playing hopscotch or football, so to speak: we can change the rules – all the rules are made on the hoof – which makes rational strategies extremely difficult to practise. But once the economy

Lecture of 29 May 1986 133

is constituted as economy, following the axiom that 'business is business', we know that 'in business there is no place for sentiment', and the rules of the game are clear. Here we have the 'as such',[32] even if – and here we should avoid making the mistake I mentioned in the first session – there are practical versions of the 'as such'. This is a link with what I was saying in the first session. There are practical versions of the 'as such', for the constitution of such spheres of existence is a constituent, fundamental law of these universes.

I shall continue with a thesis from Lukács's *History and Class Consciousness*, where he insists on the relation between the emergence of pure theories (which is very Weberian) of law, science and language, etc., and the emergence of separate spheres of activity.[33] Marx (in a text that I read a long time ago, and whose provenance I have once again mislaid), [speaks of] a 'process of apriorisation', a very interesting term, to designate the process whereby a universe is constituted as autonomous, that is, as self-founding: the very principles of this universe appear to be *a priori*, with no foundation other than its actual existence.[34] And Lukács insists on the fact that this process of appropriation and autonomisation, whereby the universe appears to itself as having no laws other than those that it accords itself, becomes the social basis for the emergence of pure, autonomous theories, rejecting as pre-scientific any idea of or attempt at totalisation, rejecting even any totalising ambition as pre-scientific. Among the presuppositions of the Chicago paradigm that I mentioned just now, there is obviously – although they don't realise it – this process of apriorisation and this sort of affirmation that there is a logic of economic calculation irreducible to any other logic.

Weber, then, insists on the fact that the process of differentiation described by Durkheim is inseparable from the creation of separate, autonomous social universes, places with a specific legal status, as manifested in a specific constitution, a fundamental law establishing them 'as such'. This process of differentiation culminates in the existence of separate fields, each of which is a place of rivalry where specific forms of power are engaged, insofar as each of the fields is the site of a struggle for a particular species of power, which is unevenly distributed within it.

Power over capital

I come now to what I see as the second phase of the construction of this notion of a field of power: the field of power seems to me to be the site

134 *Lecture of 29 May 1986*

of confrontation of different powers through agents and institutions wielding power over different fields. That was not at all clear – I'll try to rephrase it. The field of power is a site of struggles between people who do not simply have power and cultural capital (or economic, religious or artistic capital, etc.), but who have enough of the relevant form of specific capital to wield power over the other holders of this form of specific capital. To take one example: the intellectuals engaged in the struggle in the field of power will not be small holders of cultural capital, but agents whose position in the cultural field and whose cultural capital put them in a position to exercise power over the other holders of cultural capital. In other words, to comprehend the field of power, we have to deploy a preliminary distinction between the simple possession of capital and the possession of a capital conferring power over capital, that is, over the structure of a field, and thereby over the profit margins ensured by the struggle at the heart of a field.

In the case of the economic field, for instance, we can refer to a classic distinction to be found in many economists' works (in François Perroux or François Morin, for example), between what are called 'controlling shareholders' and the small shareholders who dispose simply of the juridical ownership of a small, fixed amount of capital. In the same way, in cultural matters, we can distinguish the simple owners of cultural capital from those who have a capital sufficient to determine the preservation or transformation of the structures of potential profit, for instance in the scientific field, by maintaining the dominant scientific paradigm which sustains a certain structure of the distribution of potential profit, or by transforming it radically.[35] To take a much more concrete example, since what I am saying here may seem abstract to you: authors who have attained a certain degree of consecration have, in addition to an important quantity of capital, a power over capital, a power that is given them by the size of their holding of capital, and which is manifest above all in the fact that they are able to consecrate other authors, by writing prefaces for them, publishing them, or having them published. Another example is the power of publishers, who are complex characters, able, on the basis of their economic and cultural capital, to exercise an extremely important power over the intellectual world by controlling the route into existence for authors: it is the publishers who to a certain extent consecrate an author, who make them exist or condemn them to non-existence.[36] These are examples of a second-order power, so to speak. It is not simply the possession of capital, but the power over capital.[. . .]

(I feel unhappy in saying this, because I have the feeling at every moment that I am unable to completely justify what I am saying, because on the one hand I haven't clarified everything, and on the other hand because it is over the course of the whole series that these things, which may appear to you to be dogmatic, unsubstantiated truths, will find their foundation. It is on the level of the whole schema that things which are peremptory become justified by the consequences that I can draw from these apparently peremptory affirmations. The linear aspect of spoken discourse is very awkward, because it obliges me to say in succession things that would be more convincing if I could say them simultaneously. I feel a very uncomfortable subjective feeling of arbitrariness while I am saying what I have to say.)

This distinction between [the possession of capital and] the power that possession of capital gives, even in a restricted quantity, in contrast to those who have no capital at all (which is the distinction between power, and power over power), seems important to me because it is through those who have enough power over a field to be able to mobilise the power of that field in struggles against other fields, that the struggle between fields that motivates the struggles inherent in the field of power is enacted. Concretely, if we wanted to give a rigorous definition of the dominant class (that is, of the ensemble of agents that we can classify as dominant, of the logical class of the dominant), we could say that it is constituted by the ensemble of agents who possess a sufficient quantity of the particular species of capital needed to dominate the functioning of the corresponding fields, and thereby to dominate the system of reproduction that ensures the reproduction of this field.

Power and its legitimisation

This being the case, it seems to me that there are invariants of the structure of the field of power and the struggles within this structure which I think depend on the very logic of power (although here again I am very hesitant): on the fact that, as I have said in my previous lectures, power is only really attained insofar as it is recognised, that is, misrecognised as power as such. Power is only really attained in a structure where the person exercising the power encounters the objective 'complicity' of those who suffer it. In other words, if there are invariants of the balance of power within the field of power, if we find variants of the same fundamental opposition in very different universes, it is because all power needs to legitimise itself, to have itself recognised, in order to be exercised durably. Since power has to produce belief in its own legitimacy, there is, then, room for

136 *Lecture of 29 May 1986*

a division of the labour of domination between those who exercise political, economic or military power, say, and those who consciously or unconsciously contribute to producing this condition of the exercise of power, that is, the recognition of the legitimacy of power. I am very embarrassed because I sound as if I am positing the existence of a sort of nature of power – and I believe that I am actually doing so; whereas, given my manner of thinking, I would prefer not to have to make this postulate. But this is part of my language: I cannot repeat everything that I have said in the two previous lectures about the relation between habitus and structure, about the fact that the relation of domination is deducible from what I was describing this morning; it is a relation in which the two terms do not count, in which what counts is precisely the relationship itself.

The field of power, then, is divided by the principle that, in order to be durably sustained, power must contribute to its own legitimisation, so that the field of power tends always to be organised around the opposition between political or temporal power – which, depending on conjunctures and periods, may be mainly military or economic or political, for instance – and cultural or spiritual power. I believe that it is this fundamental property, this fundamental relation between power and its legitimisation, that explains why we find invariants of the division of the labour of domination everywhere, generally as denoted in Dumézil's triad, where temporal and spiritual power are complementary and opposite in the domination that they exercise over the third character of the triad, that is, the dominated.[37] In the words of Duby, who applies Dumézil's model to a universe closer to our experience, it is the opposition between the *bellatores*, or holders of military power, the *oratores*, those who pray and speak (and in particular those who speak the language of power, who speak on behalf of power), and, finally, the *laboratores*, the dominated.[38]

To put this more simply: power of any kind can only impose itself durably on condition that it manages to be recognised as genuine by dissimulating the arbitrary nature of the force it is based on, and it is because of this that military or economic power are dependent on a properly symbolic and cultural power, which must add its own force, as it were, to their actual power for this power to become effective and [ensure] the lasting reproduction of its effects. We may then use this axiom of the dependence of actual power on a symbolic power of legitimisation to found the opposition – which is historically attested in different conjunctures and contexts – between the two powers, and the kind of division of the labour of domination, or the complementary antagonism between them.

Lecture of 29 May 1986　　　137

That said, I would now like to announce briefly what I shall be saying in the forthcoming lectures. I spoke of a 'complementary antagonism'. One of the main problems for power is that it can only be exercised if it is legitimate (first proposition), but that it cannot be legitimised by itself alone (second proposition). [. . .] (I am very embarrassed here, because I appear to be doing something that I detest in the social sciences, which is establishing a sort of transcendental genesis of the social world. I sound as if I am doing what Sartre did in his *Critique of Dialectical Reason*: I give two or three definitions and I use them to recreate history. It is a terrible way of proceeding. And yet when we want to explain things coherently it is extremely difficult not to do this, not to state a certain number of simple principles that you can combine in order to find the facts. What is the difference between adapting a sort of axiomatisation to fit a reality known in advance, that is, creating something falsely transcendental, and creating the sort of historically grounded construction that I am attempting? I am constantly worried that you will get the impression that I am creating something falsely transcendental.) [. . .]

Since the question of legitimacy, that is, of recognition, confronts all power, and since no power can operate durably unless it obtains from the dominated that sort of adherence or belief founded on misrecognition, power has to appeal to some means of legitimisation. Why does it need to appeal to some means of legitimisation? This is my second proposition. Because you cannot legitimise yourself by your own efforts alone. The paradigm that I use to explain this is the paradigm of Napoleon crowning himself.[39] Power is constantly tempted to consecrate itself, that is, to exercise its own power of recognition. When the prime minister tells the press that they should report on the prime minister in the way that the prime minister wishes to be reported on, it is no accident, it is built into power: it is one of the conditions of the existence of power to want to impose one's own image, and to be able to do so whenever possible, from the portrait of the king to the equestrian statue.[40] This temptation is nothing psychological: it is built into power, as long as you see power as I have described it, that is, as something that demands justification and recognition to avoid it being threatened. It is, then, a condition of reproducible existence [that is, the indefinite reproduction of power]. As I was saying earlier, it is part of the *conatus* of any power to want to persevere in being, to reproduce itself, to produce a representation of power implying the continuation of power (first proposition).

Second proposition: but you cannot be legitimised by yourself alone. If, as the surrealists did, I declare that I am the greatest living

138 *Lecture of 29 May 1986*

poet – I often use this example – it is too obvious that it is in my interest to say that I am the greatest living poet for the mechanism of misrecognition to function. One of the great problems for power is to get people as distant as possible from power to say that your power is legitimate. Another simple example, to give you an idea (I would like you to get the idea first, before I offer a formal definition): I can cite for instance the short circuits of legitimisation that we constantly see in the press, in weeklies like *Le Nouvel Observateur*, etc. When you are well informed, you know that the writer-journalist X always writes about Y who always writes about the writer-journalist in question. For someone who is in the know, the main effect required for legitimisation, that is, the effect of misrecognition, fails to occur: the independence, disinterestedness and unbiased nature of the person recognising towards the person recognised is not attested, and the recognition is in a way disqualified because it appears to be determined by the power, it does not appear to be a free and disinterested act of recognition.

I believe that this comes very close to the logic of Hegel, albeit rethought in historical terms. For an act of recognition to be socially effective, independently of any theories of freedom, it must appear not to be determined by the political efforts of the person recognised, which is the suspicion provoked by the mutual admiration societies that are so common in philosophy, literature and poetry. The suspicion that the writer or journalist providing a service always provokes is grounded in a fundamental anthropological argument over the nature of legitimacy.

An act of recognition will have all the more chance of being widely recognised as legitimate the more clearly it is recognised as legitimate, that is, the more its true dependence is misrecognised. For example, the celebration of Caesar's priestly rank will be the more valued the more autonomous it is. The most interesting problem is the relation between the jurists and the powers, because this is where the problem is posed most clearly. (There has been a lot of research into the question): historically, the body of jurists came to be constituted through very complicated struggles against the princes.[41] The princes thought that nobody could mete out justice better than they, they saw no reason to delegate, and there was a kind of historical struggle by the body of jurists, who were interested in their autonomy, against the princes, but also with them, since the jurists had an interest in making the princes understand that it was in their interest to respect the autonomy of the jurists, because if the jurists pronounced the same judgement as the prince while appearing to be independent of him, their judgement would be much more powerful, symbolically, than the juridical

Lecture of 29 May 1986   139

self-service offered by the prince. Likewise, if the historiographer of Louis XIV manages to appear to be independent of Louis XIV, his discourse will be much more legitimising than Louis XIV's own memoirs, which [smack of] self-praise.

Basically, what I wanted to say was that a power needs to be recognised – it must inspire belief, that is, misrecognition. Secondly, in the case of power, the maxim that 'one is never better served than by oneself' is false. If there is a case where one is ill served by oneself, it is the case of legitimisation – we need somebody else, at least, but preferably somebody as distant as possible as regards their relation to power. These are two maxims that explain why we find almost everywhere a sort of nuclear element of the division of the labour of domination, with those who dominate directly, and those who contribute to the domination through a specific exercise – the exercise of producing a discourse on the social world which serves to perpetuate the domination all the more, the more it appears to be independent of the power that it consecrates. I shall return to this next time. Thank you.

Lecture of 5 June 1986

First session (lecture): eternal false problems – The alternative of mechanism and purposiveness, and the conditions of rationality – Scientific oppositions and political oppositions – The practical mastery of structures – Imposing the right point of view
Second session (seminar): the field of power (2) – The example of the 'capacities' – Educational system, numerus clausus *and social reproduction – The search for stable forms of capital – The strategies of reproduction according to species of capital – Sociodicy and ideology*

First session (lecture): eternal false problems

[*Bourdieu starts by asking not to be recorded and explains why:*] Communication as I conceive it supposes a form of freedom that is difficult enough to achieve with such a vast audience, but the situation becomes impossible if you introduce recording, with all its implications of eternalisation and objectification. Among other factors, recording makes the experience of broadcasting [the fact of having to express myself] more difficult for me, and I think this means that the quality of what I am trying to say suffers greatly.[1]

As I have said in the past, teaching as I conceive it must be an exhibition (as when we speak of 'presenting an exposé'). If the ordinary forms of educational communication, like the majority of student productions, have as their dominant principle an extreme concern for protection (from the exam essay to the doctoral thesis, one of the principal imperatives is to expose oneself as little as possible), it seems to me that scientific communication supposes on the contrary that we take risks; this means that we are exposed to rejoinder, criticism and objectification which can be hurtful. As I try to communicate under

Lecture of 5 June 1986

141

conditions that are distinctly unfavourable, I do not want to overstep the mark beyond which this would become untenable, and if I don't want these lectures to become an obsession, I am obliged to ask you to no longer record me.

To summarise what I was trying to say last time. I showed that the social sciences are confronted with a series of epistemological pairs, of oppositions and alternatives, between which the specialists feel obliged to choose, whereas these alternatives derive their force essentially from social sources. They are social problems which tend to impose themselves as sociological problems or even as epistemological problems. This being the case, it is important to objectify them and to restore their true nature. To do this properly, we should analyse them, showing how the oppositions that constitute these social problems are distributed in the social space as a whole or within the scientific field, how the camps are pitched, on what grounds, and with what variables determining them. Since my hypothesis is that social agents, in the social field as well as in the scientific field, are not distributed at random between the poles of these oppositions, I argue that we should analyse and objectify them in order to give ourselves the strength, so to speak, to overcome them. Then we should try to objectify these patterns, which, being objective structures in the social space and the scientific field, tend to become mental structures, and therefore to seem self-evident, which makes it difficult to demolish them or call them into question. However, when people transfer them into the scientific field, or turn them into epistemological problems – as is often the case – these social problems, converted into sociological problems, become false problems and impede research, encouraging a sort of fictitious eternity born precisely of an eternally repeated historicisation.

We need to keep in mind another basic paradox: eternal problems are often problems that are constantly historicised. We can see this in the model that underlies Troeltsch's famous book on the history of Catholicism: from its origins until the present day, Catholicism has never ceased to change its meaning and direction, and it is this sort of permanent historicisation that makes it eternal.[2] Likewise, philosophical problems (those that are dealt with by name in school) are eternal because they are eternally reproduced, thanks to an unconscious historicising. This is what the philosophy teacher does: 'Plato's *Republic* helps us to understand the opposition between the RPR and the UDF.'[3] (I am joking, to avoid being nasty, but I could give real examples of updating that would be more cruel. . ..) This kind of eternity deriving from a continual re-creation is also part of the social power of these problems. The philosophers are the guardians of the

142   *Lecture of 5 June 1986*

eternal problems, and even if they certainly don't see themselves as such, I think that they function as guard dogs,[4] in particular against the sciences – formerly against the natural sciences, and today against the social sciences which annoy them even more, because sociology takes the majority of their objects and in addition is sometimes rash enough to objectify them in their work of eternalisation.

This eternalisation of problems is also grounded in the logic of the scientific field itself, which, as I have said before, proceeds by great Copernican revolutions, or permanent small revolutions, as is the case in the most advanced sciences, like physics, for instance. Often these revolutions take the form of an opposition between generations, simply because they pit the newcomers to the scientific field, who are obviously the younger ones, against the incumbents, who are already consecrated.[5] In this struggle, the eternal oppositions that I have mentioned are really useful because we can always return to the previous stage. In the social sciences for instance, emerging from a phase that, at the end of the 1960s, was stubbornly (and in my opinion stupidly: at the time I was very unhappy with this movement) objectivist and structuralist, as it was called at the time, the newcomers who wanted to establish their identity and originality tended spontaneously – spontaneity being socially conditioned – to develop theories that we might call subjectivist or constructivist. They wanted to restore the subject[6] and fall back on positions that the structuralists had attacked thirty years before. And history started up all over again... I think that we can take the risk of making a rough guess at the next fashion to come (which is not a fashion, as I said last time), it being understood that returns, so frequent in the arts, are never purely and simply reversals, unless we are completely ignorant of the history of the field, that is, strangers to the field – which is what defines the naive. People speak of a 'return to Condillac' or a 'return to Kant', which has happened so many times that it is amazing it is still possible in France,[7] but France has this privilege, grounded largely in our lack of culture, that you can start from zero all over again, time after time.

These returns are all the more pernicious for riding, navigating and surfing a wave, and at the same time allowing a slight margin of slippage to mark their originality. The logic of the field encourages pendular movements which allow and explain these returns, while helping to make it difficult to overcome the false problems. As I said last time, those who strive and even manage – it does happen – to overcome these alternatives are constantly urged by those who remain enclosed within these social problems to situate themselves in relation to the alternative they have overcome. As you can imagine, I am obviously thinking of

Lecture of 5 June 1986   143

myself, but the case is very common: Marx, Weber, Durkheim and some others are eternally solicited to situate themselves in relation to alternatives that their work has superseded. So people fabricate a young Marx to set against the old Marx (they haven't done it yet for Durkheim, but his time will come! [*laughter*]), or an objectivist Weber against a subjectivist Weber. As an important oeuvre is rich [i.e. long], it comprises different periods and can always allow people to produce this kind of distinction. Obviously – as I often say – *homo academicus* is a determining factor in these processes: he needs to classify, to feel at home and to draft lectures with easily graspable visions, and it is certainly useful in a lecture to compare and contrast Durkheim and Weber, for instance; but this leads to eternally reproducing an alternative that both had tried to overcome, which does not mean that they are not genuinely antagonistic, but that their oppositions should be placed elsewhere, in a place which can only be located if we leave these debates behind.

This is basically what I wanted to say. It is rather embarrassing to say these things in this way, but this is in fact the intellectual strategy that I have been deploying for some years now, and I cannot not say this at a certain stage in the progress of my work.

The alternative of mechanism and purposiveness, and the conditions of rationality

These alternatives are not even theses and antitheses to be transcended in the Hegelian sense; they need to be disposed of and completely ignored: the questions they raise need to be devised quite differently. Let me take the example of the alternative between mechanism and purposiveness, which I have often elaborated. It arises again today for those who use game theory to describe human behaviour; I see no problem with that, except that they invest in the philosophy of the rationalist and purposive type that I criticised last time. They make the fundamental anthropological hypothesis that social agents know what they want, in the sense that they calculate, set goals and make plans, and have a conscious mastery not only of what they are doing but of the models they are following in order to do what they are doing. We could transpose what Leibniz said of God – *Dum Deus calculat mundus fit*, 'God calculates and the world is made':[8] social agents calculate and act. Reading some of the research deploying game theory or other forms of scholarly model, we get the impression that before taking an elementary strategic decision which in general must be taken

144 *Lecture of 5 June 1986*

in a millisecond, social agents construct graphs of supply and demand, seek out the Schelling point,[9] and, if they don't find it, resolve to make their decisions without it.

At the other extreme the hypothesis of the mechanical reaction assumes that agents are automata or even physical objects like iron filings in a magnetic field. The very convenient alternative of rational calculation and mechanical reaction can go on for ever. It makes it difficult to pose the problem in the way that I phrase it, which is to ask whether social agents, in Leibniz's words, are not 'empiric in the majority of their actions',[10] that is, moved by determinations which come neither from the object nor from the subject, but from a certain obscure relationship – this is the sense of my previous analyses – between the socialised individual that I call the habitus and the social world, both structured according to homological forms.

Putting the question in these terms, we can ask under what social and historical conditions something like a rational decision can emerge. What social and historical conditions must be fulfilled so that one must and can shake off the routine automatisms whereby problems are not posed as problems (as I was saying last time), and so that the space of possibilities, the universe of choices, the consequences of those choices and the relative value of these different consequences are explicitly formulated? It is of course mainly in critical situations that we find a break in the continuity of the anticipations fuelled by our expectations of the world, or the future of the world: crises, eruptions, upsets and astonishments oblige us to question the universe, which does not mean that the conditions for a rational calculation will be fulfilled. The conditions that make a rational calculation possible include the possession of a cultural capital (obviously unequally distributed), that is, tools and rational instruments forged by history. It also needs a certain global posture towards the world that is acquired when someone is placed in the objective conditions that make rationality make sense.

I shall perhaps return to this theme of the *skholè*. This classic topic of the university tradition is I believe rooted in something true. Plato says somewhere that philosophers are distinguished from lawyers, men of action, by the fact that they have *skholè*, that is, time and leisure, *skholè* being the root of 'scholarly', 'scholastic', etc.[11] I would link this famous analysis by Plato to what Austin says somewhere in passing: that a certain number of the philosophers' favourite problems are ultimately the product of what he calls the 'scholastic view'.[12] We may think of the word *skholè* in its strong sense ('leisure'), but Austin also attributes other implications to it: there is an academic tradition, problems are posed because they have always been posed. For instance, for Austin,

Lecture of 5 June 1986   145

one constituent prejudice of the 'scholastic view' is to judge common sense always to be more stupid than the common sense developed by the philosopher. To the contrary, Austin shows (and in so doing makes explicit one of the implicit theses of analytic philosophy) that common sense is often much more knowledgeable than the scholar's common sense, and that even the most sophisticated traditional philosophical distinctions are extremely simplistic compared to the distinctions that we discover in everyday language when we know how to analyse it correctly. (This is really magnificent because it is my doctrine, and when a philosopher owns up I find it important and I am really grateful to him.)

The 'scholastic view', then, is a particular posture adopted towards the world, which is made possible by the fact of not being engaged in the urgent affairs of the world, by the fact of having time to think ahead. It is not sufficient simply to say that life's actions brook no delay, that we don't have time to decide, or that our decisions have to be made urgently. This is admitted by even the most fanatical supporters of 'rational action theory': they would say that there are cases, say for a general on the battlefield, where you can't maximise all your calculations and where you just have to decide. That is not what I mean: the important thing is that the rational posture, the rational habitus, the inclination to adopt a calculating posture when faced with life's problems, for instance before buying a flat or choosing a spouse (this is an example given by some rational action theoreticians,[13] no sacrilege can daunt them! [*laughter*]; they envisage it very seriously, even if they do admit that in this case there are other variables that manifestly elude their calculations. . .), is dependent, not only on the immediate *skholè* of the situation of decision, but also on the *skholè* that is in a way constituent, insofar as it is the condition enabling the constitution of a disposition to keep one's distance, to adopt the distant, detached gaze on the world that is the precondition of the very idea of rational calculation. Of course, these two things, the scholastic disposition and rational competence [. . .], are generally correlated insofar as, for instance, both are a condition for access to and success in the educational system. The distinction that I am making is important because the rational approach implies much more than the property of rational skill: teaching mathematical skills in school encounters a major obstacle in children from backgrounds where this approach is not common, for adopting this approach is the key condition for mastering the skills that enable the approach to succeed. (It is the same for the aesthetic disposition: this very general disposition to look at things as self-sufficient ends in themselves is independent of specific artistic competence, while being the condition for acquiring that competence.)

146 *Lecture of 5 June 1986*

This alternative of rational action and action determined by causes, then, disappears completely once we face up to the problem of the real conditions of the adoption of rational conduct. We discover that we don't have to choose between the two terms of the alternative, and having discovered that practice may be determined by principles other than those of mechanist constraint or rational project, we are led to wonder under what structural and occasional conditions a given agent obeys one or other of the principles determining an action. In other words, whereas the alternative leads to a kind of monism (people will say: 'I'm a mechanist!' Or 'I'm a rationalist!'), a scientific attempt to answer the problem, if properly posed, leads us to ask: what are the structural and incidental conditions which account for the fact that, in a given situation, a given agent will obey either mechanist constraints or rational calculations in his practice, or rather – which is more likely – obey the obscure determinations linked to the relation between his habitus and the field in which he operates?

To this question there is only an empirical response, empirical of course not meaning that theory abdicates: we can construct models with a certain number of parameters that we can vary and we will see the value that the parameters will assume in different concrete situations, and thereby the concrete form that the model will take in each case. So we escape the alternative and reach a kind of pluralist logic of practice: there are several sources of action whose importance varies according to the social agents and their situations, and therefore according to the relation between the agents and their situations. It is simple, it is disappointing, but we have put an end to an eternal *streit* [conflict] . . . in fact, we won't have finished it off, because I'm afraid they will keep on asking me: 'But is your habitus a determinist notion or not?' And I shall answer.

Scientific oppositions and political oppositions

Another currently important opposition in the social sciences is, briefly stated, the opposition between structuralists and constructivists. I shall focus the last lectures in this series on this problem because it is an important divide in the social world and because, in this case, I think it is possible to restructure the opposition in such a way as to make a genuine synthesis of the two antagonistic positions.

To give you the structuralist position in a simplified but accurate form: the holders of the structuralist position, in the ordinary social usage of the term, will say that there are objective structures, regula-

Lecture of 5 June 1986 147

tions and patterns in the social world, which mean that you cannot do whatever you fancy in the social world. They will attack what they see as 'spontaneism'. Lévi-Strauss has recently written a paper developing this opposition, qualifying those who call structuralism into question, in the pendular movement that is tending to overthrow its dominance, as 'spontaneists' challenging any regular patterns.[14] The word 'spontaneist' that he deliberately uses is most interesting because it has political overtones. It is an allusion to those who in 1968 wanted to overthrow social structures and bring anarchy out onto the streets. The defender of one pole, then, resorts to what is a classic move in any scientific conflict – he imports a political allusion, disguised and euphemised but constantly present, into the concepts that he uses in order to frighten the subject of the position that he is attacking: 'Take care, just realise what you are doing; if you give in to spontaneism you are taking sides with people who want to bring anarchy out onto the streets, who see the subject as a kind of unruly innovator overthrowing structures, waving the black flag and the red flag, or both at once.' The proponent of the structuralist position in fact invents a spontaneist position that does not really exist, but which might be the real principle behind their own position.

In the event the problems are very technical: do matrimonial exchanges have structural models as their principle, or rather strategies, that is, actions whose social agents are 'subjects'? In this debate, which could remain very theoretical and be reduced to confrontations of family trees tracing parallel and crossed cousins, we suddenly see the resurgence of a political problem that divided a generation. And it is true that, for the *doxa* – not in the recent literature that confuses everything and is of no interest[15] – the people of the generation of 1968 developed a representation of the social world as effervescent, dynamic, spontaneous and vibrant, against structuralism and its objectivist definitions of the social world in terms of fixed structures, with their prisons and enclosures.

I mention this because, as I have so often said, behind scientific oppositions there are nearly always very confused intuitive oppositions, and even metaphors. A few years ago, for instance, I had fun analysing a certain number of [*word inaudible* – someone's?] texts that were very amusing for this reason. In fact there were very few concepts involved, but there were metaphors: the fountain, the English garden as opposed to the French garden, the fountain as opposed to the channel and channelling, etc. The metaphors are important. They underlie the standpoints people take on epistemological problems and, when I said just now that I was hypothesising the existence

148   *Lecture of 5 June 1986*

of a significant relation, both statistically and intelligibly, between the agents' standpoints on these great problems and their positions in the social space or the scientific space, this is what I wanted to say: I think that these metaphors provide the mediation between the agents' positions and the standpoints adopted towards the problems. Thus, if you tend to prefer the fountain, you are an effervescent spontaneist; if you prefer the channel, you are a structuralist . . . You can see why I don't want to be recorded! [*laughter*] You can imagine people quoting me and putting '(*sic*)' afterwards [*laughter*] . . . Then all I could do would be to write: 'That's not what I meant to say at all. . .'.

Having said what needed to be said in order to give you an insight – although this brief instruction cannot really replace a long analysis – I must very rapidly explain why this opposition, which is socially very powerful but scientifically insignificant, can be at once translated and transcended in a properly scientific logic. In the logic of the pendular movement that I mentioned just now, we are bound to pass from a structuralist phase, where everyone was looking for structures everywhere, to a subjectivist phase where we try to restore the active role of the agents, saying: 'It's terrible the way structuralism has reduced agents to nothing but automata' (which is true, and is what I said during the structuralist period: the notion of habitus was constructed to challenge this reduction of agents to being the simple bearers of a structure, *Träger*,[16] as the Althusserians put it, in their over-emphasis of a very banal word in Marx). Our reaction will be to rehabilitate the subject and return to a pre-structuralist definition of the subject, instead of going further and asking ourselves whether this subject might not owe something to the structuring effect of the structure. Might not this subject be constructed as I envisage it, partly through the incorporation of the structure? In other words, should the structure/subject alternative not be abolished in favour of the dual objectification – that I have constantly repeated here – of the institution in the form of objective structures and in the form of incorporated structures? Instead of going down this route, people will talk of a 'return to the subject', that is, a return to square one, to phenomenology. Since Sartre is no longer in fashion, since he is out of date, finished and no longer chic (even philosophy teachers turn up their noses), we shall look to the social sciences for a renewed form. We shall find ethnomethodology, which is a by-product of phenomenology that has transited through the United States, which means that it has been mildly formalised and slightly simplified, and we shall import it back into France as the latest breakthrough of the avant-garde (just when it is dying in the States), as an instrument of struggle against a dominant structuralism.

Lecture of 5 June 1986 149

You can see how the movement that I have described in fast forward is more than just a question of fashion. To describe it in detail you would have to describe the field itself as well as the structural relation between the fields of French sociology and American sociology; you would have to describe the structure of the clash between the two fields, the position of the movement imported into the American field and the position of those borrowing it back into the French field. If we described all that I think we would feel despair: these things obey determinisms with a brutality that is depressing, given that we are looking at social universes whose function is to study determinisms. Obeying determinisms in these universes is a professional fault (I'm not sure if you follow my train of thought. . .); it is unfortunately in the logic of things for social agents to be moved by structural effects, but it is a great shame that these extremely simple effects, which invade our intuition and almost entirely appropriate our analyses, should be at work in the scientific fields, and I think that this justifies me in what I am trying to do with some embarrassment, which is to objectify the mental structures that the professionals of objectification use in order to objectify.

I think that this absolutely must be done, and that a twofold sociological and scientific objectification of the structures of objectification is the only effective weapon at the disposal of the social sciences if they wish to escape the laws that they describe, in order to master and control them. In other words – I keep repeating this, but it needs to be said – the social sciences have the means to make at least a small breach in the famous circle of historicism that they generate by their very existence: they need to appropriate as far as possible the objective structures that can generate the scientific agents' actions, in particular the objective structures of the fields in which the agents are situated, that is, the scientific fields and not merely the social field as a whole. In fact – this is another thing that I have said hundreds of times, but I repeat it too, because I think it is important – objectifying the social field as a whole and the position of the intellectuals in the social field as a whole [. . .] is a very neat strategy for those who want to avoid objectifying the specific field in which the true determinants and interests are situated. All this to explain that I am venturing on this terrain, not to settle accounts with my opponents, but because I think that it is the key condition for giving us at least a modicum of freedom from the structures that govern us.

Now that I have objectified the debate (the recurrent structure, the pendular movement, the social processes, etc.), what can we do with this social problem? We can establish it as a sociological problem and wonder – following the undercurrent of all my lectures this year – how

150   *Lecture of 5 June 1986*

social agents, who in one respect can be constructed as elements of a field, enfolded in the world and subject to structural determinations, can at the same time structure the world that is structuring them. [. . .] This would be a fine piece of work, once again eternally relevant, reactivating the opposition between Heraclitus and Parmenides, with structure and its reproduction at one pole, and constant change and novelty at the other. In the opposition between structure and construction, on the side of structure we will find eternity, reproduction and the absence of history, while on the side of construction there will be history, money and the subject, etc. We can say, then, that the hard structuralists 'do not understand history' (which is true for a strict structuralist). The question is knowing how we can formulate the problem of social action while escaping this alternative.

I have mentioned two oppositions, but I could have chosen others (which would take too long. . .). In fact, as I said last time, the different oppositions are not sharply divided. They function as ideological systems with a kaleidoscopic logic. Their strength lies in their capacity to escape analysis. They are like systems of myth, where none of the oppositions taken separately (masculine/feminine, hot/cold, east/west, etc.) are very strong, but a whole set of weak oppositions, loosely linked to each other in a fuzzy ensemble, creates something very powerful, because, when you move from one opposition to another, there is something like the logic of a house of cards: it all somehow balances. Behind the opposition rational choice/mechanism [?], there is liberalism [?]/collectivism, socialism. We could continue to make up others: it would give us some good exam essay topics.

The practical mastery of structures

I shall now try to recapitulate, and say how we can reply to these questions, once rephrased and better formulated, composed as sociological problems rather than social problems; in the next two lectures, I shall try to show, in a kind of concluding synthesis, how we can rethink the whole of the social field while avoiding this alternative, and how, in particular, we can resolve the famous age-old problem of social class, which seems eternal as long as it is caught in these alternatives. The problem of social class easily becomes circular, it can go round and round for ever, whereas if it is reconstructed within a genuine alternative, it can disappear. This is what I want to show next time.

Today I shall try merely to reply to the question that I have raised. First proposition: social agents really are agents – they act. This is

Lecture of 5 June 1986　　151

why I use the word 'agent' rather than the word 'actor', although it is not very attractive, with its overtones of a secret agent. There are unconscious connotations, and I know that many people find the word 'agent' vulgar. (This sort of thing does occur, sociology is often type-cast . . . I could say a lot about the avoidance of vulgar words, which is one of the obstacles to scientific construction. Philosophers, who take great care to avoid vulgar language because they have been brought up like that, find certain things impossible to think precisely because they cannot use the words that you would need in order to be able to think them – I was myself brought up in this school, I intuitively know how to play the game and I know all too well which words I should avoid using: I do not say all this vindictively, it is retrospective self-criticism.)

Social agents, then, construct the social world, but insofar as they are constructed by the social world, that is, structured by interaction with a structured world, they have in their practical experience a prac-tical mastery of the structures of this world and therefore feel at home there, so to speak; they understand spontaneously, they know how to play the game. Of course, this is not universal, it is valid for cases where they are playing one of the games where their structures were formed. The general proposition then needs to be more specific: once an agent finds himself thrust into a game whose structures he has not incorpo-rated, he will find himself ill at ease, acting against the grain. Either he will be crushed by the structures, or he will be led to question the structures. This is an important point for a structural understanding of changes in structure: social agents may be more or less well adapted to the structures of the world in which they are active. According to historically attested observation, those who create subversion often possess the property of not fitting into the pattern of the structure. For instance, in the religious field, the social agents of a prophetic type, whose discourse proposes to refashion the world differently, often have the property of inhabiting those uncertain areas of the social space where, in a way, all things are possible; and when ill-structured social agents hold a weakly structured position, they may become the source of a restructuring. (This is a classic alternative in the social world: either the structure assimilates the disturbing element, or the disturb-ing element manages to oblige the structure to restructure itself in relation to him. That was a parenthesis.)

Agents, then, construct the social world, but they are constructed by it and it is insofar as they are constructed by it that they are able to construct it, for constructing it may initially involve an act of mental construction that constitutes it as an object of perception (I showed last year that perception is a construction whose principles are structures

152   *Lecture of 5 June 1986*

that are themselves social); constructing the social world in their perception, the social agents can also work at constructing it differently in reality.

Imposing the right point of view

To take a simple example, I refer to a tradition in the sociology of law that has been developed recently in the United States: 'dispute theory'.[17] This is a trend among people who study the sources of judicial conflicts: how does the phenomenon of the trial emerge? They raise the question of how the perception of injustice emerges. A certain number of people do not perceive as unjust things that others perceive as unjust. This is banal, but, for example, a black person may not find racist aggression as unjust to the same degree as an antiracist white person. How do we move from an unnoticed, or subliminally noticed, grievance to a grievance perceived? Then, with the grievance perceived constituted as such, how do we move from the grievance perceived to an attribution of blame ('It is X's fault. . .')?

I shall take an example from some very old work of mine on Algeria.[18] As there was a war on at the time, I could not put questions on topics that were overtly political (such as colonisation). I asked people: 'There are a lot of people unemployed: what do you attribute unemployment to?' There is a first problem, however surprising it may seem, which is that unemployment may not be noticed. A considerable statistical study showed that, in regions where the notion of work as such was not formulated, where to work is to fulfil one's duties as a man (that is, to attend the assembly, to talk to the other elders, etc.), unemployment is not perceived as such, whereas it was constituted as such in the regions where work is constituted as such (for instance Kabylia, which sent a lot of immigrants to France, and had a perception of modern forms of labour). Even when work and unemployment are formulated, you still need to conceptualise the notion that unemployment is the result of some cause or other. A whole lot of people could say: 'There is unemployment because there is unemployment'; 'There is unemployment because people can't find work.' Some people said: 'There is unemployment because the women are working. It's not normal for the women to work when there are men out of work' (in France, if you put the same question, you might hear an analogous reply: 'There is unemployment because there are immigrants'[19]). I recorded and analysed a whole series of causes, from the completely magical or affective, to explanations in terms of structural causes. What I have been saying is equally valid for a grievance in everyday life: 'It's the neighbour's cat', 'It's the dustmen's fault', etc. The problems of causality are extremely complex as you know; philosophers have rightly been questioning them for generations. In their everyday life, people had relatively simple theories of causality, but that is part of the way the world is constructed.

There is, then, the perception of a grievance perceived and its attribution to a cause (obviously we are describing a linear progression in order to facilitate our analysis; it doesn't happen like that in reality). Then there is the whole process of transformation whereby the grievance perceived is attributed to a grievance socially constituted as a subject of juridical conflict. This is the decisive moment when the professionals start to intervene. To transform 'It's my neighbour who removed a fence and her goat ate my lettuce' into 'I hereby charge . . .', there is a new process of constitution and construction – the two words are important, the word 'constitution' needs to be understood in the juridical as well as the philosophical sense. This work of constitution is linked to a process of naming and blaming, but I think that, when we reach the juridical field properly speaking – and here I diverge a little from this theory of disputes – a kind of qualitative threshold is crossed: the whole logic of the field, the *nomos* of the juridical field, will – as I constantly argue – be imposed on the potential plaintiff who, from being a simple protestor, will become a litigious plaintiff and will himself be constituted by the juridical field as soon as his protest is constituted as a formal complaint. There is then a struggle between the spontaneous constitution of the grievance and the juridical constitution of the grievance. This struggle is rooted in the whole tradition of the juridical system (Racine's *The Litigants* is an example), but it has not been analysed. What the sociology of law needs to do, in my opinion, is to describe this sort of imposition of a compulsory construction.

Now to come to my second point: social agents struggle to make sense of the world; they construct the social world using the terms that it uses to construct them. In other words, the structuring they will impose on the world depends on their position in the structure (which is what I said previously: the point of view commands the vision, etc.): they will have the vision of the world that their position in the world tends to impose on them. Then, having different positions in the world, they will have divergent points of view and will confront each other, trying to impose their viewpoint, as we say. Here I think Austin is right that it is worth taking the trouble to reflect on ordinary language: we don't say that we try to 'impose our views' but that we try to 'impose

154 *Lecture of 5 June 1986*

our point of view'. We need to consider the whole: we need to consider the view and we need to consider the point of view. This is what the phenomenologists forget when they say 'you need to put yourself in their place', as in Husserl's famous analyses of subjective intercommunication. It looks impressive if we place 'put yourself in their place' in inverted commas, but we don't put ourselves in their place – if you want the view, you need the point of view! Besides, we talk of an 'impregnable point of view' [*laughter*] [. . .] People work at imposing their point of view, that is, imposing the domination of their point and position in the social space.

My history of disputes had its agenda: in these disputes, people hold a particular position. They are professionally mandated to resolve disputes. It is their profession: they have a specific power that consists in imposing the right manner of resolving disputes. They say: 'Cease your violence, cease fighting, now we shall discuss the matter, what the law says is that. . .'. They have the power to establish the point of view of the litigants as defined by the code of law, by previous judgements, by precedent, etc. We see, in this struggle for and between points of view, that there is a particular point of view: the viewpoint of the law, the right point of view. It is the right representation (which is translated in Greek as *ortho-doxy*[20]), the right vision that we have when we are in the right place, which is what you might call the viewpoint of the State. This right position is also a construction of the world, accomplished according to a certain social logic: in the struggle between points of view, in the struggle for classifications, in the struggle for visions of the world, there is an official arbiter: the juridical field.

Since I have explained this rather quickly, because of my example, I shall go over some of the ground again next time. I am saying that the agents construct the world, but I rather glossed over the second phase of my argument, which is that the agents are in conflict over this world, and I should develop this point a little further. In this conflict over the world, the juridical position is quite special: it takes part in the struggle while presenting itself as standing apart from it. I shall try then next time to show how the other alternative that I mentioned, between practical struggles and intellectual struggles, can be found in the division of labour.

Second session (seminar): the field of power (2)

In my last seminar I approached the problem of the structure of the field of power. I would like to start with a sort of critical review of what

I was saying. Reflecting on what I wanted to say today, it seemed to me – and I think this was one of the reasons for my embarrassment – that I had concentrated on what I currently find most interesting and difficult, but at the same time the least certain, forgetting to recall on the one hand the process that led me to raise the question of power and the field of power in the terms that I did, and on the other hand what aspects of the problem I found relatively easy to explain. So I was dogged by the feeling that there was a gap between my subjective feeling of urgency in what I was saying, and an acute sentiment of objective unreality, as well as the fact that you could be justified in offering some resistance to my argument, which I felt left me feeling very vulnerable. So I shall attempt to retrace my steps.

This second session is supposed to be a seminar, but, as you can see, given the structure and layout of the auditorium, it is difficult to conduct a true seminar. That said, I do try despite everything to exploit the genuine freedom of a seminar where you are not obliged to say everything and say it in the right order, where you can say something then go back over it again, where you can give examples, where there is a kind of dialogue, etc. These are all things that are very important both for the quality of what is being said and above all for the quality of communication. I think that you would find quite a few things essential, or at least very enlightening, informative and subtle, if you saw them emerge from the empirical research of somebody exposing their work, so that I could use them as a demonstration of what I had been saying *in abstracto*; then you would immediately see things otherwise. One difficulty of this sort of situation, then, is that I have to produce both the supply and the demand. In particular, since the conditions do not lend themselves to suspension of disbelief, the experience of presenting the debate can become uncomfortable.

Last time, I basically tried to get to the heart of the difficult problem of the invariants of the structure of the field of power. It was implicit in the comparisons that I used when I made reference to Dumézil and the opposition between *bellatores* and *oratores*, which I related to present-day oppositions, for example between employers and intellectuals. I presented the problem at first as very general, which gave an axiomatic and deductive turn to my argument: there are powers; any power must obtain some form of recognition; to obtain this recognition there has to be a division of the labour of domination, since, if there is one thing that a power cannot grant itself, it is the recognition of its power, for legitimacy supposes misrecognition, and perfect reflexivity is not an ideal form of consecration. I am explaining this badly, but that is more or less what I said. To put it differently: power cannot be recognised

156   *Lecture of 5 June 1986*

and cannot recognise itself without a network of legitimacy; it therefore requires a process of domination that tends to present an invariant structure, and we find, in very different historical conjunctures, oppositions of more or less similar form between the holders of the dominant power (whether economic, political or military, for instance) and the holders of a rather dominated form of power of a cultural nature, which can accord the dominant power what it cannot accord itself, namely, symbolic recognition.

As I was proceeding much too fast, I shall interrupt the analysis there. Normally, I would have continued to follow the same logic and describe what seemed to me to be the network of circulation of legitimacy. Well, let me say it straight away because I may forget to say it (and I also say it for myself because it is in the logic of what I wanted to say): I wanted to describe two major structures of the division of the labour of domination. Using Durkheim's distinction between organic solidarity and mechanist solidarity,[21] I wanted to oppose two major structures of the dominant classes or the fields of power: in some, the field of power unites the holders of power who are simply juxtaposed, as they are in segmented societies; in the others, there is a complex division of the labour of domination, as there is in our societies. I had in mind that when we speak of the 'withering away of the social classes' ('There are no longer, in our society, social classes') or, more subtly, of a transition to the 'age of managers',[22] we implicitly oppose a subtle form of the division of the labour of domination to older forms of the same, so that we believe in a withering away of the forms of domination. That is by and large what I had in mind, but it was much too complicated, and above all, lacked any introduction.

The example of the 'capacities'

So I beat a retreat. I shall say much simpler things, if not strictly in the right order. The notion of a field of power is very closely linked to the notion of species of capital. Faithful followers of my lectures will remember that two years ago I elaborated the properties of the different species of capital.[23] I tried to show how each species of capital (economic, cultural and social) has its specific properties, and in particular its specific forms of transmission. I showed that cultural capital is distinguished from economic capital by the fact that it is more difficult to mobilise immediately and to transmit. It is not hereditary, because it dies with its bearer. It is transmissible, but under very special conditions, with a considerable loss; it can be transmitted, but without

Lecture of 5 June 1986 157

the academic seal of approval that grants universal validity. You have to bear this in mind in order to understand the functioning of the field of power in which the different powers will confront each other: the different fractions that we can subdivide within the population of the holders of power will owe some of their synchronic and diachronic properties to the principal species of capital on which their power is based.

To take one example: holders of the power founded on cultural capital, those who in the nineteenth century were called the 'capacities' (a splendid word), encounter a set of specific problems that do not affect owners of real estate, for example. In the nineteenth century land could be transmitted relatively simply. Since its accumulation is slow, the holders of landed capital are very often holders of social capital, they are elders in the hierarchy of the dominant class. To own a lot of land they have to have inherited it; they are often noble, and often enjoy significant social connections, etc. This immediately gives them substance: the holders of economic capital of the landed type will almost by definition have properties in terms of cultural capital and social capital. For the 'capacities' (barristers, doctors, solicitors, etc.), the problem is very different. The capacities will have properties that are personal because, even if there is transmission of cultural capital through the family, they are acquired in one generation and are not directly transmissible; for instance, the constant temptation of the capacities to make their functions hereditary encounters more and more obstacles.

Another property affecting the capacities is the fact that cultural capital enables the production of services (medical procedures, legal advice, etc.) whose scarcity depends on the importance of the offer, which is, I believe, extremely important. In other words, the holders of cultural capital, the capacities (to whom we should add the professors), are dependent on the State, and collaborate with the State in various domains. Firstly, their privilege and control of the market depends on the control of the offer, that is, on the production of the producers, which means the State, since it delivers the diplomas. It is no accident if the capacities ceaselessly complain about the inflation of educational qualifications or, echoing a theme that returns periodically throughout the nineteenth century, continually fear the spectre of the overproduction of school graduates. As early as 1848 they say that the revolution of that year was caused by people who had educational qualifications but were frustrated failures, for instance. This obsession with the overproduction of qualified school leavers is explained when we see that the value of the cultural capital guaranteed by these qualifications depends

158 *Lecture of 5 June 1986*

on the scarcity of the producers on the market, and therefore on the limitation of the offer of services obtainable from this capital (legal services, for instance), and on controlling the production of producers, which means controlling the educational system.

Even today, when we undertake an enquiry into the educational system, we see that these categories of people are especially concerned. They score a high percentage of replies in a random sample of respondents. In an enquiry that we ran in the press,[24] asking 'What do you think of the educational system since 1968?', where people were free to reply as they wished, the capacities were over-represented, because they see themselves as 'authorised authorities' on the educational system. They justify this by implicitly saying: 'As holders of cultural capital, our opinions matter when it comes to culture.' This justification through competence is not absurd. Since it sounds convincing, it is not easy to see what it hides, which is something much more important: 'We need the State to help us to preserve our scarcity, we have a collective monopoly which is supported and upheld by the State and which remains valid as long as the State upholds it.'

I want to take some examples that may seem strange to you, but which are important. There have been debates in the United States on the subject of whether anaesthesia should be given by doctors or not. Goffman analysed it very well:[25] it is a problem that challenges the limits of the group, it is in fact a problem of *numerus clausus*: who has the right to [administer anaesthesia]?; in other words, it's a problem of statutory legal control of the market. The educational system is surely the most monstrously stratified institution, since it distinguishes people according to their diplomas, and their examination successes, etc.; there is an absolutely fantastic plethora of fine distinctions which are so many ways of controlling the market and limiting access to the market. In the juridical field we could show the same thing. For example, one American study shows that the increase in the school population and the number of holders of educational qualifications in legal studies has led to a lowering of average incomes, but also to all sorts of other consequences, such as the emergence of very important divisions between the top of the hierarchy – which manages to conserve, if not the monopoly, then at least such an important proportion of the market that its position is not threatened – and on the contrary the lower fractions of the juridical profession, which have become proletarianised. In France there is an analogous phenomenon among doctors. The overproduction of diplomas ('overproduction' means nothing in the abstract, it's always in relation to a particular state of affairs) has a global impact on the holders of diplomas, such as giving

Lecture of 5 June 1986 159

them a privileged, monopolistic right of access to a market, and also differential effects which can only be understood through an analysis of the structure of the field of the holders of diplomas that give a collective monopoly to members of the field.

In the fields that were rather corps or orders,[26] such as the Order of Doctors, we see that orders or corps tend to function as fields. For instance, if you read *Le Monde* properly (that is, if you read it sociologically, which is the only way of making it bearable), you may have seen that they recently gave the results of the elections to the Syndicat de la magistrature.[27] I am telling you this briefly because you might think that I was making things up, whereas this way you can check the details. They said that there were three trade unions (I don't remember their acronyms) . . . One union [l'Union syndicale des magistrats, USM], which has always existed, but under another name [l'Union fédérale des magistrats], was a sort of [professional] association. Not everyone was a member of a trade union, but all those who were, were members of this 'syndicate', which is the sign that we are dealing with a corps, a sort of corporation, a 'fraternity', as they say in America. This syndicate is still in existence. In May 1968 a new syndicate was created, the Syndicat de la magistrature, which produced a completely unexpected result. (In a way there were similar occurrences in higher education, in the medicine and law faculties. I won't go into detail, but I am telling you simply so that you can work out the structural analogies for yourselves and make things which might seem abstract much more concrete.)

On its appearance the Syndicat de la magistrature posed a sort of problem: it appeared to be politicising the corps of the magistrates, one of whose properties was to be extra-political, juridically neutral, etc. This field then could be outside the field while still being within the field . . . One condition was this kind of juridical neutrality: 'We are apolitical, it is out of the question for any magistrate to take up a political position.' However, at the time of the abortion debate,[28] they signed up in more than average numbers; but apart from that, 'we don't go in for politics' . . . they observed a kind of neutrality. The corps of the magistrates then found itself cleft by the emergence of this syndicate. For years this opposition lasted, until recently a right-wing union [l'Association professionnelle des magistrats] appeared, creating a polarised space in which the old union, which remains numerically dominant, occupies the central position, with a right and a left – a field that enables us to imagine almost deductively how it is organised. This is one effect of the crisis of the mode of reproduction of the capacities, which is linked to their properties. To understand what I have just been

160 *Lecture of 5 June 1986*

saying in so few words, you would need to study all the changes in the structure of the modes of reproduction within the dominant class.

Educational system, *numerus clausus* and social reproduction

After this series of parentheses, which has led me to stray from the main issue, I shall return to the specific problem of the capacities. The capacities, then, are distinguished from the other fractions, in particular those that are based on the possession of economic capital: firstly, their capital, being an individual property, dies with them; secondly, in order to function as capital, this capital needs to be rare, which demands structural conditions that depend largely on the State. This is something to add to what I said in my analyses of the specific properties of cultural capital: this capital preserves its exclusivity only insofar as access to its guaranteed form is limited, which depends largely on the State, through the mediation of the educational system. We could show in this way that the capacities have a particularly interested relation to the educational system, insofar as they feel intimately involved in it: in defending it they are in a way fighting to save their skin.

This is something that people do not understand, but if quarrels over the educational system often become extremely violent, if they take the form of struggles for ultimate values, if they are fundamentally the wars of religion of our times, it is largely because these disputes concern issues of reproduction: the educational system has become one of the great structural mechanisms of reproduction of the dominant positions, so that to control this system is the only way of controlling one's own reproduction – the more so, the more you depend on it for your own reproduction – and in reproducing the educational system of which you are a product, you reproduce the excellence that you attribute to yourself. In other words, educational disputes take on the form of wars of religion, in a life or death struggle, because the stakes are in a way absolute; what is at stake (I am simplifying a little, I could nuance my argument, but I just want to launch the idea) is the reproduction of what I am, and what I am worth, through the reproduction of the market where the value of my capital is rated.

If for instance we just get rid of Latin – this is an example that I often use – those who have invested in Latin are like the holders of Russian bonds: overnight, their capital, earned by years and years of work, is devalued, has lost all value. Likewise, the holders of linguistic capital. Commentators with a somewhat rationalistic-economistic vision of the legitimate bases of conflict often describe linguistic battles as irrational,

Lecture of 5 June 1986 161

as if there were reason on the one hand and passion on the other. In fact there is also an economic reason in this affair: if, for example, we change the mode of acquisition of the language or languages in competition, we transform the whole structure of the distribution of the rival species of capital. This is the case for instance in ex-colonial countries, such as Algeria, where three languages, Berber, Arab and French, are in competition: if you change the educational system you change the balance of power between those with small savings and those with a major portfolio of linguistic capital. This enables us to see that the motives of the struggle are not emotional at all. More exactly, they are emotional, but just as much as economic struggles are. No more, no less. They are not irrational, they are reasonable, without being rational.

The holders of cultural capital inhabit quite a strange and special position, because of the unusual vulnerability of their capital. Since this capital goes hand in hand with a certain mode of reproduction and its particular logic, it is constantly threatened by any crisis in the mode of reproduction that might entail the disqualification of the holders of the traditional form of this capital. This means that their relation to the educational system becomes determining, as does their relation to the State which acts in a way to guarantee the stability of the mode of reproduction or the mode of succession – we tend to forget, but in fact the educational system is a mode of succession. Just as some will protest against a wealth tax,[29] others will protest against any reform of the baccalaureate. Although it is not immediately obvious, they follow the same logic, and I think that one virtue of a rigorous construction is to confront things that common sense separates and to separate things that common sense confuses.[30] The State's bureaucratic decisions do then have great importance, in that they can affect the monopoly; they can for instance increase the number of people who share the monopoly or on the contrary restrict it with a *numerus clausus* (the *numerus clausus* plays an absolutely crucial part in this logic).

By allowing numbers to increase through a sort of pedagogical *laissez-faire*, we encourage a process of devaluation of diplomas and their holders, and a process of intensification of competition between holders of qualifications, with everything that competition implies: open conflicts that won't have been seen before (like those emerging among the magistrates), and inadmissible forms of competition. For instance, in the United States there has been much debate among attorneys over whether they should be able to advertise their services. This is very interesting because they could propose to extend juridical rights,

162 *Lecture of 5 June 1986*

to give juridical rights to all (I don't know if I am getting through to you, I would like you to understand what I am hinting at. . .); they could become militant, since militantism can be an admissible form of winning the market over (that's what I wanted to say, but didn't want to say. . .). There are all sorts of current forms of militantism whose progressive contribution cannot be denied. It can be very important for blacks to have legal aid, to have at their disposal free forms of defence against discrimination. That said, this has the effect of increasing demand, and in a period when the offer is increasing a lot, it is important to increase the demand. These ideas can fire the imagination of the magistrates when the offer increases and the demand declines, which means that the most noble ideas can have their source in mechanisms which are less noble.

(Given my philosophy of history, I find no problem in this, and I would be very worried if our supreme values arose from illumination; it is much more healthy to realise that they arise from interest, under certain conditions, which does not mean that they are reducible to those interests. That was a short parenthesis, but I distinguish between two great philosophies of humanity [one for whom progress is achieved by exceptional moral individuals and the other which explains it through the existence of properly social mechanisms which show that morality too is driven by interest[31]].)

To return to my argument: the producers of services based on cultural capital are very closely linked to the State, in several ways: through the State they can control the production of producers but also (as I have implicitly shown in the example of militancy) the creation of demand, since they are able to impose measures that stimulate increased demand (if you say 'we need legal aid for all abused women', you create a juridical demand). I have developed this point at length because it is a good example, but we could do the same thing for each group defined by the dominant possession of a particular form of capital.

The search for stable forms of capital

The capacities also have a third reason to feel implicated in everything public and bureaucratic, everything run by the State: it is the fact that the fragility of their capital, linked to the fact that it is a kind of 'equity release' (in fact that is what I was trying to say just now: it is 'equity release' compared to the other forms of capital), obliges them to back up their capital, in order to preserve it, with other forms of capital.

Lecture of 5 June 1986 163

Flaubert's father, for instance, bought up some land [he acquired economic capital in the form of real estate] and encouraged his son to study. The capacities have these two strategies – or they try to marry off their daughters. In the nineteenth century, for instance, these strategies of perpetuation aimed to acquire stable forms of capital, especially real estate, since everybody knows how to buy land, whereas it is much more difficult to buy into business. This is still true nowadays: when I studied the savings patterns of the different dominant categories, [I observed that] the capacities, as in Flaubert's day, don't know how to invest in industry. They invest in land, which is no doubt less suitable than it was in the nineteenth century, when the land produced a reliable income as well as social capital, and sometimes noble titles, etc.

To preserve their stability, another important strategy lies in cultivating relations with the bureaucratic field, the State, the higher civil service and the political field. These holders of cultural capital have a privileged access to the political field – which explains a lot about our most recent political life[32] – which gives immediate access to the bureaucratic field of the higher civil service, which allows them to control indirectly a whole host of affairs. Through the political power, you can act on the bureaucratic power and use this to get a certain number of measures enacted, but also to gain all sorts of personal advantages, for instance in protecting people, or assembling a clientele, which is one of the aims of any power .[. . .]

To sum up: given that a general property of all species of capital is never to be self-sufficient, we cannot oppose fractions of the governing class, as people sometimes do, by using simple divisions into holders of real estate, holders of financial investment, and holders of cultural capital of such and such a kind, etc. In fact I believe that one condition of legitimate and complete belonging to the dominant class is the possession of several species of capital (in different proportions). What divides the fractions, separating for instance artists from business managers, is – as I have repeatedly said in these lectures[33] – the structure of the capital, that is the relative proportion of the volume of the different species of capital in the total volume of capital possessed. That said, the holder of a particular form of capital generationally acquired must add other species of capital to this in order to become a fully paid up member of the field of power. The *parvenu* or 'self-made man' who has acquired his capital in one generation will not become a full member of the dominant class until he has added [another species of capital] to this capital, and this is also true of cultural capital (you only have to see how Proust, that is, [the world of the] salons, speaks of academics. . .).

164   *Lecture of 5 June 1986*

One manner of acquiring social capital, and also something more, is marriage. (I hesitate to say certain things because I am afraid that you will reduce them to examples of folk wisdom.) Marriage is one of the real entrance tickets for a *parvenu*. Also, one of the major pledges you can give to the dominant universe is to marry one of its daughters (or one of its sons, in the – much more improbable – case of the intragenerational accession of a woman to the dominant class); you have to 'plight your troth' (I might return to this point if anyone wants me to).

Given the specific properties of cultural capital, the holders of this capital are terribly dependent on the State if they wish to fulfil their destiny and perpetuate themselves, given that the State is able to control the educational system (public or private – I could go on for hours about this). They are dependent on the bureaucratic space and the political space, since these can convert cultural capital into other, more durable forms of capital. It has often been noted that barristers, doctors and professors are over-represented in the representative institutions of politics. These are things that we tend to understand too quickly: we note the fact they are good speakers, but not all the people who are good speakers want to trade their words in that market place . . . What are the real reasons that explain this interest in politics? That is more or less what I want to explore.

The strategies of reproduction according to species of capital

To recapitulate. As I have developed this example of the capacities at such length (which I had not intended to do), this has distorted my whole argument. What I wanted to say was, in order to understand what I mean by the 'field of power', and the logic of the struggles that are played out within this field, you need to bear in mind that the different species of capital are each endowed with specific properties. These specific properties explain that the strategies of reproduction and perpetuation in the dominant positions are very variable according to the type of capital possessed. This means that the holders of different species relate differently to their own reproduction. I came out with various ideas, but not in any order: the idea that we can only understand the field of power and what occurs within it if we take into account the fact that it is constantly concerned with its own reproduction. This is almost an axiom: that we can understand most of the strategies of social agents as strategies of reproduction.

For example, during the whole of the nineteenth century, the capacities had a far lower level of fecundity than the other fractions of the

Lecture of 5 June 1986 165

dominant class. If you have been following my argument, you will immediately see the explanation, especially if you bear in mind the link I have tried to establish elsewhere between the different strategies of reproduction within a single group.[34] The principal feature unifying these different strategies being the habitus, there is a link – which I shall state very briefly – between the strategies of biological reproduction and the more general strategies of reproduction, those of investment, succession and matrimony, among others. All these strategies contribute to one system, and constitute a coherent whole to such an extent that there is hardly any sense in studying, for example, customs of succession without studying strategies of fecundity or matrimonial strategies.[35] The historical studies that ignore this system risk understanding nothing. For instance, one aspect of the strategies of biological reproduction may be the effect of compensating for the difficulties of the strategies of succession; or, on the contrary, the strategies of succession may have the effect of compensating for the failure of the strategies of reproduction. Using the example that I always take because it is simple, to have only daughters in a system of male primogeniture is a catastrophe;[36] you have to make up for it in other ways and use very subtle matrimonial strategies in order to try to obtain, through the daughters, what you would have had through a son.

Reproduction is a kind of constituent imperative – you might almost say an axiomatic imperative . . . A dominant class is statutorily concerned with its own reproduction, it thinks of little else. Which does not mean that it is conceptualised as such. A sentence by Balzac that I quoted as an epigraph to the first work on reproduction I published happens to say more or less that: 'Reproduction is the problem of all power' or 'Duration is the problem of all power.'[37] How to last, how to perpetuate yourself? In other words, the major political question concerning the problem of power is 'How to last?' The modes of durability of the different powers are one of the major principles of differentiation between them. To raise the question of power is to raise the question of the mode of reproduction. The different fractions of the dominant class, in the different areas of the field of power, are distinguished by the species of capital that constitutes the dominant part of their capital, and thus by their different relations to the system, to the mechanisms of reproduction available, and by their different relations to the dominant mode of reproduction, it being understood that 'mode of reproduction' means the ensemble of the systems and mechanisms of reproduction available, and the relation that the different groups entertain with these different mechanisms of reproduction – I think this is a reasonably rigorous definition.

166 *Lecture of 5 June 1986*

Yet another example: for the recent period running from 1880 to our own times, there has been a great change in the dominant class, which is the change in their mode of reproduction, driven by the increasing importance of the educational system in the system of the mechanisms of reproduction – to such an extent that today even the economically dominant fractions need to pass through the educational system, at least to legitimise their mode of reproduction and even to secure it. (I shall consider here only the mode of reproduction with an educational component – I want to make this clear, because people simplify and say: 'Bourdieu says that it is the educational system that reproduces'; what I do say is that the educational system *contributes to* reproduction.) As I tried to establish in an article on employers that I published a few years ago,[38] even those fractions whose position, whose membership of the dominant class and position in the field of power, depend on their possession of economic capital – a capital more easily transmissible, within the limits of the laws of succession and a certain number of secondary constraints – tend more and more to use the educational system to ensure their own reproduction, partial or total. For example, the strategies of reproduction that the bourgeois families of the eighteenth century resorted to in order to ensure the reproduction of the family, with all its offspring – one inherits the business, another becomes a bishop, the third a military man, etc. – have been much transformed and diversified with the emergence of the necessity and possibility of resorting to the educational system for the reproduction of all or some of their lineage.

Generally speaking, then, we need to take account of the existence of different species of capital and different relations to the mechanisms of reproduction. When you have a good theoretical construction, you suddenly understand differently things that seemed banal. I hope that I am able to create this kind of effect today. I make this announcement (if we were at the circus, it would be accompanied by a drum roll) because, when you are not completely immersed in the scientific field, you can find banal things that are in fact quite astonishing, and vice versa. (I am constantly worried that you might be wondering: 'Why does he keep going on about a topic that is so self-evident.' It is often, it seems to me, because there must be a gap between your system of constructing the object of study and the system that I deploy either implicitly or explicitly.)

Lecture of 5 June 1986   167

Sociodicy and ideology

What separates the holders of different species of capital, or – to be more precise – of structures of capital dominated by different species, are the different modes of reproduction. While it is true, as I have said, that any dominant class tends by its very existence to work for its own reproduction as a dominant force, we can understand that, in the struggle for classification which I mentioned just now – that is, in the political struggle to impose a legitimate point of view on the social world – the dominant tend always to propose what Weber in a magnificent formula calls a 'theodicy of their own privileges',[39] or, more simply, a sociodicy. Let me briefly explain. Theodicy (for Leibniz) is not the judgement of God, it is the justification of God, it is the attempt to justify the existence of God:[40] how is God possible if evil exists? If we wanted to give a simple, practical definition of ideology (assuming that we feel we must preserve the term. . .), we could say that it is a theodicy of privilege, that is, a coherent discourse, claiming to be systematic, destined to justify a dominant social group in their domination, in their existence as dominant. This means that an ideology always takes the form of a constative utterance disguising a performative: 'That is how things are, all is fine and good, and all must remain that way.'

It transpires from what I have been saying that theodicies will vary according to the privileges. This is what I was driving at: the dominant tend to develop theodicies of their privileges that are a function of the structure of their capital and the dominant space. Thus the capacities, whom I have dealt with at considerable length, will situate their theodicy in what I call 'the ideology of giftedness', that is, in an incoherent but sociologically very powerful combination of meritocracy and – dare I say – charismatocracy, since to be gifted is to be charismatic. In fact the professional ideology of the teacher is a combination of an ideology of giftedness ('highly talented pupil') and an ideology of merit ('hardworking'), with hardworking of course being slightly inferior to being gifted ('serious but not brilliant' as opposed to 'brilliant'[41]). This professional ideology is in fact consubstantial with the educational system.

'Ideology' is not a good word, and I never use it, except to explain how to understand it. The word makes us think of ideas at work. However, what we call 'ideologies' may be practices, they are not necessarily discursive. It is the idea of an ideologist, or even a professor of philosophy, to believe that in order to dominate you have to make speeches, and that ideologies are ideologies. The best 'ideologies' are mechanisms. The educational system is thus a formidable ideology

168 *Lecture of 5 June 1986*

in a practical state; it constantly propagates the ideology of gifted-ness, saying that the most talented are the best, that the best are the most talented. This is why I place the word 'ideology' between quota-tion marks. What we should remember is that the holders of different species of capital tend to mirror themselves in different justificatory systems. Nevertheless, there are invariants. In any case, the point is to say that this is how things are, and how they should be, and things are fine like that: this naturalising is the essence of all theodicies. It is naturalisation as a form of universalisation. Marx said that 'ideology is the universalisation of particular interests',[42] and the primary ideologi-cal strategy consists in saying: 'I am what I should be because what I am is universal.' The universalisation of particular interests takes a particularly powerful form when the universal is one with nature.

In the case of the landed aristocracy, we find an ideology of blood and earth (we could preserve the term ideology, but only to designate the explicit form of the justificatory discourse which emerges when reproduction is called into question). These ideologies of blood and earth can be assigned to authors who emerged in Germany in the 1830s,[43] when the privileges of the *Junkers* [members of the landed gentry in Prussia] were called into question and a certain number of automatic processes of transmission were at least contested by critical, rationalist philosophers. We therefore have an explicitly formulated discourse, produced by professional ideologues. This is again what I was saying in the lecture just now: a major division opposed the practical responses and the discursive responses produced by what we would nowadays call right-wing intellectuals, who composed a dis-course forming the justificatory praxis of the dominant – heritage, blood and so on. This is practical logic, these are the main instruments and weapons of groups whose power is based on reproduction through land and heritage. To know your genealogy, to know if a particular person is an heir or not, is often capital. What is in your genealogy will become blood and earth, and this will inspire orators to preach blood and earth.

In the case of what we might call the culturocracy of the capacities, we will find practical mechanisms of legitimisation and justification, which are all the more powerful because they are produced without being seen or enunciated. They reproduce while dissimulating their contribution to reproduction, and they legitimise in terms of the defini-tion that I give of legitimacy: legitimacy is the misrecognition of the arbitrary. The educational system, for instance, is a formidable 'ideo-logical machine' (in inverted commas), because it ensures reproduction in a manner that is invisible – until some sociologist comes along to show what it is doing by bringing to light its contribution to social reproduction. Thus the ideology of giftedness hardly needs help in establishing itself, and when it is established, it is reactionary. There is a ritual debate over the inherited nature of intelligence: is it in the genes or is it in society? People fight over it, and there is always a biologist to say that there is nothing in the genes, it is all in our history. This fine debate is one of those that I was referring to just now: it arises when the ideology of giftedness is threatened in its practice. Otherwise all you have to do is write 'brilliant' in the margin of an essay and everything works like clockwork: in fact [writing] 'brilliant' is an absolutely extraordinary practical ideological act (I could develop that further).

To conclude: the different species of capital lead in very different ways to different forms of discourse justifying privilege, it being understood that any justificatory discourse is always a naturalising discourse. Finally we might make a slight adjustment to Weber's excellent formula that ideology is a theodicy: we might say that justificatory discourses are sociodicies of naturalisation: they are discourses that justify historical phenomena, such as unequal distribution, through naturalisation. They transform the *nomos* into *phusis*:[44] they transform what arises through human law or distribution into something that arises from nature. They transform things that are arbitrary, in the sense of being contingent on or produced by history, into things that are necessary, in the sense of being natural. This general and generic logic of sociodicy is rooted in species of capital.

Next time I shall look into different properties of capital, especially properties concerning the structure of the field of power.

Lecture of 12 June 1986

First session (lecture): the space of positions and the space of standpoints – The representation of the social world at stake – A collective construction – A cognitive struggle – Making the implicit explicit – The specificity of the scientific field
Second session (seminar): the field of power (3) – Boundaries of the fields and right of entry – The example of the literary field – Flow of capital and variations in the exchange rate – Establishing a new mode of reproduction – Maxwell's demon

First session (lecture): the space of positions and the space of standpoints

Today I am going to continue with what I had started to say about the notion of the field, and recapitulate the properties that are inherent in the fact that fields are fields of struggles rather than simply fields of forces. I had already said that a certain number of these properties can be deduced from the fact that fields are fields for the struggle to transform the field of forces, since the strength that the different agents or institutions dispose of in their struggles corresponds to their position in the field of forces. We need to consider this doubly antagonistic relation as a whole: the agents have the ability to construct and transform a position which is itself constructed by its position in the field.

I think that one of the problems raised by the fields where what is at stake is something cultural (as in the case of the religious, artistic or scientific fields) is the fact that we need to take into account both the existence of a *motus*, an inclination for struggle, movement and change, and also the direction of this change. On this point, I have so far only indicated the area in which I am seeking the answer. It seems to me that the distinction between the space of positions and the space of standpoints, which I have proposed on several occasions, is important here, the space of positions being what I call a field of forces, and the space of standpoints being the space of the strategies employed by the rival holders of the different positions, strategies whose aim may be to transform the space of positions, this space being homologous with the space of standpoints. The space of standpoints, in fields like the juridical or scientific fields, is charged with all their past struggles, in such a way that it defines the direction in which the field will head. To put this simply: to understand how a scientific or an artistic field changes, we need to see that its motor is in the field of positions, guided by a sort of *angelus rector*[1] [guardian angel], whereas what defines its orientation is to be found in the field of standpoints. (I shall return to this point again later, because I fear sometimes that you are asking yourselves questions that anticipate the moment for me to give the answers; I am trying therefore to answer in advance, but this is not always easy.)

So we need to consider two things in conjunction: the agents construct the social world, but using building blocks provided for them by the social world; these building blocks can be incorporated into the habitus in the shape of patterns of perception. Social agents work either in cooperation or in opposition to transform the structure, but it is the structure that determines the standpoints they take up in order to transform the structure. Another way of saying the same thing: social agents struggle to establish the sense of the world – this is the struggle for classification that I have mentioned; they fight not only over the meaning of the world, but over the principles to use in constructing that meaning, and this cognitive battle for the principles of vision of the world derives from interests that are not cognitive. Those who insist on the fact that the social world is a construct forget its materialist dimension; this construction does not operate in a vacuum; it emerges from a certain position in the social world.

The representation of the social world at stake

The social world, then, is itself at stake in the struggle; there is no social field in which the truth is not simultaneously a weapon in the conflict and its object. This is, I think, an anthropological presupposition. It is possible, as Habermas and others have done, to turn this empirical observation into a sort of transcendental presupposition[2] and identify a kind of universal claim to validity, particularly in the philosophical or scientific fields. I think that [whether we establish it as an empirical

172 *Lecture of 12 June 1986*

observation or a transcendental presupposition] is a question of intellectual strategy or philosophical opinion. These two ways of expressing the same thing are philosophical universes apart, but that does not matter much for the viewpoint that interests me, which is that of a scientific construction. It makes no difference then whether we say either that there is a sort of universal claim to truth made by all the social agents who take part in a game, and in particular in the scientific field, or simply that there is no scientific game in which the claim to truth is not both a tool and an issue, in the sense that somebody with truth on their side has an advantage, which, in certain fields, can even provide important social leverage.

The truth of the social world is a bone of contention in the social world, and the political field is obviously one of the universes where this struggle to impose one's point of view, to make others see, believe and act according to one's viewpoint, takes on its most transparent form. It has a particular position in the universe of possible fields because of its strikingly polemical dimension. We can see the political field and the scientific field as two extreme poles. In the political field (especially when the politics are of the Machiavellian type), the struggle comes out into the open, whereas in the scientific field the struggle is masked by the very logic of the forms that it must express itself through (this is its Durkheimian side: the structure imposes constraints, robbing the individual agents of any chance of absolute freedom), and, at the same time, it is a *constructum*, liable to be transformed at any moment.

We could then say that the world is our construction, to counter the idealist tradition, which sees the world as my representation. Some currents of social phenomenology go as far as this radical subjectivism. For Schütz for instance, the social world tends to be reduced to the experience that social subjects have of it: there is no transcendence of the social, there is a sort of radical anti-Durkheimianism. This whole movement has in a way been constructed against Durkheim's idea of a 'collective consciousness', against his claim to establish sociology as a science, with an object irreducible to psychology, against the concept that constraint is a criterion of the reality of the social, and against the idea that the social world presents itself, and should be studied, as a thing, etc. All these properties which Durkheim used to characterise the social world and establish it as the specific object of sociology are revoked by the radically subjectivist tendency, whose clearest expression is to be found I think in Schütz, but which can also be found in many ethnomethodologists. These theories tend to consider the world as a pure construction of the mind, and we might paraphrase the title of Schopenhauer's book, *The World as Will and Representation*,[3] to say

Lecture of 12 June 1986   173

that they see the social world as no more than the representation that the agents have of it: it exists only insofar as the agents perceive it [and only in the way that they perceive it]. I wanted to remind you of the two poles of this alternative in order to show what we adopt and what we reject from it, when we try to supersede it.

A collective construction

The social world, then, is not my representation, but our construction. It is a collective construction, that is, the end product of a collective effort of negotiations and transactions (ethnomethodologists will agree with me thus far) carried out under constraint (which is the point where we differ). The truth is that social agents negotiate and confront antagonistic strategies. Thus the pedagogic relationship that is established in the classroom is the product of negotiations between the pupils and the teacher, whom they may or may not heckle. Interactionist sociologists or ethnomethodologists, especially Goffman, have the merit of showing that the social power games which we observe on the microsociological scale of a simple classroom (or, another example, in the relation between doctor and patient) are the product of a collective process; they have as their subject a kind of *us* in the making, where the social agents, without being aware of it, are using strategies of negotiating and bargaining.

However, this position is only partially true (which means that it is false). In fact it describes these balances as the result of negotiations produced between interchangeable subjects (whose properties are not characterised), whereas these negotiations are actually contracted between socially composed individuals, each endowed with a habitus and holding a different position, each with different interests and resources and forming different relationships on the occasion of any particular negotiation. In other words, the balance of power that may be observed between spouses in the domestic unit, between the different branches of an extended family or between dominant and dominated clans owe their objective properties to the very structure where they were produced, and we cannot imagine describing these transactions and their work in constructing the world without taking into account the incorporated properties of those involved and the social conditions they are subject to.

We might think of Mehan's analyses,[4] for example, of the relationships negotiated in the classroom: without even being aware of it, the analysts reintroduce properties of habitus and position that do

174 *Lecture of 12 June 1986*

not figure in their theories (this often happens: people do better in their scientific practice than in their declared theories). To explain the negotiations they are obliged to take into account the fact that the teacher, a woman surrounded by male pupils and separated from them by only a relatively small difference in age, has a reduced margin of manoeuvre; there are certain strategies (that would be available to a man, for instance) that she cannot use. In short, they draw on all sorts of secondary variables which are inherent in the very structure on which the negotiations are based, and these micro-modifications of the structure are the root of major structural changes. One of the motors of change is the ensemble of all these infinitesimal, small-scale moves, which, when added, accumulated and integrated, ultimately lead to major changes, for instance through threshold effects. Overcoming the alternative of structuralism and constructivism, as I constantly do, nowadays also means overcoming the alternative between structure and history that unfortunately haunts the minds of most of the people who practise the social sciences, but is a sad trope of academic teaching imposed upon scientific reality.

These negotiations and acts dealing with the social world are based socially on individual acts of construction, but these acts of construction call on individual agents who are embedded in relationships which are themselves structured, in such a way that the constructions are collective constructions. This is why I said: 'The world is our representation', which is not a very good formula; we ought to say that the social agents work collectively, in a collaboration (which may be conflictual, as in the case of a negotiation) that does not appear to be one, but is designed to transform the structures which are the very source of their transformative intentions.

A cognitive struggle

Another important proposition: as I was saying just now, the struggles over the social world are cognitive struggles. I often say the same thing in different ways. My feeling that research in the social sciences needs this kind of work on language helps in a way to justify my manner of proceeding. My experience is that I have often found that I suddenly understood something that I had been saying for ages when I formulated it differently. I hope that I can produce the same effect in my present exercise in communication and that those who might not have understood what I was saying when I called these struggles 'symbolic' will immediately understand if I say that they are cognitive struggles.

Lecture of 12 June 1986

As soon as we say 'cognitive struggles' we slip into an intellectualist logic and think of acts of discursive cognition in the strong sense of the term. However, as I have tried to argue, there are acts of cognition that are non-discursive. This is the sense implied in my expression of 'the logic of practice'. One of the functions of the notion of habitus, as a system of behavioural patterns, is to remind us that social agents can follow a practical procedure, below any level of consciousness, in order to know and construct the social world, because they are able to do it in a practical fashion. Thus in the case of the classroom negotiations that I mentioned, the social agents in conflict may have no explicit idea of the cognitive goal, which is to decide who is the true master of the day: does a schoolmaster cease to be a master if she is a schoolmistress?

It is true that these things come to the surface from time to time. I remember for instance a very pretentious debate some years ago between leading academics and the most eminent representatives of the economic world (as they were described in the reports in *Le Monde*): at least 20 per cent of their time was spent wondering whether the world might have changed because our children (in fact, those of the bourgeoisie) had had only schoolmistresses for masters . . . You would need all of Flaubert's talent to be able to recount the way in which these things were concretely set out in their naively triumphal bourgeois discourse, but what they were saying, to put it crudely, was: 'Busy modern men as we are, being rarely at home, our children are left to the devices of women at home as well as in school; under these conditions, how are we going to be able to reproduce the virility that is one of the conditions of fulfilling the exalted functions that we fulfil?' [*laughter*]. This is the kind of problem that our most eminent men tend to discuss . . . Feminisation is a process that progresses imperceptibly, then becomes visible at a given moment (as in the paradox of the grain of sand), for there is a threshold effect, a moment of awareness. We then get a debate in *Le Monde*. To describe concretely how things happen: Ménie Grégoire discusses it one morning [*laughter*], then there is an editorial by Ivan Levaï, then an editorial by Serge July, and then, finally, a learned article in *Le Monde* provides a summary[5] [*laughter*].

In short, a series of discontinuous and diffuse experiences becomes a social problem and, obviously, the 'sociologists' hasten to discuss this social problem. (A particular problem for sociologists is that they want to play the game. Whatever they do or say, their would-be scientific discourse is immediately absorbed into the run of play and exploited in accordance with people's strategies and interests. The natural sciences do not have this problem: they don't have to worry that the planets might hijack their arguments. One problem for the social sciences is

176 *Lecture of 12 June 1986*

that the internal games of even the most autonomous scientific field fascinate the other social agents; which means that this scientific autonomy is constantly under threat. I shall return to this point.)

The construction of the social world, then, is collective, which means that it is the product of a process in which many people, with different interests and balances of power, are engaged. I make this clear in order to signal my difference from the dominant philosophy of neoclassical economics, which offers us isolated individuals, without relations (other than market relations), and is thereby only able to account for collective effects using a logic of aggregation, which is a purely additive, physicalist and statistical logic. In the logic that I adopt, collective productions are not obtained through an additive aggregation of interchangeable elementary particles; the individuals are not isolated, they are inserted in objective relations, in spaces whose structures govern their actions. In a very asymmetrical balance of power, the resulting collective may thus owe 90 per cent of its properties to the dominant force in the structure, and we will never understand the result if we rely on recording a simple addition of the elements present. In other words, in any interaction between individuals, whatever its object, the whole structure is present in the habitus of the agents. (I make this clear in order to suggest the consequences of things which I sometimes say rather rapidly and which you might be tempted to find banal, but which are in fact very different from other ways of thinking.)

These collective constructions may be standpoints, they may be cognitive, gnoseological constructions, without forasmuch being acts of cognition in the reductive sense that we habitually understand them. 'Cognitive' does not imply 'intellectual', for there are practical kinds of cognition. This is what I wanted to say with the example I started to develop, showing how feminisation had called into question a collective image in the depths of our unconscious and brought to the surface a new image of the schoolmaster and the schoolmistress. We could analyse the common representation of a certain number of social agents at a certain moment in time (the policeman, the schoolmaster and the judge, for instance).

This collective work may operate below the level of discourse, since these representations owe a considerable part of their collective force precisely to the fact that they are infra-discursive, remaining implicit and often being rooted in very ancient emotional experience. The founding fantasy of the elementary educational universe which formed us and which we love so much resurfaces when we speak of education. We can see the most eminent minds regress towards infantile modes of thought when they start to speak of education, because they are

Lecture of 12 June 1986   177

returning to their cognitive and affective complexes (the smell of glue, the sound of chalk on the blackboard, etc.). I was saying last time why pedagogical struggles are always dramatic for those categories of agents who owe everything to the school. But another explanation for the climate of tragic pathos and religious warfare that prevails in discussions over the educational system is the fact that agents engage in discussions of the founding experiences of the social world, like the experience of the world of school or of teacher–pupil relations, which are both socially and psychologically impregnated with transposed forms of their relations with their father or mother. On this point we should remember all those nineteenth-century literary accounts of the first day in school. They make their own contribution to heightening the primary experience because they are recycled back into the schools as if they were extracts from a primary school text book. This explains things that I have been saying for some time: education and apprenticeship deposit in each of us little springs that may long lie dormant and yet may still at certain moments be reactivated. I hesitate to do so, but I could take the example of Chevènement, who for reasons that largely escape him (he is the son of a primary school teacher, he has a deep educational unconscious), was able to reactivate all those little springs and make a whole nation move backwards with him[6] [*laughter*]. There you are. That was less of a parenthesis and more of an illustration of things that I have been saying in my previous lectures.

Making the implicit explicit

The struggles over the social world, then, are cognitive struggles, which does not necessarily mean they are intellectual. They are often practical struggles in which the agents engage practical, infra-discursive constructions that may then be brought up to the level of discourse by the specific work of agents like writers or sociologists, who take it upon themselves to make these practical constructions explicit (to define a primary school teacher, for instance). These cognitive struggles may also be based on theoretical constructions. The struggles over the social world engage a sort of division of labour in which the ordinary agents, those who do not have a mission to offer discursive visions of the social world, find themselves confronted with the professional producers of discourse on the world and in particular the social world.

There are in fact fields specialising in the production of discourse on the social world, the judicial field first and foremost. As I said last time, jurists are professionals who have been mandated, or, more exactly

178   *Lecture of 12 June 1986*

(since the jurists had to fight with the princes before they gained the right to lay down the law), who have mandated themselves to deliver the right and orthodox vision, to say how we should see the world, to put this into words and present a right-thinking discourse, explicitly composing an experience claiming – with a reasonable likelihood of success, as Weber says – to be recognised as *the* legitimate vision.

I would like here to expand on what is implied in the passage from a practical construction (for instance the ideal schoolmistress of the 1980s) to the explicit theoretical construction of a social model or portrait, as figure or stereotype. We could take the example of the judge. In the years that have followed May '68 we have seen a number of debates about red judges.[7] A collective process, in which journalists have played a considerable part, has composed a new image of the judge, instead of the fantasy image we had, which tended to resemble one of Daumier's caricatures, picturing a gentleman with a bonnet on his head. At a certain moment in time, this fantasy became collectively reworked. Some people mocked these images, others defended them, and then this practical work was able at a certain moment to pass into the discursive order, which marks a kind of qualitative leap. I must insist on this point: there is a veritable act of creation, and I think that the passage from the implicit to the explicit is an extremely important leap. The people who guard this passage dispose of a very important specific power. They have the capacity to transform the practical, confused, fuzzy and vague experience that constitutes the essence of our experience of the social world into an explicit, composed, formal, codified and accredited discourse that enables us to reach an agreement by using the same language. In differentiated societies, there obviously exist several forms of explication of this type, which is rather a good thing: given the power that making explicit confers, it would be terrifying if one category of 'explicators' managed to seize the monopoly of this work of making explicit.

In the ideology of the professional explicators, this work is described as 'creation'. We could speak of 'producers', as we sometimes do for the artistic field: this has a reductive, deflationary effect which has the virtue of undermining the professional ideology of the professional explicators, but at the same time – we should always be wary of radical breaks, they are often too extreme – we have to recognise that there is some truth in the ideology of creation. In fact, this passage from the implicit to the explicit seems unimpressive because what has been made explicit was already there beforehand: what is the benefit of this explication if it merely announces something that we knew already? This is typical of the prophecy effect: the prophet tells people something

Lecture of 12 June 1986 179

that they knew already, but which had not yet found expression. It is a genuine conversion, a change in ontological status that can exercise a formidable imposition of force. The implicit experience of the agents may thereby find itself transformed: the agents may have the impression that they are discovering the truth of their lived experience in an explication which is, however, not the implicit experience in which they were living.

This is what I call *allodoxia*, which is when we are mistaken in our object of study. This is possible because of the fact that the implicit is liable to have several explanations: there is some indeterminacy linked to the approximate nature of the habitus, which is not the product of a precise rule, but is always 'roughly' adjusted. This practical indeterminacy of the practical standpoints renders them vulnerable to enforced explication; for an explication to succeed, the person made explicit needs to recognise themselves in the explication: you can't say just any old thing. This is what Max Weber shows when he speaks of affinities between the great religious traditions and some social group or other:[8] the peasant religions have a lot to do with a sort of paganism and with the feeling of impotence of the traditional peasant, and we will find it difficult to preach a religion that would be very suitable for a Confucian bureaucrat to a traditional peasant. That said, the margin of tolerance is such that it might well work. It is really important to see that this passage from the implicit to the explicit is determined, but at the same time there is a margin of freedom, tolerance and indeterminacy that allows allodoxical explications, especially in politics.

I take the rather crude example of the permanent debate over the political opinions of the dominated, in particular the manual workers, the working classes: how can we explain that, in different conjunctures, the same workers can identify either with messages of a materialist, communist type, or with fascistic, nationalist ones? It is simply that the same practical experience (with variants) is open to relatively different explications. This empowers the specific producers of discursive representations of the social world: they have the power to transform practical constructions, to represent them (the word 'representation' is crucial). In fact, the professionals have the monopoly of representation and of the passage to the explicit, which is the passage to representation in every sense of the term. This relative autonomy of representation in relation to practical experience is then the Archimedean point starting from which and pressing on which we can apply the political leverage.

I should qualify what I have just said, for fear that you might see my analysis as a Machiavellian representation of politics ('All representers

180   *Lecture of 12 June 1986*

are wicked') and think that these people use their power of explication of the implicit experience of the social world entirely for their own benefit. This is partly true, but the leap from the implicit to the explicit is so perilous that they really have no need to deliberately traduce it in order to misrepresent it. It is so difficult to explicate practical experiences . . . I think that the work of explication is the equivalent of giving birth for Socrates; or even more difficult. The good sociologist bases his work on indices provided by the discourse of his respondents, but the discourse used by individuals to describe themselves is nearly always an alienated discourse [that is, already explicated by others].[9] There is no literature less working class than the literature written by workers. It is the same thing with writings on the primary school written by émigrés from the lower classes who have tried their luck in Paris and then returned to their country village to launch into populism, having failed to succeed on the Left Bank.[10] This literature, extracts from which are destined to be collected in primary school anthologies, has marked our public consciousness. Sociologists note it down naively, thinking that they are recording popular experience, when in fact they are recording the populist discourse reformulated by popular experience in response to a populist sociologist hoping to discover the truth of popular experience [*laughter*]. (But if I say that, people are going to say that I'm the one who is prejudiced. . ..)

The distortion [between the implicit and its explicated version] is therefore self-evident. What is not self-evident is the genuine miracle of true explication, for it is a considerable undertaking to help people, without forcing them, to find the means to say precisely what they are unable to say because they don't have the words to say it with, and the words that we supply them with are often words taken from outside their experience. All the language that is readily available, like the sets of adjectives which I often use, is constructed in ignorance of what really ought to be said. This is an important point: the distortion is not the result of disrespect or ill will, but of the most powerful social mechanisms, in particular the mechanisms of misrecognition. 'Misrecognition' is not the right word (I'm trying to think of a better one . . . you could try, too). That said, perhaps all the words used to express what I am trying to say are wrong: they express the relation of the people who produce them to their object rather than the object in question. 'False consciousness', for instance, is a myth: it supposes that there is a [true] consciousness; it supposes a theory of revolutionary consciousness; it supposes the awakening of consciousness and therefore ultimately intellectuals who will bring consciousness to those who do not possess it. This is a typical intello-centric bias: it supposes that

Lecture of 12 June 1986 181

there are some people who are unconscious and others who will bring them consciousness.

What happens in this alchemical passage from the implicit to the explicit is very obscure, and both parties contribute to the mystification. In this encounter between two habitus, one important element of the mystification is the non-analysed habitus of the analyst: whether the analyst going to meet the people (which is his mission) is driven by populist nostalgia, an émigré's guilty conscience or an outburst of goodwill, his work of explication will in any case express his relation to this object much more than the object itself, and will thereby encourage allodoxical effects. The strategies of condescendence that I often evoke[11] are thus the source of many sociological errors. There are ways of speaking of the dominated (women, peasants, workers, etc.) that are very difficult to avoid for those who are subjected to this condescendence because they signal such good intentions [*laughter*]. I wanted to say this so as not to pass too quickly over something central to scientific practice, the interview being one of the fundamental operations of social science (but the point may also affect the way we read and analyse documents).

The specialised fields are places where constructions of the social world that have the particular force of the explicit are produced: since the explicit is there, and spelt out in words, we end up thinking that we are living what we are meant to be living because someone has said it, and said it with authority. I remember (and I repeat it once more in an attempt to get people to understand it) that when I read some phenomenological analysis by Sartre, I always felt that it was formidably intelligent. It was so well expressed that you said: 'Well, yes, that is how I experience life.' You did have the vague feeling that it wasn't really quite like that, that you had never experienced an emotion in the way that Sartre described it, but the description was so powerful that it could overcome what Sartre himself called the absolutely arbitrary 'Certainty'[12] that I had really experienced. He could then explain away the famous lived experience that he was supposedly making explicit. The fact that sociologists and ethnologists receive the approval of their respondents does not mean that they are right. Nor, moreover, does the fact that they are disapproved mean that they are wrong, for in fact the populist argument that the people have the right to invent their own definition is absurd. For instance, we find it is a classic reaction in fully colonised countries to say, in the name of a mysterious participatory experience, that only the natives can analyse their societies. You see: we tread on ground where the political stakes constantly threaten to overwhelm the cognitive imperatives. In fact all these (perhaps rather

182   *Lecture of 12 June 1986*

long-drawn-out) analyses do at least have the advantage of illustrating
the imbrication of the cognitive and the political in the social world.

The specificity of the scientific field

In the struggle for the legitimate knowledge of the social world, which
is always one dimension of any political conflict, explicit and implicit
experience, the discursive and the infra-discursive, confront each other,
with the discursive benefiting from the specific force of revelation or
consecration. In this space, the law has a particular position because
it is invested with all the properties that I have attributed to discourse,
in particular the self-verification effect gained by discourse when faced
with something implicit. This self-fulfilment effect is multiplied in
the case of the legal discourse, since it is accompanied by constraint
(the verdict is a discourse that will be executed, that is, accomplished
and verified). At the same time, I should remind you once more of
the fundamental axiom that I announced at the start of this lecture
(I mention it because you might think of this objection yourselves): the
legal discourse, which is the supreme example of symbolic efficacy in
any discourse, can only be verified insofar as it consecrates something
that pre-exists it. This is the debate on morality and the law. The legal
discourse is verifiable insofar as it proclaims what will be proclaimed,
insofar as it imposes something that is self-evident.

I haven't said what I wanted to say today at all [*laughter*], but there
is one last point that I do want to make. Political struggles concerning the social world tend to take two very different forms depending
on whether the struggles are practical issues for the habitus, such as
the cognitive manoeuvres of the kind involving the schoolmistress,
or theoretical struggles in a scholarly field, where one of the most
important scientific and political questions is how the correspondence
between the autonomous (legal, scientific or political) spaces and the
social space is established. I merely raise the question.

In conclusion, I would like to indicate a problem (which is in fact
the essence of what I would have liked to say today. . .) that I'll try
to return to next time. My analysis may have lost sight of one thing,
which is the specificity of the scientific field.[13] This question is no doubt
legitimate, but it is interested. We should always suspect ourselves.
Might it be precisely because we belong to a field that we want to make
an exception of it and treat it differently? Don't we run the risk of being
the victims of an official representation of the scientific field and the
professional ideology that it produces?

Lecture of 12 June 1986   183

Having admitted this suspicion as a caveat, we can now ask ourselves whether the general laws of the fields that we have discovered so far are valid for the scientific field. Is the scientific field the site of a struggle to impose a truth, where everybody wields the force that corresponds to their position in the balance of power? Do these laws apply to the scientific field, and, if this is the case, is it not self-destructive or at least paradoxical to have announced everything I have so far as if it were gospel truth? In other words, if social science follows its logic through to the end (which is to proceed to analyse the social universe in which it is produced), does it not ruin itself as a science? Can the sociologists, who are the most vulnerable to this relativist or historicist counter-attack, carry their analysis of the scholarly social fields through without destroying the very foundations of their claim to establish a scholarly discourse? This is obviously a very old problem, which has exercised the minds of many final-year pupils. Today from time to time the press pick up this problem as the last word in philosophical thinking, although it was all formulated in the 1880s by Marx (who is obviously attacked in this kind of analysis).

Finally, I would like to try to formulate the problem more clearly. I might express it in these terms: does the logic of the mechanisms producing the social truths and challenges of the particular struggles that we call 'scientific', that is, those oriented towards the production of the truth of the social world, contradict the claim of the agents engaged in this struggle to express the truth? Or are there particular social conditions [. . .] in which the very logic of the game tends to enable social agents to transcend the social limits ascribed to the social conditions of production of discourse on the world? I shall return to this next week.

Second session (seminar): the field of power (3)

[. . .] I shall now attempt to recapitulate what I have been saying during the previous sessions about the field of power, and try to put some order into the argument before taking it further. I have said that I was calling 'the field of power' a field of forces involving agents of institutions holding different powers or different species of capital, and that this field of forces was at the same time a field of struggles to transform the balance of power instituted in the field, these being struggles between the holders of different powers to gain the upper hand. What are the limits of these fields and how are they constructed? There is no absolutely universal, theoretical answer to this entirely legitimate question. It is up to historical research to determine in each

184   *Lecture of 12 June 1986*

case what belongs to a field or doesn't, and whether its limits are clearly traced or not. One of the virtues of a theoretical schema is precisely to propose a set of systematic questions about reality, and above all about extremely different realities.

The *numerus clausus* that I mentioned last time involves precisely this question of limits. As we can see, it appears only in certain critical states of the struggles within a field. Resorting to the *numerus clausus* (sometimes I stick my neck out but, believe me, I know when I am doing it . . . I think I have had my fair share of hesitation and remorse, so you can take my word for it) is a sign of crisis and weakness, in the sense that a field of power is normally preoccupied with the reproduction of its own existence. Almost by definition, a field of power is organised to work at its own reproduction. Which means that, in a successful field of power – a field of power in the organic state as Auguste Comte[14] would have said – the question of the *numerus clausus* need not arise: the mechanisms of reproduction there are such that there is no problem of a mismatch – no problem of illegal access to the practice of medicine, for instance, or no problem of intrusion by people whose properties are unsuitable, etc. The *numerus clausus* is an explicit juridical resort, which is an admission of weakness in a way, since it is declared, whereas, if you have followed my argument in the previous lectures, you will understand that what we might call the automatic mechanisms of reproduction, such as the educational system, are much more powerful since they do what they have to do but in a manner that prevents us from seeing that they are doing it – the very operation of reproduction goes unchallenged because it is not even noticed. As I said last time, the manner of reproduction of the educational system, in its euphoric and triumphal phase (before the emergence of the specific contradictions typified, I believe, in the events of May '68), has precisely this property of being an 'ideological' mechanism while disguising the fact that it fulfils this function, or fulfils it in such a way that these things do not impinge on our consciousness.

One weakness of all theories of ideology, not least that of Marx and his followers, is their tendency to describe the mechanisms of domination as being oriented in some way by the will: there is always a kind of purposiveness or teleology, individual or collective. They think of the reproduction of the established order as a product of the will oriented towards reproduction, whose supreme form would be publicity or propaganda. There is a whole genre of simplistic denunciation which has every sign of progressive virtue but which in fact is extremely naive, and leaves the essential untouched. Analysing this critically, we could go so far as to describe it as a kind of complicity, because if you

Lecture of 12 June 1986   185

mount a strong attack on something that has very little presence, while remaining silent over something that has a much more powerful presence, you divert people's attention away from the latter, and this really is how to fulfil an ideological function.

There are many indignant rebuttals like this, and they have become something of a speciality for intellectuals: lacking insight into these obscure mechanisms, they don't just fail to illuminate them, they plunge them into deeper obscurity. The case of the educational system is typical, precisely because it concerns one of those mechanisms whose efficacy goes partly unnoticed due to the fact that it can only be grasped at the level of statistical aggregations and it escapes indigenous intuition: everyone will know a concierge's daughter who is enrolled at Polytechnique – the probability must be very slight, but if you look hard enough you are bound to find one. These are examples that are opposed to scientific analysis: I could give you terrible examples of analyses perceived as refutations of the statistical analyses that show the correlation between social origins and academic success!

One property of the mode of reproduction that I mentioned last time – which I refer to as 'having an educational component', where the educational system plays a very important part – is that it is a statistical mode of reproduction: it does not reproduce the son of the king mechanically, it reproduces one of the sons of the king statistically; it is not the king who chooses him, etc. The relation between the generations, between the titular heads and their successors, then, is a statistical relation, and not the kind of mechanical relation that you would see blatantly in the case of a transmission of power through the right of primogeniture. (In such cases, the apparently very enlightened minds of the followers of the Frankfurt school, who are ruthless critics of modern society, fail to notice the more profound mechanisms, those that function silently in an implicit state; yet we can clearly see that explication does nonetheless reveal things hitherto completely unnoticed. I rest my case.)

Boundaries of the fields and right of entry

A field, then, has limits. However, the question of limits is more or less of an issue depending on the field and the state of the field. When it has to call for explicit, patent juridical interventions, I think this shows that the successful, normally invisible mechanisms of reproduction are no longer fulfilling their function. In a way, resorting to the *numerus clausus* is an admission of weakness, above all in societies

186 *Lecture of 12 June 1986*

that proclaim the values of equality and democracy, since the *numerus clausus* announces a drive to reproduce that can only assert itself tacitly, as something self-evident, as opposed to the notion of 'equal opportunities' for instance: equal opportunity being almost a founding value, announcing an authoritarian limitation of opportunity is a sort of contradiction.

Be that as it may, the question of limits cannot be raised *a priori*. It is contentious, and the limits – usually statistical – beyond which the force of a field ceases to take effect can in certain circumstances become designated boundaries, that is, juridical acts, for the boundaries are an arbitrary division in a *continuum*: they draw a line that separates what is inside from what is outside. I am sure that I have already said this,[15] but in the case of social boundaries it may be of interest to recall a comic example. The humourist Alphonse Allais made fun of the problem of boundaries: 'Imagine a father pulling the alarm cord on the train to declare that his son had just had his third birthday and ought to pay a supplement because he had benefited from a reduction for children under three!'[16] There are similar jokes about baggage weighing more or less than 30 kilos: it is obvious that the juridical act establishes arbitrary boundaries whose function is precisely to avoid conflict over boundaries and limits. This brings me to what I was saying about the habitus: in the absence of an explicitly fixed limit, the customs officer will judge a habitus. If he is in a bad mood, he will say: '29.85 kilos: you have to pay'; if he is in a good mood, he will let you through with 32 kilos. This mode of operation generates conflict. It is fine in societies that have time to haggle and in civilisations that can function in terms of the habitus. In fact we ought really to study the link between forms of society and their degree of codification. The role of the law is universally to erect clear, decisive, unequivocal and universal boundaries, leaving no latitude for dispute.

Depending on the field, it may happen that its boundaries are established. For instance, when the field of the medical professions experiences some crisis, there are, as I mentioned last time, debates to decide whether, for instance, delivering anaesthetic is a medical act or not. In the case of the juridical field, there are debates over which category of legal official can accomplish which category of legal act. These problems can be studied historically. Studying the theoretical model, we find that what is at issue in every field is the reproduction of the field, which is often connected with access to the field. For instance, the right of entry to the artistic field is less juridically controlled than the right of entry to the academic field. The academic field is quite strongly controlled by legal texts and academic diplomas, etc. Unlike

Lecture of 12 June 1986 187

the field of business, the artistic field does not require entrants to have economic capital or inheritance – which explains some of the artistic changes in the nineteenth century[17] – and unlike the administrative field, it does not require as a condition of entry any diploma or (as in the days when the administrative field was less dependent on educational codification than it is today) patronage, favour or the protection of a senior member. The academic field, earlier than the other fields, required statutory qualifications. The field that retained open entry was the artistic field: you could enter it without diplomas or qualifications.

As soon as you make a study, like those of Ponton or Charle,[18] say, comparing the presence of diplomas in different milieux, you notice that the artistic and literary field is characterised by its weak overall possession of educational capital. The lax entry requirements of this universe make it liable to overflow. It is a universe where imposing a *numerus clausus* is out of the question: everybody can enter, including women and Jews, for instance. Even in the most segregated societies, it is one of the places where Jews have been able to enter, which helps to explain the over-representation of Jews in these universes. Since entry is not restricted, the effects of the surplus production of graduates of secondary education will have an immediate impact, and one of the most powerful factors of transformation in the artistic field is the purely morphological effect of the growth in the number of (artistic or literary) producers, because not only are the peaks in surplus production not restrained, but the artistic field serves as a sort of refuge for all the surplus production! This point, which is important for understanding the evolution of the literary field, is always forgotten in traditional literary histories, because it is difficult to delineate (it requires very complicated statistical work), but also for ideological reasons: we prefer not to know this sort of thing: it threatens our sublimated image of the artist and the artistic life. I could go further, but I shall leave it at that.

I think that these two or three examples, presented as a digression, will have shown you how we might use the notion of the field to help us think about the problem of boundaries. Afterwards, we might consider the means that the different fields use in order to regulate their boundaries. Agents may act as gate-keepers to control the boundaries in formal fashion, like customs officers charging a tariff on entry, but there can be much more subtle forms of exclusion and elimination: who then takes on this role? Is it publishers, gallery owners. . .? So we have a set of questions, and these general questions become specific by definition when we work empirically.

The example of the literary field

As I was saying, the field of power is the sort of construction that you are obliged to posit in order to understand a certain number of phenomena. I should perhaps have admitted at the outset, in order to help you understand, that I had been led to think along those lines as I worked on the literary field, or more precisely, on the emergence of an autonomous literary field and, even more precisely, within this autonomous literary field, on the defenders of art for art's sake, that is, the writers who took as the very principle of their existence their autonomy from the outside world. It very soon appeared to me that this autonomy was not, as the artists believed, autonomy from the social world as a whole, but rather autonomy from that universe where the artists evolved, which we normally call the dominant class, but which – as I said last time – I prefer to call the field of power. I have been led to speak of the field of power in order to explain a major property of the artistic field and of those who are engaged in it. You cannot understand this property if you do not resituate the artistic field within the field of power. The point is that the artists are agents who collaborate in their own domination – who have power, but in a dominated position.

Let me start my explanation by showing you a little diagram [*Bourdieu draws the following diagram on the board*]:

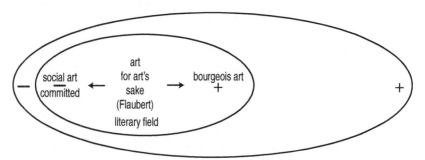

I have drawn the limits of the fields but, as I have just said, they are subject to debate. To simplify, a literary or artistic field comprises the dominant and the dominated, and people defending 'art for art's sake', who are in a central position, neither dominant nor dominated. People like Flaubert, for instance, occupy this central position: they define themselves both against what they call 'bourgeois art' ('bourgeois drama', etc.) and against social or committed art. They want to oppose both camps at once.

Lecture of 12 June 1986 189

But a certain number of the fundamental properties of the writers cannot be understood at the level of this space, which is itself enclosed within the greater space that I have called the field of power and which itself contains both dominant and dominated positions, the whole ensemble of the artistic or literary field being situated in a dominated position within the field of power. [. . .] Clearly, we have to imagine a space even greater than the field of power, the social space, with a high and a low, a plus (+) and a minus (-), the field of power being situated in the dominant positions of the social space as a whole.

This diagram, like all diagrams, is dangerously simplistic, but if you keep it in mind you will better understand the ensemble of what I am trying to say, which is why I have decided to show it to you. It enables us for instance to understand a problem that I referred to this morning: the people who explicate the experiences of people who are placed here [*Bourdieu shows positions in the social space*], or claim to do so. It is simple: when they speak of this [*positions in the social space*], are they not essentially speaking of that [*positions in their own field*]? What I was saying just now in the abstract becomes concrete: when he speaks of the workers, is Leroux not speaking of his relation to Flaubert? Under the guise of speaking of [*Bourdieu points out a position in the social space*], is Zola not speaking of his relation to Mallarmé or some other Symbolist poet? Which does not mean that he is not also speaking of these [*in the position designated on the diagram*] or for them (with all the ambiguity of the word 'for'. . .).

This kind of diagram leads us to wonder what are the mediating forces that establish this relation – which is the only one they invoke. The spokesmen direct the attention of the analyst, the observer or their rival towards their direct relation with those whose speech they record, those spoken for; whereas in fact it is the relation between the spokesmen that is the real mediation or screen between the spokesmen and those spoken for; and the spokesman speaks more or less – here again there is no general rule, but a general question about this relation – the spokesman can always be asked how much of his discourse is determined by his relation to other spokesmen, although he steadfastly claims that his discourse is determined solely by his relation to his questioners. I think that it was useful to give you the diagram to help you to understand what I am saying.

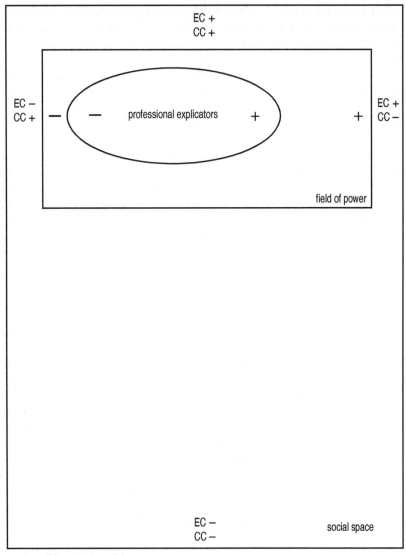

EC economic capital
CC cultural capital

Flow of capital and variations in the exchange rate

The field of power, then, is that space where the holders of different species of capital confront each other, one of the goals of the confronta-

Lecture of 12 June 1986   191

tion being to determine the hierarchy among these conflicting forces. Although the metaphor is slightly risky, we might say that at every moment the different species of capital are in a balance of power. For instance, in the field of power today, economic capital is the dominant species of capital. Among the indicators we dispose of to try to define the hierarchy among the species of capital, or the hierarchy among the fields founded on the primacy of one or other species of capital, there are the movements, that is, the flow from one field to another: say, for example, someone who during their lifetime passes from the university field to the administrative field, from the administrative field to the political field, and from the political field to the business field. These flows are indicators and we may suppose that the social agents concerned indicate the dominant pole through their displacements (they emigrate towards the dominant pole). Here things are simple: we put the business field and the economic field at the + pole and the intellectual and artistic field at the - pole. Another statistical indicator is to be found in intermarriages: the circulation of women follows the same directions and gives the same hierarchy of fields as the circulation of the men during their careers. At a certain moment, then, there is between the different species of capital a sort of exchange rate that defines the structure of the balance of power between holders of the different species of capital.

One of the goals of the struggle within the field of power is to change these exchange rates. For instance, a petition of the type 'Ten eminent scientists mount a protest in defence of. . .' is a struggle to raise the exchange rate of scientific capital against measures which aim overall to lower it structurally, by using political and administrative power. When, for instance, we read in the history books of a 'Republic of the professors',[19] it means that, structurally, the exchange rate of cultural capital is rising: in the struggles within the dominant class, the same quantity of cultural capital enables you to obtain more than the previous generation would have obtained. This internal structure of the field of power is then a state of the balance of power between the holders of different species of capital which, themselves, govern the struggles destined to transform them. This struggle to impose the dominant species of capital (or to revalue a species of capital) may be deduced from what I was describing just now: it assumes the guise of an effort to change the representation of the different forms of capital, which leads us back to what I was discussing last time on the sociodicy of privilege and the legitimate reasons for domination, which are the very essence of the internal political debates of the dominant class.

For the nineteenth century, for instance, Charle describes at length the struggle to codify access to the senior civil service,[20] that is, to replace

192 *Lecture of 12 June 1986*

the extremely antiquated modes of transmission of charges, inherited from the monarchy (with forms of patronage or quasi-succession, etc.), with codified forms, mediated by examinations and competitions perceived as legitimate. This struggle divided people according to the properties they possessed. To take a simple example – Charle's very fine analysis illustrates perfectly what I was saying just now: the people who were struggling to introduce competitive examinations and bureaucratic forms of selection were themselves characterised by an ensemble of properties that distinguished them from the other members of the dominant class. They were more Protestant, had more universally recognised diplomas, were more progressively inclined by their origins, etc. In other words, we find here a typical illustration of what I was saying just now: the standpoints adopted in a field with a view to changing the power relations in that field are determined by the position held in the balance of power that constitutes the field in question. The people who took up the position, at more or less the same time, for the creation of Sciences Po[21] had very different qualities: they tended to be more provincial, Catholic and conservative . . . Obviously, in these struggles within the field of power, not everybody is mobilised directly. The people who were fighting for the introduction of the competitive examination and those who were fighting at the same time to set up Sciences Po may never have met each other. And yet their action only makes sense if we consider the whole of the space on which they wanted to act.

(What I am presenting you with here is slightly mad. I was going to say that it is subjectively the pinnacle of my intellectual effort: it is my most risky and difficult enterprise. It contradicts common intuition, which is at once very close to it and far from it, and I run some risk of appearing at once dogmatic and unrealistic. I think that if we developed the argument completely, we could give quite a luminous explanation of a lot of things that would otherwise be dispersed, incoherent and hopelessly muddled . . . I am obliged to say this so as not to feel too upset by what this makes me feel. . ..)

Establishing a new mode of reproduction

The field of power, then, is the sort of thing that we have to construct if we want to understand phenomena like the one I have just described (which is, as you will see, most abstract and absurd, but at the same time it does enable us to understand something very fundamental). I was referring to the struggles to set up new schools: between 1880

Lecture of 12 June 1986 193

and 1900 there was quite an effort in the field of power to transfer the dominant mode of reproduction away from the family model (with transmission of patrimony, etc.) towards establishing a new mode of reproduction in which the educational system, with its statistical logic, becomes the principal intermediary between generations (when I say 'effort . . . to' it is purposive and quite false, I should say 'effort whose objective result was to. . .', but my sentences are awkward enough already. . .). The motives for constructing this new mode of reproduction were not neutral, since the different agents engaged in the field of power had unequal interests in this new mode of reproduction. The supporters of Sciences Po [political science], Centrale, Polytechnique [both for engineers] or the École normale were extremely different and didn't share the same interests in this enterprise. Furthermore, at a second degree, they had very unequal interests in the different educational qualifications. For instance – you can check this very easily today through a study of the *grandes écoles*[22] – the different members of the dominant class, defined in the terms I have suggested, have very unequal interests in the different institutions of higher education. To simplify: what is objectively required and objectively offered by the Polytechnique or the École normale is very different from what you get at HEC or Sciences Po.

The specifically educational filter, which is the academic field, imposes its specific law unequally, depending on the sector. The more you move away from Ulm-science [science at the École normale] towards HEC [business studies at Hautes Études commerciales], the more the specificity of this filter diminishes. This means that those who have the greatest interest in the full application of the specificity of the educational system – that is, the professors, nowadays the science professors – have a much greater interest in reinforcing the sector of the educational system that tends to favour their reproduction, whereas those who, having less educational capital, and especially educational capital with a specifically scientific dimension, will have a much greater interest in reinforcing the other pole of the field, that is, Sciences Po and the ENA [École nationale d'administration, forming senior civil servants]. Now something that may seem very abstract as we see it today can be seen at work historically when we study the people who worked to reinforce, on the one hand, the importance of educational criteria among the conditions of reproduction and, on the other hand, the differential in the educational system between the most and the least academic. People like [Émile] Boutmy, who backed the creation of Sciences Po, are distinguished in a lot of aspects from those who supported the reinforcement of the scientific type of school. They relate

194 *Lecture of 12 June 1986*

to each other in the same ways that the institutions that they support relate to each other.

This is not all . . . One of the most mysterious things in the social order as we see it today is that it all seems to happen as if there were a space of dominant positions, a space of fields, with, from the dominant on the right to the dominated on the left, the business field, the administrative field, the academic field and then the intellectual and artistic field. And it all seems to happen as if the field – whose global structure is linked to the relative value in the balance of power of the corresponding species of capital – found its reproductive process through the mediation of a homologous field of educational institutions. In other terms, what is reproductive is not one *école* or the other (it is not the École normale that reproduces professors, the École polytechnique engineers or Centrale managers. . . although this is not entirely false, because we can find significantly high percentages there. . .), but the homology between two systems of differences.

One problem is how this works concretely in terms of a logic of individual choices (this kind of structural model does not prevent us from understanding how the agents function, far from it). It provides the system of constraints within which the social agents, who are not atomic particles, follow certain pathways. They will pass written and oral examinations, they will fare well or badly, they may do well in the written tests and badly in the orals, they will be attracted by this or that, they will feel a vocation for Sciences Po or the ENA, they will be rejected by Sciences Po and have to settle for a law degree, etc. There will then be a series of social constructions, transactions or negotiations, as I said just now (an examination, even a written examination, is a negotiation: there is a *captatio benevolentiae*, a 'display of goods', with 'inflation', 'bluff' and 'deflation', etc.). The agents concerned on both sides will engage in this work (they will attribute marks, that is, market prices, etc.), while obviously being unaware of these structures (I would need many hours to articulate these structures explicitly). They will act in a way as if they were activating this structure.

Maxwell's demon

Physicists invoke Maxwell's famous demon to answer the question: 'Why is it that the hottest particles go to one side. . .?' This is how the educational system works.[23] It all happens as if, when we look at the overall picture, the individual agents, being children of one or another social origin, come to face this space of institutions with a perception of the space that is itself structured by the position they hold in the space and that predisposes them to perceive one thing rather than another, and to not even see certain institutions, which nevertheless exist. The son of a mathematics professor has very little chance of seeing HEC (or, if he does see it, he will see it as the smallest of business schools). Social agents come to confront this universe with their inertia or impetus and their *conatus*, linked to the position and trajectory of their whole family, which is a kind of springboard from which to leap further, or to fall. They will be selected, or rather ('being selected' is too passive) they will select themselves (in the case of their vocation) and be selected (in the case of co-optation), with both operations, self-selecting and being selected, functioning according to the intuitions of the habitus. Thus in examinations, not to mention competitive examinations and co-optation, the sympathy of the habitus plays a major part. The agents will be recruited in such a way that at the end of the day it all happens as if the global structure of the dominant positions had found its reproduction through the mediation of a structure homologous with the educational institutions.

To continue, and to return to the analogy of Maxwell's demon: this truly astonishing system has the effect of bringing together in the *écoles* people who have much in common. It all happens as if the principle of this sort of selection (and it is here that the image of Maxwell's demon is important) were a kind of mechanism or process (I find this very difficult to express, I keep feeling that I should find other words to describe it) intended to make us believe that the process is designed to bring together as many people as possible having as much in common as possible: sharing the same tastes in painting and music and a very strong probability of having the same political opinions, etc. There is a system of differences – you will always hear: 'The Polytechnician compares to the HEC man as the. . .' – with all its side effects, for instance the extraordinary effect of socialisation exercised by the *grandes écoles*: they create lifelong affinities, friendships (and marriages, now that they are mixed) and social and other connections. After graduating from a *grande école*, these people will never again find a universe where they will have at their side so many people with whom they have so much in common, without having had to ask or even feel the need. I am not making this up; it has been investigated and analysed. These people have never asked themselves: 'Was my room mate[24] or my fencing partner (depending on the *école*) the son of this or that family, did he share my religious beliefs or not?' If this kind of question can be completely blindsided and erased, it is in particular because the whole process is the product of a whole set of mechanisms. The strength of

196 *Lecture of 12 June 1986*

the unconscious attractions and co-optations is multiplied precisely by the fact that they are unconscious. They are unchosen elective affinities, whence that kind of feeling of a paradise lost that is so striking in the reminiscences of old boys of the Écoles normales or the École polytechnique ('The best years of my life!'). . . It is a Rousseauist social world, a world without resistance or asperity, since these people have the greatest number of things in common – with just enough differences, of course, to avoid noticing that they have everything in common.

This is what I wanted to say, what I find most important, but in order to reach this point I have had to pass through all the mediations. Let me say once again that I have not done so from a feeling of rampant scepticism in my audience, but rather, following a somewhat irrational strategy, I have launched into the most troubled waters in order to try to be a bit more convincing. So be it. Next time, I shall try once again to go back over . . . because I had promised myself that I would feel free more than ever in these second sessions [of my course] not to follow a linear sequence.

Lecture of 19 June 1986

Practical struggles and struggles among theoreticians – The struggles of the professional explicators – Science of science and relativism – Science as a social field – A rationalist relativism – The vulnerability of social science – The Gerschenkron effect – The problem of the existence of social classes – 'Class': a well-constructed fiction – Constructed classes and infra-representational classes – The constructivist phase

Practical struggles and struggles among theoreticians

I shall extend this last lecture over two hours in order to give a certain unity and closure to what I have been saying this year. I shall attempt to approach on the one hand the problem of the specificity of the scientific field and on the other hand [. . .] the problem of the clash of perspectives between structuralists and constructivists over the absolutely central problem of the social classes.

First of all I would like to pick up what I was saying last time. I was distinguishing between two types of struggle: practical struggles, which do not necessarily involve a representation of the aims and objects or the circumstances of the struggles, and struggles which are grounded in an explicit, objective position. This distinction corresponds, by and large, to the opposition between the struggles that are played out in the specialised fields of cultural production and those that are at play in our ordinary, everyday existence in the social field as a whole. As I also said, the struggles may take an individual or a collective form: I shall return to this distinction when I come to deal with the problem of the social classes.

What I wanted to point out was the fact that the practical character of our everyday struggles entails a number of consequences affecting

198 *Lecture of 19 June 1986*

the analysis that we can subject them to. I think that all those who have taken an interest in these everyday struggles, in particular the interactionists and the ethnomethodologists, who have acted as the sociologists of everyday life, make a similar mistake. Setting themselves the aim of creating a sociology of our everyday life and experience of the social world, they could not help seeing the strategies, struggles, conflicts and bluffs, in short, all the practices intended among other things to inflate the subjective image or, as Goffman says, to present the self in a particularly favourable light.[1]

The basic mistake that they seem to me to have made is to have presented practical struggles as if they were conscious strategies and intentional struggles. This mistake arises from ignorance of the distinction between what is practical and what is theoretical (or represented). Those who make this mistake tend to locate in the conscious minds of the agents something that is in fact produced by the argument the analyst uses to explain the agents' practices. I have often pointed out this fundamental anthropological error. Researchers in the social sciences wanting to give a reason – as they said in the seventeenth century – for practices must produce a scientific construction or at least a discursive argument designed to render intelligible practices that are not necessarily intelligible even to themselves. An error almost automatically inherent in scientific practice is to forget that these constructions are produced by the scientists themselves, and to constitute them as objective explicative principles, turning what are innate practices into a determining anthropological principle, one devised by the scholar in order to explain the practices.

So we need to distinguish between everyday struggles and the struggles as they unfold in the field of the professionals, which includes the professionals and their analyses. The professionals of explication paradoxically overlook their own work of explication. Which is why I insisted last time on what is, when you come to think of it, the rather extraordinary character of the work of making explicit: the analytic process forces a kind of transmutation on what it is analysing. Paradoxically, in their theory of ordinary experience the analysts ignore what is the ordinary substance of their own experience, that is, theorising. When you live in a theoretical universe, a universe of discourse, however elementary, you forget to constitute discourse as an object of your discourse. This is an elementary paradox: to constitute practice, you have to constitute it as non-theoretical, that is, as non-discursive, non-reflexive. And this is the same process that makes us discover practice as practice and theory as theory.

Lecture of 19 June 1986 199

This particular practice, which is the practice of the agents of reflection [who are the professionals of reflection], we might say, must be constituted as such in order to avoid operating that kind of projection which, moreover, is inspired by a sort of humanist good will and generosity (intellectuals often think that there is no action nobler than thinking of others in their own image): they are positing this relation to practice that is excluded from practice and making a gift of it to the agents involved in the practice. This gift seems to me to generate major theoretical errors and prevents people from raising the most fundamental issue of social science and social life, the problem of the passage from the implicit to the explicit, which is the problem of politics in particular, but one which only exists, it seems to me, if you over-emphasise the gap between practice and theory.

The struggles of the professional explicators

I said just now that the opposition between practical struggles and theoretical struggles corresponded 'by and large' to the opposition between ordinary action in the social field and the specific activity that is at work in the professional fields. I say 'by and large'; it is obvious that there is not a sort of initiatory break between ordinary agents unable to think or analyse, lacking reflexive resources, and scholars who would be reflexive through and through. One reason, as I have just said, is that the scholars do not reflect on the social conditions of their reflection and the whole set of practical and theoretical presumptions involved in holding a theoretical attitude.

To speak of 'theoretical practice' as the Althusserians did[2] is to resort to a terrible expression which disguises everything I have been trying to make explicit. It had the success of all those slogans like Gramsci's 'organic intellectual' or Mannheim's 'unattached, rootless intellectual'[3] which express the professional ideology of the intellectual. These slogans for self-satisfied intellectuals immediately scored a considerable success, whereas the analyses that I attempt to offer are disagreeable for those who are their object (as I can tell from the social effects that they produce), and they are immediately turned back against their author, suspected of forgetting that he is himself the object of these analyses (as if that were possible. . .). In short, the specialised social fields are the site of a rather peculiar practice, which has an unconscious mind of its own. That said, if the fundamental law of these fields is to raise to the level of discourse practices, thoughts and relations with the world that others leave in a practical state, this

200 *Lecture of 19 June 1986*

does not mean that agents outside these fields don't have 'thoughts'; as I ceaselessly repeat, non-discursive thoughts may in certain circumstances have a specific efficacy infinitely greater than thoughtful thoughts.

The universes of the specific production of discourse in the different fields of cultural production (religious, philosophical, legal, political and scientific, and so on) are therefore so many worlds in which the meaning of being in the world is explicitly debated. They propose learned visions of the world, often claiming to be coherent systems, whether this be the approximate coherence of religious and legal systems, or the provisional coherence of scientific systems. These universes that propose visions of the world claiming coherence, which are in any case tributary to a regime of permanent explication and discursive debate, are multiple: they are not a universe but a multiverse (I think that this is very important). And if we wanted to pass a normative judgement, we might say that the dominated – those who, among all the agents who are not professional explicators, are the most lacking in explicative resources and the social conditions that empower explication – may in fact find opportunities in the multiplicity of fields of cultural production and the existence of contradictions, or at least tensions, between these fields.

As I shall not return later to the field of power, I will at least add a word now to conclude one of the arguments I was pursuing. The field of power as I have defined it is a site of confrontation between the agents who dominate the various fields of cultural production. It is a site both of objective tensions and explicit struggles between the different fields and those who dominate them. The notion of a field of power has the function in particular of clearly displaying one of the effects of analysing society in terms of fields: it reveals the fact that inside the social world there exist autonomous spheres of existence, universes or worlds, and that these have different fundamental laws and systems of interest. Thus the notion enables us to understand one of the most important factors of historical change, which is the structural tensions between the different fields and the explicit struggles between the dominant agents of the different fields, in particular the dominant agents of the fields of cultural production. In certain states of the field of power, these struggles – between science and religion, between jurists and social scientists, etc. – may take the form of palace warfare. These struggles are extremely important: they are one of the factors transforming our vision of the world and can thereby help to transform the world, if the transformed visions of the world become social forces by becoming grand narratives capable of mobilising social groups.

Lecture of 19 June 1986 201

Another important effect of the division into fields, and of the rivalry arising from the confrontation of these fields, is to affect the way that intense struggles within each field can under certain conditions become synchronised, so to speak, with more general, practical struggles. Let me clarify this point, which is relatively important. It is an old problem of political theory, in particular in the Marxist tradition, to wonder whether the dominated can really access all the resources necessary for the raising of consciousness, to use the language of that tradition. It is, according to Kautsky's term I believe, the problem of 'consciousness from without':[4] where can this famous raising of consciousness (a fictitious notion that, as I have said, I do not believe in at all[5]) come from? How can the dominated access the resources for the raising of consciousness of their position in the social space? This question, which fascinates intellectuals and immediately stimulates intello-centrism, has provided the matter for endless discourse, and it is in this arena that we find all the ideologists that I mentioned just now, from Gramsci to Mannheim, via Sartre.

I think that the notion of field, and the idea that there exist autonomous fields with specific aims and a structure independent of the structure of the social field as a whole, enable us to formulate the problem in a realistic way. In fact a property common to the different fields is the way they tend to polarise, that is, to organise themselves according to a fundamental opposition between the holders of specific capital and those who possess less of it. Even if it assumes different forms in different fields, this opposition may be found as easily in the religious field as in the field of cultural production or the legal field, which shows that within these universes, which occupy dominant positions in the social space, there is still an opposition between the dominant and the dominated.

Thus, while there was a high and a low, a + and a - , in the social field in the little diagram that I drew in my last lecture, you could find, within the space situated in the dominant position of the social space seen as a whole, oppositions designated by a + and a - between the holders of capital and those lacking specific capital. I think you can see what I am getting at: it is something difficult to understand in traditional logic, in particular traditional Marxist logic which recognises only one form of capital and is unaware of the structural effects detected by the notion of the field; for instance the alliance that the intellectuals (as holders of a particular form of capital generating profits of a particular type) may strike up with the dispossessed. This paradoxical alliance between capitalists and the dispossessed is explained if we see that there are dominated positions subsisting within the dominant social universes.

202 *Lecture of 19 June 1986*

Alliances which are inexplicable if judged according to identities of condition can be understood if we judge according to homology of position: the intellectual and artistic fields as a whole occupy a dominated position within the field of power; the social agents concerned are, globally speaking, dominated dominators; they are the most dominated among the dominant, and all the more because they hold a dominated position in this globally dominated universe.

Now we can understand how those holding a dominated position in the dominant space may, under certain conditions and in certain circumstances, have at least a propensity (for obviously we are dealing with potential, stochastic [uncertain, arbitrary] laws, not with mechanist determinisms at all) to find themselves objectively inclined to sympathise with the dominated in general. In the light of this analysis, then, certain alliances are comprehensible and we become able to find a solution to the famous problem of the initial accumulation of cultural capital that is needed precisely in order to pass from practical struggles to theoretical struggles or struggles based on representation, which is an important issue for understanding the birth of the new forms of struggles that start to appear in industrial societies in the nineteenth century.

Science of science and relativism

These different fields of cultural production which share a common claim to universality (this is another of their properties: religions are universal, the law is a rational law, science is by definition universal, etc.), these universes which commonly proclaim themselves to be producers of truths – specific truths, maybe, but truths nonetheless – appear, at first, to be social universes that obey the general laws of social universes, which are organised according to power relations and animated by struggles tending to preserve or transform these power relations. The question that then arises is whether a social science that characterises the universes of production of truth as ordinary social universes does not itself fall into relativism: does it not annihilate its foundations and its ambition to constitute the other universes as objects of sociological knowledge? This proposition (which I may be formulating in a more explicit fashion than is customary) has generated a relentless and exhausting ongoing polemic against social science and sociology in particular, especially when the latter follows its work through to a conclusion and pushes objectification to the point of objectifying the professional objectifiers themselves. That is what sociology has taken care not to do and what I have attempted to do; this may be my historical contribution.

Try as you might, you will not find much of a sociology of the intellectual in Marx. In Durkheim there is none at all; in Weber there is a smattering.[6] The sociology of the intellectual, strangely, remains a sort of private game reserve which is always situated between the sociology and theory of knowledge and a sort of discreet self-praise for intellectual creators. Very often, for instance, the history of science or the history of ideas and theories lapses into hagiography (as history often does). I have had occasion to attend colloquia on the history of science where aged scholars narrated the history of even older scholars, hoping that one day their own history might be told in its turn [*laughter*]. This point shows us how easily an enterprise of objectification can degenerate into an enterprise of celebration. I don't think we need at all costs to be the 'man with the hammer', in the words of the prophet [Nietzsche],[7] but it is sometimes very useful to be able to wield a hammer to shatter conventional wisdom, to break down that kind of conformist self-satisfaction that any scientific universe tends to breed. Most speeches (like eulogies, for instance) are self-congratulatory speeches by proxy; one whole aspect of the scientific life is a euphemised and therefore authorised form of self-congratulation.

The hammer may come in useful, but is the iconoclastic intent sufficient? Can we attribute a scientific function to a science of science, a social science of science and in particular of social science? Or is this just some spiritual consolation for an idle researcher? Most often when scientists want to engage in mathematics they practise the history of mathematics. That is fair enough, we all need to make a living . . . Is [the science of science] a spare-time job, an alternative life even, or does it really have a scientific function? I have tried to take this question seriously, and what I want to try to demonstrate or at least argue for today is the fact that for me the science and the social history of the social sciences[8] are a fundamental element of science in general, and above all of social science.

The field of the social sciences is obviously particularly vulnerable to the kind of self-reflecting mirror image that is involved in any science of science. Once the social sciences took it upon themselves to target the production of ideas as an object of science they laid themselves open to all kinds of relativism: historicism (wherein the historian destroys the foundations of his own science by recalling the historical foundation of his own scientific practice), but also sociologism, ethnologism, and the like. In other words, the social sciences run the risk of finding themselves in the situation of Baron Munchhausen,

204 *Lecture of 19 June 1986*

who destroys his own foundations in a way, since he can only pull himself out of the water by tugging at his own hair.[9] For me Baron Munchausen symbolises the transcendental solution: when you are in the pits all you can do is imagine a transcendental consciousness that turns the question into the answer: 'The reason is, Reason. . .'. What is left for you to do if you are not satisfied with the Munchausen solution? Are you doomed to accept radical historicism? Does an analysis that objectifies the academic world including the person producing it, as I do in *Homo Academicus*, destroy its own foundations and its own claims to scientific validity? I think not, and I shall try to prove it.

Science as a social field

In general, people who discuss science or the sociology of science oscillate between the two extreme positions that were announced in this very place only four days ago,[10] in a form that I found caricatural, but which is nonetheless sociologically valid. There is first a professional scholarly ideology, idealising the scientific profession, according to which scholars are pure, disinterested and concerned with the future of humanity; they are self-reflexive, know what they are doing, and are in control of the orientation of their practice and method, etc. This scientific hagiography, which was particularly strong in Renan's day (*L'Avenir de la science*, etc.[11]), has indeed tended to lose some of its social force in recent times. This is because science has revealed a certain number of properties which were less visible in its early, triumphal phases.

It is also because the social sciences, which developed as humble and rather embarrassing offshoots of the natural sciences, while hiding under their umbrella, have developed some ideas against nature – and ideas moreover against the natural sciences: the sciences, including the natural sciences, have a history; scientific concepts have a history; there are successive definitions of the truth that we can describe rigorously and historically; there are different stages in the history of Reason, and what has changed are not only the scientific truths but, something much more important, what Foucault called the regimes of truth,[12] that is, the modes of validation, the socially recognised procedures for having a 'validity claim', which is the claim for validity inherent in membership of the scientific community, acknowledged. Under these conditions, we can and we must do what many historians of science have done and describe what were at a certain moment the require-

Lecture of 19 June 1986 205

ments in terms of proof and demonstration, coherence, instrumentalisation, operationalisation and scientific verification.

The social sciences, then, have organised a kind of return of the scientific repressed, an important repression that, like all professional ideologies, represents a mystification, but a functional mystification, for the scientific life perhaps needs such an illusion about the real foundations of scientific practice in order to exist. This is one of the problems posed by the sociology of science: the return of the repressed may produce social effects that it may not always control. In fact social science does not control its own effects. I have implied that the natural sciences have shown that they are not in control of their own effects, in particular the social application of the techniques they invent, but this is also true of the social sciences. I think (and truly believe) that the social sciences have social effects which are much more powerful than people, even the sociologists themselves, generally believe, and which completely escape the control of the producers of would-be scientific discourse.

Among these effects (I can say this because it has often been used in argument against me) are the effects of 'cynicisation': even if, behind the particular lucidity of certain researchers, there may be a moral indignation (which is the absolute opposite of cynicism) against what they describe, social science may encourage a certain cynicism by bringing the repressed back to light, revealing the real motives, the scientific battles and the 'underbelly' of the pure and perfect universe which the scholars present to the outside world, and in which they profoundly believe, this belief being one of the conditions of the functioning of the scientific field. It is a fundamental problem: could the social world still function if the sociologist managed to produce the full truth of the social universes and get people to know, believe and acknowledge that representation? Insofar as the social universes are motivated by an *illusio*, the scientific practice that sheds light on the social conditions of production of this *illusio* might tend to disperse this very *illusio*. I shall not follow this idea through to the end because it is obviously utopian, there's no danger of it happening, it is so unlikely and, moreover, to believe that scientific analysis could destroy the illusion is to make the mistake I mentioned just now, confusing the theoretical and the practical: the *illusio* is a practical *illusio*.

A scholarly experience of the truth of practices and a practical experience of this truth may perfectly well coexist: we may know very well that a sport is just a game with a set of rules and yet we invest wholeheartedly and naively in that sport; otherwise life would be impossible for sociologists! [*laughter*] I have raised issues that are naive, but are

206 *Lecture of 19 June 1986*

at the same time felt by people to be fundamental. I deal with them as if they were the ultimate questions raised by master thinkers who believe they have found the hole in the floor through which the whole of sociology will collapse into the void [*laughter*]. I have raised these problems briefly to show that there is nothing metaphysical in them and they are relatively approachable.

All that being said, social science reveals that the scientific field is a field that obeys the ordinary laws of fields: there are stakes, interests, battles, conflicts of interest, power relationships, monopolies, alliances, collusion, you name it. . . To give you one example out of thousands, I think of a typical article published a few years ago where Michael Pollak told the story of Paul Lazarsfeld, a sociologist who helped to rationalise the scientific practices of the social sciences. The article was entitled 'Paul Lazarsfeld, Founder of a Scientific Multinational'[13] (the analogy with a multinational is I believe well justified) and aimed to show how this man, armed with a specific capital and a personal mission, succeeded in constructing a sort of multinational of temporal and scientific power, which provided the basis for constructing a definition of scientific practice dominant enough to disqualify all competing definitions. In order to understand the logic of the scientific field, it is important to recognise that the structure of the power relationships at its heart gives this field a specific form. It has accumulated a particular form of capital which would not be valid in another field (even, for example, in the scientific disciplines, where there is a hierarchy of disciplines, the capital accumulated in the highest discipline is not automatically convertible into the capital of a discipline of inferior rank[14]).

Thus these different universes have their specificity, and possession of a specific capital by a researcher or an institution exercises a specific form of domination: its power always has a relationship with the truth. Someone who manages to concentrate a sufficient amount of the sounding brass and ready cash of a specific capital is able to wield not only the power of nomination or promotion, but also the power to promulgate the truth and, thereby, to censor any rival claims to the truth. I wanted to recall these extremely basic things, which have been said over and over again in the history of science, to be sure that you could follow clearly what I have to say today.

A rationalist relativism

The scientific fields, then, are fields of struggle in which there are specific stakes, as well as relations of domination which are specific but

Lecture of 19 June 1986　　207

which remain relations of domination. The question that arises then is: how is it that truth can have a history? If truth has a history, is it a veritable truth? It seems to me that the fittest manner of formulating the question of the relation of history to truth is the following: what particular characteristics are, or should be, adopted in the struggles within a field like the scientific field for the struggle to result in imposing a certain regime of truth? A few years ago I wrote an article that was an attempt to overcome this age-old alternative of Reason and History, and to try to determine what should be the social logic of a field for the social agents, struggling with temporal interests as they would elsewhere (vanquishing opponents, being the first into print, etc.), to contribute to the progress of Truth and of Reason, without even needing to explicitly desire to do so. I'll give you the reference for this article because I am going to describe it very quickly and inadequately (teaching is a terrible thing because you can't explain things that you have already written and you find it difficult to discuss those you haven't yet written, otherwise they would already be written [*laughter*] . . . Actually, when I say 'you' I mean 'I' [*laughter*]): 'La spécificité du champ scientifique et les conditions sociales de progrès de la raison', *Sociologie et sociétés*, vol. 7, no. 1, 1975, pp. 91–118; it was published in a much more elaborate and fully argued form in June 1976 in *Actes de la recherche en sciences sociales*, nos. 2/3, pp. 88–104.

I'll read you the opening sentence of the article, which contains the essence of what I have to say, and then comment on it:

Having tried elsewhere to describe the logic of the functioning of the fields of symbolic production (the intellectual and artistic field, the religious field and the field of high fashion, etc.) we intend here to determine how these laws are specified in the particular case of the scientific field; more precisely, under what (social) conditions generic mechanisms, like those which in any field govern the acceptance or rejection of new entrants [*Bourdieu explains:*] (controlling entry to the field is one of the determining factors of its self-reproduction), or competition between different producers, can determine the emergence of scientific truths – which are social products, but relatively independent of the social conditions of their reproduction. (I say '*relatively* independent'). I am driven by the conviction, itself a product of history (it is important to say that the conviction which I intend to develop has its own historical origins), that it is in history that we need to seek the reason for the paradoxical progress of a thoroughly historical reason that is nonetheless irreducible to history.[15]

208 *Lecture of 19 June 1986*

There you are. That is the last word I have to say on the question, and I shall try to provide some argument for it. Basically the thesis that I defend is a sort of relativist rationalism, that is, an attempt to overcome, without resorting to the Munchausen bluff, the antinomy/ies linked to the historicity of Reason.

Let me be a little more precise: in order to be a winner in the scientific field, which is the site of a particular form of struggles, you need to be right according to the current historical definition of Reason at that moment in the historical field. In the scientific field, the strongest reason tends to be the most reasonable reason. More precisely, the scientific field is a universe where it is more likely than elsewhere that the person who is most right is the strongest, the reason of the person who is most right being defined according to a historical norm of Reason, which is itself a product of the specific history of the field concerned. That said, how do we explain the fact that these struggles take a form which is not common to the other universes? How is it that we find universes which base their practical reason on dialogue and scientific exchange, which some people, Habermas for example,[16] tend to constitute as implying a tacit recognition of a claim to rational validity, thus implying a sort of Munchausian postulate of rationality? How can it happen that universes which base their reason, their *nomos*, on Reason can emerge, and what are their properties?

I think that we need to distinguish two levels that the theoreticians of science or the history of science either ignore or accept as separate. There is first of all, it seems to me, the problem of the motor of change in the scientific fields, the problem of how and why change is produced. If we were to survey the various current theories on the question, we would sometimes find among them a transfigured version of Hegel's *Selbstverwirklichung* ['self-realisation' or 'self-accomplishment']: a sort of internal logic of scientific, artistic or philosophical ideas generating its own developments according to its own laws.[17] We find this theory in the domains of law and art. This theory of autonomous self-propulsion is ultimately one aspect of the professional ideology of the specific producers. Other theorists, apparently more subtle and realistic, would say that there is a kind of natural selection, involving a conflict of ideas where the better idea is the stronger. In fact they forget to question the conditions that need to be fulfilled for the better idea to have that strength. Spinoza's proposition, 'The true idea has no intrinsic strength',[18] remains true: for the true idea to have a little strength, it requires the existence of very special universes in which the logic of the social world is itself so constituted that an argument can find strength there.

Lecture of 19 June 1986   209

I think that if we look at the question of the motive force of the field (how does the field change?), we cannot avoid taking into account the level where we find the drives and passions of the *libido sciendi*, that is, motive forces that lie beyond the scientific intent, but which are enshrined in the logic of the struggles and make the scientific field fundamentally a field like any other. In a text published in *Cahiers pour l'analyse* that I have already mentioned,[19] Foucault explicitly excludes the level of analysing change in philosophy or science. He speaks of a 'doxic level', and for him the social strategies that target theoretical and transcendental issues are not the object of a rigorous search for knowledge.[20] In my opinion this leaves us with a discourse lacking motive force: we don't see why or how these universes can be transformed. It seems to me that the dynamism of the scientific fields is to be found in the logic of their struggles, but that the specific orientations and forms of this dynamism cannot be deduced from a mere knowledge of the social interests and goals defined in the struggles between the social agents engaged in the different fields. So we have to introduce another level, whatever we call it. I think in fact that this is what Foucault calls the '*épistémè*',[21] and I call 'the space of possibilities' (which we could also call the 'problematics'), that is, the universe of what are the pertinent questions at any given moment of time, a universe obviously destined to be bound by the constraints controlling the legitimate means of replying to legitimate questions.

This kind of space of possibilities is a space of objective potentials, things to discover, directions that need to be taken. Something commonly observed in the history of the sciences is that there are moments when, to use the metaphor of iron filings in a magnetic field, a transfer of the whole set of filings occurs: everyone rushes into a certain sector of the space of possibilities. Belonging to a scientific field or an artistic field (in this case it makes no difference) means having the knowledge (actually much more practical than explicit) of the 'menu' of interesting and pertinent questions, which are unknown to the 'naive' painter[22] or scientific autodidact. This knowledge of the key orientations is inseparable from a knowledge of the legitimate means of appropriation and validation of the ambition to resolve the questions raised.

This space of possibilities, which are at the same time objective potentials, defines both what may be done and, rather than what may not be done, what cannot even be thought within the framework of the given problematics. Kojève, for instance, was very insistent on this point:[23] the most powerful effect of a space of possibilities is to render impossible a certain number of problems, which will retrospectively appear to be fundamental, and expose the limits of that space.

210 *Lecture of 19 June 1986*

A reflexive science must feel the nostalgic urge to study the limits of the space of possibilities, precisely to try to escape them: one function of the sociology of sociology as I conceive it is to try to become as acutely aware as possible of the space of possibilities whose agents are both exploiters and victims, and at the same time to explore the limits of the space of possibilities, hoping to overcome them. Thus, while I was trying in these last lectures to show you how our thinking about the social world was enclosed in an alternative that is very powerful scientifically, because that alternative is so powerful sociologically, I was trying to think my way out of the box in which contemporary sociologists are enclosed.

The vulnerability of social science

I think that sociology is especially vulnerable to social pressure: since its aims are targets for struggles that leave nobody indifferent, we are not allowed the autonomy that is willingly accorded to astronomers. Once the theological problems have been settled, scientists may live in peace, whereas sociologists will never be left in peace, for what they have to deal with is much too important. Whether they conclude that there are social classes or that these do not exist, they will always upset as many people as they enthuse. Their autonomy is never taken for granted, so strong is the pressure of social questions that are jostling on the threshold wanting to be treated as sociological questions. Consequently, this effort to think about the space of possibilities is particularly important in the social sciences. But if sociologists are particularly vulnerable, they are also in control of the most powerful instrument of objectification, and consequently they can turn this instrument of objectification against themselves (and this is not one of your Munchausen devices) and keep the change left over from the transcendental transaction (in the sense of Malraux saying 'art is the change from the absolute':[24] we no longer have God, but we have the change in our purse).

I think that the historicist-rationalist solution which I have to offer is something like the change left over from transcendental absolutism: how do we replace that faintly Prussian absolutist verdict (and its transcendental solution, Reason) with a progressive and progressist historical solution? How do we set in operation the rational struggle to further the constitution of the scientific universe as a universe of truth? Researchers always affect to look down on the struggles of scientific politics, but seen from a position like the one I am defending, these struggles of scientific politics, these struggles to improve the regime

Lecture of 19 June 1986   211

of truth, are important. This seems absurd because we are not used to thinking of the scientific field as a social field, we are not used to thinking of it in terms of movement and mobilisation, or, if we do happen to think of it this way, it is always ultimately to defend our more or less universalised corporatist interests.

I am proposing something that should enable us to escape the all-or-nothing alternative of a rampant, rationalising Reason or a sad historicism knowing that Reason is bound by history and that what is true today will be discredited tomorrow. I think that we can make the best of our knowledge of the (sometimes fatal) constraints that hamper the production of truth, in order to access the truth of these conditions and thereby master them in theory and perhaps in practice. One obstacle to the type of politics I am defending is that people immediately interpret it in terms of ordinary logic. In fact it is a law of the social world that people who are committed to a professional ideology of disinterest (in this case, of disinterested science) tend to have an extremely sociologistic and pessimistic philosophy towards others, whether unconsciously or explicitly, and conducting a social science of the social sciences and cultural productions is hindered by the fact that it seems to confirm this pessimistic vision that each member of the field has of the others.

I don't know if you follow what I am trying to say: using sociological pretexts to reduce things to objectification is a tactic used in all fields, but especially in the scientific field and the sociological field where the people are, at least in principle, professionals of objectification. The sociology of the intellectual has been treated like this and it is true that Aron's famous book, *The Opium of the Intellectuals*, considered to be one of the classics of the sociology of the intellectual, is a typical product of the strategy used by one sector of the intellectual field against another: it is the vision that the right-wing intellectual spontaneously forms of the left-wing intellectual. Similarly, at the same time (I always quote this example because it is so typical[25]), Simone de Beauvoir, in 'La pensée de droite aujourd'hui',[26] expressed the classic vision that the left-wing intellectual has of the right-wing intellectual. They both had in common their refusal to objectify the positions from which they were adopting their opposing views, within the field as a whole, thus preventing them from discovering their bias in seeing what they saw and in not seeing what they didn't see but that the other saw in them.

Scientific observation, then, comes up against an additional difficulty: it constantly encounters things that are already objectified (rumours, for instance). Above all, a part of scientific production involves either partial objectifications or more global objectifications but which lead

212   *Lecture of 19 June 1986*

to a kind of nihilism. For instance, there is at present what we might call an ultra-subjectivist movement, which I think was largely inspired by the article that I quoted,[27] and which tends to claim that scientific production is pure rhetoric,[28] and ultimately that scientific discourse is characterised by a rhetoric of truth: just as novelists produce an impression of reality, so scientists produce an impression of truth, and all that matters at any given moment is identifying the right regime of truth and being in tune with it, that is, showing scientific conformity and knowing how to produce the external signs of truth. This is not always a mistake: it represents one possible strategy in the scientific field, suitable for certain positions. That said, I think that the very excess of these falsely radical objectifications (with the polarising effects that I often mention), and their unrealistic nature, make them accomplices of non-objectification and hagiographic self-representation. That's it [for the first session].

The Gerschenkron effect

(*[We have not been able to reconstitute the start of the second session, but Bourdieu started by responding to questions that had been handed to him during the break:*] [. . .] Between what I have in mind and see quite clearly before coming [to give my lecture], and what comes out of my mouth when I am on stage here, there is a considerable gap, which does distress me. I wanted to tell you this, and to thank those of you who have been kind enough [to pass me your comments(?)], which have been a help to me.)

To finish what I was saying before. In a word, I wanted to say that although the position of sociology and the social sciences is extremely vulnerable, especially when they aim to objectify themselves, sociology may nonetheless benefit from its extreme vulnerability to sociological analysis in order to gain more control over the social determinisms that handicap it. In other words, I think that we should exploit sociology's inherent vulnerability to historicist or relativist [arguments (?)] by using a sociological knowledge of the social conditions of sociological production to create more lucid insights into scientific practice, which will also give us a better knowledge of the limits of the validity and utility of sociological production.

Maybe I would do better not to raise one last, dreadful problem, since it might give us yet another reason to cast doubt on the scientific credentials of the social sciences, a reason that has not occurred to our opponents – although heaven knows there are enough of them,

Lecture of 19 June 1986 213

but if my theory of vulnerability is right, the more criticism we attract, the better it will be for us – and one which is perhaps the worst threat to confront the social sciences: it is the fact that the social sciences are newcomers to science; for its late arrival makes sociology vulnerable to the dominant scientific models. I call this the 'Gerschenkron effect'. Gerschenkron was a major historian who showed that the rather strange form taken by capitalism in Russia is due to the fact that it developed quite a long time after the beginnings of capitalism in England and France.[29] This time-lag has had an effect, among others, on the ways in which this tardy capitalism has been able to become conscious of its own backwardness.

For me, the 'Gerschenkron effect' designates all those perversions that enter the social sciences because of the symbolic domination they suffer at the hands of the so-called 'advanced' sciences. In general, the strategies that are most powerful socially are those which generate the most profit with the least economic expenditure, in sociology and even in history, by mimicking the scientificity of the sciences which have preceded the social sciences, draping themselves in the external clothing of scientificity as formulated in a certain truth regime. Formalisation, with the use of more or less well handled mathematical or computerised procedures, for instance, enables the production of artefacts that do have a legitimate scientific usage. In a way, I think that the social sciences, which started late, failed to really take off because they managed to persuade people that they had already taken wing: they may pass themselves off as post-Galileo and post-Einstein, although they are often pre-Galileo. It is possible to be ignorant of economic markets and still lead people to believe, especially [. . .] by playing with equations, that one understands the mechanisms of economics.

We might say that one of the least questionable criteria of the scientific quality of a universe is its capacity to assert its autonomy against external interference and refract external pressure, for example, in order to transform social problems into scientific problems. But in the case of the social sciences, even this criterion is not easy to use, given the fact that it is possible, in the name of a simplistic representation of the natural sciences, to produce an artefact satisfying the dominant definition of science, and pay lip service to autonomy. This is what I call the phenomenon of the false break. I have shown, for example, how we may understand Heidegger's use of rhetoric in *Being and Time* as being objectively oriented towards producing the appearance of a break between the problems as posed by Heidegger and the problems raised in the wider world, in the Germany of the 1920s and 1930s, outside him: he does in fact raise these questions, but in a

214 *Lecture of 19 June 1986*

language that makes him seem to be interested in something entirely different.[30] In the domain of law, the rhetoric of the false break rules triumphant; juridical discourse is grounded in this neutralising intent, which enables social conflicts to be translated into clashes of argument. In the case of the social sciences too, these effects are at work, and so we cannot even use this criterion, which leaves social science vulnerable to the feeblest arguments of the most elementary philosophers. Burying their heads in the sand, the sociologists take refuge in positivist [. . .] approaches, or on the contrary theorising ones (which come to the same thing: you can swear allegiance to a general theory and be ignorant of all its details. . .). It seems to me that the social sciences will not succeed in this way; on the contrary, they should deliberately face up to the awareness that they have no foundations [. . .] and above all that they are more exposed than the other sciences to all the factors of heteronomy.

(I was for some considerable time a proponent of the idea that I should adopt a superior, Wittgensteinian attitude, and reject all question of foundations.[31] My strategy in fact was to answer the philosophers' objections by saying: 'Laugh if you like, . . . but I have work to do. . .'. I now think that this strategy – which may have its social use, because many philosophers are not worth much more of an answer – is not right. But it is true that, in my heart of hearts, I am obliged to admit that I lack foundations [*laughter*]. I don't know if I should say that in public, but when all is said and done, to be loyal to my convictions, I think I must.)

The problem of the existence of social classes

Unfortunately, I have once more calculated the relation between what I had intended to say and the rhythm of my argumentation very badly. I shall take the risk of attempting to conclude with an overview of what I did want to say. The problem of the validation of the claims to scientificity and the particular form taken by this question of validation in the case of the social sciences, which I raised rather *in abstracto*, is raised very concretely whenever a sociologist offers a representation of the social world. Take the example of an analysis like the composite description of a social universe that I presented in *Distinction*. One objection that may be made to this is that the description is in fact a construction: to engage in his research the scholar creates a construction, which thereby invites comparison with rival constructions. It will be easy enough to find constructions in the scientific field itself that contradict the one he has to offer. These rival constructions can become more or less efficient, in the sense that a sociologist or a historian offering a representation of the social world may find validation in the facts, even if it is not necessarily a scientific verification.

Marxism, for instance, has become a social force and has been, as it were, incorporated into reality, so that when we question people on the existence of social classes, they respond in terms of a reality transformed by Marx. However, this validation does not imply that these Marxist theories are true. In this way the propositions of the social sciences can become rallying cries, transforming reality by becoming part of it. Our theories of the social world have this property, that they are able to be incarnated in the social world, and there are those who would argue that this means that the social sciences are not scientific.

In this respect, scientific representations of the social world, which is a site of struggles, are thus open to all the relativisations that I mentioned just now. In addition to being in competition with each other, they are in competition with the partial representations (we can't call them 'spontaneous theories', that is too much of a verbal transgression) that agents present in the form of practical images (so to speak, words fail me. . .) in their behaviour. Unlike other scholars, sociologists see their constructions confronted with practical or discursive constructions made by social agents, and this can lead to a kind of nihilism, as we see in the debate over the problem of social classes.[32] This is a problem that has given rise to discussions very similar to the ancient quarrels over universals (which have moreover returned to fashion in modern philosophy[33]), raising the question of the reality of concepts: is there something in reality that corresponds to the notion of 'dog'?

The contemporary philosophers who reflect on this problem of the reality of universals seem to me to make distinctions that we might make use of when dealing with the problem of social classes. In fact they say that the question of the existence of universals confronts us with the choice between a Platonism that ultimately grants reality to universals, and a nominalism that grants these universals no reality, other than that of being thought by those who think them. Thus we could say of the 'social classes' either that they exist in reality, that they do really exist, or that they are pure fictions invented by the scholar. A famous article by Raymond Aron on the notion of class[34] is very typical of the second position: class is a convenient scientific fiction.

The philosophers warn us that, when we are debating the reality of universals, we may be understanding two different things: we may be wondering about the reality of the reality designated by universals (the

216 *Lecture of 19 June 1986*

existence of dogs), or about the reality of the concept that designates this reality (does the word 'dog' exist?). Once we make this distinction, the problem of social class looks a little different. There will be a clash between those who say: 'Classes are only an artefact, a fiction, a nominal construction, and since one nominal construction is worth another, we can see this as relativism', and those who say: 'Classes are constructions whose objective correlate exists in reality and can be discussed.' That said, we need to take into account the fact that, when we speak of social classes, these classes are an exception in the notion of class . . . The word 'class' is the concept par excellence . . . it is extremely difficult to conceptualise . . . Let us say that our question for the concept is whether what it refers to exists. This question can be decided when we have a specific concept. If we wonder whether the dog as concept exists or whether the ensemble designated by the concept 'dog' exists, we know where we are. But when it is a question of classes and social classes, things are much less simple. Does social class exist? Does the conceptual reality 'class' exist? Let us start with another, simpler question. Does the reality designated by the notion of class exist? The answer is yes (I shall say more about this: we can supply arguments and show that what I am constructing exists), but does the notion 'class' exist in reality, and does the scholar find it ready-made in reality or does he himself compose the totality of what he observes under the name of class? In the case of a specific class, if you bear in mind everything that I have said previously, you will see that the question has to be put differently: it is possible that this is a reality that does really exist in people's minds and also in the form of groups constituted as real classes. The alternative of nominalism and realism is thus more difficult to resolve than it seems. I am finding it difficult to explain this in five minutes: it is one of the most difficult problems in philosophy because ultimately it makes us think about our own thinking. I find that the notions of class and the social world confront us with a series of paradoxes similar to Gödel's 'incompleteness theorems'.[35] They are insurmountable antinomies that it is better to constitute as such, to avoid constantly oscillating from a nominalist position to a realist position. There you are. I have more or less formulated the question.

'Class': a well-constructed fiction

Now, it is relatively easy to demonstrate that what sociologists designate by the name of 'classes' does exist in reality, as long as you think

Of what I call 'class' in *Distinction*, for instance, not as a class that exists as such in reality, but as a construction by scholars that is clearly grounded in reality – *cum fundamento in re*, as the scholastics said. A conception of reality founded in reality does not imply the reality of the conception. In fact the passage from the concept of reality to the reality of the concept, which is the common leap operated by our logicians' illusion, occurs in the present case with particular force. I said this once and everybody laughed; so I shall say it again, with all due reflection: the mistake Marx makes is to consider that the class he constructs (as long as it is well constructed, that is, *cum fundamento in re*) exists in reality, that is, in people's minds, in institutions, dispositions and [political (?)] movements, etc., whereas it is relatively easy to show that class exists as a well-constructed fiction, as a well-composed theoretical ensemble.

Constructing a social space and its divisions requires updating the principles of differentiation which enable this space to be regenerated and reproduced theoretically; an adequate theory of the social space, such as the one that I attempted to offer in *Distinction*, will take account of the existence of differences in the social world. We may note an infinity of differences in the social world: people are different from one another in thousands of ways; there are objective differences and then subjective differences (people love to differ: they are already objectively different, and they transform their differences into distinctions). Taking these differences into account, sociologists wonder how they might reproduce them theoretically (as is their scientific mission), but in an economical way (the geographer does not draw a map as large as the country it depicts. . .). A certain sociography, which does have its uses, is tempted to offer an infinite description of differences ('Farmers may be small, medium or large, and then there are their different modes of production. . .'). Constructing a social space, on the contrary, means constructing a simple model that enables us to use a small number of variables, articulated with one another, to regenerate the space of these differences, that is, the structure of distributions. That is what I was trying to do [in *Distinction*]: there is a social space, in which social agents are situated and defined by the positions that they occupy.

To construct this space we need two or three articulated variables: the total volume of capital possessed and the structure of this capital. For we may say that the relative weight of the different species of capital in the total volume already enables us to situate people in two dimensions, the vertical dimension of the space (the total volume of capital) and its horizontal dimension (the structure of the capital).[36]

218   *Lecture of 19 June 1986*

A third important dimension is what we might call the history of the capital, or in other terms, its provenance: how the capital of the social agents concerned has evolved in volume and structure over a period of time. To construct this space we may take elementary indices, since one problem in the construction of any model is the empirical construction of the parameters and indicators that enable as much information as possible to be condensed and summarised.

Having constructed the space in this manner, we can situate each social agent in a region of the space, and their position in the space gives us a very strong prediction of their practices, of consumption and other kinds. Here we have a realist model, and using this space as a basis we can differentiate classes, that is, regions in this space, which has nothing to do with geographical space (a banal but important point): people very close to one another in this social space may be very distant in geographical space,[37] and vice versa (see also my analysis of strategies of condescendence, which are based on a distance in social space that defies proximity in physical space). To divide up the regions of this space I shall draw circles with a felt-tip, my hypothesis being that the smaller the circle, the more the people enclosed within this circle will share common properties, both actual and potential. The theoretical classes that I shall construct by a process of division will correspond to sets of agents endowed with similar properties, both actual and potential, and will therefore enable reliable prediction of their future behaviour, all the more so, since the classes that I divide up in this way are classes of agents defined by holding the same position in the space and possessing the whole set of pertinent properties associated with this position, including especially those dispositions that are the tendentious products of this very position.

If we recall that this position is at once the volume, the structure and the 'past' of the capital, and if we bear in mind the fact that objective structures become incorporated structures, that is, a habitus, we may say that the whole set of agents belonging to the same class will be characterised by 'ownership' of the same habitus: the agents enclosed in the same class each possess the same system of dispositions. At the risk of appearing very mechanist and providing ammunition for those who would like to punish the wicked determinist that I am (we should reflect on this, although science is not obliged to judge, but determinism does imply constantly accepting limits), I consider that the habitus as a system of dispositions is at once what Leibniz called a *lex insita*,[38] an immanent and inherent law, and a *vis insita*, an immanent and inherent force: the habitus, as the word 'disposition' well says, is a disposition to act according to certain laws; it is at once a propensity to

Lecture of 19 June 1986   219

act (in which case, knowledge of the agents' habitus provides a prediction) and a propensity to act in a certain direction.

Constructed classes and infra-representational classes

We can clearly see that class, as defined in these terms (that is, as an ensemble of pertinent properties that account in the most economical way for the differences that constitute a social universe), is a fiction, a construction very different from the ordinary constructions produced by agents in their everyday struggles. People constantly produce classes; the class of 'queers', for instance, that I mentioned:[39] the insult classifies, everyday life produces classification. These classes always claim a basis in reality, and claiming validity is I think a universal feature of social struggles, and not only of scientific struggles. (There are I think two historical universals in practice: the claim to truth in everyday struggles and the claim to neutrality in everyday exchanges. I said two universals, but this is not an attempt to reintroduce the transcendental through the back door.) These everyday classes to which people consign each other are obviously quite different from the sociologist's classes: they are partial, they are based on constructing only a fraction of the social space, they do not perceive the space as a whole. The classes constructed by scientific discourse may pride themselves on obtaining the consensus of researchers insofar as they are based on reality and on operations of construction reproducible in such a way that any researcher possessing the same data will obtain the same results – which is the classic criterion for scientific verification.

That said, we are dealing with a universe that is slightly bizarre, because the classes constructed with a basis in reality at this level already have a particular property. The notion of a disposition implies in particular that people with identical dispositions should be favourably disposed towards one another. As I said just now, we are talking about the disposition to act and to perceive. Thus the habitus associated with a class of positions implies that the whole set of agents situated in the same region of space will have a tendency to create real links with one another and constitute themselves as groups. The more closed my circle, the more constructed my class, the higher the rate of endogamy and the whole set of classic indices of the construction of real groups: *connubium*, marriage, *commercium* – in short, all the signs of communication and cooperation.

The groups constructed by the scholar will have all the more chance of being practical groups the better constructed they are: if their

220   *Lecture of 19 June 1986*

construction conforms to the theoretical presuppositions that I have elaborated, the classes constructed on the basis of reality should tend to be practical groups. These classes, then, do have some existence in reality, in a practical state. They may even exist as semi-consciously constructed groups, in the form of what Weber called 'status groups',[40] that is, groups that reinforce the spontaneous affinities or sympathies of the agents' habitus with a systematic avoidance of mismatching and a systematic search for homogamy, in the general sense of the term, through all the mechanisms of rational co-optation which enable the group to control its reproduction as tightly as possible.

Here we already encounter something complicated, which escapes the order of the natural sciences. A well-constructed social class has a good chance of existing in reality as a class, which does not mean that it exists as a consciousness of class – which would be a very wrong assumption. I think that even if we said that the struggle to avoid mismatching is a tactical form of class consciousness, this would already be a mistake, because 'class consciousness' supposes representation, etc. The class, then, will exist in an infra-representational mode as a real group, and this is something very disturbing. I said just now that dispositions are predictable. I can predict, because I suppose that holders of the same position have the same dispositions to act, and therefore [given the fact that dispositions are both *lex insita* and *vis insita*] the same tendencies and orientations. There is then in the notion of disposition something that the scholastics called *esse in futuro*, that is, a potential: the disposition is an essence that harbours its own future. (Take care, this exaggerates the determinist side of my argument; I don't have enough time to correct the bias, so I'll leave it to you to make the necessary compensation yourselves.)

A well-constructed classification is a predictive classification: unlike a random, descriptive classification, a good classification is one where the people grouped into the same class will have a whole lot of common properties beyond the properties that have been used to classify them. [In zoology, if you group into the same class] all the animals which, shall we say, fly, or eat grain, you can deduce from this a whole lot of other things. A sociological construction is of the same order: if it is well devised, you can deduce from two fairly abstract criteria (the global volume of capital, and its structure) what the agents grouped in the same class like, that is, a whole lot of things which were not specific criteria for the construction of the classes.

But the most paradoxical thing is that you can deduce their propensity to rally and gather together into groups, in other words their propensity to respond to actions aiming to construct them as a group.

Lecture of 19 June 1986 221

On the one hand you note that a certain number of the practices they are disposed to follow are accretive practices, practices of assemblage, and on the other hand, through analysis of their dispositions, you grasp something that it is tempting to render as 'classes' in the traditional, Marxist sense of the term: you detect their tendency to assemble if someone tries to rally them. In so doing you repeat Marx's error, treating them as if they have already assembled, and you say: 'They really are classes.' It is very complicated. I repeat: in a first move, you assemble them, but you say to yourself 'Take care, I am a scholar, I know that I am the one who has produced their assemblage, they are not a class in reality (the correlate of the concept of dog exists, but the concept of dog does not exist in reality).' And then, in a second move, when your classes are neatly constructed, you say to yourself: 'But, in the end, they exist much more than I would have thought, since not only do [the agents] spontaneously come together in operations that are very important for the reproduction of the group, but in addition, among the characteristics that I correctly discern in their current behaviour, there is the essential property of being ready to assemble, or to be mobilised if someone mobilises them.' In so doing, you have passed from the class constructed on paper by the scholar, that is, the class that is theoretical but well based in reality (it is not class-fiction, which would not be taken seriously), to the real class, and so to the proletariat and the whole Marxist mythology. In this way you gloss over the fundamental problem of the construction of the class qua class, of the process that takes us from this kind of virtual class with a propensity to assemble, to the rallying cry of 'Proletarians of all countries, unite!'[41]

The constructivist phase

Now I shall finish off very rapidly. Everything is so intricately bound up together that I don't know whether I shall manage to unpick it all. So far I have described the objective phase of the scientific procedure, that is, the structuralist phase where the scientist acts as God the father. You can erect a crash barrier against this temptation to take yourself for God the father by objectifying the probability of this temptation, which is inherent in the scientific field, as in all the dominant fields: one property of all the fields I have been discussing since the start of the lecture (the religious field, etc.) is that they are founded on *skholè*, leisure, and its distance from practice; those who become involved in the theoretical fields tend to forget the distance between

222 *Lecture of 19 June 1986*

theory and practice and to make the mistake that I mentioned at the outset, setting up their vision of the social world as a reality of the social world, placing in the minds of the social agents their representation (scientific or not) of these practices. We may call this the 'scientistic error' or the 'Marxian mistake'. It is a sort of ethnocentrism on the part of the theoretician. We criticise the social sciences, saying, for instance: 'You are a son of. . .', 'Yours is a bourgeois sociology' or 'Yours is a sociology for mandarins', which is a way of reducing the production of discourse to the most general social properties of its author; at a slightly more refined level the discourse can be related to the specific properties engaged in the space of its specialised production. But in both cases we forget something much more fundamental: the fact that it belongs to the space of the production of discourse, that is, the universe of theory, the mental world that tells 'monumental' lies, in the words of the poet [Jacques Prévert].[42] I think that the 'divine theorist' temptation is linked to the first phase. I am telling you this to show you how sociology enables us to overcome certain errors generically associated with belonging to the social universe in which science is produced.

This theorising vision tends to disqualify the whole of classic sociology, with its triumphant objectification: the scholars are convinced that they must construct their science in opposition to what Durkheim called 'pre-notions', or Marx 'ideology'.[43] This objectivist standpoint is in a way the point of honour of the scholar. Wanting to be a scholar means wanting the kind of gratification provided precisely by the status of scholar. 'You are naive, you are trivial, I know truths about you that you don't know', 'I have deciphered the enigma that you are for yourself.' For the followers of Althusser this exploited the idea of the break as initiation,[44] with the notion of the break taking on the function that it has in initiatory philosophies. Moreover, Bachelard's term 'rupture' had for the Althusserians become a 'break', a much more overdetermined term. This pleasant vision that the scholar has of himself, which is no doubt one of the motive forces of the scientific vocation in the social sciences, leads to the fundamental error of theorising, which I define as passing from a constructed class to a real class. But that is not the end of it: in so doing, the scholar disqualifies the practice of the social agents constructing their rival social world. The more inexperienced, insecure and uncertain of his validity the sociologist is (it would be the same for a psychoanalyst or a philosopher), the more strongly he will tend to assert his divorce from the layman, and in thus defending his self-esteem he will make a whole lot of scientific mistakes.

Lecture of 19 June 1986 223

Disqualifying the ordinary experience of the social world and the contribution by social agents to its construction, which is one of the elementary rewards of theorising, prevents us from going beyond this objectivist stage. Firstly, it prevents us from asking about the objectification of the interests associated with this objectivist procedure (which I have done in passing) and, secondly, it prevents us from going beyond this objectivist phase to call into question the space that I have constructed. I think that the space which I have constructed does objectively exist. It exists independently of the representation that the agents have of it. It also exists independently of the construction that I have made of it: it is independent of my thought, which is one of the criteria of reality. That said, it is at the same time an object of people's perceptions and struggles, and the sovereign, divine representation that I claim to offer will itself become an object of struggle: it can become part of reality again. If you question relatively cultivated people about representations of social space, there is a good chance that you will find *grosso modo* the structure that I offered in *Distinction*, all the more so since this structure has been absorbed into the categories used by INSEE.[45] In other words, a scientific construction is liable to pass into reality (categories deriving from scientific research may end up being printed on your identity card) without forasmuch being validated.

This process reminds us that what the scholar constructs is a state of dispute over the social world, that is, dispute over the way to construct it. The structuralist or objectivist phase should then give way to a wholly constructivist phase, where we remember that the social world is a goal to be negotiated, that the very existence of 'classes' is an object of dispute, and that different visions are in confrontation: agents can disagree, firstly, about the actual existence of these classes and, secondly, if they accept the existence of these classes, about the way to divide them up and the principles of their classification. These struggles have an impact. Like the scientific argument itself, they can lead to action.

This is where, to speed things up (and finish my argument), I return to objectivism. Objectivist science must renew itself by taking into account the debates over objectivism which confront scientific description, like it or not. This means that a science of the social world must include a theory of struggle, based on a theory of the power relationships within which these struggles are waged. We can, for instance, suggest that the symbolic power available in the struggles to change the social world or preserve it will depend, firstly, on the symbolic capital held by the individual or the group proposing a conservative or transformational vision of the social world and, secondly, on the level of realism, that is, on the foundation in reality of the proposed representation. Between two conflicting visions of the social world, the two principles of differentiation then will be, on the one hand, the symbolic authority held by the two parties and, on the other, the level of realism, that is, of predictability, of the two conflicting visions. Objectivism, then, needs to be superseded, but it is in a way insurmountable. To pass objectivism by would be to note that the social world is constructed without seeing that those who construct it are constructed by it and contribute to its construction in proportion to the place that it allows them; it would also be to resign yourself to a sort of relativism, denying any reality to the social world.

One last point: we can clearly see that class is going to be a key issue in these struggles, and that the analysis which I have to offer allows us to face the question of the specific conditions of the specific research needed in order to pass from a kind of virtual, would-be class to a class mobilised in action, if indeed it does exist, or to some delegate, proxy, spokesperson or movement able to say: 'I am the class.' The question as to how all this political work can even come to exist can only be debated if you have done the research that I have tried to accomplish. Well, there you are... I have attempted to say what I wanted to, however briefly and awkwardly.

Situating the Later Volumes of General Sociology *in the Work of Pierre Bourdieu*

Julien Duval

This fifth volume continues the publication of the Course in General Sociology that Pierre Bourdieu delivered during his first five years of teaching at the Collège de France from 1982, at the rate of eight to ten two-session sessions each year. It contains the lectures given during the academic years 1985–86.

In the words that he used during his very first lecture, the 'Course in General Sociology' presents the 'fundamental lineaments' of his work.[1] The first year of lectures following his inaugural lecture of April 1982 was relatively short. It concentrated on the question of the constitution and classification of groups and 'social classes'. It functions as a kind of prologue to the whole course. During the second year, Bourdieu explained how he envisaged the object of sociological study and developed his thinking on knowledge and practice, then he started to present the major concepts of his sociological approach, expounding their underlying theoretical assumptions as well as the function that he assigned them in the general economy of his theory. He devoted a whole series of lectures to the concept of the habitus, taking account of the fact that the subject in sociology, unlike the subject in philosophy, is a socialised subject, that is, one invested by social forces, and he showed how that concept enabled us to think about social action without falling into the alternative of mechanism and purposiveness. He then made a first, 'physicalist' approach to the concept of the field, presenting it as a field of forces, and leaving to a later stage in the lectures the analysis of the dynamics of the field seen as a field of struggles aiming to modify the field of forces.

The third year focused on the concept of capital. Bourdieu reminds us of the link between this concept and the concept of the field, and then goes on to elaborate the different forms of capital (which are linked to the variety of the fields), as well as the different states of

226   *Situating the Later Volumes of* General Sociology

cultural capital. He pays particular attention to the codification and objectification of capital: this is designated as one of the sources of the coherence of the social world and an important source of the divergence between pre-capitalist societies and our differentiated societies. The fourth year tackled the concept of field in terms of a field of struggles, insofar as it is the object of perceptions by the social agents, these perceptions being generated by the relation between the habitus and capital. In this fourth year, Bourdieu developed the project of a sociology of social perception, conceived as an inseparably cognitive and political act in the struggle between social agents to define the *nomos*, the legitimate vision of the social world. The fifth year, which forms the present volume, continues to develop these analyses, but as he prepares to conclude the course of lectures, Bourdieu also seeks to link the two aspects of the concept of the field (the field as field of forces and as field of struggles) through the simultaneous mobilisation of three major concepts. The symbolic struggles aim to transform the field of forces. To understand them we need to introduce the notion of symbolic power and symbolic capital, or the symbolic effect of capital, which is constituted in the relation between habitus and field, a relation of *illusio*. The fifth year finishes with questions arising from the position of the social sciences in the symbolic struggles that aim to impose a certain representation of the social world, and with the idea that the social sciences should combine both structuralist and constructivist perspectives in order to study the social world, which is both a field of forces and a field of struggles that aim to transform it but are also conditioned by it.

Coherence over five years

This five-year-long course of lectures enabled Bourdieu to look back over the theoretical system that he had been progressively constructing. Shortly before the start of this course, and before his election to the Collège de France, he had published two sizable volumes of synthesis, *Distinction* (1979), comprising all his research on culture and social class in France, and *The Logic of Practice* (1980), comprising his investigations in Algeria and the theory of action that he derived from them. The Course in General Sociology covers both research enterprises at once, and aims to elaborate a social theory as valid for pre-capitalist as for highly differentiated societies. Rejecting the usual division between anthropology and sociology, it not only displays the coherence of these various research projects but also promotes the unity of the social

Situating the Later Volumes of General Sociology 227

sciences. In 1984–85 and 1985–86 in particular, Bourdieu is a sociologist enquiring into the process that leads from pre-capitalist to differentiated societies, while drawing attention to their continuity. More than once, he points out how pre-capitalist societies act as analysts of our societies: they 'zoom in' on relations between the sexes, they show 'close up' the symbolic struggles that are less perceptible but still at work in differentiated societies (25 April 1985); and he emphasises, for example, what his analyses on social class owe to his work on kinship relations in Algeria (2 May 1985).

The work of synthesis is also applied to the concepts. One of the objectives of his teaching in fact is to 'show the articulation between the fundamental concepts and the structure of the relations that link those concepts'.[2] In a concern to clarify, part of the course during the second and third years consists in presenting the three key concepts in succession, with some lessons using the first drafts of the generally rather short theoretical summaries that Bourdieu published in his review *Actes de la recherche en sciences sociales* at the end of the 1970s and the beginning of the 1980s, on the species and states of capital, on the properties of fields, on the effects of the corps, etc. But even at this stage of the course, the concepts remained linked to each other. The concept of capital, for instance, is first introduced in relation to the concept of field and the habitus reappears when the notion of 'information capital'[3] is introduced. The question of codification and institutionalisation, tackled during the third and fifth years respectively, as was the question of the field of power, links up with the relations between capital and the field; and the problem of perception, central to the fourth year, involves the relation between the habitus and the field directly. Countering the temptation of selective borrowing from Bourdieu's sociology, this Course in General Sociology reminds us how far the concepts of habitus, capital and field have been thought through as '"systemic" concepts because their use presupposes permanent reference to the complete system of their interrelationships'.[4]

If Bourdieu takes pains to recapitulate his arguments (more and more often as his teaching progresses), it is because he fears that his concern to 'produce a discourse whose coherence would emerge over a period of years' might escape his audience (1 March 1984). In addition to the spacing out of the lectures over a period of years, there is the fact that Bourdieu is addressing an 'intermittent public' (ibid.) that changes over those years. His style of teaching, moreover, leaves room, within a pre-established canvas, for potential and sometimes quite substantial improvisations and 'digressions'. Finally, the exposition cannot follow a perfectly linear course: its nature is to circulate in

228 *Situating the Later Volumes of* General Sociology

a sort of theoretical space that authorises different pathways. When he starts the fourth year of his teaching, for instance, Bourdieu says that he hesitated between several possible 'pathways' (7 March 1985).

The lectures were not intended to be published, at least not in their given form,[5] but their 'overall coherence' will perhaps be more apparent to the readers of the transcriptions than it would have been to the audience at the time. The time spent in reading the published lectures is not the same as that devoted to their preparation or that of their oral delivery. Reading acts as a kind of accelerator of the process of thinking that informs the lectures. The juxtaposition of the five volumes, for instance, will show up the loop operated very discreetly in one of the last lectures of the Course in General Sociology, as Bourdieu returns to the 'notorious problem of the social classes, which is absolutely central for the social sciences' (5 June 1986), that was at the heart of the first year of his teaching (1981–82). This return to the point of departure, as it might seem on first analysis, demonstrates the coherence of the whole of the course. It allows the reader to measure the distance travelled and become aware of the questions that have been investigated or that have taken on another dimension through the developments proposed in the meantime.

It may also suggest an approach to reading the lectures. The first year, in the spring of 1982, was presented as a reflection on classification and the social classes. The arguments that Bourdieu deployed there drew on insights gained from *Distinction*, but were also based just as much on the research that he was finishing at the time: in particular his book on language, and his analyses of the process of naming or the performative power invested in words under certain social conditions; Bourdieu thus added considerable depth to his theory of the social classes.[6] The movement of the Course in General Sociology could then be understood as a manner of expanding, exploring and generalising the thoughts on the subject of the social classes that he expounded during the first year. For the second and third years, Bourdieu explored his theoretical system, to return in the last two years to the question of the symbolic struggle over the principles of perception of the social world, whose division into classes is a sort of special case. Competition within the 'field of expertise' and the very particular power of the State in matters of nomination are generally two major aspects of the symbolic struggle in our differentiated societies, which the problem of social classes forces us to face.

Read in this way, the lectures do not come full circle. Far from returning to the point of departure in an attempt at closure, the final return to the social classes represents an opening out and a progres-

Situating the Later Volumes of General Sociology   229

sion that are linked to a form of generalisation. It is less of a loop and more of a 'spiralling'[7] movement that he achieved over five years. The image of the 'spiral', like that of the 'constant reworking' of research[8] that Bourdieu also used to describe his manner of working, is relevant not only to the structure of the course. It also applies to the numerous echoes that reverberate from one lecture to another. Because he is afraid of seeming to repeat himself, Bourdieu sometimes specifically emphasises the fact that these are not identical 'repetitions': 'I do sometimes take different routes that pass through the same point' (17 April 1986); 'I have said this in an earlier lecture, but I shall now rework the theme in a different context' (18 April 1985); 'Two years ago I elaborated the argument about the objective dimensions in a lecture . . . I mention this in case you want to make the connection' (15 May 1986). There are themes that recur (for instance the discussion of purposiveness and mechanism and the critique of decision theory, both broached in 1982, recur in 1986) and the same examples may be used to illustrate different analyses: thus the careers of nineteenth-century regionalist authors are referred to within the literary field in which they fall (25 January 1983), but are related later to the space where they originate and terminate in order to show the contribution of these writers to a certain educational mythology (12 June 1986).

The 'improvisations' of the second sessions

The year that the third volume comprises corresponds to the moment when Bourdieu's teaching at the Collège de France settled into a stable form. From the start of his appointment in 1982, Bourdieu had been obliged to abandon the standard format of this institution, which was to deliver a one-session lecture and, at a different time and in a smaller hall, deliver a seminar of the same duration. Researchers who worked alongside him remember how the first seminar session broke down in an atmosphere of great disorder, since the room could not hold the numbers of the public who flooded in.[9] After this experience, Bourdieu decided in 1982–83 to deliver his teaching in the form of two successive session-long sessions with no distinction between a 'lecture' part and a 'seminar' part.

He proceeds somewhat differently in the years published in volumes 3, 4 and 5. As he notes regularly in the course of the lectures, the formula of the open lecture to an anonymous and heterogeneous audience reduced to the role of listener is an ongoing problem for him: he finds this framework ill-suited to what he is trying to transmit (a

230   *Situating the Later Volumes of* General Sociology

'method' rather than a body of knowledge in the literal sense),[10] and he refuses to conform to it entirely. He cannot resist the temptation to launch into partly improvised digressions, which lead him very often at the end of a lecture to regret[11] not having said everything that he had intended, and having to postpone certain developments until the following session. At regular intervals he also continues, as he did already during the first two years, to reply to written questions submitted to him during the interval or at the end of the lecture, and which enable him to have at least some contact with his listeners.[12] But at the start of the year 1983–84 he reintroduced a distinction between the two sessions of his teaching on Thursday mornings:[13] while the first session, from 10.00 a.m. to 11.00 a.m., was spent on 'theoretical analysis' (1 March 1984), the second, from 11.00 a.m. to 12 noon, showed a change of subject and tone.[14]

Since he did not feel able at the Collège de France to organise a real seminar, he tries in the second session to give an idea of what a seminar would be, showing how an object of study might be constructed and how a problem might be elaborated, and above all how his theoretical formulae and formulations could be deployed in concrete operations, which is the essence of the craft of the scientist – the art of detecting the theoretical issues to be found in the most singular or banal details of everyday life (1 March 1984). With only a few exceptions, the second sessions of the lectures published in the later volumes are devoted to 'work in progress' (19 May 1984), 'tentative essays, reflections on risky topics' (26 April 1984), or 'improvisations' (17 April 1986). Bourdieu 'allows himself more freedom' than in the first session (15 May 1986), in particular to depart from a 'linear itinerary' (12 June 1986) and a 'sustained discourse, with long-term coherence' which would run the risk of being 'slightly enclosed and totalising (some would say slightly totalitarian)' (17 April 1986). As far as possible, he looks for some degree of correspondence between 'the applied studies of the second session and the theoretical analyses of the first session' (1 March 1984). Thus in the fourth year the 'theoretical analyses' concern the perception of the social world and the second sessions focus on a social category, the painters who, with Manet, accomplish a revolution in vision and perception (23 May 1985): the lectures develop in particular the notion of the *nomos*, while the second sessions draw attention to the 'institutionalisation of anomie' operated by modern art.

The second sessions are generally devoted to research that Bourdieu is presenting for the first time. In 1984–85 it is his research into the field of painting carried out with Marie-Claire Bourdieu. In the years immediately after these lectures, he published the first articles arising

Situating the Later Volumes of General Sociology   231

from this.[15] At the end of the 1990s he devoted two whole years of his teaching to it.[16] The lectures given in 1985 enable us to judge that this research, probably started at the beginning of the 1980s,[17] was already well under way, even if it still lacked, for instance, the analysis of Manet's works that he was to offer in the 1990s. In 1985 Bourdieu was working in parallel on *The Rules of Art*, which appeared in 1992, and the object of this research seems to lie above all in 'a series of analyses of the relations between the literary field and the artistic field' (7 March 1985): the study of the relations between the painters and the writers takes a central place in the exposition, and some developments refer quite directly to the analyses of the 'invention of the life of the artist' undertaken in the framework of the research on Flaubert and the literary field.[18] At this time Bourdieu was very concerned to show that the process of autonomisation affects the whole range of the artistic field and cannot therefore be entirely grasped in research focusing on a single sector (such as painting, literature, or music).

In 1983–84 and in 1985–86, the second sessions concentrate on more limited research projects, which usually last for no more than two or three successive sessions. The first piece of research presented, which Bourdieu says he has 'found while rummaging through [his] notes' (1 March 1984), is his analysis of a 'hit parade' published by the magazine *Lire* in April 1981. He may well have used the lecture to draft the text that appeared as an article a few months later as an appendix to *Homo Academicus* in November 1984.[19] Four years later, he would link it up with the analysis of a sort of 'Chinese game' that he had given a few years earlier.[20] He speaks of a sort of '"masterpiece", such as those made by a medieval craftsman', and presents his approach in these terms:[21]

> I'd say: There's the material, in front of you; it's available to everyone. Why is it badly constructed? What does this questionnaire mean? What would you do with it? . . . You have to question the sample: who are the judges whose judgements led to this list of best authors? How were they chosen? Isn't the set of authors implied in the list of judges chosen and in their categories of perception? . . . And so an idiotic survey of no scientific object if, instead of reading the results at face value, one reads the categories of thought projected in the results they produced . . . you're dealing with already published results that needed to be re-constructed.[22]

At all events, this research into the ranking list is more than just an exercise in method or style. Bourdieu also uses it as an opportunity

232   *Situating the Later Volumes of* General Sociology

to reflect on the properties of the intellectual field, its weak institutionalisation and its vulnerability in the face of a journalistically procured 'social action'. The choice of a limited and easily accessible but also very well chosen and intensively exploited object of study may have something to do with the fact that Bourdieu must certainly have reflected during these years on how he could best continue to engage in empirical research. For his election to the Collège de France brought with it new obligations and necessarily reduced his presence in his research centre,[23] as well as at the École des hautes études en sciences sociales – an institution which, unlike the Collège de France, allows its teachers to direct doctoral theses.[24] His availability for the kind of research that he had been practising since the 1960s was no doubt restricted, even if the enquiry into private housing that he had started during the first half of the 1980s (2 May 1985), like *The Weight of the World*, shows that he managed to launch important new collective research projects based on first-hand material.

Among other research projects presented in the second sessions, several are distinguished by the fact that they are based on literary texts, an approach that Bourdieu had previously practised only in his analysis of *Sentimental Education*.[25] He studies Franz Kafka's *The Trial* (22 and 29 March 1984), Virginia Woolf's *To the Lighthouse* (15 and 22 May 1986), and, rather more briefly, Samuel Beckett's *Waiting for Godot* (19 April 1984) and Kafka's *Metamorphosis* (22 May 1986).[26] He appears to show more interest in literary material and analysis than previously. The analysis of *The Trial* led to a paper read after the end of the academic year 1983–84 in a multidisciplinary colloquium organised at the Centre Pompidou on the occasion of the sixtieth anniversary of Kafka's death.[27] It is possible that this interest in literature is linked to the writing of *The Rules of Art*. Bourdieu does more than find a kind of allegory in *The Trial*, he also in a way practises the 'science of works' whose principles are developed in this book in 1992, in the way that he links the 'Kafkaesque' vision of the world to the insecurity that characterises the literary field that produced it (and Kafka's position in that field). A few years later he notes a slight change in his attitude to literature: he gradually frees himself from the temptation, felt strongly at the beginning, in a context where the scientific nature of sociology was insecure, to distance himself from his own literary education and tastes.[28] In the lectures he retains his concern to circumscribe the place allocated to literary analysis ('I shall not develop this further – since I have already done my little literary turn, you would find that I was going too far' [15 May 1986]), but his sociologist audience are invited to reflect on their relation to literature.

Situating the Later Volumes of General Sociology   233

Explaining his reflections on the 'biographical illusion' exploited by William Faulkner and Alain Robbe-Grillet in particular, Bourdieu draws attention to the 'intellectual double life' led by sociologists, who can make a personal reading of the nouveau roman without drawing conclusions for their professional practice (24 April 1986), and he emphasises how much the repression of the 'literary' by sociologists owes to their position in the space of disciplines; the particular form taken by the opposition between the arts and the sciences in the nineteenth century masks the advantage that writers have over researchers on questions such as the theory of temporality.

Announcing later research

As it intersperses Bourdieu's presentation of projects in progress with reminders of his previous research, the Course is driven by a dynamic in which the contemporary reader can see the bones of some of the studies that Bourdieu was to undertake in the second half of the 1980s, and even during the 1990s.

Above all, the present volumes announce the whole range of the lectures that Bourdieu was to give at the Collège de France from 1987 to 1992. It is no accident if the lecture that opens the third volume remarks in passing on the failings of the French edition of Max Weber: this author will often be referred to during the year 1983–84.[29] A little earlier, moreover, Bourdieu had published in the daily newspaper *Libération* a text entitled 'N'ayez pas peur de Max Weber!' (Who's afraid of Max Weber?!'),[30] which seems to have been triggered by his preoccupations at the time. In his lectures Bourdieu comments on extracts from *Economy and Society*,[31] discussing codification, the notion of the 'discipline' or the sociology of law, which he knows only from the German or English editions. Weber's observations on *Kadi*-justice and the justice of Sancho Panza or Solomon are frequently referred to in the lectures. It is probably during the years that he was giving these lectures that Bourdieu's interest in Weber and the sociology of law developed so strongly. The theme of the *vis formae*, which was never mentioned during the two previous years, is referred to on several occasions during the year 1983–84. His article on the 'force of law' would be published in 1986,[32] that is, during the year of teaching that closes the present set of volumes and which contains references to research in the sociology of law (15 May 1986, 5 June 1986), as well as reflections on the juridical field, which would be at the heart of his teaching for 1987–88.

234   *Situating the Later Volumes of* General Sociology

It is not only the law but also more generally the State that becomes the central object of his reflection. The formula that Bourdieu uses to widen Weber's definition of the State ('an enterprise [. . .] that claims the monopoly of legitimate physical coercion') recurs frequently in his lectures in the early 1980s. His critique in 1983–84 of linear interpretations of the process of rationalisation (29 March 1984) prefigures the reflections to be developed a few years later in his lectures on the genesis of the State. The references to the State are very numerous in the last sessions of the fourth year. Indeed, the main theme of social perception leads into a study of the State's monopoly of authorised perception. The analysis of certification also implicates the State, defined in this case as a 'field of expertise, or the field of agents in competition for the power of social certification' (9 May 1985), and the last lecture of the year finishes by acknowledging that a sociology of symbolic struggles should question this 'last analysis' that the State represents. Bourdieu notes that the State has become a major concern for his arguments even before starting his lectures on the State[33] in 1989–90: already in 1987–88 he entitled his course 'Concerning the State'.

The article (1990) and then the book (1998) that he devoted to 'Masculine Domination'[34] may also be seen being sketched out in the lectures. During the year 1985–86 several developments relate to the political dimension of masculine domination or the 'androcentric unconscious' of Mediterranean societies. It is in 1985–86 too that he comments on *To the Lighthouse* (which became an important reference in his later writings on the relations between the sexes); he is particularly attracted to its feminine vision of masculine investment in social games.

While it is more difficult to detect in the lectures the signs prefiguring the work that Bourdieu would publish in the 1990s, today's reader, seeing Bourdieu's methodological reflections on the difficulty of retrieving and explaining the experience of social agents (12 June 1986), cannot help thinking of the organisation of the collective enquiry that culminated in 1993 in *The Weight of the World*. Likewise, it is tempting to connect the study of the 'hit parade' with the analyses that Bourdieu would apply ten years later to the 'grip of journalism';[35] although he does not use this expression in 1984, he sees in the ranking list the sign of a transformation of the balance of power between the intellectual field and the journalistic field in favour of the latter. However, the media and Bourdieu's relations with them were significantly transformed in the ten years or so that separate the analysis of the 'hit parade' (that Bourdieu published only in his review, and in an appendix to an academic work) from the brief polemical work that he was to publish at the end of 1996 for a wider readership,

Situating the Later Volumes of General Sociology   235

On Television, which is partly a book about 'media-friendly intellectuals'.[36] Essentially, we could say that the lectures published here do slightly pre-date the turning point represented by the privatisation in 1986 of the most popular channel, TF1. At the beginning of the 1980s, the spirit of public service inherited from the beginnings of television remained fairly strong.[37] Bourdieu was still liable to participate in television broadcasts from time to time or to take part in a debate with leading journalists. In 1985, for instance, he intervened in a forum organised by the Comité d'information pour la presse dans l'enseignement,[38] and encouraged by his Collège de France colleague Georges Duby, he started to participate in the 'educational television' project that would lead to the creation of 'la Sept' (Channel 7), which gave birth to Arte.[39]

The framework of the Collège de France

To understand the space where Pierre Bourdieu was situated in the years from 1983 to 1986 we have to think of the Collège de France. Georges Duby was one of his closest colleagues. Their relationship went back a long way: Duby was one of the founders of the review *Études rurales* in which Bourdieu had published a substantial article (more than a hundred pages long) at the beginning of the 1960s, when he was almost unknown.[40] In the lectures for 1986 where he elaborates the notion of the 'field of power', Bourdieu often quotes his medievalist colleague's book, *Les Trois Ordres, ou l'imaginaire du féodalisme* (1978). He also refers to the analyses of Indo-European triads developed by Georges Dumézil, who had retired in 1968 after nearly twenty years teaching at the Collège de France (he died in 1986). Bourdieu discusses Claude Lévi-Strauss's arguments even more often (although Bourdieu referred to his anthropological studies continuously throughout his career, even when he no longer attended his seminar). Lévi-Strauss retired from the Collège de France in 1982, but a lecture that he gave in 1983 marks a moment of tension between the two men, as reflected in one of Bourdieu's lectures in 1986 (5 June 1986). Bourdieu's lectures also contain glancing allusions to or passing discussions of research by younger professors at the Collège de France: Emanuel Le Roy Ladurie (18 April 1985), Jacques Thuillier (2 May 1985), whom Bourdieu had known from the École normale supérieure, and Gérard Fussman (28 March 1985).

Bourdieu played his part in the life of the institution. He refers twice to seminars or colloquia which united participants from the different

236   *Situating the Later Volumes of* General Sociology

historical and literary disciplines represented at the Collège de France (22 May and 19 June 1986). He participated until his retirement in various events of this nature. In 1984–85 he urged his audience to go to the lectures that Francis Haskell had come to deliver at the Collège de France (18 April 1985, 2 May 1985). Bourdieu's lectures do not refer to any of the works of the 'Collège scientists', but when the right returned to power in 1986,[41] Bourdieu joined several of them (the biologist Jean-Pierre Changeux, the physicist Claude Cohen-Tannoudji, the pharmacologist Jacques Glowinski and the chemist Jean-Marie Lehn) in signing a 'solemn appeal' to the government, which intended to reduce the public funds allocated to research. In addition, the lectures are contemporary with the preparation of the 'Propositions for the education of the future' that the President of the Republic (François Mitterrand) had asked the professors of the Collège de France to prepare in 1984 and which was remitted in March 1985.[42] Bourdieu was the editor in chief, and even to some considerable extent, the initiator of the project.[43]

During these years, one of the members of the Collège de France whose lectures were most popular was Michel Foucault. Bourdieu was to explain much later what attracted him to and what distanced him from Michel Foucault,[44] whose seminar at the École normale supérieure he had attended. In the 1980s, Foucault and Bourdieu joined forces in appealing to the French government to support Polish trade unionists, but the lectures published here bear witness to a mixture of esteem and distance. Although Bourdieu makes explicit reference to Foucault's work, such as his notion of *épistémè*, the fourth and fifth years' lectures are marked by an ongoing critique of the analyses of power elaborated by the philosopher: in particular the formula 'power springs from below' is seen as showing naive thinking, inspired above all by a spirit of contradiction (17 April 1986). Bourdieu's lectures had already finished just over a month before Foucault's death at the end of June 1984. Bourdieu joined André Miquel and other professors from the Collège de France to attend the ceremony in Paris that preceded his funeral.[45] He published two notices in homage to 'a friend and colleague', one in *Le Monde* and the second in *L'Indice*.[46]

The intellectual field in the first half of the 1980s

The lectures also show the influence of the contemporary intellectual field outside the Collège de France.[47] They contain allusions to major figures from previous decades, such as Jean-Paul Sartre and

Situating the Later Volumes of General Sociology   237

Jacques Lacan, who had died in 1980 and 1981 respectively, and Louis Althusser, who was interned in November 1980 after murdering his wife. In one of his lectures Bourdieu alludes to the contemporary journalistic debate over finding a 'successor' to Sartre.[48] The dominant figures of the moment who combine intellectual recognition with public notoriety are a group of fifty-year-olds that include Bourdieu, with, principally, Michel Foucault, Jacques Derrida, Gilles Deleuze (and Félix Guattari).[49] They became known during the years preceding May 1968 and shared what Bourdieu calls an 'anti-institutional mood' (2 May 1985). These 'consecrated heretics', according to another of Bourdieu's formulae,[50] took their distance from traditional philosophy and the traditional university. In the first half of the 1980s, they often found themselves signing the same appeals or petitions. However, a younger generation emerged and started to relegate them to the past: in autumn 1985 an essay much hyped by the media took as its target the 'anti-humanist '68 thinking' that they allegedly represented.[51] Bourdieu alludes to this book in one of his lectures (5 June 1986), and on several occasions mentions the thematics of the 'return to Kant' and the 'return to the subject' that its authors stand for.

If he mentions only in passing the development of the 'postmodernism' that dates from the second half of the 1970s (in discussing research into the sociology of science, whose relativism he criticises), he does make several references to the appearance, at roughly the same time, of the 'nouveaux philosophes': 'From the moment that someone intrudes into the space, even a "new philosopher", their existence creates a problem and provokes thought, although that thought may make people think askew, not to mention the fact that it may cause people to burn energy that could be more usefully employed elsewhere' (18 April 1985). The attitude to adopt in the face of this new type of rival, and more generally in the face of the threats that seem to confront 'philosophy' at this time, then provoke debate; several allusions in the lectures reveal Bourdieu's reservations, as he takes his distance from Deleuze's declarations on the 'nouveaux philosophes' (which he finds counter-productive) or from the Estates General of philosophy organised by Jacques Derrida.[52] His analysis of the 'hit parade', however, shows his awareness of the accelerating structural transformations at work at this time,[53] and of the danger they represent for the perpetuation of the intellectual model that he incarnates.

At the beginning of the 1980s, his own status in the intellectual field changed, but according to a logic that is not easy to characterise unequivocally. His election to the Collège de France, for example, or the success of *Distinction*, which made its mark as an important book

238　　*Situating the Later Volumes of* General Sociology

with an impact well beyond the circle of specialists, increased the recognition of his work, but at the same time made him the incarnation of a discipline and a body of thought that many intellectual schools of thought attacked for being a 'determinist' or even 'totalitarian' 'sociologism'. Among these various criticisms and attacks (which on occasion find an echo in the lectures published here), we could mention, even if they are only a few examples among others, those emanating from collaborators or intellectuals connected with the review *Esprit* or the book that appeared in 1984, *L'Empire du sociologue*.[54]

The subspace of sociology

We find this ambiguity in the subspace of sociology. Since his work was already at a stage that authorised a retrospective viewpoint, Bourdieu sometimes ventures in his lectures to grasp and formulate the general sense of his enterprise; he can insist on the efforts that he has made, in opposition to 'economic and economistic analysis', to highlight 'the decisive role of the symbolic in social exchanges', 'all those conflicts that history is full of and whose stakes are never reducible to their material dimensions' (22 March 1984 and 30 May 1985); he may also point out that his 'historical contribution' will have been to 'take his work as a sociologist to its conclusion, that is the objectification of the professionals of objectification' (19 June 1986),[55] or to 'show due respect to anything that could help us think more deeply about the social world' (14 March 1985). Moreover, he starts working on a synthesis (which includes these lectures) and popularisation. In parallel with his research, Bourdieu started to publish books designed to give accessible insight into his work: in 1980 for the first time he collected in one volume oral presentations given in diverse circumstances.[56] In 1983, one of his first students, Alain Accardo, published the first book that undertook to lay the major concepts of his sociology before a readership of students and militants.[57] His international reputation also grew. Thus, just before starting the fifth year of his lectures, he spent a month travelling round the United States, where he gave fifteen seminars and lectures in American universities (San Diego, Berkeley, Chicago, Princeton, Philadelphia, Baltimore, New York University). In the years that followed, he made similar tours in other countries.

This growing consecration does not mean that he started to exercise a 'mastership'. In sociology, as in the whole of the intellectual field, the growing recognition that Bourdieu attracted seemed to generate even fiercer forms of rejection. In the first half of the 1980s, there were several

Situating the Later Volumes of General Sociology   239

attempts to describe his sociology as 'out of date', with some talk of an 'actor's last farewell'. The attacks were mounted, in particular, in the name of a 'methodological individualism' that claims to explain social phenomena on the basis of a desocialised *homo sociologicus*. Their leader was Raymond Boudon, who, having been in the 1960s one of the principal importers into France of the 'methodology' of Paul Lazarsfeld (which Bourdieu attacked on epistemological grounds),[58] developed in the 1970s an analysis of educational inequalities challenging the views imposed by *The Inheritors* and *Reproduction*. If Bourdieu in these lectures repeats his criticism of 'methodological individualism' on several occasions, or points out his divergence from the view of his work that it propagates, it is because this current of thought, which was making inroads in the United States at the same time, had entered a particularly aggressive phase. In 1982 Presses Universitaires de France published a *Dictionnaire critique de la sociologie*, edited by Raymond Boudon and François Bourricaud, whose project 'to scrutinise the imperfections, uncertainties and flaws of sociological theories, but also the reasons for their success', is an attack on Marxist- or structuralist-inspired sociology.

Bourdieu's remarks on the 'ultra-subjectivism' and 'facile radicalism' that are emerging in the sociology of science are a response to the appearance in 1979 of the book *Laboratory Life*.[59] Based on the ethnographical study of a laboratory of neuroendocrinology, this book claims to found an approach explicitly different from the analyses that Bourdieu had been offering since the mid-1970s on 'the scientific field and the social conditions of the progress of reason'. Bourdieu rejects this approach, which radicalises to the point of relativism the thesis according to which scientific facts are socially constructed. The authors' insistence on the scientists' search for credibility and their reliance on rhetorical apparatus leads them to ignore the fact that not all strategies are possible in the scientific field (28 March 1985 and 19 June 1986). Some fifteen years later, by which time this 'new sociology of science' had developed considerably, Bourdieu would return to this criticism.[60]

In these lectures Bourdieu also discusses the imports into sociology that took place in the 1980s. These years saw a wave of translations in France of a German contemporary of Durkheim, Georg Simmel, and the 'discovery' of interactionism and ethnomethodology, 'heterodox' currents of American sociology dating from the 1950s and 1960s. At the intersection of sociology and philosophy, the work of the Frankfurt School, largely unknown in France before the 1970s, was also published copiously at the start of the 1980s, particularly by

240   *Situating the Later Volumes of* General Sociology

Payot at the instigation of Miguel Abensour. In one lecture Bourdieu offers in passing an analysis of these imports of the 1980s (5 June 1986). Although he mocks the provincialism that leads the French to translate research when it has gone out of fashion in its native land, he cannot help being irritated by these imports when they are introduced by more or less declared rivals in the sociological space and presented as innovations that require immediate attention. In fact they are sometimes explicitly opposed to his own sociology, despite being authors that he had read long before and whom he had helped to make known in France (most of Goffman's work had been translated in the 1970s and 1980s by Éditions de Minuit), and above all whom he had already integrated into his approach.

The political context

The concern to offer teaching that was theoretical but not divorced from the most concrete reality inspires frequent allusions to the political context of the times, to the questions and problems constituted as such in the media and in the political world. Bourdieu finds an almost perfect example of his reflections on the 'science of the State' in the unemployment figures published by INSEE. This statistical indicator in fact became a central stake in contemporary political debate: the unemployment rate was very low until 1973 but then rose continually until the mid-1980s. Among other things, the arrival in France of mass unemployment helped to foreground the question of immigration – the electoral scores of the Front National after 1982 are only the most spectacular manifestation of this. In this way 'current affairs' are a direct illustration of one of the ideas developed by Bourdieu: it is the principles underlying the vision of the social world (and in the event the question of whether the division between immigrants and non-immigrants can replace the division between rich and poor) that are at stake in the struggle. In the first half of the 1980s the growing stigmatisation of immigrants inspired a mobilisation of opposition opinion that Bourdieu associated himself with. Thus he signed a text of support for the march for equality and against racism that took place in autumn 1983,[61] and he played a part in the activities of SOS Racisme, close to the Socialist Party, launched in 1984. In November 1985, for example, he took part in a meeting with the association during which he warned them of the danger of an 'ethico-magical movement' and denounced those who analyse immigration in terms of cultural difference, because this provides a smokescreen

Situating the Later Volumes of General Sociology   241

hiding the economic and social inequality between Frenchmen and immigrants.

The lectures also include echoes of the rise of neoliberalism, whose acceleration at the start of the 1980s was symbolised by the accession to power of Margaret Thatcher in Great Britain and Ronald Reagan in the United States. The economists of the 'Chicago School', mentioned on several occasions by Bourdieu, are said to have encouraged economic policies which, contrary to the interventionist policies employed in the post-war decades, consider, in a now-famous formula, that the State (or at least its 'left hand') is 'the problem, not the solution'. When at one moment he discusses the difference between private charity and public welfare (9 and 23 May 1985), Bourdieu mentions the attacks that the Welfare State was subjected to at the time. In the last lecture published in the fourth volume (30 May 1985), the connection that he establishes between the tragedy that had just occurred at the Heysel stadium and the politics of the 'Iron Lady' announces the theme of the 'law of conservation of violence' that he will use to confront the neoliberal politicians in the 1990s.[62] Moreover, the lectures often echo events and situations that are being discussed in the 'foreign affairs' columns of the French media at the time. Thus Bourdieu alludes to the Iranian revolution or the Irish troubles and offers elements of reflection on them based on his theoretical analyses.

At a national level, the period corresponds to François Mitterrand's first seven-year mandate. The lectures make few allusions to internal political events, apart from some critical comments on the restoration of the school of the Third Republic sought and proposed by the socialist minister of education, Jean-Pierre Chevènement (12 June 1986).[63] The last lecture of the Course makes a few (anecdotal) references to the return of a right-wing government as a result of the legislative elections of March 1986. We can, however, note that, without alluding to this in his lectures, Bourdieu did take public stands on some aspects of the policies implemented by successive governments: he signed several petitions condemning the position of the socialist government towards events in Poland,[64] but also an appeal relating to conditions in prisons and, after the return of the right to power in 1986, appeals against cuts in the budget for research and against the proposal to halt the construction of the new opera house at the Bastille.

The Lecture of 19 June 1986 that concludes the final volume brings Bourdieu's five-year Course in General Sociology to a close. It was the first general introduction to sociology ever given at the Collège de France. The following year, Bourdieu took advantage of the opportunity that members of the Collège have to suspend their teaching

242 *Situating the Later Volumes of* General Sociology

temporarily. He started his lectures again in 1988 with a new title, 'À propos de l'État' ('On the State'). This marks the start of a five-year cycle devoted to the analysis and deconstruction of this institution and, more generally, the start of a period when Bourdieu's lectures at the Collège focus on specific themes: after the sociology of the State[65] came the sociology of the economic field, the sociology of domination, the sociology of a symbolic revolution in painting;[66] then, in a sort of conclusion to his teaching, he analysed research into the sociology of science in general and the sociology of sociology in particular,[67] as if to remind his audience, in opposition to a certain kind of radical relativism, that it is possible, given the right social circumstances – precisely those that constitute the scientific field – to produce truths that are not reducible to the social world that produces them.

Summary of Lectures of 1985–86

The relation of immediate complicity established between the habitus and the social fields is one of cognition, but of a quite particular form: the practical sense that orients the ordinary practices of everyday existence (as opposed to those used in moments of crisis) operates through a kind of bodily confrontation with the world, below consciousness and discourse, objectification and representation. It is the habitus – as the socially constituted source of the perception and appreciation of the social world – that determines *itself* and determines the world to determine it. The people who have what we call a 'feel for the game', the model of practical mastery that agents have of a game whose structures they have incorporated, see what 'has to be done' (or said) and they read into the present moment of the game the future that it is pregnant with, they note the 'objective potential' that it comprises and this triggers a response absolutely irreducible to the rational strategy of a consciously calculating mind. (This is why, for instance, we cannot explain variations in practice in matters of fertility without referring to people's differential sensitivity to security or insecurity, or their different practices in matters of disputes and law suits without taking into account their differential sensitivity to offence or injustice.) We may say that agents do exercise choices, but only if we bear in mind the fact that they do not choose the grounds for those choices at every moment. It follows that we cannot allow interpretation of these acts of recognition, obedience or submission provoked by the symbolic powers to remain trapped within the alternative of a purely mechanist reaction to constraint, a 'voluntary servitude' based on 'bad faith', or the 'false consciousness' of the 'subjects' voluntarily helping to produce the machinery of their own servitude.

Symbolic power is a power that can only operate with the collaboration of the person subjected to it; but this complicity, far from being a

244 *Summary of Lectures of 1985–86*

conscious or deliberate concession that could be revoked by a simple change of mind, is rooted in the fundamental investment – interest in the game, or *illusio* – involved in membership of a field, that is, in a habitus whose structures are adapted to the structures of the field. All forms of symbolic credit or discredit exist only through and for the belief that constitutes them, but this belief is itself the product of a whole individual and collective history: symbolic capital, whether in the case of Benveniste's *fidēs*, Weber's charisma, or more generally the charms of power and the powerful, becomes capital of one kind or another when it is perceived according to the categories of perception and appreciation that it imposes, so that its arbitrary nature is mis-recognised and it is recognised as legitimate. Like the stigma attached to the colour of somebody's skin or their ethnic or religious identity, symbolic capital is made by the gaze, but to change the gaze, you have at least – although this alone is not sufficient, because of the *hysteresis* of the habitus – to change the social conditions producing the gaze, that is, the structure of the distribution of capital.

When the cognitive structures that are the source of our experience of the social world are themselves a product of our experience of this world, we find history communicating with itself, in a way, below the level of discourse and consciousness. The social order is written into our bodies, and the magic of the symbolic power that operates through social orders or judgements draws on the fact that these appeal to long-term dispositions, the coiled springs of socialisation that are the incorporated, somatised form of this order with all the regulations, prohibitions or injunctions that it imposes. We also show in passing that the compelling presence of the unavoidable alternative of the individual and the collective, which is rooted deep in our everyday or semi-scientific thoughts, locked into appearances and enclosed in the ceaselessly recurring oppositions of political struggles – such as liberalism and socialism, individualism and capitalism – prevents us from forming an adequate notion of an agent who would be defined precisely by overcoming this opposition: the real agent, armed with his whole history written into him in the form of incorporated properties, can be defined equally well either as a collective entity individualised by incorporation, or as a biological individual 'collectivised' by sociali-sation; and he is just as distant – although in different ways – from collective realities as is the abstract individual, totally lacking in social qualities and any economic and legal context, who is his exact oppo-site. In addition, insofar as he is endowed with a system of creative dispositions that enable endless innovation, but within the limits of the implicit principles of the habitus, that practical *ars inveniendi*, he is

Summary of Lectures of 1985–86 245

just as far from being the simple 'appendage' of social structures that certain structuralists have made of him as he is from being the constituent subject of the idealist tradition.

However, reminding ourselves that social agents construct the social world by applying to it patterns of perception and appreciation which are socially constituted, and which orient their strategies and thereby the reproduction or transformation of the structures, does not mean we have to return to an intellectualist representation of action and the agent that would lead us to place in the conscious mind of the agent the rational constructions or discursive models needed to account for their practices. The work of constructing social reality, in which social agents participate even when they are arguing and haggling over the definition of social realities (over their existence or non-existence, the legitimate way of identifying them, or the value that should be attributed to them, etc.), is mostly undertaken as part of the ordinary action of everyday existence, that is, in a practical way and without passing through representation and explanation. The social definitions of health or physical or mental illness, of delinquency or crime, are collective constructions in which the whole set of agents engaged in the medical field, including the patients, collaborate, as do the whole set of agents involved in the judicial field – police force, lawyers, judges and the accused. These practical constructions, which are elaborated through countless daily transactions, negotiations, confrontations and interactions, of which the most typical are classificatory notions such as proper and common names designating collective entities and identities – clans, tribes, nations, regions, professions or social classes – present themselves to the analyst as given, as ready-made for some scientific activity reduced to a recording exercise. The effect of imposition that results from this is never so visible as when researchers take as their instrument of analysis something they ought rather to submit to analysis, when they accept a definition of their object that is implied in the definition preconstructed by the population concerned (for instance a list of writers) or basing their statistical analysis on systems of classification borrowed uncritically from the universe being analysed.

Social agents fight over the sense of the social world and thereby help to construct it. Among these cognitive struggles, we should distinguish those, like the law, where the goal is to enunciate the legitimate principles of division of the world, and where the professionals of explication confront one another, driven by the generic and specific interests involved in holding a position in a juridical, religious, political or scientific field, or a field of cultural production. This obliges

246   *Summary of Lectures of 1985–86*

us in passing to raise the question of the specificity of the scientific vision of the social world and the social conditions that need to be fulfilled, particularly in the practical determination of the weapons used and the goals pursued in the competition, in the struggles (whose drive and motivation are no doubt less pure than the hagiographers allege) to manage to favour the emergence of social products relatively independent of the social conditions of their production. Far from threatening sociology in its very foundations, the fact that sociology can take itself as an object is the founding principle of a methodical attempt to attain a reflexive mastery of the social determinants of scientific practice. The act of assuming vulnerability may be transformed into a privilege. Social science, in its objectivist or structuralist phase, records objective patterns independent of individual consciousness and will, in order to express the effect of structural constraint that gives the social world a reality independent of thought. In so doing, it reduces the representations that agents make of their world, and even their experience of it, to the level of appearance and illusion. Awareness of the particularities of the position of the scholar, the man of *skholè* [leisure] tempted by what Austin called a 'scholastic vision', leads us to make a second break with the vision that was itself born of a break with the common vision. Just as it was necessary to transcend the particular view linked to a particular position in the social world in order to accede to an overview allowing us to objectify the first-degree viewpoint over the social world, so we need to transcend the transcendental vision of the objectivist moment in order to reintroduce, as an integral part of the objective reality of the social world, the different, contrasting and even contradictory viewpoints that are in conflict over this world: the objectivist construction that allows us to situate the different perspectives over the social world as viewpoints taken from clearly determined points in this world is in no way invalidated by an analysis that moves to a higher level in order to take these struggles over the world and its objectivity into account, and assign them their proper place in the active construction of this world. If we overcome the fictitious opposition between a structuralist objectification and a subjectivist constructivism, we can also set ourselves the goal of grasping both the objective structure of the social universes (the social field as a whole or some particular specialised field) and the properly political strategies that agents produce with a view to making their viewpoint triumph. And this without forgetting that the whole world of construction, whether practical or theoretical, individual or collective, whereby the agents (particularly institutional groups like the professional corps) participate in producing social realities and inscribing them into the lasting objectivity of the structures, is oriented by the perception they have of the social world, which depends on their position in these structures and their dispositions, themselves fashioned by the structures.

Notes

Editorial Note

1 Pierre Bourdieu, *Science of Science and Reflexivity*, trans. Richard Nice (Cambridge: Polity, 2004).
2 Pierre Bourdieu, *On the State*, trans. David Fernbach (Cambridge: Polity, 2015).
3 Pierre Bourdieu, *General Sociology*, vol. 1, *Classification Struggles*, trans. Peter Collier (Cambridge: Polity, 2018), vol. 2, *Habitus and Field*, trans. Peter Collier (Cambridge: Polity, 2019).
4 See the editors' note in Bourdieu, *On the State*, pp. xi–xii.

Lecture of 17 April 1986

1 In the last lecture of the previous year (30 May 1985), Bourdieu had explained why the formula 'a sociology of symbolic forms' constituted a 'barbarism'. The concept of a 'symbolic form' proposed by Ernst Cassirer in *The Philosophy of Symbolic Forms* (New Haven: Yale University Press, 1998) follows a neo-Kantian tradition and is to be understood as a universal, transhistorical form.
2 Bourdieu may have in mind the analyses of forms of power and influence (in particular those exercised by 'leaders' over 'followers') developed by Bertrand Russell in *Power: A New Social Analysis* (London: Allen & Unwin, 1938).
3 The notion of 'propaganda', for example, is central to the Frankfurt School. It is used by Max Horkheimer and Theodor Adorno in *Dialectic of Enlightenment*, trans. John Cumming (London: Verso, 1997), and by Jürgen Habermas in *The Structural Transformation of the Public Sphere*, trans. Thomas Burger and Frederick Lawrence (Cambridge: Polity, 1989).
4 The Greek word *charisma* is often translated as 'grace'.
5 See the Lecture of 30 May 1985, in Pierre Bourdieu, *General Sociology*, vol. 4, *Principles of Vision*, trans. Peter Collier (Cambridge: Polity, 2022), pp. 244, 307.
6 Pierre Bourdieu and Yvette Delsaut, 'Le couturier et sa griffe', *Actes de la recherche en sciences sociales*, no. 1, 1975, pp. 7–36.

Notes to pp. 7–12 249

7 'Music, by a natural bent, is that which at once receives an adjective ... No doubt the moment we turn an art into a subject (for an article, for a conversation) there is nothing left but to give it predicates.' Roland Barthes, 'The Grain of the Voice', in *Image, Music, Text*, trans. Stephen Heath (London: Fontana, 1977), p. 179.

8 Claude Lévi-Strauss, 'Introduction à l'oeuvre de Marcel Mauss', in Marcel Mauss, *Sociologie et Anthropologie* (Paris: PUF, 2008), pp. ix–lii.

9 M. Mauss and H. Hubert, 'Esquisse d'une théorie générale de la magie', in *Sociologie et Anthropologie*, p. 119.

10 On the relations between social structures and mental structures, see Pierre Bourdieu, 'The Kabyle House or the World Reversed', in *The Logic of Practice*, pp. 271–83; on the relations between economic structures and economic dispositions, see Pierre Bourdieu, *Algérie 60* (Paris: Minuit, 1977) and *Esquisses algériennes* (Paris: Seuil, 2008); on the effects of the disintegration of social structures on mental structures, see Bourdieu (with Abdelmalek Sayad), *Le Déracinement. La crise de l'agriculture traditionnelle en Algérie* (Paris: Minuit, 1964).

11 See Pierre Bourdieu, *Forms of Capital*, trans. Peter Collier (Cambridge: Polity, 2021), Lecture of 29 March 1984, pp. 137, 335, re Jean-Paul Sartre, *Critique of Dialectical Reason*, vol. 1, trans. Alan Sheridan-Smith (London: Verso, 2004), p. 723: 'The old violence is absorbed by the inertia-violence of the institution.'

12 In his lectures for this year, 1985–86, Bourdieu refers several times to these analyses by Michel Foucault and his formula: 'Power comes from below; that is, there is no binary and all-encompassing opposition between rulers and ruled at the root of power-relations, and serving as a general matrix – no such duality extending from the top down and reacting on more and more limited groups to the very depths of the social body. One must suppose rather that the manifold relationships of force that take shape and come into play in the machinery of production in families, limited groups, and institutions, are the basis for wide-ranging effects of cleavage that run through the social body as a whole. These then form a general line of force that traverses the local oppositions and links them together; to be sure, they also bring about redistributions, realignments, homogenizations, serial arrangements, and convergences of the force relations. Major dominations are the hegemonic effects that are sustained by all these confrontations.' Michel Foucault, *A History of Sexuality, Volume 1: An Introduction*, trans. Robert Hurley (New York: Pantheon Books, 1978), p. 94.

13 Edmund Husserl, *Ideas: A General Introduction to Pure Phenomenology*, trans. W. R. Boyce Gibson (London: Routledge, 2012).

14 Ibid., §46.

15 Bourdieu is referring principally to the 'seminar' sessions of his lecture course, which during the previous year he had devoted entirely to an analysis of the 'Impressionist revolution'. See *Principles of Vision*.

16 The reference may well be to 'The Spirit of Christianity and its Fate' (1798–99), where Hegel invokes 'this important period in which men strove by various routes to revert from barbarism, which followed the loss of the state of nature, to the unity which had been broken'. G. W. F. Hegel, *Early Theological Writings*, trans. T. M. Knox (Philadelphia: University of Pennsylvania Press, 1971), p. 182.

250   *Notes to pp. 13–18*

17 An article on this topic had appeared a few years earlier in the review *Actes de la recherche en sciences sociales*: Danièle Léger, 'Les utopies du "retour"' (no. 29, 1979, pp. 45–74).

18 If it is difficult to determine which philosopher Bourdieu is thinking of, it is possible that he is in fact invoking his own research on Algeria, although the sentences that follow the 'quotation' given in this lecture suggest a modification of the previous formula: 'The traditional order is only viable on condition that it is chosen, not as the best possibility, but as the only possibility, on condition that all the "lateral possibilities" are ignored, since they contain the greatest threat, through the simple fact that they would make the traditional order, held as necessary and immutable, as one possibility among others, that is, as arbitrary. The very survival of traditionalism is at stake, as traditionalism unaware of its status as a choice unaware of it choosing.' Pierre Bourdieu, 'Traditional Society's Attitude towards Time and Economic Behaviour', in *Algerian Sketches*, trans. David Fernbach (Cambridge: Polity, 2013), pp. 52–71.

19 An allusion to the Frankfurt School, which Bourdieu had already referred to at the start of the lecture. Theodor Adorno and Max Horkheimer speak, for instance, of the 'mystification of the masses' in *Dialectic of Enlightenment*.

20 A few weeks after this lecture, in June 1986, the principal themes broached in these second sessions became the central focus of an issue of *Actes de la recherche en sciences sociales*, 'L'illusion biographique' (nos. 62–3) and of a brief article with the same title published there by Bourdieu (pp. 69–72). See Pierre Bourdieu, 'The Biographical Illusion', trans. Y. Winkin and W. Leeds-Hurwitz, *Working Papers and Proceedings of the Center for Psychosocial Studies (Chicago)*, 14, 1987, pp. 1–7.

21 The term and the process of 'deconstructionism' became current in philosophy and literary analysis after the publication in 1967 of Jacques Derrida's *Of Grammatology*, trans. Gayatri Chakravorty Spivak (Baltimore: Johns Hopkins University Press, 1997).

22 In 1968, the first two parts of *The Craft of Sociology*, for instance, were devoted to the 'break [with preconstructed objects]' and to the demands of 'constructing the object'. Pierre Bourdieu, Jean-Claude Chamboredon and Jean-Claude Passeron, *The Craft of Sociology: Epistemological Preliminaries*, trans. Richard Nice (Berlin and New York: Walter de Gruyter, 1991).

23 Alain Robbe-Grillet, *Le miroir qui revient* (Paris: Minuit, 1984), p. 208. [*Ghosts in the Mirror*, trans. Jo Levy (London: Calder, 1988); my translation here.]

24 In the Lecture of 24 April, Bourdieu expands on this brief allusion, which he refers to *Macbeth* but also to William Faulkner's novel, *The Sound and the Fury* (1929).

25 This is no doubt a reference to a passage in Ferdinand Saussure's *Course in General Linguistics*, trans. Wade Baskin (New York: Columbia University Press, 1995), p. 70: 'The signifier, being auditory, is unfolded solely in time, from which it gets the following characteristics: a) *it represents a span*, and b) *the span is measurable in a single dimension*; it is a line.'

26 An allusion to the distinction established by Heidegger in *Being and Time* between lived history (*Geschichte*) and historical enquiry (*Historie*). Martin Heidegger, *Being and Time*, trans. John Macquarrie and Edward Robinson (Oxford: Blackwell, 1962).

27 David Hume, *Treatise of Human Nature* (London: Penguin, 1969), Book 1, Part 4, Section VI: 'Of Personal Identity', pp. 299–310: 'But further, what

Notes to pp. 18–23 251

must become of all our particular perceptions upon this hypothesis? All these are different, and distinguishable, and separable from each other, and may be separately considered, and may exist separately, and have no need of any thing to support their existence. After what manner therefore do they belong to self, and how are they connected with it? For my part, when I enter most intimately into what I call myself, I always stumble on some particular perception or other, of heat or cold, light or shade, love or hatred, pain or pleasure.'

28 An allusion to the revival in the seventeenth century of the classical genre of the 'Characters', of which the best-known example is the work by La Bruyère, *Caractères, ou les Moeurs de ce siècle* (1688).

29 The example refers no doubt to Molière's 'comedy of character', *Le Misanthrope ou L'Atrabilaire amoureux* (1666).

30 Immanuel Kant, *Critique of Pure Reason*, trans. Paul Guyer and Allen W. Wood (Cambridge: Cambridge University Press, 1998), 'Transcendental Analytic', Book I, Chapter II, Second Section, §16, p. 248: 'I am therefore conscious of the identical self in regard to the manifold of the representations that are given to me in an intuition because I call them all together my representations, which constitute one.'

31 Later on, Bourdieu spells out the names of the authors of the tendency he is thinking of: Saul Kripke and Paul Ziff. The 'theory of possible worlds' was elaborated by Leibniz in his *Theodicy* (1710).

32 The problem is part of the notion of 'multipositionality' developed by Pierre Bourdieu and Luc Boltanski on the subject of 'Les professeurs de l'Institut d'études politiques' in *La production de l'idéologie dominante* (Paris: Seuil, 2008).

33 Bourdieu is probably thinking of the case of André Chastel, holder of the chair of 'Art and Civilisation in Renaissance Italy' at the Collège de France from 1971 to 1984, who was a contributor to *Le Monde* for over forty years.

34 Bourdieu develops his analysis of the naive painters in *The Rules of Art*, trans. Susan Emanuel (Cambridge: Polity, 1996), pp. 244–7, 385.

35 This example is developed in Pierre Bourdieu and Monique de Saint Martin in 'La Sainte famille. L'épiscopat Français dans le champ du pouvoir', *Actes de la recherche en sciences sociales*, nos. 44–5, 1982, pp. 2–53.

36 In 1980 an issue of *Actes de la recherche en sciences sociales* (no. 35) had been devoted to the question of identity. Roger Brubaker's text appeared a good time later in the same review: 'Au-delà de l'"identité"', trans. Frédéric Junqua, *Actes de la recherche en sciences sociales*, no. 139, 2001, pp. 66–85.

37 Saul Kripke, *Naming and Necessity* (Oxford: Blackwell, 1980).

38 In the Lecture of 9 November 1982, *Habitus and Field*, pp. 109–10, and the Lecture of 8 March 1984, *Forms of Capital*, pp. 41–2, re: Bertrand Russell, 'On Denoting', *Mind*, 14, 1905, pp. 479–93.

39 Paul Ziff, *Semantic Analysis* (Ithaca: Cornell University Press, 1967), p. 104.

40 Pierre Bourdieu, 'Les rites comme actes d'institution', *Actes de la recherche en sciences sociales*, no. 43, 1982, pp. 58–63; 'Rites of Institution', in Bourdieu, *Language and Symbolic Power*, trans. Gino Raymond and Matthew Adamson (Cambridge: Polity, 1991), pp. 117–26.

41 Pierre Bourdieu, *The Logic of Practice*, trans. Richard Nice (Cambridge: Polity, 1990), pp. 170–2.

42 André Chamson (1900–83) was a historian, essayist, novelist, Academician and Director General of the Archives de France. His memoirs had been published posthumously two years earlier: *Il faut vivre vieux* (Paris: Grasset, 1984).

252   ·   *Notes to pp. 24–29*

43 Pierre Bourdieu and Monique de Saint Martin, 'Les catégories de l'entendement professoral', *Actes de la recherche en sciences sociales*, no. 3, 1975, pp. 68–93; Bourdieu, 'The Categories of Professorial Judgement', in *Homo Academicus*, trans. Peter Collier (Cambridge: Polity, 1988), pp. 194–225. The analysis of obituaries was resumed by Bourdieu in *The State Nobility*, trans. Lauretta C. Clough (Cambridge: Polity, 1996), pp. 35–53. Bourdieu invokes some reactions to this work in *Sketch for a Self-Analysis*, trans. Richard Nice (Cambridge: Polity, 2004), p. 43.

44 Jean-Paul Sartre, *Being and Nothingness*, trans. Hazel Barnes (Abingdon: Routledge, 2003), pp. 134–40. The sentence from Malraux is 'The terrible thing about Death is that it transforms life into Destiny.' André Malraux, *L'Espoir* (Paris: Gallimard, 1937), p. 225; *Man's Hope*, trans. Stuart Gilbert and Alastair Macdonald (New York: Grove/Atlantic, 1979).

45 See Pierre Bourdieu, 'L'Invention de la vie d'artiste', *Actes de la recherche en sciences sociales*, 1, no. 2, 1975, pp. 67–93; 'The Invention of the Artist's Life', trans. E. R. Koch, *Yale French Studies*, 73, 1987, pp. 75–103; *The Rules of Art*, pp. 4–43.

46 Eugène Nicole, 'Personnages et rhétorique du nom', *Poétique*, no. 46, 1981, pp. 200–16.

47 The *cursus honorum* ('honours race') in ancient Rome defined the order in which the different public magistratures (access to which was controlled by very strict rules of age) could be held successively. It became formalised only in 180 BC.

48 Until 1999 all households in France received a visit at regular intervals from the census officers. The principal information required from each member of the household was their surname, first name, profession, date of birth, position in the household and nationality.

49 Bourdieu had used the word *census* the previous year (Lectures of 9 and 30 May 1985, in *Principles of Vision*).

50 See for example the Lecture of 28 March 1985, in *Principles of Vision*.

Lecture of 24 April 1986

1 As early as 1965, in his introduction to *Photography: A Middle-brow Art*, Bourdieu does not oppose the subjective to the objective, but explains that sociology should work to recapture the objectification of subjectivity: 'the description of objectified subjectivity refers to the description of the internalization of objectivity'. *Photography: A Middle-brow Art*, trans. Shaun Whiteside (Cambridge: Polity, 1990), p. 4.

2 Derived from the same Greek word, the terms of *noesis* and *noema* refer, respectively, to the act of thinking and the object of thought. Edmund Husserl defines their use in phenomenology in *Ideas*, 'Noesis and Noema', §87–96.

3 Émile Benveniste, *Dictionary of Indo-European Concepts and Society*, trans. Elizabeth Palmer (Chicago: Hau Books, 2016), Book I, pp. 75–90.

4 Greek verbs, like the French, can take an active form and a passive form, but also a 'middle' form which is generally close to the reflexive form in French, indicating that the subject of the verb suffers the action.

5 Benveniste, *Dictionary of Indo-European Concepts and Society*, p. 85.

6 Ibid., pp. 86, 87.

Notes to pp. 30–39 253

7 Ibid., p. 90.
8 Ibid., p. 87.
9 Ibid., p. 88.
10 Bourdieu had already drawn attention to this passage from Weber's *Economy and Society* in his Lecture of 3 May 1984, *Forms of Capital*, pp. 233, 349 note 39.
11 Benveniste, *Dictionary of Indo-European Concepts and Society*, pp. 135–8.
12 Claude Lévi-Strauss, 'Le sorcier et sa magie' (1949), in *Anthropologie structural* (Paris: Plon, 1958), pp. 183–203.
13 Benveniste, *Dictionary of Indo-European Concepts and Society*, p. 139.
14 For example: 'For our purposes here, the personal call is the decisive element distinguishing the prophet from the priest. The latter lays claim to authority by virtue of his service in a sacred tradition, while the prophet's claim is based on personal revelation and charisma.' Max Weber, *The Sociology of Religion*, trans. Talcott Parsons (Boston: Beacon Press, 1993), p. 46.
15 Weber speaks of a 'charisma of office', *Economy and Society*, 2 vols, trans. Ephraim Fischoff et al. (Berkeley: University of California Press, 2013), vol. 2, pp. 1139–41.
16 Robert A. Dahl, *Who Governs?* (New Haven: Yale University Press, 1961). Bourdieu had referred to this book already at the start of his Lecture of 7 March 1985, *Principles of Vision*, p. 2.
17 See the Lecture of 2 November 1982, *Habitus and Field*, especially pp. 82–8.
18 Bourdieu and Delsaut, 'Le couturier et sa griffe'; Bourdieu, 'The Production of Belief: Contribution to an Economy of Symbolic Goods', in *The Field of Cultural Production*, trans. Randal Johnson (Cambridge: Polity, 1993), pp. 74–111.
19 M. Mauss and H. Hubert, *A General Theory of Magic*, trans. Robert Brain (London: Routledge, 2001).
20 Mauss's *General Theory of Magic* starts by examining 'the elements of magic' (the magicians, the acts, the representations), after which he affirms the unity of the whole: 'At the same time the whole adds up to much more than the number of its parts. The different elements which we have dealt with consecutively are, in fact, present simultaneously. Although our analysis has abstracted them they are very intimately and necessarily combined in the whole.' Ibid., p. 107.
21 Jean-Paul Sartre, *Anti-Semite and Jew*, trans. George J. Becker (London: Grove Press, 1960). One formula has remained very famous: 'It is the anti-Semite who makes the Jew' (p. 69).
22 Rudolf Otto, *The Idea of the Holy*, trans. John W. Harvey (Oxford: Oxford University Press, 1958).
23 This may be a reference to the following phrase: 'The fetish of the art market is the master's name affixed to the work.' Walter Benjamin, 'Eduard Fuchs, Collector and Historian', trans. Edmund Jephcott and Howard Eiland et al., in *Selected Writings, vol. 3, 1935–1938* (Cambridge MA: Harvard University Press, 2002), p. 283. Bourdieu had already referred to this phrase the previous year, in his Lecture of 23 May 1985.
24 It is this 'historical anamnesis' that Bourdieu studies in *The Rules of Art*: 'It is a matter of describing the gradual emergence of the entire set of social mechanisms which make possible the figure of the artist as producer of that fetish which is the work of art – in other words, the constitution of the artistic field [. . .] as the locus where belief in the value of art – and in that power to create

254 *Notes to pp. 39–45*

value which belongs to the artist – is constantly produced and reproduced' (pp. 291–2).

25 Sartre, *Being and Nothingness*, pp. 70–94.

26 See above, Lecture of 17 April 1986, note 9.

27 On 23 April 1986, Jacques Chirac had participated in a political broadcast (the television programme *L'heure de vérité* [The moment of truth]) for the first time since his nomination as prime minister a month earlier. He had declared that the two priorities of his government were 'social order' and security.

28 François Bonvin, 'Systèmes d'encadrement et demandes des familles dans l'enseignement privé. Deux collèges secondaires dans leur marché', thèse de 3e cycle, Université Paris-V, 1978; 'L'école catholique est-elle encore religieuse?', *Actes de la recherche en sciences sociales*, no. 44, 1982, pp. 95–108.

29 Pierre Bourdieu and Alain Darbel, 'La fin d'un malthusianisme?', in Darras, *Le partage des bénéfices* (Paris: Minuit, 1966), pp. 135–54; Pierre Bourdieu, 'The Future of Class and the Causality of the Probable', trans. M. Grenfell, in A. Christoforou and M. Lainé (eds.), *Re-Thinking Economics: Exploring the Work of Pierre Bourdieu* (London: Routledge, 2014), pp. 233–69.

30 The word 'fiction' comes from the Latin verb *fingere*, which means 'to falsely invent', 'to forge out of bits and pieces' but above all 'to fabricate'.

31 Bourdieu returns to the role of symbolic capital in the economic field in *The Social Structures of the Economy*, trans. Chris Turner (Cambridge: Polity, 2005).

32 Bourdieu is no doubt thinking of passages like the following: 'The essential fact of modern times is the advent of democracy. It is incontestably true that in the past, as described by its contemporaries, we find the shadow of coming events; but those indications which are perhaps most interesting would have been noted then only had they known that humanity was moving in that direction; now the trend of that movement was at that time no more marked than any other, or rather it did not yet exist, since it was created by the movement itself – that is, by the forward march of the men who have progressively conceived and realised democracy. The premonitory signs are therefore, in our eyes, signs only because we now know the course, because the course has been completed. Neither the course, nor its direction, nor in consequence, its end were given when these facts came into being: hence they were not yet signs.' Henri Bergson, *The Creative Mind*, trans. Mabelle L. Andison (New York: The Philosophical Library, 1946), p. 24.

33 The French translation of Julian Barnes's novel had just been published at the time this lecture was given (*Le Perroquet de Flaubert*, trans. Jean Guiloineau [Paris: Stock, 1986]).

34 See Lecture of 30 May 1985, *Principles of Vision*, pp. 230, 305 note 18.

35 William Shakespeare, *The Tragedy of Macbeth*, V, 5.

36 Wolf Lepenies, 'Der Wissenschaftler als Autor – Buffons prekarer Nachruhm', in *Das Ende Der Naturgeschichte. Wandel kultureller Selbstverstandlichkeiten den Wissenschaften des 18. Und 19. Jahrhunderts* (Munich: Carl Hanser Verlag, 1976), pp. 131–68, and published after this lecture: Wolf Lepenies, *Les Trois Cultures. Entre science et littérature. L'avènement de la sociologie* (Paris: Éditions de la Maison des sciences de l'homme, 1990), especially pp. 2–3. Bourdieu had treated at greater length the questions of style and writing in the sciences in the framework of his analysis of the space of disciplines during the second year of his lecture course (Lectures of 23 November 1982 and 30 November 1982, *Habitus and Field*, pp. 165–72 and pp. 183–5).

Notes to pp. 46–56 255

37 The audience laugh because they know that Minuit is one of Bourdieu's publishers.
38 Robbe-Grillet, *Le miroir qui revient*, p. 126.
39 'L'Illusion biographique' had not yet been published when this lecture was given; it appeared in June 1986.
40 Marcel Dassault had died at the age of ninety-four on 17 April 1986, a few days before this lecture was given.
41 See above, Lecture of 17 April 1986, p. 24.
42 Annie Ernaux, *A Man's Place*, trans. Tanya Leslie (London: Fitzcarraldo Editions, 1992).
43 Louis Marin, 'Pouvoir du récit et récit du pouvoir', *Actes de la recherche en sciences sociales*, no. 25, 1979, pp. 23–43.
44 The passage that follows makes reference to Jean-Paul Sartre's approach in *The Family Idiot: Gustave Flaubert 1821–1857*, trans. Carol Cosman (Chicago: University of Chicago Press, 1981–1991), an unfinished book whose first two volumes cover Flaubert's childhood and youth, the analysis concerning society and literature in Flaubert's time emerging only in the third volume. Against this approach, Bourdieu opposed his own analysis of Flaubert (*Habitus and Field*, pp. 271–2; *The Rules of Art*, pp. 1–43), as well as his own self-analysis, which is an exemplary illustration of his approach applied to himself (*Sketch for a Self-Analysis*).
45 Founded in 1894 and dissolved in 1910, Le Sillon was a political movement of Catholic inspiration which pleaded for an entente between the Church and the Republic, and offered the workers an alternative to the anti-clerical left.
46 On ('vertical' and 'horizontal') displacements in the social space, see Pierre Bourdieu, *Distinction*, trans. Richard Nice (London: Routledge, 1984), especially pp. 109–10.
47 We might quote, for example: 'This unity, which is the being of the man under consideration, is a free *unification*, and this unification can not come *after* a diversity which it unifies. But to be, for Flaubert, as for every subject of "biography", means to be unified in the world. The irreducible unification which we ought to find, which is Flaubert, and which we require biographers to reveal to us – this is the unification of an original project, a unification which should reveal itself to us as a *non-substantial attribute*.' Sartre, *Being and Nothingness*, p. 582.
48 'If I want to mix a glass of sugar and water, I must, willy nilly, wait until the sugar melts. This little fact is big with meaning. For here the time I have to wait is not that mathematical time which would apply to the entire history of the material world, even if that history were spread out simultaneously in space. It coincides with a certain portion of my own duration, which I cannot protract or contract as I would like. It is no longer something *thought*, it is something *lived*.' Henri Bergson, *Creative Evolution*, trans. Arthur Mitchell (Mineola, NY: Dover, 2012), pp. 10–11.
49 See in particular Bourdieu's *Homo Academicus*, and *Distinction*, pp. 71–2 and 110–11 (as well as a work published after these lectures, *The Rules of Art*).

256   *Notes to pp. 58–64*

Lecture of 15 May 1986

1 The principal users of the notion of the habitus are: in philosophy, Aristotle, the scholastics (Thomas Aquinas in particular) and Edmund Husserl and, in the social sciences, Émile Durkheim, Marcel Mauss and Norbert Elias.
2 Ludwig Wittgenstein, *Philosophical Investigations*, trans. G. E. M. Anscombe et al. (Chichester: Wiley-Blackwell, 2009), §82, p. 43: 'What do I call "the rule according to which he proceeds"? – The hypothesis that satisfactorily describes his use of words, which we observe; or the rule which he looks up when he uses signs; or the one which he gives us in reply if we ask him what his rule is? – But what if observation does not clearly reveal any rule, and the question brings none to light? For he did indeed give me an explanation when I asked him what he meant by "N", but he was prepared to withdraw this explanation and alter it. – So how am I to determine the rule according to which he is playing? He does not know it himself. – Or, more correctly, what is left for the expression "the rule according to which he proceeds" to say?'
3 See the Lecture of 9 November 1982, *Habitus and Field*, pp. 105ff.
4 Weber, *Economy and Society*, vol. 1, p. 4; he also speaks of 'an almost automatic reaction to habitual stimuli' and 'an uncontrolled reaction to some exceptional stimulus' (p. 25).
5 Gilbert Ryle, *The Concept of Mind* (New York: Barnes & Noble, 1962), pp. 86–7.
6 Pierre Bourdieu, *Outline of a Theory of Practice*, trans. Richard Nice (Cambridge: Cambridge University Press, 1977), pp. 27–8.
7 See the Lectures of 2 and 9 November 1982, *Habitus and Field*, pp. 89–96, 102–7.
8 Bourdieu is thinking of a 'phylactery': the speech bubble used in cartoon books which is meant to show what the character is saying or thinking.
9 Erich Auerbach, 'The Brown Stocking', in *Mimesis: The Representation of Reality in Western Literature*, trans. Willard R. Trask (Princeton: Princeton University Press, 1971), pp. 525–53 [translator].
10 Bourdieu returns to this analysis of the calendar in his lectures on the State (*On the State*, pp. 7–11).
11 As does Auerbach [translator].
12 Bourdieu regularly mobilises this 'sociological Proust' in *Distinction*. After these lectures his review published an article by Catherine Bidou-Zachariasen, 'De la "maison" au salon. Des rapports entre l'aristocratie et la bourgeoisie dans le roman proustien', *Actes de la recherche en sciences sociales*, no. 105, 1994, pp. 60–70, and in the collection *Liber*, Jacques Dubois, *Pour Albertine. Proust et le sens du social* (Paris: Seuil, 1997).
13 Bergson and Proust were born barely two years apart, and shared the same interest in memory and lived time, which gives rise to much reflection on the influence that the former may have had on the latter, on their convergence and divergences.
14 See the two previous lectures.
15 The quotation is perhaps borrowed from the following passage: 'To predict is not to see in advance, denying the event its radical novelty, reducing it to a *déjà vu* as the regular manifestation of some permanent essence.' Jean Cavaillès, *Sur la logique et la théorie de la science* (Paris: Vrin, 1997), p. 80.
16 Edmund Husserl, *The Phenomenology of Internal Time-consciousness*, trans. James S. Churchill (Bloomington: Indiana University Press, 2019).

Notes to pp. 65–71   257

17 See the Lecture of 29 March 1984, *Forms of Capital*, pp. 127ff.
18 Bourdieu often quotes this phrase from Leibniz: 'The present is big with the future' (from *Theodicy*, trans. E. M. Huggard, project Gutenberg ebook §17147, 2005, §360).
19 Sartre, *Critique of Dialectical Reason*, vol. I, pp. 293ff.
20 'The reader may perhaps already perceive that knowledge through the senses is something of a science: he will have to understand later that any science consists in perceiving things more exactly.' Alain, *Quatre-vingt-un chapitres sur l'esprit et les passions* (Paris: Camille Bloch, 1921), p. 19. Referring to this passage, Maurice Merleau-Ponty writes 'Perception is an incipient science.' *Phenomenology of Perception*, trans. Donald A. Landes (London: Routledge, 2014), pp. 56–7.
21 'Indeed, in three-fourths of our actions we are nothing but empirics.' Gottfried Wilhelm Leibniz, *The Monadology*, trans. Robert Latta, Global Grey ebook, 2018, §28.
22 Étienne de la Boétie, *Discours de la servitude volontaire* (Paris: Gallimard, 1983).
23 This remark, often quoted by Bourdieu, is inspired by the following passage: 'a truly philosophical criticism . . . does not however consist, as Hegel thinks, in discovering the determinations of the concepts of logic at every point; it consists in the discovery of the particular logic of the particular object.' Karl Marx, 'Critique of Hegel's Doctrine of the State', in *Early Writings*, trans. Rodney Livingstone and Gregor Benton (London: Penguin, 1992), pp. 158–9. One French translation is closer to the wording quoted by Bourdieu: 'Ce n'est pas la Logique de la Chose mais la Chose de la Logique qui est le moment philosophique.' Karl Marx, *Critique du droit politique hégélien*, trans. Albert Baraquin (Paris: Éditions sociales, 1975), p. 51 [translator].
24 Ziff, *Semantic Analysis*, p. 8.
25 See the Lecture of 9 November 1982, *Habitus and Field*, pp. 107ff.
26 Louis Althusser, 'Idéologie et appareils idéologiques d'État (Notes pour une recherche)', *La Pensée*, no. 151, 1970, pp. 3–38; reprinted in *Positions* (Paris: Éditions sociales, 1976), pp. 67–125.
27 Wittgenstein, *Philosophical Investigations*, §132 and 38 (the German reads 'wenn die Sprache leerläuft' and 'wenn die Sprache *fiert*').
28 'Methodological individualism' is a sociological current which studies collective phenomena as the result of individual actions. Bourdieu deals with this at greater length in the next lecture, 22 May 1986.
29 Bourdieu may be thinking in particular of James Coleman, with whom he co-edited *Social Theory for a Changing Society* (Boulder: Westview Press & Russell Sage Foundation, 1991).
30 This may refer to Pierre Bourdieu, 'Avenir de classe et causalité du probable', *Revue française de sociologie*, 15, no. 1, 1974, pp. 3–42; Bourdieu, 'The Future of Class and the Causality of the Probable'.
31 'Even if the crag is revealed as "too difficult to climb", and even if we must give up the ascent, let us note that the crag is revealed as such only because it was originally grasped as "climbable"; it is therefore our freedom which constitutes the limits which it will subsequently encounter.' Sartre, *Being and Nothingness*, p. 504.
32 'For example, a grimacing face suddenly appears pressed against the outside of the window; I am frozen with terror. [. . .] In the state of horror, we are

258   *Notes to pp. 71–75*

suddenly made aware that the deterministic barriers have given way. That face which appears at the window, for instance – we do not at first take it as that of a man, who might push the door open and take thirty paces to where we are standing. On the contrary, it is presented, motionless though it is, as acting at a distance. The face outside the window is in immediate relationship with our body; we are living and undergoing its signification; it is with our own flesh that we constitute it [. . .] Consciousness plunged into this magic world drags the body with it in as much as the body is belief and the consciousness believes in it.' Jean-Paul Sartre, *Sketch for a Theory of the Emotions*, trans. Philip Mairet (London: Methuen, 1981), pp. 84, 86–7.

33 'The serious attitude involves starting from the world and attributing more reality to the world than to oneself; at the very least the serious man confers reality on himself to the degree to which he belongs to the world. It is not by chance that materialism is serious; it is not by chance that it is found at all times and places as the favourite doctrine of the revolutionary. This is because revolutionaries are serious. They come to know themselves first in terms of the world which oppresses them, and they wish to change this world.' Sartre, *Being and Nothingness*, p. 601.

34 The allusion is probably to Pierre Legendre, *Jouir du pouvoir. Traité de la bureaucracie patriote* (Paris: Fayard, 1985).

35 See in particular *Distinction*, the chapter on 'Cultural Goodwill', pp. 318–71.

36 Dr Cottard is a character in *In Search of Lost Time* who appears in *The Way by Swann's* and frequents the 'little clan' of the Verdurins (the Guermantes way of the noble salons). He strives, with some difficulty and much care, to hold his place there, especially in the cultural domain. Marcel Proust, *In Search of Lost Time*, vol. 1, *The Way by Swann's* (London: Penguin, 2003).

37 During the break Bourdieu had written on the board a reference to Harold H. Kelley and John L. Michela, 'Attribution Theory and Research', *Annual Review of Psychology*, 31, 1980, pp. 457–501.

38 On this point, see especially *Classification Struggles*, pp. 12–13, 18.

39 'A. borrowed a copper kettle from B. and after he had returned it was sued by B. because the kettle now had a big hole in it which made it unusable. His defence was: "First, I never borrowed a kettle from B. at all; secondly, the kettle had a hole in it already when I got it from him; and thirdly, I gave him back the kettle undamaged." Each one of these defences is valid in itself, but taken together they exclude one another.' Sigmund Freud, *Jokes and their Relation to the Unconscious* (Harmondsworth: Pelican, 1978), p. 100.

40 The references that Bourdieu has noted on the board are as follows: Irene Frieze, 'Perceptions of Battered Women', in Irene Frieze et al. (eds.), *New Approaches to Social Problems* (San Francisco: Jossey-Bass Publishers, 1979), and Lenore Walker, *The Battered Woman* (New York: Harper & Row, 1979).

41 Saul Kripke, *Wittgenstein on Rules and Private Language: An Elementary Exposition* (Oxford: Basil Blackwell, 1982).

42 Pascal Engel, 'Comprendre un langage et suivre une règle', *Philosophie*, no. 8, 1985, pp. 45–64.

43 On this point, as on several topics discussed in this part of the lectures (including the commentary on *To the Lighthouse*), see Pierre Bourdieu, *Masculine Domination*, trans. Richard Nice (Cambridge: Polity, 2001).

44 See in particular the first year of Bourdieu's lectures at the Collège de France, *Classification Struggles*.

Notes to pp. 75–82 259

45 Jean-Paul Sartre, 'Élections, piège à cons', *Les Temps Modernes*, no. 378, 1973; reprinted in *Situations X. Politique et autobiographie* (Paris: Gallimard, 1976), pp. 75–87.

46 Bourdieu is alluding implicitly to Courbet's painting *The Origin of the World* (1866), which represents a nude woman whose genitals are at the centre of the picture. In 1989 a female artist, Orlan, painted a similar picture but representing a man, with the title *The Origin of War*.

47 Virginia Woolf, *To the Lighthouse* (Harmondsworth: Penguin, 1974). Page references given in the text are to this edition [translator].

48 I have had to change Bourdieu's commentary occasionally, to adapt it to the actual text and order of events of the novel, which Bourdieu seems to have misremembered [translator].

49 The poem recited is Alfred Lord Tennyson's 'The Charge of the Light Brigade', relating an incident in the Crimean War at the Battle of Balaclava (1854) where 500 British cavalrymen rode bravely and suicidally to their death.

50 Even if the formula itself is not to be found there, we might refer to the passage that Bourdieu devotes to war in his analysis of the sense of honour: 'From the "Rules" of Honour to the Sense of Honour', *Outline of a Theory of Practice*, pp. 10–15.

51 In fact, in the passage quoted, rather than fighting in the Crimean War, Ramsay imagines himself leading a polar expedition. The Antarctic explorer Ernest Shackleton had recently died at the South Pole in January 1922, having refused to abandon his ice-bound ship. *To the Lighthouse* was first published in 1927 [translator].

52 In fact, a judge or a statesman [translator].

53 See Bourdieu, 'Rites of Institution', in *Language and Symbolic Power*, pp. 117–26. For longer developments of this question, see in particular the Lecture of 16 November 1982, *Habitus and Field*, pp. 137–40.

54 This analysis no doubt owes a lot to the fact that Bourdieu, like most of the boys in the south-west of France, played rugby and remained a passionate fan of this 'virile' sport all his life. He refers explicitly to this in certain texts, in particular to illustrate metaphorically the 'feel for the game'.

55 See Bourdieu's analysis of *L'Éducation sentimentale* in the Prologue to *The Rules of Art*, in particular the section 'The Question of Inheritance', pp. 9–19.

56 See the Lecture of 8 March 1984, *Forms of Capital*, pp. 52–3, and 321 note 24, on this allusion to Plato.

57 On the occasion of the publication of *Masculine Domination*, Bourdieu alluded to some observations noted during a survey of house purchases ('A Contract under Duress', in *The Social Structures of the Economy*, pp. 148–84): 'We have been led to note that in the event of the purchase of a house, in every milieu, the men do not stoop to inform themselves, they leave to the women the trouble of putting questions, asking for prices, and if it turns out alright, that's fine, but if it doesn't, it's their fault. In thousands of little details like this, the women take a back seat or are sidelined, and all the more so when they are from a humble background. Social origins double this effect.' 'L'homme décide, la femme s'efface', interview with Catherine Portevin, *Télérama*, no. 2532, 22 July 1998.

58 For this reason Bourdieu will entitle the first part of his book *Masculine Domination*, 'A Magnified Image'. The reference to Plato is probably to *The Republic*, where, faced with the observation that the nature of justice seems

260   *Notes to pp. 82–91*

to be written in 'small writing' in 'the individual', Socrates proposes to find a 'larger copy of the same writing' by studying it at the level of the 'whole city', for since 'a city is something bigger than an individual', 'justice will be on a larger scale in what is larger, and easier to find out about.' Plato, *The Republic*, trans. Tom Griffith (Cambridge: Cambridge University Press, 2000), Book 2, 368c-e, pp. 49–50.

59 Bourdieu, 'The Kabyle House or the World Reversed', in *The Logic of Practice*, pp. 271–83.

60 See Bourdieu, *Outline of a Theory of Practice*, esp. 'Matrimonial Strategies and Social Reproduction', pp. 58–71.

61 Immanuel Kant, *Anthropology from a Pragmatic Point of View*, trans. Robert B. Louden (Cambridge: Cambridge University Press, 2012), p. 103.

62 Bourdieu may be thinking of texts like Joel Feinberg's 'Legal Paternalism', *Canadian Journal of Philosophy*, 1, no. 1, 1971, pp. 105–24; Gerald Dworkin, 'Paternalism', *The Monist*, no. 56, 1972, pp. 64–84; Bernard Gert and Charles M. Culver, 'The Justification of Paternalism', *Ethics*, 89, no. 2, 1979, pp. 199–210.

63 See Bourdieu, *Distinction*, especially pp. 402–5.

64 A reference to an enquiry into museums that Bourdieu and researchers from his Centre had carried out in 1964 and 1965, and which had led to the publication of *L'Amour de l'Art* in 1966. See Pierre Bourdieu and Alain Darbel, *The Love of Art: European Art Museums and their Public*, trans. C. Beattie and N. Merriman (Cambridge: Polity, 1990).

65 Le Laboratoire d'anthropologie sociale was the research centre set up by Claude Lévi-Strauss in 1960 at the Collège de France and the École pratique des hautes études.

Lecture of 22 May 1986

1 This analysis had been presented in the Lecture of 24 April 1986, and was based on Benveniste, *Dictionary of Indo-European Concepts and Society*, pp. 85–90.

2 See Maurice Merleau-Ponty, *Résumés de Cours. Collège de France (1952–1960)* (Paris: Gallimard, 1968), and *La Prose du Monde* (Paris: Gallimard, 1969).

3 See, for example, the development of the 'feel for the game' in the Lecture of 2 November 1982, *Habitus and Field*, pp. 78–80.

4 Sartre, *Being and Nothingness*, pp. 485ff. 'The world by means of its very articulation refers to us exactly the image of what we are.'

5 See the Lecture of 12 October 1982, *Habitus and Field*, p. 25.

6 Bourdieu is thinking of Michel Foucault, Gilles Deleuze or Jacques Lacan, who all, in their different ways, developed variations on the themes of desire and/or power.

7 In the middle of the 1980s, while liberalism was gaining ground with Ronald Reagan in power in the United States and Margaret Thatcher in the United Kingdom, the theme of the return of the individual, and a retreat to the private sphere after the exhaustion of collective action, inspired many enquiries and articles in the press. Essays published on the theme included: Gilles Lipovetsky, *L'Ère du vide. Essais sur l'individualisme contemporain* (Paris: Gallimard, 1983), and Alain Laurent, *De l'individualisme. Enquête sur le retour de l'individu* (Paris: PUF, 1985). In sociology, Marxism lost ground and some critics started to talk

Notes to pp. 91–100 261

of a 'return of the individual' or a 'return of the actor', based in particular on the works of Raymond Boudon or Michel Crozier.

8 *Habitus* is the past participle of this verb, as Bourdieu had pointed out in his Lecture of 29 March 1984, where he defined it as 'something having-been-acquired'. See *Forms of Capital*, pp. 133 and 334 note 11.

9 See the Lectures of 1983–84, especially the Lecture of 19 April 1984, *Forms of Capital*, pp. 156–84.

10 'Methodological individualism', as noted above, consists in studying collective phenomena as the result of individual actions. The expression, which had been used by the philosopher Karl Popper and the economist Joseph Schumpeter, found new fortune in French sociology with Raymond Boudon, who invested in it in the 1970s. It is Boudon whom Bourdieu seems to have principally in mind in the argument that follows. Boudon's methodological individualism is one part of his critique of Durkheimian and Marxist sociologies, perceived as incarnations of a 'holistic' (from the Greek, meaning 'whole' or 'total') position.

11 Sartre, *Being and Nothingness*.

12 Bourdieu had raised the question of racism in the Lecture of 24 April 1986, referring to the analyses developed by Jean-Paul Sartre in *Anti-Semite and Jew*.

13 Maurice Merleau-Ponty, *Les Aventures de la dialectique* (Paris: Gallimard, 1955). This book, written after Merleau-Ponty had left Jean-Paul Sartre's review *Les Temps Modernes*, includes a discussion of Sartre's philosophical (and political) positions.

14 Lévi-Strauss, 'Le sorcier et sa magie'.

15 An allusion to Mauss and Hubert, 'Esquisse d'une théorie générale de la magie'.

16 J. L. Austin, *How to Do Things with Words* (Oxford: Oxford University Press, 2009).

17 The *angelus rector* draws on the idea, still present in Kepler, of a 'guardian angel' presiding over the movement of the planets.

18 For example: 'When the activities of the body that need to be exercised in the service of the mind are oft *repeated*, they gain an increasingly higher degree of adequacy, because the soul acquires an increasingly greater familiarity with all the circumstances concerned, and becomes more and more at home in these external manifestations, so that it accedes to an ever-increasing capacity of immediate corporeal translation of its internal determinations, and consequently transforms the body more and more into its property, its useful instrument; in such a way that this gives birth to a *magical* relationship, an immediate influence of the mind on the body.' G. W. F. Hegel, *Encyclopédie des sciences philosophiques*, vol. III, *Philosophie de l'esprit*, trans. Bernard Bourgeois (Paris: Vrin, 2008), addendum to §410, p. 513; 'The *most unmediated* magic is, more precisely, that exercised by the individual mind on *its own corporality*, making this the submissive and passive executor of its will' (addendum to §405, p. 467). [My translation from the French; the addenda are not included in English editions.]

19 Otto, *The Idea of the Holy*.

20 See Bourdieu, *Distinction*, and the analysis of the struggle between position and disposition in the Lecture of 2 November 1982, *Habitus and Field*, pp. 72ff.

21 For development of this topic, see the Lecture of 10 May 1984, *Forms of Capital*, pp. 241–68.

262   *Notes to pp. 102–112*

22 Karl Marx, *The Ethnological Notebooks*, ed. Lawrence Krader (Assen: Van Gorcum & Co. BV, 2nd edition, 1974), p. 335.
23 Sartre, *The Family Idiot*, vol. III, *passim*. Sartre associates commitment to art for art's sake with neurosis (and with the radical failure of social and aesthetic ambition).
24 See in particular the Lecture of 7 December 1982, *Habitus and Field*, pp. 221–2.
25 Bourdieu, *The Logic of Practice*.
26 The annals of the Collège de France have not enabled us to identify this series of seminars. According to Bourdieu's indications, we are led to think that they might have included, apart from Georges Duby (chair of the History of Medieval Societies from 1970 to 1991), Emmanuel Laroche (chair of Asia Minor studies from 1973 to 1985), Jean Leclant (chair of Egyptology from 1979 to 1990), and perhaps also Gilbert Dagron (History and Civilisation of the Byzantine World from 1975 to 2001) and Jacques Gernet (chair of Social and Intellectual History of China from 1975 to 1992).
27 'Was woman anything other than an illusion, a sort of veil, screen . . . or rather a lure, go-between and intermediary? . . . in this military society, was not courtly love in truth a love for men? I am willing to give at least a partial answer: I am convinced that, in serving his wife it was the love of the prince that the young men aspired to, with their humble, devoted compliance. Just as they bolstered the morality of marriage, the rules of refined love came to reinforce the rules of feudal morality . . . Under the discipline of courtly love, was masculine desire not exploited for political ends?' Georges Duby, 'À propos de l'amour que l'on dit courtois', in *Féodalité* (Paris: Gallimard 'Quarto', 1996), p. 1420.
28 On this point, see also Michel Foucault who, in his *History of Sexuality, Volume 1*, also analysed this process of the autonomisation of sexuality in the nineteenth century.
29 In English in the text. The notion was introduced into the social sciences by Robert K. Merton, 'The Self-Fulfilling Prophecy', *Antioch Review*, 8, no. 2, 1958, pp. 193–219. Bourdieu, however, attributes it to Popper (see the Lecture of 14 March 1985, *Principles of Vision*, pp. 25 and 279 note 19).
30 See the Lecture of 30 May 1985, *Principles of Vision*, pp. 239 and 307 note 44, where Bourdieu cites Descartes on God as being true, rather than a deceiver, and the guarantor of our knowledge. See Descartes, *Meditations on First Philosophy*, especially Meditation V.
31 Romain Rolland, *Jean-Christophe*, trans. Gilbert Cannan (New York: Henry Holt and company, 1911), p. 17. See the Lecture of 15 March 1984, *Forms of Capital*, pp. 89 and 327–8 note 46.
32 G. W. F. Hegel, *Elements of the Philosophy of Right*, trans. H. B. Nisbet (Cambridge: Cambridge University Press, 1991), pp. 12–14. See the Lecture of 8 March 1984, *Forms of Capital*, pp. 45 and 321 note 16.
33 See Bourdieu, *Homo Academicus*.
34 We are not certain we have accurately transcribed this remark, but it is likely that Bourdieu was thinking of exclusion procedures such as those practised in particular by the French Communist Party in the 1950s.
35 In the Lecture of 22 March 1984, where he analyses *The Trial*, Bourdieu had already alluded to the letter Kafka had addressed to his father, but not sent, in 1919, and which was published in the 1950s. See *Forms of Capital*, pp. 126, 333 note 54. Franz Kafka, *Letter to his Father*, trans. Ernst Kaiser and Eithne Wilkins (New York: Schocken Books, 1966).

Notes to pp. 112–116 263

36 Published during Kafka's lifetime (in 1915), the novella had been written in 1912 (during the same period as the novella 'The Verdict'). The main character is a young office worker who still lives with his parents and his sister. The plot of the story is announced in its famous *incipit*: 'As Gregor Samsa awoke one morning from uneasy dreams he found himself transformed in his bed into a gigantic insect.' Franz Kafka, *Metamorphosis and Other Stories*, trans. Willa and Edwin Muir (Harmondsworth: Penguin, 1961).

37 The Greek term *anamnesis* designates the action of recalling something to memory. Plato uses it to defend his theory of reminiscence, according to which 'knowledge is simply recollection' (*Phaedo*, 72c) of what the soul has contemplated in the heaven of Ideas. The word has passed into the vocabulary of medicine and psychoanalysis (the cure aims to make the patient recall an unconsciously repressed past). In the 1990s, Bourdieu often used it to designate the part of sociological work concerned with a repressed collective past deposited in unconscious form in our vision of the world (*The Rules of Art*, pp. 108, 290–5, 312; *Masculine Domination*, chapter 2), or the social past of the researcher (*Sketch for a Self-Analysis*).

38 Bourdieu went on to organise a similar enquiry whose results were published in *The Weight of the World*, trans. Priscilla Parkhurst Ferguson et al. (Cambridge: Polity, 1999).

39 See the Lecture of 24 April 1986, pp. 28–40 above.

40 Bourdieu may be thinking of Sigmund Freud, 'A Child is Being Beaten', in *On Psychopathology*, trans. James Strachey (Harmondsworth: Penguin, 1979), pp. 159–93.

Lecture of 29 May 1986

1 See above, Lecture of 15 May 1986, note 21, 'Indeed, in three-fourths of our actions we are nothing but empirics.' Leibniz, *The Monadology*, §28.

2 For Spinoza, 'Desire is appetite with a consciousness of itself', where appetite corresponds to man's effort to 'persist in his being' and is 'nothing else than the essence of man'. Baruch Spinoza, *Ethics*, trans. Andrew Boyle (London: Dent, 1986), Part III, Definitions of the Emotions, I, p. 128. It is no doubt psychoanalysis, and the writers variously inspired by it (like Gilles Deleuze and Félix Guattari), that Bourdieu has in mind when he refers to recent usage of the word.

3 Concepts developed by Saint Augustine in *The City of God* and adopted by Pascal: 'All that is in the world is concupiscence of the flesh, the concupiscence of the eyes, and the pride of life. *Libido sentiendi, libido sciendi, libido dominandi.* Unhappy the accursed land which these three rivers of fire inflame rather than water!' Pascal, *Pensées*, ed. Louis Lafuma, trans. John Warrington (London: Dent, 1960), §696.

4 The *conatus* ('effort' in Latin) designates the fact that 'Everything in so far as it is in itself endeavours to persist in its own being.' Spinoza, *Ethics*, Part III, Proposition VI, p. 91.

5 Later, in one of his lectures at the Collège de France in 1993, Bourdieu proposed a 'table of the grand classes of strategies of reproduction'. 'Stratégies de reproduction et modes de domination', *Actes de la recherche en sciences sociales*, no. 105, 1994, pp. 3–12.

264 *Notes to pp. 117–123*

6 Bourdieu had already dealt with 'decision theory', albeit in a slightly different perspective, in the second year of his course. See the Lecture of 9 November 1982, *Habitus and Field*, pp. 100–26.

7 'Marginalism' in the strict sense refers to the introduction of marginal reasoning into classical economic thought from the 1870s, along with the concepts of marginal utility and productivity. Here the word should no doubt be understood as a simple synonym of 'neoclassical economics', and in opposition in many respects to Marxist economics.

8 'We presuppose labour in a form in which it is an exclusively human characteristic. A spider conducts operations which resemble those of a weaver, and a bee would put many a human architect to shame by the construction of its honeycomb cells. But what distinguishes the worst architect from the best of bees is that the architect builds the cell in his mind before he constructs it in wax.' Karl Marx, *Capital*, trans. Ben Fowkes (Harmondsworth: Penguin, 1990), vol. I, part 3, chapter 7, 1, pp. 283–4.

9 Herbert A. Simon, *Administrative Behavior: A Study of Decision-Making Processes in Administrative Organization* (New York: Macmillan, 1947), pp. 67–9.

10 Allen Newell and Herbert A. Simon, *Human Problem Solving* (Englewood Cliffs: Prentice Hall, 1972), pp. 70–3.

11 The astronomer Tycho Brahe (a near contemporary of Giordano Bruno, who was executed by the Inquisition in 1600 for defending the heliocentric hypothesis of Copernicus) is famous above all for the compromise he attempted to formulate in order to preserve the geocentric hypothesis while integrating certain objections to it.

12 'No social order is ever destroyed before all the productive forces for which it is sufficient have been developed, and new superior relations of production never replace older ones before the material conditions for their existence have matured within the framework of the old society. Mankind thus inevitably sets itself only such tasks as it is able to solve, since closer examination will always show that the problem itself arises only when the material conditions for its solution are already present or at least in the course of formation.' Karl Marx, 'Preface' to *A Contribution to the Critique of Political Economy* (Moscow: Progress Publishers, 1977).

13 Bourdieu probably has in mind Aaron Cicourel's research into expert programmes in medicine. An article had been published in French six months before this lecture: 'Raisonnement et diagnostic: le rôle du discours et de la compréhension classique en médecine', *Actes de la recherche en sciences sociales*, no. 60, 1985, pp. 79–89.

14 Heidegger, *Being and Time*. [Heidegger's expression is 'In-der-Welt-sein'/'Being-in-the-World' (translator).]

15 Sartre, *Being and Nothingness*, p. 472.

16 Marcel Proust, *In Search of Lost Time*, vol. 4, *Sodom and Gomorrah*, trans. John Sturrock (London: Penguin, 2002), pp. 505–21.

17 The reference here is to the concentration of economists of neoclassical inspiration in the Department of Economics at the University of Chicago from the 1960s onward: monetarists, theoreticians of rational anticipation, of public choice, etc. Gary Becker and Milton Friedman are the best known 'members' of this school.

Notes to pp. 124–132   265

18 Immanuel Kant, *Groundwork of the Metaphysics of Morals*, trans. Mary Gregor and Jens Timmermann (Cambridge: Cambridge University Press, 2012), pp. 21–55.
19 Erving Goffman, 'Symbols of Class Status', *The British Journal of Sociology*, 2, no. 4, 1951, p. 297; Goffman, *The Presentation of Self in Everyday Life* (Harmondsworth: Penguin, 1969), pp. 172, 186.
20 The formula 'learned ignorance' which Bourdieu refers to is associated with Nicholas de Cusa's 1440 work *On Learned Ignorance*, which explains how 'to know' is 'to be ignorant of', appealing notably to Socrates who 'knew nothing but his own ignorance'.
21 An allusion to Arthur Schopenhauer's *The World as Will and Representation*, trans. E. F. J. Payne (New York: Dover, 2000).
22 Plato develops the theory of the 'philosopher-king' in Book V of *The Republic*. Lenin reactivates this theory in the sense that he condemns spontaneism and considers that the Party must guide the workers, providing them with 'political knowledge'. The French Communist Party in 1966 notoriously reproached Louis Althusser with using his 'epistemological break' to resuscitate the figure of the 'philosopher-king'.
23 Bourdieu had mentioned this movement in the social sciences during the previous lecture, 22 May 1986.
24 A reference to the 'battle of the gods and the giants' waged between materialism (the friends of the earth) and idealism (the friends of Ideas) in Plato's *The Sophist* (§246).
25 This seminar session and the two others that follow, concerning the field of power, are based on a text that Bourdieu had just written but did not publish during his lifetime. The text, which was found in his archives, was published after his death: 'Champ du pouvoir et division du travail de domination. Texte manuscrit inédit ayant servi de support du Cours au Collège de France, 1985–1986', *Actes de la recherche en sciences sociales*, no. 190, 2011, pp. 126–39.
26 Bourdieu is referring allusively to a branch of American political science whose iconic representative was Robert A. Dahl, author of the 1961 book *Who Governs?*
27 The lectures were given at the Sorbonne in 1913–14. Émile Durkheim, *Pragmatism and Sociology*, trans. J. C. Whitehouse (Cambridge: Cambridge University Press, 1983), p. 94.
28 Ibid., p. 95.
29 Ibid.
30 Bourdieu is thinking of Mauss's 'Essay on the Gift' (1923–24), which he commented on at greater length in his lectures of 1992–93 devoted to the creation of the economic field. In this text, which ends strikingly in a 'conclusion on general sociology and morality', Mauss points out, among other things, that 'societies have progressed insofar as they themselves, their subgroups, and lastly the individuals in them, have succeeded in stabilising relationships, giving, receiving, and finally giving in return'. Marcel Mauss, *The Gift*, trans. W. D. Halls (London: Routledge, 2006), p. 105.
31 The reference may be to the sections 'Religious Ethics, World Order, and Culture' and 'Relation to Politics, Economics, Sex, Art' in Weber's *The Sociology of Religion*. Weber deals with the tensions that emerge between 'the systematization of religious obligations in the direction of an ethic based on inner religious faith' and 'the reality of the world . . . with the increasing

266 *Notes to pp. 133–140*

systematization and rationalization of communal relationships . . . of particular autonomous spheres of life' (p. 209), 'which themselves become systematized with their own laws', as 'the material development of an economy on the basis of social associations flowing from market relationships generally follows its own objective rules' (p. 217) . . . and 'art becomes an autonomous sphere' (p. 243).

32 Bourdieu had already emphasised these points in his Lecture of 22 March 1984, *Forms of Capital*, pp. 97–126.

33 Georg Lukács, *History and Class Consciousness: An Essay in Marxist Dialectics*, trans. Rodney Livingstone (Cambridge MA: The MIT Press, 1972).

34 Bourdieu is no doubt thinking of a sentence in Engels' correspondence that he quotes on other occasions. 'The jurist imagines that he is operating with a priori propositions, while the latter are *after all* only reflections of the economic process.' Friedrich Engels, Letter to Conrad Schmidt in Berlin, London, 27 October, 1890, trans. Sidney Hook, in Marx-Engels Correspondence, 1890, at www.marxists.org.

35 See Bourdieu, 'The Specificity of the Scientific Field and the Social Conditions of the Progress of Reason', trans. R. Nice, in Ch. C. Lemert (ed.), *French Sociology, Rupture and Renewal Since 1968* (New York: Columbia University Press, 1981), pp. 257–92.

36 In a text written after these lectures, Bourdieu describes the editor as a 'dual character who has to be able to reconcile art and money, the love of literature and the search for profit' and 'who has the absolutely extraordinary power to ensure *publication*, that is, to give a text and an author access to *public* existence'. 'Une révolution conservatrice dans l'édition', *Actes de la recherche en sciences sociales*, nos. 126–7, 1999, pp. 3–28; 'A Conservative Revolution in Publishing', trans. R. Fraser, *Translation Studies*, 1, no. 2, 2008, pp. 123–53.

37 In his work on comparative mythology, Georges Dumézil advances a theory of 'trifunctionality' (religion, war, production). See in particular *L'Idéologie des trois fonctions dans les épopées des peuples indo-européens* (Paris: Gallimard, 1968), and *Les Dieux souverains des Indo-Européens* (Paris: Gallimard, 1977).

38 Georges Duby, *Les Trois Ordres, ou l'Imaginaire du féodalisme* (Paris: Gallimard, 1978).

39 Bourdieu had already referred to this paradigm in his lectures. See in particular the Lecture of 2 June 1982, *Classification Struggles*, pp. 98–9.

40 On this point, see the Lecture of 12 May 1982, *Classification Struggles*, pp. 33–4.

41 Bourdieu devoted a complete series of lectures to analysing the juridical field (lectures for the academic year 1988–89) as well as an article: 'La force du droit. Éléments pour une sociologie du champ juridique', *Actes de la recherche en sciences sociales*, no. 64, 1986, pp. 3–19; 'The Force of Law: Toward a Sociology of the Juridical Field', trans. R. Terdiman, *Hastings Law Journal*, 38, no. 5, 1987, pp. 814–53.

Lecture of 5 June 1986

1 If, in spite of this request, we publish *in extenso* this recording of his lecture that Bourdieu made for his personal use – since he used the lectures and seminars less as occasions to expound what he has 'already thought' than as incitements

Notes to pp. 141–144 267

to pursue his reflection by expounding it – it is because, apart from the innate interest of this exposé (which it is preferable to reproduce exactly rather than reconstituted from partial and inaccurate notes), the reticence that he reveals to his audience in justifying this ban goes further than the case in point and serves as a warning that affects our manner of reading the whole series of lectures, emphasising in particular the fact that we must not take 'literally' a text which is the transcription of an oral discourse partly improvised, and incomplete.

2 Ernst Troeltsch, *Oeuvres*, vol. III, *Histoire des religions et destin de la théologie* (Paris: Cerf/Labor et Fides, 1996), chapter 'Que signifie "essence du christian-isme"?'

3 The Rassemblement Pour la République and the Union pour la Démocratie Française were the two main right-wing parties in France in the 1980s.

4 This may be a glancing allusion to Paul Nizan's book on the philosophers, *Les Chiens de garde* (Paris: Rieder, 1932).

5 Pierre Bourdieu, 'Le champ scientifique', *Actes de la recherche en sciences sociales*, no. 2, 1976, pp. 88–104; 'The Specificity of the Scientific Field'.

6 On this point and other aspects mentioned later in this lecture, see Pierre Bourdieu and Jean-Claude Passeron, 'Sociology and Philosophy in France since 1945: Death and the Resurrection of a Philosophy without Subject', *Social Research*, 34, no. 1, 1967, pp. 162–212.

7 Bourdieu is no doubt using the example of Kant because he was in vogue in the middle of the 1980s. Philippe Raymond, for example, published in *Commentaire* in 1985 an article entitled 'Le retour à Kant et la philosophie politique' (no. 30, pp. 651–7).

8 *Die philosophischen Schriften von Gottfried Wilhelm Leibniz* (Berlin: C. I. Gerhard, 1875–90; reissued Hildesheim, 1960–61), vol. 7, p. 191.

9 A notion from game theory proposed under the name of the 'focal point' by Thomas Schelling in *The Strategy of Conflict* (Cambridge MA: Harvard University Press, 1960). It is the solution (for example to try to manage to meet) which two people who are unable to communicate with each other will tend to select.

10 See above, Lecture of 15 May 1986, note 21.

11 'The latter [the philosophers] always have what you mentioned – time. They carry on their conversation unhurriedly, in peace and quiet discussion . . . The duration of the discussion doesn't bother them: it could be long or short. Their only concern is to reach the truth. A speaker in a law court, however, is differ-ent: his allotted time is slipping away and forcing him to hurry his speech. Nor can he talk about whatever strikes his fancy: he's got an adversary standing over him, wielding necessity in the form of a document stating what the issues of the case are, which is read out to ensure that the speaker confines himself to these issues.' Plato, *Theaetetus*, §172e–173a.

12 'My general opinion about this doctrine is that it is a typically scholastic view, attributable, first, to an obsession with a few particular words, the uses of which are over-simplified, not really understood or carefully studied or cor-rectly described; and second, to an obsession with a few (and nearly always the same) half-studied "facts". (I say "scholastic", but I might just as well have said "philosophical"; over-simplification, schematisation, and constant obsessive repetition of the same small range of jejune "examples" are not only not pecu-liar to this case, but far too common to be dismissed as an occasional weakness of philosophers.) The fact is, as I shall try to make clear, that our ordinary

268 *Notes to pp. 145–158*

words are much subtler in their uses, and mark many more distinctions, than philosophers have realised; and that the facts of perception, as discovered by, for instance, psychologists but also by common mortals, are much more diverse and complicated than has been allowed for. It is essential, here as elsewhere, to abandon old habits of *Gleischaltung*, the deeply ingrained worship of tidy-looking dichotomies.' J. L. Austin, *Sense and Sensibilia* (Oxford: Clarendon Press, 1962), p. 3.

13 An allusion to Gary S. Becker, *The Economic Approach to Human Behaviour* (Chicago: University of Chicago Press, 1978), chapter 11, 'A Theory of Marriage'; Becker, *A Treatise on the Family* (Cambridge MA: Harvard University Press, 1993).

14 Claude Lévi-Strauss, 'L'ethnologie et l'histoire', *Annales ESC*, 38, no. 6, 1983, pp. 1217–31. This is the text of the Marc Bloch lecture that Lévi-Strauss had given in June 1983; Bourdieu had already commented on this lecture: Pierre Lamaison, 'De la règle aux stratégies: entretien avec Pierre Bourdieu', *Terrains*, no. 4, 1985, pp. 93–100, reprinted in *In Other Words* (Cambridge: Polity, 1990), 'From Rules to Strategies', pp. 59–75.

15 An allusion no doubt to the essay by Luc Ferry and Alain Renaut, *La Pensée 68. Essai sur l'anti-humanisme contemporain*, which had been published by Gallimard in November 1985.

16 See the Lecture of 14 March 1985, *Principles of Vision*, pp. 16 and 278 note 6.

17 See the special issue 'Dispute Processing and Civil Litigation', *Law and Society Review*, 15, nos. 3–4, 1980–81. Bourdieu refers especially to the following articles: Lynn Mather and Barbara Yngvesson, 'Language, Audience and the Transformation of Disputes', pp. 776–821; William L. F. Felstiner, Richard I. Abel and Austin Satat, 'The Emergence and Transformation of Disputes: Naming, Blaming, Claiming', pp. 631–54; and Dan Coates and Steven Penrod, 'Social Psychology and the Emergence of Disputes', pp. 654–80.

18 Pierre Bourdieu, Alain Darbel, Jean-Paul Rivet and Claude Seibel, *Travail et travailleurs en Algérie* (Paris: Mouton, 1973).

19 The ten years preceding these lectures were characterised by a very large increase in unemployment in France and followed a period marked by new waves of immigration (originating in Morocco and Tunisia from the 1960s onward, and from sub-Saharan Africa a little later). At the time of these lectures, the National Front, which in 1982 and 1984 had scored its first electoral victories, linked the two phenomena.

20 The word 'orthodoxy' is formed from two Greek words, *orthos*, 'right', and *doxa*, 'opinion'.

21 This opposition is the central thesis of Émile Durkheim's *The Division of Labour in Society*, trans. W. D. Halls (London: Palgrave Macmillan, 2013).

22 This is no doubt a reference to the type of thesis defended by James Burnham in *The Managerial Revolution* (London: Lume Books, 1941), or in the 1960s by John Kenneth Galbraith in *The New Industrial State* (Princeton: Princeton University Press, 2007).

23 Lecture of 3 May 1984, *Forms of Capital*, pp. 213–40.

24 This enquiry, conducted in 1969, is referred to in particular in Bourdieu's 1972 conference paper entitled 'Public Opinion Does Not Exist', in *Sociology in Question*, trans. Richard Nice (London: Sage, 1993), pp. 149–57.

25 Goffman, *The Presentation of Self in Everyday Life*, pp. 38–9: 'The difference between the front maintained by a nurse and the front maintained by a doctor

Notes to pp. 159–165 269

is great; many things that are acceptable for nurses are *infra dignitatem* for doctors. Some medical people have felt that a nurse "under-ranked" for the task of administering anaesthesia and that doctors "over-ranked"; were there an established status midway between nurse and doctor, an easier solution to the problem could be found.'

26 On the difference between 'corps' and 'field' and on the passage from the logic of the corps to the logic of the field, see Pierre Bourdieu, *Manet: A Symbolic Revolution*, trans. Peter Collier and Margaret Rigaud-Drayton (Cambridge: Polity, 2017).

27 B. L. G., 'Politisation chez les magistrats', *Le Monde*, 29 May 1986. The article sums up the results of the professional elections that had taken place in May 1986 in the following terms: 'Reduction of influence of the Union syndicale des magistrats (USM, moderate), progress of the Syndicat de la magistrature (SM, left-wing), breakthrough by the Association professionnelle des magistrats (APM, right-wing). These are the results . . ., which confirm the politicisation of the magistrature.'

28 Bourdieu may perhaps have in mind a manifesto of March 1971 which, just before the 'Manifesto of the 343', attacked a proposal to liberalise the law on abortion and was signed in particular by magistrates (alongside doctors, teachers and the military).

29 This is a reference to the tax introduced in 1982 by the French socialist government, which was called the 'solidarity tax on wealth' after 1989.

30 Bourdieu may have more or less clearly in mind the formulas quoted by Émile Durkheim in *The Rules of Sociological Method*, trans. W. D. Halls (New York: Free Press, 2014): 'The scientist often distinguishes between what the layman confuses' (p. 149); with a bad concept 'we run the risk of confusing the widely differing species and of linking types extremely dissimilar' (p. 83).

31 In the 1990s, Bourdieu returned on several occasions to the problem of morality being interested or disinterested: through his analysis of the genesis of the literary field (which distinguishes between the phase of 'heroic beginnings' and the phase where disinterest is institutionalised in the field); in his lectures on the scientific field (*Science of Science and Reflexivity*; or in more general texts ('Is a Disinterested Act Possible?', in *Practical Reason* [Cambridge: Polity, 1998], pp. 75–91).

32 Bourdieu is no doubt thinking of the over-representation of the liberal and teaching professions, which he mentions explicitly a little later.

33 See Bourdieu, *Distinction*, chapter 'The Sense of Distinction', pp. 260–317.

34 Bourdieu is alluding to his studies of peasant celibacy (collected in *The Bachelors' Ball*, trans. Richard Nice [Cambridge: Polity, 2007]). In the following development he draws on his research on reproduction strategies, which he progressively widened to include other groups outside the peasant class. See especially Pierre Bourdieu, Luc Boltanski and Monique de Saint Martin, 'Les stratégies de reconversion. Les classes sociales et le système d'enseignement', *Informations sur les sciences sociales*, 12, no. 5, 1973, pp. 61–113; 'Changes in Social Structure and Changes in the Demand for Education', in Salvador Giner and Margaret Scotford-Archer (eds.), *Contemporary Europe: Social Structures and Cultural Patterns* (London: Routledge and Kegan Paul, 1977), pp. 197–227; Bourdieu, 'The Future of Class and the Causality of the Probable'; also *Distinction*, and, after these lectures, 'Stratégies de reproduction et modes de domination', *Actes de la recherche en sciences sociales*, no. 105, 1994, pp. 3–12.

270   *Notes to pp. 165–173*

35 See the article 'Les stratégies matrimoniales dans le système des stratégies de reproduction', *Annales*, nos. 4–5, 1972, pp. 1105–27, republished as 'The System of Matrimonial Exchanges in Traditional Peasant Society', in *The Bachelors' Ball*, pp. 11–37.
36 Ibid.
37 'Self-preservation is the aim of all power.' This sentence from *Le Médecin de campagne* (1833) is quoted by Bourdieu as an epigraph to 'Reproduction culturelle et reproduction sociale', *Informations sur les sciences sociales*, 10, no. 2, 1971, p. 45; 'Cultural Reproduction and Social Reproduction', in Richard Brown (ed.), *Knowledge, Education, and Cultural Change* (London: Tavistock, 1973), pp. 71–112.
38 Pierre Bourdieu and Monique de Saint Martin, *Le Patronat* (Paris: Maison des sciences de l'homme, 1978).
39 See the Lecture of 19 April 1984, *Forms of Capital*, pp. 171, 338–9 note 31, and Weber, *The Sociology of Religion*, pp. 102, 113. [Weber's term is actually a theodicy of 'good fortune' as opposed to a theodicy of 'disprivilege' (translator).]
40 The word 'theodicy' is formed from two Greek words, *théos* and *dikè*, which mean, respectively, 'God' and 'judgement' or 'judicial action' – it can therefore also be understood to refer to the judgement of God. Its origin is to be found in the title of Leibniz's book published in 1710: *Theodicy: Essays on the Goodness of God, the Freedom of Man and the Origin of Evil*. Leibniz intends, against 'those who arraigned the Divinity or who made thereof an evil principle', to 'present his supreme goodness', to 'conceive of a power ordered by the most perfect wisdom'. *Theodicy*, project Gutenberg, Preface, §53. Leibniz does not define (nor does he use) the term theodicy in his book, but he did in 1715 write that it meant 'the doctrine of the justice of God'.
41 An allusion to Bourdieu's analyses of the adjectives used in teachers' reports. See in particular Bourdieu and de Saint Martin, 'Les catégories de l'entendement professoral'; and 'The Categories of Professorial Judgement', in *Homo Academicus*, pp. 194–225.
42 See the Lecture of 1 March 1984, *Forms of Capital*, pp. 28, 318–19 note 46, referring to *The German Ideology*.
43 On these points, see the Lecture of 18 January 1983, *Habitus and Field*, pp. 295ff.
44 A reference to the opposition in classical Greek thought between nature (*phusis*) and the law (*nomos*), which is of human origin.

Lecture of 12 June 1986

1 See above, Lecture of 22 May 1986, note 17, on Kepler.
2 Jürgen Habermas, *The Structural Transformation of the Public Sphere*; and *Knowledge and Human Interests*, trans. Jeremy J. Shapiro (Cambridge: Polity, 1987).
3 Arthur Schopenhauer, *The World as Will and Representation*, trans. E. F. J. Payne (New York: Dover, 2000).
4 Hugh Mehan, *Learning Lessons: Social Organization in the Classroom* (Cambridge MA: Harvard University Press, 1979). This is an ethnographic study of a primary school class with a female teacher (which explains Bourdieu's following remarks).

Notes to pp. 175–187 271

5 The problem, then, is gradually taken up by the agents who have the greatest power of consecration in the journalistic space: Ménie Grégoire was a radio presenter whose broadcasts on Radio Luxembourg attracted a wide audience and dealt with social, family and sexual problems; Ivan Levaï was a journalist whose various functions included, especially at the time of these lectures, many years spent on editorials and press reviews on the Europe 1 and France Inter radio stations; Serge July was the director of *Libération* and the man mainly responsible for transforming the newspaper in the first half of the 1980s into a rival of the leading papers of the daily press, with *Le Monde* remaining the most influential. On *Libération*, see Pierre Rimbert, *Libération. De Sartre à Rothschild* (Paris: Raisons d'agir, 2005), and on *Le Monde*, see Patrick Champagne, *La double dépendance* (Paris: Raisons d'agir, 2016).

6 This lecture took place a little less than three months after the left had lost the legislative elections, leading Laurent Fabius's socialist government to resign. Jean-Pierre Chevènement had for nearly two years been minister of education in this government. In this position he had set as his aim to 'bring 80% of an age group to the level of the baccalaureate', but had also pursued policies reminiscent of the school at the beginning of the Third Republic (for example in restoring 'civic instruction').

7 An article on the 'red judges' had appeared in *Actes de la recherche en sciences sociales*: Pierre Cam, 'Juges rouges et droit du travail' (no. 19, 1978, pp. 2–27).

8 See the chapter on 'Castes, Estates, Classes, and Religion', in Weber, *The Sociology of Religion*, pp. 80–94.

9 In the enquiry published in 1993 under the title *The Weight of the World*, which is based mainly on a series of interviews, Bourdieu considers the enquiry relationship at length, and in particular the sociological interview, that is, the specifically sociological work of making explicit the implicit experience of the social world of the respondents. See in particular the closing chapter, 'Understanding', pp. 607–26.

10 Bourdieu had referred to the trajectory of these émigrés in the literary and artistic fields during the second year of his lectures. See the Lectures of 18 January 1983 and 25 January 1983, *Habitus and Field*, pp. 292–3 and pp. 339–42.

11 See in particular the Lecture of 14 December 1982, *Habitus and Field*, pp. 247–8.

12 Jean-Paul Sartre, *The Imagination*, trans. Kenneth Williford and David Rudrauf (London: Routledge, 2012), Part 1.

13 Bourdieu had already published an article on this topic at the time of this lecture ('Le champ scientifique'). He returns to this point in the last year of his lectures at the Collège de France, which he published as *Science of Science and Reflexivity*.

14 Auguste Comte contrasted 'critical' periods with the 'organic' periods that came to close previous revolutions, in *Cours de philosophie positive*, vol. VI (Paris: Bachelier, 1842), *passim*. Bourdieu and Jean-Claude Passeron used this distinction in *Reproduction*, trans. Richard Nice (London: Sage, 1977).

15 See in particular the Lecture of 28 April 1982, *Classification Struggles*, pp. 9–10 and 159 note 11.

16 See Alphonse Allais, 'Un honnête homme dans toute la force du mot', in *Deux et deux font cinq* (Paris: Paul Ollendorf, 1895), pp. 69–72.

17 See the analyses that Bourdieu devoted to the artistic revolutions of the nineteenth century in the literary field (*The Rules of Art*) and in the field of painting (*Manet: A Symbolic Revolution*).

272   *Notes to pp. 187–199*

18 Rémy Ponton, 'Le champ littéraire en France de 1865 à 1905', EHESS, 1977; 'Naissance du roman psychologique', *Actes de la recherche en sciences sociales*, no. 4, 1975, pp. 66–81; Christophe Charle, *La Crise littéraire à l'époque du naturalisme. Roman, théâtre, politique* (Paris: Presses de l'École normale supérieure, 1979).

19 'The Republic of the professors' is an expression used to refer to the Third Republic, when a considerable proportion of the major political leaders, such as the members of parliament for the radical left and the socialists, were teachers. For the origin of the expression, the book by Albert Thibaudet, *La République des professeurs* (Paris: Grasset, 1927) is often cited.

20 Christophe Charle, *Les Hauts Fonctionnaires en France au XIXe siècle* (Paris: Gallimard-Juillard, 1980).

21 'L'École libre des sciences politiques' was created in 1872. In 1987 Bourdieu published in his review an article on the birth of this institution: Dominique Damamme, 'Genèse sociale d'une institution scolaire: l'École libre des sciences politiques', *Actes de la recherche en sciences sociales*, no. 70, 1987, pp. 31–46.

22 See Bourdieu, *The State Nobility*.

23 For developments of this analogy with Maxwell's demon, see Pierre Bourdieu and Monique de Saint Martin, 'Agrégation et ségrégation. Le champ des grandes écoles et le champ du pouvoir', *Actes de la recherche en sciences sociales*, no. 69, 1987, p. 17, and Bourdieu, *Practical Reason*, pp. 20–4.

24 The French word *coturne* is a slang expression from the École normale supérieure, referring to the fellow student with whom one shares a room (a *turne*) in this residential institution.

Lecture of 19 June 1986

1 Goffman, *The Presentation of Self in Everyday Life*.

2 See in particular Louis Althusser, *For Marx*, trans. Ben Brewster (London: Verso, 2005), where the formula is used to designate a philosophical procedure.

3 Only a partial French translation of Karl Mannheim's work was available at the time of these lectures. This is the standard English translation: 'As regards the first way out, unattached intellectuals are to be found in the course of history in all camps. Thus they always furnished the theorists for the conservatives who themselves because of their own social stability could only with difficulty be brought to theoretical self-consciousness. They likewise furnished the theorists for the proletariat which, because of its social conditions, lacked the prerequisites for the acquisition of the knowledge necessary for modern political conflict. Their affiliation with the liberal bourgeoisie has already been discussed. This ability to attach themselves to classes to which they originally did not belong was possible for intellectuals because they could adapt themselves to any viewpoint and because they and they alone were in a position to choose their affiliation, while those who were immediately bound by class affiliations were only in rare exceptions able to transcend the boundaries of their class outlook.' Karl Mannheim, *Ideology and Utopia*, trans. Louis Wirth and Edward Shils (London: Routledge & Kegan Paul, 1954), p. 141. The notion of the 'organic intellectual', which is set up in opposition to that of the unattached intellectual, is taken from Antonio Gramsci: 'Every social group, coming into existence on the original terrain of an essential function

Notes to pp. 201–206 273

in the world of economic production, creates together with itself, organically, one or more strata of intellectuals which give it homogeneity and an awareness of its own function not only in the economic but also in the social and political fields.' From 'Prison Notebooks', in *An Anthology of Western Marxism*, ed. Roger S. Gottlieb (Oxford: Oxford University Press, 1989), p. 113.

4 Lenin uses the term in *What is to be Done?*, quoting a text written by Kautsky in 1901–2: 'The vehicle of science is not the proletariat, but the *bourgeois intelligentsia* [K. K.'s italics]: it was in the minds of individual members of this stratum that modern socialism originated, and it was they who communicated it to the more intellectually developed proletarians who, in their turn, introduce it into the proletarian class struggle where conditions allow that to be done. Thus, socialist consciousness is something introduced into the proletarian class struggle from without [*von Aussen Hineingetragenes*] and not something that arose within it spontaneously [*urwüchsig*].' V. I. Lenin, *What is to be Done?* (1902), trans. Joe Fineberg and George Hanna, Marxists Internet Archive.

5 Bourdieu expressed his criticism of the notion of 'awakening of consciousness' several times in his lecture courses: in the Lecture of 26 May 1982, *Classification Struggles*, pp. 64ff., and more briefly in this year 1985–86 in the Lectures of 24 April, 15 May and 12 June 1986.

6 Bourdieu is no doubt thinking principally of the discussion of the 'intellectual strata' (and, for instance, the 'proletaroid intellectuals') in the section 'Intellectualism, Intellectuals, and Salvation Religion' of Weber's *Economy and Society*, vol. 1, pp. 500–17.

7 A reference to the subtitle of Friedrich Nietzsche's *Twilight of the Idols, or, How to Philosophise with a Hammer*, trans. Richard Polt (Indianapolis: Hackett, 1997).

8 In the 1990s two issues of *Actes de la recherche en sciences sociales* were devoted to 'L'Histoire sociale de sciences sociales'.

9 *The Adventures of Baron Munchausen* is a German tale from the end of the eighteenth century. In one much-read episode, the Baron, whose horse is sinking in quicksand, pulls himself out by tugging at his own hair, in a kind of allegory of false logic.

10 This was the colloquium 'Science, the Renaissance of a History: international colloquium Alexandre Koyré', organised at the Collège de France, 10–14 June 1986 (the proceedings of the colloquium were published in 1987 in a special number of the review *History and Technology*).

11 Ernest Renan, *L'Avenir de la science. Pensées de 1848* (Paris: Calmann-Lévy, 1890).

12 'Each society has its regime of truth, its "general politics" of truth: that is, the types of discourse which it accepts and makes function as true; the mechanisms and instances which enable one to distinguish true and false statements, the means by which each is sanctioned; the techniques and procedures accorded value in the acquisition of truth; the status of those who are charged with saying what counts as true.' Michel Foucault, 'Truth and Power', in *Power/Knowledge: Selected Interviews and Other Writings 1972–1977*, trans. Colin Gordon (New York: Pantheon, 1980), p. 131.

13 Michael Pollak, 'Paul Lazarsfeld, fondateur d'une multinationale scientifique', *Actes de la recherche en sciences sociales*, no. 25, 1979, pp. 45–59.

274   *Notes to pp. 206–213*

14 On these points, and more generally on the developments in this first session that deal with the scientific field, see, in addition to the two articles cited by Bourdieu a little later, the lectures that he delivered in 2000–1, his last lecture series, published under the title of *Science of Science and Reflexivity*.
15 See Bourdieu, 'The Specificity of the Scientific Field'.
16 Bourdieu had referred to these analyses by Jürgen Habermas in the previous lecture, 12 June 1986.
17 Bourdieu had developed his arguments on these kinds of analyses in the Lecture of 3 May 1984, in *Forms of Capital*.
18 'A true knowledge of good and evil cannot restrain any emotion in so far as the knowledge is true, but only in so far as it is considered as an emotion.' Spinoza, *Ethics*, Book IV, proposition 14.
19 Michel Foucault, 'On the Archeology of the Sciences: Response to the Epistemology Circle', in *Essential Works of Foucault 1954–1984*, vol. 2, trans. Robert Hurley et al. (New York: The New Press, 1998), pp. 297–333.
20 'But there is also *doxological illusion* each time one sets forth description as the analysis of the conditions of the existence of a science. This illusion has two aspects. It admits that the actuality of opinions, instead of being determined by the strategic possibilities of conceptual games, refers directly to the divergences of interests or mental habits among individuals; opinion would be the irruption of the nonscientific (of the psychological, of the political, of the social, of the religious) in the specific domain of science. But, on the other hand, it presumes that opinion constitutes the central nucleus, the fulcrum from which the entire ensemble of scientific statements is deployed; opinion would manifest the impact of fundamental choices (metaphysical, religious, political) of which the diverse concepts of biology, or of economics, or of linguistics, would only be the positive, superficial version, the transcription into a determinate vocabulary, the mask blind to itself. The doxological illusion is one manner of eliding the field of a mode of knowledge as the site and law of formation of theoretical opinions.' Ibid., p. 329.
21 Michel Foucault, *The Order of Things* (London: Tavistock, 1970).
22 See Bourdieu's analysis of le Douanier Rousseau in *The Rules of Art*, pp. 244–6, 385–6.
23 See Alexandre Kojève, *L'Idée du déterminisme dans la physique classique et dans la physique moderne* (Paris: Le Livre de Poche, 1990).
24 *La Monnaie de l'absolu* is the title of the third volume of André Malraux's *Psychologie de l'art* (Paris: Skira, 1949); *The Psychology of Art*, vol. 3, *The Twilight of the Absolute* (New York: Pantheon, 1950).
25 Bourdieu had mentioned it in particular at the start of his first lecture course, in the Lecture of 12 May 1982, *Classification Struggles*, pp. 43–4.
26 This response to Raymond Aron's book appeared in two issues of *Les Temps Modernes* in 1955 (nos. 112–13, pp. 1539–75 and nos. 114–15, pp. 2219–61), and was then republished in *Privilèges* (Paris: Gallimard, 1955), and later as *Faut-il brûler Sade?* (Paris: Gallimard 'Idées', 1972).
27 This refers to the article on 'Le champ scientifique'.
28 Bourdieu went on to develop his critique of 'the strong programme' in the sociology of science in his last series of lectures at the Collège de France. See *Science of Science and Reflexivity*, pp. 18–20.
29 Alexander Gerschenkron, *Economic Backwardness in Historical Perspective* (Cambridge MA: Harvard University Press, 1962). On the 'Gerschenkron

Notes to pp. 214–222 275

effect' see also Pierre Bourdieu, *Choses dites* (Paris: Minuit, 1987), pp. 51–3; 'Le champ scientifique', pp. 101–2; Lecture of 2 November 1982, *Habitus and Field*, pp. 98–9.

30 Pierre Bourdieu, *The Political Ontology of Martin Heidegger*, trans. Peter Collier (Cambridge: Polity, 1991).

31 Ludwig Wittgenstein, *On Certainty* (Oxford: Blackwell, 1969).

32 From his first lecture, Bourdieu raises the question of the social classes in terms of the problematics of classification (Lecture of 28 April 1982, *Classification Struggles*, p. 5). He returns to the same problem in this last lecture, in order to call attention to the complexity of the analysis enabled by mobilising the conceptual system he has expounded in the years intervening.

33 The 'quarrel of universals' (often presented, as Bourdieu does here, in terms of reflections on the concept of 'dog') was a great debate in medieval scholastic philosophy. After being marginalised during the Renaissance and in continental philosophy for several centuries, it was revived from the end of the nineteenth century in analytic philosophy, notably by Bertrand Russell, from whom Bourdieu borrows the example 'the king of France is bald', used on several occasions when discussing social class in the second year of these lectures (see *Habitus and Field, passim*).

34 Raymond Aron, 'Classe sociale, classe politique, classe dirigeante', *Archives européennes de sociologie*, 1, 1960, pp. 260–81; reproduced in part in Pierre Birnbaum and François Chazel (eds.), *Sociologie politique. Textes* (Paris: Armand Colin, 'U2', 1978), pp. 103–7.

35 In 1931 Kurt Gödel argued that no formal system could prove all truths about the arithmetic of natural numbers and that although such a consistent system could make statements that are true, some would be unprovable, and such a system could not demonstrate its own consistency [translator].

36 Bourdieu has in mind the diagram of the 'space of social positions' published in *Distinction*, pp. 128–9, and republished in simplified form in *Practical Reason*, p. 5.

37 On the relations between the social space on the one hand, and the space of interactions and geographical space on the other hand, see Bourdieu, *Distinction*, p. 124 and *passim*; *The Weight of the World*, pp. 123–9; and *Pascalian Meditations*, trans. Richard Nice (Cambridge: Polity, 2000), pp. 182–5.

38 Bourdieu had developed and justified this borrowing from Leibniz in the Lecture of 15 March 1984, *Forms of Capital*, pp. 67–96.

39 See the Lecture of 19 May 1982, *Classification Struggles*, pp. 62–3, and the Lecture of 28 March 1985, *Principles of Vision*, p. 54.

40 Weber, *Economy and Society*, vol. 1, pp. 305–7.

41 Karl Marx and Friedrich Engels, 'The Demands of the Communist Party in Germany', in Karl Marx, *The Revolutions of 1848* (Harmondsworth: Penguin, 1973), p. 109 [translator].

42 'You shouldn't let intellectuals play with / matches / Because Dear Sirs when you leave it alone / The mental world / Dear Sirs / Is not very bright / And once left on its own / Works in arbitrary ways / To look after itself / And generously benefit construction / Workers / An auto-monument? Say it again Dear Sirs / When you leave it alone / The mental world / Is Monumentally / Mendacious.' Jacques Prévert, 'You shouldn't', in *Paroles* (Paris: Gallimard, 'Folio', 1972), p. 219.

43 See the Lecture of 8 March 1985, *Principles of Vision*, pp. 7–8, 277.

276 *Notes to pp. 222–230*

44 An allusion to the notion of the 'epistemological break' introduced by Louis Althusser at the beginning of *For Marx*, which was intended to be a more radical version of Gaston Bachelard's 'epistemological rupture' (*La Formation de l'esprit scientifique* [Paris: Vrin, 1938]).

45 In 1982 the revision by INSEE of the 'nomenclature of the socio-professional categories' had drawn in particular on the findings of *Distinction*. Bourdieu had developed this point earlier, in the Lecture of 28 March 1985, *Principles of Vision*, pp. 45, 282.

Situating the Later Volumes of *General Sociology* in the Work of Pierre Bourdieu

1 Lecture of 28 April 1982, *Classification Struggles*, p. 11.

2 Ibid.

3 'The notion of habitus means that there is a sort of information capital that structures and is structured, that functions as a principle of structured practices without these structures that can be found in the practices having existed before the production of the practices in the form of rules' (10 May 1984).

4 A formula employed in Bourdieu et al., *The Craft of Sociology*, p. 35.

5 Bourdieu would certainly have revised the text as was his habit, but an aside ('In fact, what I have to say does exist, or I hope that it will, in book form' [25 April 1985]) and later indications ('This chapter . . . tends to leave aside the specific logic of each of the specialized fields . . . that I have analyzed elsewhere and which will be the subject of a forthcoming book.' *The Rules of Art*, p. 380; see also *On the State*, p. 367) suggest that he envisaged publishing one or several volumes. The Course in General Sociology is perhaps one of the lecture courses that were not published for lack of time (on this point see Pierre Bourdieu and Yvette Delsaut, 'L'esprit de la recherche', in Yvette Delsaut and Marie-Christine Rivière, *Bibliographie des travaux de Pierre Bourdieu, suivi d'un entretien sur l'esprit de la recherche* (Pantin: Le temps des cerises, 2002), p. 224. *Pascalian Meditations* (like the volume on the 'theory of fields' that he had nearly finished) was an opportunity to publish some developments from the lectures.

6 The reflections delivered during this first year, 1981–82, were to furnish the substance of an important later article: 'The Social Space and the Genesis of Groups', *Theory and Society*, 14, no. 6, 1985, pp. 723–44.

7 'And if I rework the same themes and return several times to the same objects and the same analyses, it is always, I think, in a spiralling movement which makes it possible to attain each time a higher level of explicitness and comprehension, and to discover unnoticed relationships and hidden properties.' *Pascalian Meditations*, p. 8.

8 See Bourdieu and Delsaut, 'L'esprit de la recherche', p. 193.

9 As noted earlier, this incident explains why the first year of lectures, published in the first volume, *Classification Struggles*, is shorter than the following four (and perhaps also why the second year, *Habitus and Field*, is the longest: Bourdieu had probably envisaged a greater number of sessions in 1982–83 to make up for the sessions that he had not been able to provide in spring 1982).

10 Bourdieu, *Classification Struggles*, p. 4.

11 On the other hand he is sometimes very pleased with this (see for example the Lecture of 2 May 1985).

Notes to pp. 230–234   277

12 'These questions are very useful for me psychologically because they give me the feeling that I have a better idea of your expectations' (23 May 1985).
13 As a result, the lectures published in this volume all last more or less two sessions, whereas in 1982–83 some lectures lasted considerably longer than the time allotted.
14 Between the two sessions Bourdieu observed a formal break (or an 'interval', as he somewhat ironically calls it, perhaps to remind us of the objectively rather theatrical nature of the occasion).
15 Pierre Bourdieu, 'L'institutionnalisation de l'anomie', *Les cahiers du Musée national d'art moderne*, 19–20, 1987, pp. 6–19; 'La révolution impressioniste', *Noroît*, no. 303, 1987, pp. 3–18.
16 Bourdieu, *Manet: A Symbolic Revolution*.
17 See the indications given on this subject in the Lecture of 14 March 1985.
18 Bourdieu, 'The Invention of the Artist's Life'.
19 'The Hit Parade of French Intellectuals, or Who is to Judge the Legitimacy of the Judges', in *Homo Academicus*, pp. 256–70.
20 Pierre Bourdieu, 'Un jeu chinois. Notes pour une critique sociale du jugement', *Actes de la recherche en sciences sociales*, no. 4, 1976, pp. 91–101, and 'Associations: A Parlour Game', in *Distinction*, pp. 546–59.
21 'I'm rather like an old doctor who knows all the diseases of the sociological understanding', Interview with Pierre Bourdieu by Beate Krais (December 1988), in *The Craft of Sociology*, p. 256.
22 Ibid., pp. 256–7.
23 We may note that it was in 1985 that Bourdieu ceased to direct the Centre de l'éducation et de la culture.
24 In fact, between 1983 and 1997 Bourdieu's graduates completed only half as many theses as between 1970 and 1983 (fourteen as opposed to twenty-nine).
25 Bourdieu, 'The Invention of the Artist's Life'.
26 Bourdieu refers more briefly to Dostoevsky's *The Gambler* (29 March 1984). During this period he also published an article on Francis Ponge: 'Nécessiter', in 'Francis Ponge', *Cahiers de L'Herne*, 1986, pp. 434–7.
27 Pierre Bourdieu, 'La dernière instance', in *Le siècle de Kafka* (Paris: Centre Georges Pompidou, 1984), pp. 268–70. Reprinted in *Choses dites*.
28 Pierre Bourdieu, *Images d'Algérie. Une affinité élective* (Arles: Actes Sud/Sinbad/Camera Austria, 2003), p. 42.
29 The index of the two volumes of the *General Sociology* confirms this: Marx, Durkheim and Weber are the authors that Bourdieu refers to most often (they are followed by Sartre, Kant, Hegel, Flaubert, Lévi-Strauss, Plato, Goffman, Kafka, Foucault and Husserl). It is Weber who is cited the most (116 citations against eighty-six and eighty-one for Marx and Durkheim), particularly in 1983–84.
30 Pierre Bourdieu, 'N'ayez pas peur de Max Weber!', *Libération*, 6 July 1982, p. 25.
31 In 1962–63, when Bourdieu was teaching at Lille, he had devoted a lecture course to Max Weber and invited his students to read and translate passages from *Economy and Society*. In the 1960s he had made copies of selected passages for his students and researchers. It was only in 1971 that Plon published a partial translation of the book.
32 Bourdieu, 'The Force of Law: Toward a Sociology of the Juridical Field'.
33 Bourdieu, *On the State*.

278 *Notes to pp. 234–236*

34 Pierre Bourdieu, 'La domination masculine', *Actes de la recherche en sciences sociales*, no. 4, 1990, pp. 2–31; *Masculine Domination*.

35 On this reflection (preceded by 'L'évolution des rapports entre le champ universitaire et le champ du journalisme', *Sigma*, no. 23, 1987, pp. 65–70), which includes an analysis of journalism in terms of field, see in particular 'L'emprise du journalisme', *Actes de la recherche en sciences sociales*, nos. 101–2, 1994, pp. 3–9; 'Journalisme et éthique' (Communication à l'ESJ Lille, 3 June 1994), *Les Cahiers du journalisme*, no. 1, 1996, pp. 10–17; 'Champ politique, champ des sciences sociales, champ journalistique (Cours du Collège de France, 14 novembre 1995)', *Cahiers du Groupe de recherche sur la socialisation* (Lyon: Université Lumière-Lyon 2, 1996), republished in English in Rodney Benson and Erik Neveu (eds.), *Bourdieu and the Journalistic Field* (Cambridge: Polity, 2005), pp. 29–47; *On Television*, trans. P. Parkhurst (Cambridge: Polity, 2011); 'Return to Television', in *Acts of Resistance: Against the New Myths of our Time*, trans. Richard Nice (Cambridge: Polity, 1998), pp. 70–7; 'À propos de Karl Kraus et du journalisme', *Actes de la recherche en sciences sociales*, nos. 131–2, 2000, pp. 123–6.

36 Patrick Champagne, 'Sur la médiatisation du champ intellectuel. À propos de *Sur la télévision*', in Louis Pinto, Gisèle Sapiro and Patrick Champagne (eds.), *Pierre Bourdieu, sociologue* (Paris: Fayard, 2004), pp. 431–58.

37 During the period of these lectures, Bourdieu participated in two sessions of the TV talk show *Apostrophes* (for *Language and Symbolic Power* and *Homo Academicus* and then for the report by the Collège de France on education) and presented two of his books (*Language and Symbolic Power* and *Homo Academicus*) on two television news programmes (one 'regional' and the other 'night-time').

38 Drawing on his analyses of the fields of cultural production, he introduces a sociological reflection on the themes of the disaffection of 'the young' with the press and on the relations between journalism and the educational institution. See Philippe Bernard, 'Exercice illégal de la pédagogie', *Le Monde*, 16 May 1985.

39 See *Pierre Bourdieu & les médias. Rencontres INA/Sorbonne (15 mars 2003)* (Paris: L'Harmattan, 2004). In the years following the lectures (and therefore after the growth of the private channels in France), Bourdieu was one of the instigators of the movement 'Pour que vive la télévision publique' (Long live public television). See Pierre Bourdieu, Ange Casta, Max Gallo, Claude Marti, Jean Martin and Christian Pierret, 'Que vive la télévision publique!', *Le Monde*, 19 October 1988.

40 Remi Lenoir, 'Duby et les sociologues', in Jacques Dalarun and Patrick Boucheron (eds.), *Georges Duby. Portrait de l'historien en ses archives* (Paris: Gallimard, 2015), pp. 193–203.

41 Although the socialist François Mitterrand remained President of the Republic, legislative elections in 1986 compelled him to share power with a right-wing prime minister, Jacques Chirac.

42 'Propositions pour l'enseignement de l'avenir. Rapport du Collège de France' (Paris: Minuit, 1985), a 48-page pamphlet; see also *Le Monde de l'éducation*, no. 116, 1985, pp. 61–8).

43 On the origins, drafting and reception of the report, see the research in progress by P. Clément (for a first draft: 'Réformer les programmes pour changer l'école? Une sociologie historique du champ de pouvoir scolaire',

Notes to pp. 236–241 279

doctoral thesis in sociology, Université de Picardie Jules-Verne, 2013, chap. 2, pp. 155–240).

44 Bourdieu, *Sketch for a Self-Analysis*, pp. 78–81.

45 Bourdieu mentions this ceremony in *Manet: A Symbolic Revolution*, pp. 318–19.

46 Pierre Bourdieu, 'Le plaisir de savoir', *Le Monde*, 27 June 1984; 'Non chiedetemi chi sono. Un profilo di Michel Foucault', *L'Indice,* October 1984, pp. 4–5.

47 For a detailed analysis of the philosophical field at the time of the lecture course, see Louis Pinto, *Les philosophes entre le lycée et l'avant-garde. Les métamorphoses de la philosophie dans la France d'aujourd'hui* (Paris: L'Harmattan, 1987).

48 See also Pierre Bourdieu, 'Sartre', *London Review of Books*, 2, no. 22, 1980, pp. 11–12.

49 By this time, this intellectual recognition already included the American universities. In Foucault's case, for instance, there was a wave of translations in 1977 in the United States. At this time, Bourdieu, who was slightly younger and the only one not to call himself a 'philosopher', lagged behind rather in this respect.

50 Bourdieu, *Homo Academicus*, pp. 105–12.

51 Ferry and Renaut, *La Pensée 68. Essai sur l'anti humanisme contemporain.*

52 On this point see Benoît Peeters, *Derrida* (Paris: Flammarion, 2010), pp. 369–80.

53 This model is that of the intellectual combining genuinely intellectual recognition with notoriety for a fairly broad educated public. The beginning of the 1980s (which corresponds for instance to the moment when François Maspero sold his publishing house) was a period when publishers started to deplore the scarcity of scholarly authors able to sell in quantity, in a context where academic specialisation seemed to be increasing.

54 Collectif Les Révoltes logiques, *L'Empire du sociologue* (Paris: La Découverte, 1984).

55 We can also refer to his remark on the 'slightly Cubist' character of his sociology (9 May 1985).

56 Bourdieu, *Sociology in Question.*

57 Alain Accardo, *Initiation à la sociologie de l'illusionnisme social. Invitation à la lecture des oeuvres de Pierre Bourdieu* (Bordeaux: Le Mascaret, 1983; republished Marseille: Agone, 2006). This book was followed by a collection of texts edited by Alain Accardo and Philippe Corcuff: *La Sociologie de Bourdieu* (Bordeaux: Le Mascaret, 1986).

58 On the opposition between methodology and epistemology, see *The Craft of Sociology*, pp. 6–7, 11–12. On Bourdieu's relation to Paul Lazarsfeld's enterprise, see *Sketch for a Self-Analysis*, pp. 72–5. On the 'methodological imperative' that tends to unite the different stages of Raymond Bourdon's sociology, see Johan Heilbron, *French Sociology* (Ithaca: Cornell University Press, 2015), pp. 193–7.

59 Bruno Latour and Steeve Woolgar, *Laboratory Life: The Social Construction of Scientific Facts* (London: Sage, 1979).

60 Bourdieu, *Science of Science and Reflexivity.*

61 On the public positions he adopted during this period, see Pierre Bourdieu, *Interventions 1961–2001: Science sociale et action politique* (Paris: Agone, 2002), pp. 157–87.

62 See, for instance, Bourdieu, *Acts of Resistance*, p. 40.

280 *Notes to pp. 241–242*

63 Jean-Pierre Chevènement was minister of education under Prime Minister Laurent Fabius from 1984 to 1986. He hoped to revive the original mission of the Republican school, which, in addition to promoting civic and lay values, was to level out social inequalities [translator].
64 In 1986, activists belonging to Solidarność, the Polish workers' trade union, demonstrated in favour of the release of political prisoners and organised strikes, which defied the regime of General W. Jaruzelski and paralysed the country. Bourdieu and some colleagues signed a petition protesting against the French government's lack of supporting action [translator].
65 Bourdieu, *On the State*.
66 Bourdieu, *Manet: A Symbolic Revolution*.
67 Bourdieu, *Science of Science and Reflexivity*.

Index

Abensour, Miguel, 240
abortion, 159
abstract individuals, 90–2
abstraction, 49, 90–2, 119
academic field, 186–7, 193–4; *see also* intellectual field
Accardo, Alain, 238
acclamation, 32–3
accumulation, 157, 202
Actes de la recherche en sciences sociales, 227
action, 41, 58–60, 68–71, 94–6, 114–25, 143–6, 225, 226
administrative field, 187, 191, 194
admiration, 7, 36
adjectives, 7, 180
advertising, 43, 161–2
ageing, 56–7
aggregation, 176, 185
agricultural societies, 12, 13
Alain, 66
Algeria, 152, 161, 226, 227
alienation, 12, 15, 71, 72, 79, 101, 180
Allais, Alphonse, 186
alliances, 201–2, 206
allodoxia, 179, 181
Althusser, Louis, 68, 126, 148, 199, 222, 237
amor fati, 101–2
analytic philosophy, 19–20, 35, 145
anarchism, 99, 147
anomie, 230

anonymity, 52–3
anticipation, 64–7, 71, 72, 144
anthropology, 29, 30, 33, 45, 60, 198, 226–7, 235; *see also* ethnology
apparatus, 69–70
appropriation, 23, 42, 72, 133
arbitrariness, 5, 50, 136, 168–9, 186
Aristotle, 58
army *see* military
Aron, Raymond, 211, 215
art
    art for art's sake, 188
    artistic capital, 134
    artistic field, 3, 16, 38–9, 46, 170–1, 178, 186–90, 194, 202, 209, 231
    bourgeois art, 188
    and fetishism, 38–9
    modern art, 230
    perception of, 7–8
    and power, 103–4
    relation to literature, 231
    revolution in, 230
    signatures, 6, 39
    social art, 188
    and social class, 72–3, 103–4
    and taste, 7–8
artificial intelligence, 120–1
aspiration, 72, 80
atheism, 110
attribution, 29, 49–50, 73
Auerbach, Erich, 61
Austin, J. L., 95, 144–5, 153–4

282   *Index*

authorised perception, 234
authority, 23, 30–2, 34, 97, 107–9, 181,
    224
autobiography, 16–17, 27
autonomisation, 133, 231
autonomous fields, 107, 132–3, 188, 201

Bachelard, Gaston, 125, 222
bad faith, 39, 70, 93
balance of power, 135, 161, 174, 176, 183,
    191–2, 194, 234
Balzac, Honoré de, 61, 165
baptism, 22–3, 48
baraka, 32, 33, 36, 39
Barnes, Julian, 44
Barthes, Roland, 7
basism, 126
beauty, 85, 106
Beauvoir, Simone de, 211
Becker, Gary, 128
Beckett, Samuel, 232
behaviouralism, 60–1
Benjamin, Walter, 38
Benveniste, Émile, 6, 29–34, 35–6, 87
Bergson, Henri, 44, 56, 63, 131
biography, 16–18, 23–7, 43–7, 51–7, 233
biological ageing, 56–7
biological individuals, 20–1, 48–9, 91
biological reproduction, 165, 166
bishops, 21, 42
blame, 73, 152–3
bodily structures, 12
body, the
    bodily postures, 95–6, 97, 104
    bodily structures, 12
    embodied censorship, 100–1
    and gender, 95–6
    and habitus, 88, 89, 97
    Hegel's conception of, 96–7
    king's two bodies, 51
    and the political, 95–6, 104–6, 110–11
    and power, 32–3, 35, 36–7, 75, 90,
        95–6, 104–6, 110–13
    relationship with the social world, 42,
        88–90, 94–7
    and sexuality, 75, 104–6

socialised body, 90, 96–7
    see also biological individuals
Boivin, François, 42
Boudon, Raymond, 239
boundaries, 185–7
Bourdieu, Marie-Claire, 230
bourgeois art, 188
bourgeoisie, 54, 72, 103–4, 166, 175
Bourricaud, François, 239
Boutmy, Émile, 193
Brahe, Tycho, 119
brands, 43
Buffon, Comte de, 45
business field, 187, 191, 194

calendars, 62
capacities, 156–65, 167, 168
capital
    accumulation of, 157, 202
    appropriation of, 23
    artistic capital, 134
    concentration of, 37, 39
    cultural capital, 3–4, 64, 91, 134, 144,
        156–64, 191, 202, 226
    distribution of, 2, 144, 161
    economic capital, 3–4, 134, 156–7, 160,
        163, 166, 187, 191
    educational capital, 187, 193
    flow of, 190–2
    hierarchy of forms of, 190–1, 194
    history of, 218
    information capital, 227
    landed capital, 157, 163
    linguistic capital, 160–1
    magical capital, 33–4
    power over, 133–5
    production of, 37
    relation to the field, 225–6, 227
    relation to the habitus, 226, 227
    religious capital, 134
    reproduction of, 160–2, 164–9, 192–4
    social capital, 3, 157, 163–4
    species of, 2, 3, 129, 130, 156–7, 161,
        163–9, 190–1, 227
    specific capital, 134, 201, 206
    stable forms of, 162–4

structure of, 163, 167, 217–18
symbolic capital, 3–5, 7, 23, 28–9,
  34–40, 43, 63–4, 87, 223, 226
total volume of, 217–18
transmission of, 156–7, 166, 168, 185,
  193
capitalism, 213
Catholicism, 55, 141, 192
causality, 45, 59, 73, 97, 152–3
Cavaillès, Jean, 64
censorship, 53, 82–3, 100–1
censuses, 25–6
centralism, 126
certification, 50, 113, 234
champions, 32, 34
Chamson, André, 23
Changeux, Pierre, 236
charisma, 4, 5, 32, 33–5, 85, 105–6, 167
Charle, Christophe, 187, 191–2
Chevènement, Jean-Pierre, 177, 241
Chicago school, 123, 133, 241
childhood games, 9, 79
childishness, 78–9
Chinese game, 231
Chirac, Jacques, 41
choice, 15, 92–4, 122, 144, 150; *see also*
  decisions
chronological time, 44–5, 54
circularity, 4, 8, 128, 150
circumcision, 49, 81
citizenship, 25–6, 50
civil service, 80, 100, 163, 191–2, 193
classification, 26, 104, 154, 167, 171,
  219–24, 225, 228
codification, 25, 26, 53, 117, 121, 178,
  186–7, 192, 226, 227, 233
cognition
  and choice, 92
  cognitive relations, 7, 28, 63, 88, 90
  cognitive structures, 2, 11–12
  cognitive struggles, 154, 174–7
  and misrecognition, 4–6, 15
  relation to knowledge, 63–4
Cohen-Tannoudji, Claude, 236
collective construction, 173–4, 176
collectivism, 126, 127, 150, 173–4, 176

colonisation, 110, 152, 161, 181
common sense, 16, 52, 56, 145, 161
commonality, 7–8, 195–6
communism, 179
competition, 129–30, 161, 192, 195, 207,
  215, 228
complicity, 6, 8, 9, 15, 31, 135, 184–5
Comte, Auguste, 184
conatus, 116, 137, 195
condescendence, 181, 218
Condillac, Étienne Bonnot de, 18, 142
conditions of production, 3, 6, 51–3, 183
confidence, 30–2
conflict, 1–2, 23, 73, 160–1, 186, 208; *see*
  also war
consciousness
  class, 124, 220
  collective, 172
  consciousness-raising, 201
  false, 180–1, 243
consecration, 38, 40, 98, 112, 134, 137,
  182
conservatism, 12, 14, 21, 192
consistency, 21–7, 47–51, 69
conspiracy theories, 4
constructed classes, 219–21
construction
  collective construction, 173–4, 176
  practical constructions, 177–9, 182
  of the social world, 151–2, 153, 171,
    173–4, 176, 223
  theoretical constructions, 23–4, 124,
    166, 177–8, 182
constructivism, 125, 142, 146, 150, 174,
  197, 223, 226
continuity, 10, 23, 122–3, 227
controlling shareholders, 134
Copernicus, Nicolaus, 119
corps, effect of, 227
credit, 29–34
crime, 19
criminal records, 25, 26
crises, 11, 19, 67, 110–11, 144, 161
culture
  cultural capital, 3–4, 64, 91, 134, 144,
    156–64, 191, 202, 226

284 *Index*

culture (*cont.*)
  cultural production, 197, 200–2
  and power, 103–4, 136
  and social class, 72–3, 103–4, 226
curriculum vitae, 25, 26, 27, 47, 53, 54, 57
cursus honorum, 25, 26, 53
customary law, 102
cynicisation, 205

Dahl, Robert A., 35
Dasein, 88
Dassault, Marcel, 48
Davidson, Donald, 74
decision theory, 117–23, 143–6, 229
decisions, 60–1, 71, 117–23, 150, 229; *see also* choice
deconstruction, 16, 22, 71
delegation, 32, 34, 100
Deleuze, Gilles, 237
deliberation, 69, 117, 120, 121–4
Derrida, Jacques, 237
Descartes, René, 92, 97, 123
designer labels, 6, 39–40
desire, 75, 84–5, 88, 90, 104, 116, 117; *see also libido*
despair, 110–11
destiny, 24, 101, 106
determination, 40–2, 70–1, 74, 146
determinism, 59, 126, 146, 149, 212, 218, 220, 238
differentiated societies, 2, 29, 130–2, 226–7
digressions, 61
discipline, 101–2, 111
disinterest, 138, 204, 211
disorder, 41–2, 47, 63
dispositions, 58–60, 67, 71, 74, 80, 95, 98–101, 218–21
dispute theory, 152–4
distribution
  of capital, 2, 144, 161
  of power, 133, 161
division of labour, 9, 41, 80–5, 95, 104–5, 113, 114–15, 117–18, 136, 154–6, 177
domestic violence, 74, 101

dominant classes, 129–30, 135, 156, 160, 163–7, 188, 191–2
doxa, 10, 13–15, 36, 147
dualism, 64, 97, 125
Duby, Georges, 106, 136, 235
Dumézil, Georges, 136, 155, 235
Durkheim, Émile, 32, 92, 131–3, 143, 156, 172, 203, 222, 239

economic capital, 3–4, 134, 156–7, 160, 163, 166, 191
economic field, 131–3, 134
economic individuals, 91
economic power, 87, 130, 136
economic theory, 60–1, 82, 91, 117, 123, 134, 176, 213, 241
education, 9, 26, 42, 61, 113, 145, 157–62, 164, 166–9, 173–7, 184–5, 192–6, 236
educational capital, 187, 193
effects
  of capital, 7–8
  of the corps, 227
  Gerschenkron effect, 212–14
  of language, 95
  nomination effect, 112–13
  of power, 4–8
  prophecy effect, 178–9
  Pygmalion effect, 6, 113
  of science, 205
  self-fulfilment effect, 107, 182
  symbolic effects, 4, 7–8, 36, 182
  threshold effects, 174, 175
  verdict effect, 106–10, 112
emotions, 71, 93–4
empiricism, 18, 146
energy, 116, 132
Engel, Pascal, 74
entry requirements, 185–7, 207
Ernaux, Annie, 52
Esprit, 55, 238
eternal problems, 38, 128, 140–3
eternalisation, 50, 51, 128, 140–3
ethnicity, 37–8, 40, 87–8
ethnologism, 29, 34, 203
ethnology, 7, 12, 16, 29, 33–7, 46, 104, 239; *see also* anthropology

Index

ethnomethodology, 3, 9–11, 13–14, 16, 148, 172, 173, 198, 239
euphemisation, 53, 203
events, 17, 25, 44, 47, 54–5, 59, 63
everyday struggles, 197–8, 219
examinations, 158, 192; *see also* qualifications
exchange economy, 132
exchange rates, 190–2
exclamations, 7
exclusion, 41, 103, 110, 187
exclusivity, 7–8, 160
experience, 9–12, 18, 26–7, 71, 109, 177–82, 189, 223, 234
expertise, 121, 228, 234
explication, 177–82, 189, 198–202

false break, 213–14
false problems, 61, 97–8, 140–3
family, 25, 51, 107–10, 111–13, 166, 193; *see also* kinship
fascism, 13, 179
fashion, 6, 39–40, 91, 127, 142, 148–9
Faulkner, William, 45, 47, 49, 53, 233
fear, 66, 71, 88, 93
femininity, 75–6, 79–80, 82, 86, 104–5
feminisation, 175, 176
feminism, 11, 74, 76, 112
fertility, 42
fetishism, 6–8, 15, 29, 34, 38–40
fidēs, 6, 28–34, 35, 37–8, 87, 113
fields
  academic field, 186–7, 193–4
  administrative field, 187, 191, 194
  artistic field, 3, 16, 38–9, 46, 170–1, 178, 186–90, 194, 202, 209, 231
  autonomous fields, 107, 132–3, 188, 201
  boundaries of, 185–7
  business field, 187, 191, 194
  differentiation of, 130–3
  economic field, 131–3, 134
  field of cultural production, 201, 245
  field of expertise, 228, 234
  field of forces, 1–2, 170–1, 183, 225, 226

  field of power, 2, 128–39, 154–7, 163–9, 183–5, 188–93, 200–2, 227, 235
  field of struggles, 1–2, 127, 170–1, 183, 225, 226
  intellectual field, 3, 134, 186–7, 191, 193–4, 202, 232, 234
  juridical field, 153–4, 158–9, 171, 177–8, 186, 233
  literary field, 16, 46, 187–90, 229, 231
  logic of, 116, 124, 125–8, 142, 153
  political field, 163, 172, 191
  relation to capital, 225–6, 227
  relation to habitus, 1–2, 20–1, 36, 40–1, 58–9, 87, 98, 116, 226
  religious field, 2–3, 131–2, 151, 170, 201
  right of entry, 185–7, 207
  scientific field, 16, 125–8, 134, 141–2, 170–2, 182–3, 197, 205–12
  structure of, 2, 40–1, 128, 171, 201
  transformation of, 170–1, 192, 208–10, 226
Flaubert, Gustave, 24, 54, 55, 81, 103, 163, 188, 189, 231, 232
folk theories, 16, 35
forces, field of, 1–2, 170–1, 183, 225, 226
formalisation, 213
Foucault, Michel, 9, 204, 209, 236, 237
Frankfurt school, 4, 15, 185, 239
free will, 101
freedom, 92, 93, 101–2, 172
Freud, Sigmund, 73, 107, 113, 116
Front National, 240
functionality, 34, 99–100
Fussman, Gérard, 235
future, 31, 64–7, 71, 72, 107, 220

game theory, 143
games
  childhood games, 9, 79
  cumulative and discontinuous play, 65
  feel for the game, 64, 66–7, 92, 118
  and gender, 75–6, 77–82, 103–4, 234
  investment in, 36, 72, 75, 81
  rules of, 9, 36, 60, 132–3, 205

286   *Index*

games (*cont.*)
  and social class, 103–4
  social games, 41, 75–82, 88, 103–4,
    124, 173, 234
  and war, 76, 77–9
  see also play
gate-keepers, 187
gaze, 38, 94, 103
gender
  and bodily behaviour, 95–6
  and the division of labour, 9, 41, 80–5,
    95, 104–5
  and education, 174, 175, 176
  femininity, 75–6, 79–80, 82, 86, 104–5
  feminisation, 175, 176
  and games, 75–6, 77–82, 103–4, 234
  gender relations, 31, 43, 71, 74–85, 98,
    102–4, 227, 234
  and identity, 49, 50
  masculinity, 75–6, 77–82, 85, 104–7,
    234
  and power, 31, 43, 71, 74–6, 80, 83–5,
    98, 102–4, 234
  and socialisation, 41, 79–82, 103
  and violence, 74, 101
Gerschenkron effect, 212–14
Geschichte, 18, 44
giftedness, 4, 167–8, 169
gifts, 132
Glowinski, Jacques, 236
Gödel, Kurt, 216
Goffman, Erving, 124, 158, 173, 198, 240
Gramsci, Antonio, 38, 199, 201
Greek, 28–30
Greek civilisation, 130
grievances, 152–4
group-formation, 220–1
Guattari, Félix, 237

Habermas, Jürgen, 171, 208
habitus
  in Aristotle and scholasticism, 58, 91
  and the body, 88, 89, 97
  changing of, 67–8
  and choice, 92–4
  and determination, 40–2, 70–1, 74

  and freedom, 101
  and individuality, 90–2
  and knowledge, 63–4
  and perception, 63, 88, 171, 226, 227
  relation to capital, 226, 227
  relation to field, 1–2, 20–1, 36, 40–1,
    58–9, 87, 98, 116, 226
  and rules, 58–60
  and sensitivity, 40–2
  structure of, 68
  as system of dispositions, 218–19
  and time, 60–7, 71
  and unity, 19, 20–1
happiness, 12, 33, 84
Haskell, Francis, 236
Hegel, G. W. F., 12, 44, 46, 69, 96–7,
    110, 138, 143, 208
Heidegger, Martin, 62, 88, 93–4, 122,
    123, 213–14
Heraclitus, 150
heresy, 14, 128
heterodoxy, 14
historicism, 141, 183, 203, 204, 210–11,
    212
history, philosophy of, 56, 69, 131–2
homo sociologicus, 239
honour, 45, 77, 82, 96
Hume, David, 18
Husserl, Edmund, 10, 13, 28, 64–5, 154

idealism, 90, 125, 172–3
ideas, history of, 203
identity
  and gender, 49, 50
  legal identity, 50
  multiple identities, 20, 48
  national identity, 25–6, 50
  and nomination, 21–7, 38–9, 47–51, 81
  properties determining, 25–7, 49–50
  unity of the self, 17, 18–21, 24, 26–7,
    50
identity cards, 25–6, 47, 223
ideology, 167–9, 184–5, 201, 222
illusio, 36, 41, 42, 72, 75, 77–9, 80, 87, 88,
    103–4, 205, 226
immigration, 240–1

Index

287

implicitness, 177–82, 199
incompleteness theorems, 216
indeterminacy, 126, 179
individuality, 20–7, 47–51, 70, 89, 90–2, 126, 127, 239
inertia violence, 9
information capital, 227
infra-representational classes, 219–21
inheritance, 81, 157, 161, 168; *see also* succession
injustice, 74, 152
insecurity, 42
instinct, 102, 117, 123
institutionalisation, 227, 230, 232
instrumentalism, 68, 73, 75
insurance, 19, 31
intellectual field, 3, 134, 186–7, 191, 193–4, 202, 232, 234; *see also* academic field
intention, 5, 97
interactionism, 3, 173, 198, 239
interviews, 44, 52–3, 101, 112
intimidation, 88, 90, 95–6, 104, 109, 110
intrusion, 20
investment, 36, 72, 75, 81, 116, 163, 165
irrationalism, 123–4, 160–1

Jews, 38, 98, 187
journalism, 101, 138, 232, 234, 237; *see also* press
Joyce, James, 17, 47
judges, 100, 178
juridical field, 153–4, 158–9, 171, 177–8, 186, 233
juridical neutrality, 159
juridical rights, 162
justice, 100, 138–9, 233

Kabyle society, 9, 23, 77, 82, 95, 104–5
Kadijustiz, 100, 233
Kafka, Franz, 111–13, 232
Kant, Immanuel, 18–19, 45–6, 83–4, 86, 97, 123, 124, 142, 237
Kantianism, 2, 97, 123
Kantorowicz, Ernst, 51
Kautsky, Karl, 201

kinship, 60, 64, 227; *see also* family
knowledge
    acquisition of, 40
    common sense, 16, 52, 56, 145`, 161
    and decision-making, 118–19
    expert knowledge, 121
    feel for the game, 64, 66–7, 118
    and habitus, 63–4
    and practice, 225
    practical knowledge, 64, 66, 121, 122, 124–5, 175
    relation to cognition, 63–4
    scientific knowledge, 22, 126–8
    of the social world, 2, 115, 182
    sociology of, 203
Kojève, Alexandre, 209
kred, 30–4, 35
Kripke, Saul, 22, 24, 48, 74

La Boétie, Etienne de, 68
labour, division of, 9, 41, 80–5, 95, 104–5, 113, 114–15, 117–18, 136, 154–6, 177
Lacan, Jacques, 237
land, 157, 163, 168
language
    and action, 95
    effects of, 95
    and explication, 180
    linearity of, 17
    linguistic capital, 160–1
    mechano-purposive nature of, 70
    and oppositions, 105
    performative language, 228
    philosophy of, 35–6, 47
    political language, 105
Latin, 29–30, 160
law
    and boundary-creation, 186
    customary law, 102
    and the false break, 214
    and imposition of points of view, 152–4
    judges, 100, 178
    juridical field, 153–4, 158–9, 171, 177–8, 186, 233

288 *Index*

law (*cont.*)
juridical neutrality, 159
juridical rights, 162
legal discourse, 182, 214
legal disputes, 73, 152–4
legal identity, 50
legal individuals, 91
and rules, 60
sociology of, 152–4, 233
Lazarsfeld, Paul, 206, 239
Le Monde, 20, 159, 175, 236
Le Roy Ladurie, Emanuel, 235
left-wing politics, 13, 74, 100, 211
legal aid, 162
legal discourse, 182, 214
legal field *see* juridical field
legal identity, 50
legal individuals, 91
legitimacy, 2, 4–5, 7, 130, 135–9, 155–6,
166, 168–9, 191
Lehn, Jean-Marie, 236
Leibniz, Gottfried Wilhelm, 19, 66, 67,
115, 143, 144, 167
Lenin, Vladimir, 126
Lepenies, Wolf, 45
Lévi-Strauss, Claude, 7, 34, 60, 64, 69,
94–5, 147, 235
liberalism, 126, 127, 150
libido, 75, 79, 90, 116; *see also* desire
life stories, 16–18, 23–7, 51–7
linearity, 17, 44–5, 46–7
linguistic capital, 160–1
literary field, 16, 46, 187–90, 229, 231
lived experience *see* experience
logic, 20, 47–9, 69, 211
lost paradise, 12–13, 14
Lukács, Georg, 133

magic, 32, 33–4, 35, 36–7, 94–5, 97, 112
magical capital, 33–4
male domination, 31
Malraux, André, 24, 210
mana, 32, 33, 36, 39
Manet, Edouard, 230, 231
manipulation, 6, 68, 70
Mannheim, Karl, 199, 201

Marin, Louis, 53
markets, 52, 157–9, 160–2, 213
marriage, 60, 83, 163, 164, 165, 219
Marx, Karl, 69, 80, 102, 117, 120, 133,
143, 148, 168, 183, 184, 203, 215,
217, 221, 222
Marxism, 80, 92, 117, 124, 201, 215, 221,
239
masculinity, 75–6, 77–82, 85, 104–6,
234
materialism, 171, 179
Maupassant, Guy de, 44
Mauss, Marcel, 7, 8, 36–7, 39, 94,
131–2
Maxwell's demon, 194–6
May 1968, 13, 147, 184
meaning, 45, 171
mechanism, 60, 63, 64, 69–70, 80, 143–6,
218, 225, 229
medicine, 158–9, 186
Mehan, Hugh, 173–4
memory, 4, 54, 65
mental structures, 11–12, 94–6, 141
Merleau-Ponty, Maurice, 88, 94
methodological individualism, 51, 70,
91–2, 126, 127, 239
militantism, 162, 238
military, 95–6, 136
military power, 136
Miquel, André, 236
miracles, 33, 95
misrecognition, 4–6, 15, 135, 138–9, 155,
168, 180
Mitterand, François, 236, 241
models, 60, 64, 143–4, 217–18
modern art, 230
modernism, 18
monopolies, 158–9, 161, 179, 206, 234
moral philosophy, 19, 123, 124
morality, 131, 162
Morin, François, 134
motive forces, 19, 94, 208–9
Munchausen, 203–4, 208, 210
murder, 111, 112
music, 7, 231
myth, 64, 104–5, 125, 126, 150

narrative, 16–18, 44–7, 61–2
national identity, 25–6, 50
nationalism, 179
natural sciences, 91, 142, 175, 204–5, 213
naturalisation, 168, 169
negotiation, 173–4, 175
neoclassical economics, 176
neo-Kantianism, 2
neoliberalism, 241
neutrality, 159
Nicholas of Cusa, 124–5
Nicole, Eugène, 24–5
Nietzsche, Friedrich, 203
noema, 29
noesis, 28–9
nominalism, 215–16
nomination, 21–7, 38–9, 47–51, 81, 228
nomination effect, 112–13
nomos, 2, 36, 49, 153, 169, 208, 226, 230
norms, 60, 64, 83, 86–7
nostalgia, 12–13, 14, 181, 210
nouveau roman, 16–17, 45, 46–7, 233
Nouvel Observateur, 33, 138
novels, 16–17, 18, 24–5, 27, 44–7, 61–2,
    76–82, 106–10
numerus clausus, 158, 161, 184, 185–7

obedience, 29–30, 31, 70, 96–7, 109
obituaries, 240, 2
objectification, 2, 89, 117–18, 128, 140–2,
    148, 149, 202–4, 210–12, 222–3, 226
objective potentials, 59, 209
objective structures, 11, 94–6, 118, 141,
    146–8, 218
objectivism, 28–32, 89, 96, 125, 127, 142,
    147, 221–4
oppositions, 15, 64, 82, 91–2, 104–5,
    125–8, 141–50, 155–6, 174, 201
order, 41–2, 47, 63
orthodoxy, 13–15, 128, 154
Otto, Rudolf, 38, 98
overproduction, 157–9, 187

paganism, 179
panic, 66, 71
paradise, 12–13, 14

Parmenides, 150
paternal power, 106–10, 111–13
paternalism, 5, 31, 84, 108, 109
peasants, 12, 179
perception
    authorised perception, 234
    categories of, 1–2, 3–5, 7–8, 11
    and habitus, 63, 88, 171, 226, 227
    patterns of, 7, 59, 171, 245
    and power, 4–5, 7–9, 15
    of present and future, 65–7
    social perception, 226, 234
    of the social world, 2, 9–12, 87, 151–2
performative language, 228
Perroux, François, 134
perspectivism, 126
petite bourgeoisie/petit bourgeois, 72–3,
    80, 103
phenomenology, 9–12, 13–14, 65, 109,
    148, 154, 172, 181
philosopher king, 126
photograph albums, 25
Plato, 82, 84, 124, 126, 128, 141, 144,
    215
play, 20, 65, 77–81; *see also* games
pleasure principle, 100, 108
points of view *see* viewpoints
political field, 163, 172, 191
political oppositions, 104–5, 146–50
political power, 136
political representation, 115
political struggles, 128, 167, 182
Pollak, Michael, 206
Ponton, Rémy, 187
populism, 180, 181
positions, 95, 98–101, 170–1, 194, 217–18
positivism, 17, 33, 214
possibilities, space of, 15, 144, 209
possible spaces, 19–20, 22
possible worlds, 24
postmodernism, 237
potestas, 30, 31
power
    and art, 103–4
    balance of, 135, 161, 173, 176, 183,
        191–2, 194, 234

290 *Index*

power (*cont.*)
  and the body, 32–3, 35, 36–7, 75, 90,
    95–6, 104–6, 110–13
  over capital, 133–5
  and charisma, 5, 85, 105–6
  competition for, 129–30, 192
  and culture, 103–4, 136
  desire for, 90, 96, 107
  and the differentiation of fields, 130–2
  distribution of, 133, 161
  economic power, 87, 130, 136
  effects of, 4–8
  and *fidēs*, 28–34
  field of, 2, 128–39, 154–7, 163–9,
    183–5, 188–93, 200–2, 227, 235
  and gender, 31, 43, 71, 74–6, 80, 83–5,
    98, 102–4, 234
  and legitimacy, 4–5, 7, 130, 135–9,
    155–6, 191
  military power, 136
  paternal power, 106–10, 111–13
  and perception, 4–5, 7–9, 15
  political power, 136
  primordial power, 111–13
  realist conception of, 35–6, 129
  reproduction of, 137, 165, 184–5,
    192–4
  and responsibility, 97–8, 103
  and sexuality, 85, 105–6, 107–8
  site of, 5–6, 9–10, 35, 37, 39, 68, 80, 90,
    95, 97–8
  and social class, 103–4, 129, 156
  spiritual power, 131, 136
  struggle for, 129–30, 134
  symbolic power, 4–8, 15, 28–9, 32–6,
    39–42, 87, 90, 94–6, 107–13, 136,
    223, 226
  temporal power, 131, 136, 206
  thrill of, 71, 75
  and truth, 107–10, 112
practical constructions, 177–9, 182
practical knowledge, 64, 66, 121, 122,
  124–5, 175
practical problems, 120
practical struggles, 154, 177, 182,
  197–202

practice
  and knowledge, 225
  relation to theory, 124, 198, 221–2
  theory of, 114–17, 120–1, 123
pre-capitalist societies, 9, 12, 29, 30–1,
  95, 110–11, 132, 226–7; *see also*
  Kabyle society
preconstruction, 16, 22
prediction, 64–7, 107, 109–10
present time, 60–7
press, 35, 137, 138, 159, 175; *see also*
  journalism
priesthood, 34–5, 100
primitive societies *see* pre-capitalist
  societies
primordial power, 111–13
private time, 62
privilege, 76, 79, 80, 82–3, 103, 167–9,
  191
problems
  eternal problems, 38, 128, 140–3
  false problems, 61, 97–8, 140–3
  non-existence of, 119–21, 123
  social problems, 141–3, 150, 175–6
production
  of capital, 37
  of classes, 219
  conditions of, 3, 6, 51–3, 183
  cultural production, 197, 200–2
  overproduction, 157–9, 187
  of qualified people, 157–62, 187
  of representations, 114–15
  see also reproduction
professional explicators, 177–82, 189,
  198–202
progressivism, 21
projection, 64–6, 199
propaganda, 4, 68, 184
proper names, 21–7, 38–9, 47–51, 52, 53,
  228
prophethood, 34–5, 100, 178–9
prosopography, 130
protection, 30–2, 79
protention, 64–6
Proust, Marcel, 12–13, 17, 24–5, 49, 52,
  63, 72–3, 122–3, 163

psychoanalysis, 35–6, 82, 90, 106, 112, 113
psychology, 63, 73, 172
public time, 62
publishing, 52–3, 134, 187
punishment, 19
purposiveness, 44, 70, 143–6, 184, 225, 229
Pygmalion effect, 6, 113

qualifications, 26, 112–13, 157–62, 187, 193

Racine, Jean, 153
racism, 37–8, 87–8, 93–4, 152, 240–1
ranking lists, 231–2, 234, 237
rarity, 7–8, 157–8, 160
rational decision, 117–23, 143–6
rationalisation, 234
rationality, 42, 60–1, 91, 117–25, 143–6, 206–11
reaction, 41, 59–60, 63–4, 69, 73, 144
Reagan, Ronald, 241
real estate, 157, 163
realism, 35–6, 61, 83, 125, 129, 216, 218, 224
reality principle, 83, 100, 108
rebellion, 89, 98, 109–10; *see also* revolution
recognition, 4–8, 15, 135–9, 155–6
recording, 17–18, 27, 51–3, 140–1, 148, 189
relativism, 183, 202–4, 206–10, 212, 216, 237, 239
religion
   affinities with social groups, 179
   Catholicism, 55, 141, 192
   and conservatism, 21
   and education provision, 42
   peasant religion, 179
   priesthood, 34–5, 100
   and progressivism, 21
   prophethood, 34–5, 100
   religious capital, 134
   religious field, 2–3, 131–2, 151, 170, 201

requirement to include on census forms, 26
Renan, Ernest, 204
representation
   and biography, 53
   monopoly of, 179
   political representation, 115
   production of, 114–15, 179–80
   of the social world, 2, 11, 81, 115, 147, 171–3, 179–80, 214–15, 226
representatives, 115
reproduction
   biological, 165, 166
   of capital, 160–2, 164–9, 192–4
   and the education system, 160–2, 166, 168–9, 184–5, 192–4
   new modes of, 192–4
   of power, 137, 165, 184–5, 192–4
   social, 126, 160–2, 169
   strategies of, 116, 164–6, 184, 185, 192–4
responsibility, 6–7, 50, 84, 97–8, 103
retention, 65
revolution, 11, 71, 89, 93–4, 109, 230
right of entry, 185–7, 207
right-wing politics, 14, 159, 168, 211, 241
rites of institution, 22–3, 27, 49–51, 81–2
rites of passage, 22–3, 49, 81
ritual, 23, 50–1, 64
Robbe-Grillet, Alain, 16–17, 47, 233
Roman civilisation, 26, 130
Rousseau, Henri ('Le Douanier'), 20
rules
   and action, 58–60, 68–9, 120
   and decision-making, 120
   following of, 58, 68–9, 74
   of the game, 9, 36, 60, 132–3, 205
   and habitus, 58–60
   of kinship, 60
   and law, 60
Russell, Bertrand, 3, 22
Russia, 213
Ryle, Gilbert, 58, 59, 63, 74

sacredness, 38, 40, 98
Sancho Panza, 233

Sartre, Jean-Paul, 9, 38, 39, 54, 56, 66, 70–1, 75, 89, 93–4, 103, 122, 137, 148, 181, 201, 236–7
Saussure, Ferdinand de, 17, 45
scarcity *see* exclusivity; rarity
scholasticism, 58, 91, 144–5, 217, 220
Schopenhauer, Arthur, 116, 125, 172
Schütz, Alfred, 10, 172
science
  effects of, 205
  history of, 203, 206, 208
  natural sciences, 91, 142, 175, 204–5, 213
  and quality of writing, 45–6
  and relativism, 202–4, 206–10, 237, 239
  science of science, 202–4
  scientific field, 16, 125–8, 134, 141–2, 170–2, 182–3, 197, 205–12
  scientific knowledge, 22, 126–8
  scientific oppositions, 125–8, 146–50
  scientific struggles, 127–8, 183, 219
  scientism, 126, 222
  as social field, 204–6, 211
science fiction, 24
security, 42
Selbstverwirklichung, 208
selection, 195–6
self, unity of, 17, 18–21, 24, 26–7, 50; *see also* identity
self-evidence, 9–13, 14, 141, 186
self-fulfilment effect, 107, 182
self-made man, 4, 163, 164
sensitivity, 40–2, 50, 59, 63, 74
seriousness, 71, 72, 75, 76, 81–2, 89, 93, 103
sexuality, 75, 82, 85, 104–6, 107–8
Shakespeare, William, 45
shock, 66, 68
signatures, 6, 39, 48–9
Simmel, Georg, 239
Simon, Herbert, 118–19, 122
skholè, 144–5, 221
social ageing, 56–7
social art, 188
social capital, 3, 157, 163–4
social class, 103–4, 124, 129, 131,

150, 156, 197, 210, 214–24, 225, 226, 228–9; *see also* bourgeoisie; dominant classes; petit bourgeoisie; working classes
social games, 41, 75–82, 88, 103–4, 124, 173, 234
social norms, 60, 83
social perception, 226, 234
social problems, 141–3, 150, 175–6; *see also* problems
social reproduction, 126, 160–2, 169
social structures, 8–9, 10–12, 95, 110, 146–7
social world
  constructed by social agents, 151–2, 153, 171, 173–4, 176, 223
  experience of, 9–12, 109, 177–82, 189, 223
  explication of, 177–82, 189, 198–202
  knowledge of, 2, 115, 182
  perception of, 2, 9–12, 87, 151–2
  position in, 124
  relationship with the body, 42, 88–90, 94–7
  representation of, 2, 11, 81, 115, 147, 171–3, 179–80, 214–15, 226
  self-evidence of, 9–13, 14
  struggle for legitimate vision of, 2, 154, 167, 171–2, 177–8, 226
socialisation, 8–9, 15, 41, 79–82, 90–2, 96–7, 99, 101, 102, 103, 104, 195, 225
socialised body, 90, 96–7
socialised individuals, 59, 90–2
socialism, 127, 150
sociodicy, 167–9, 191
sociologism, 203, 211, 238
solidarity, 156
Solomon, 233
somatisation, 104, 110–13, 244
sorcerers, 34, 37, 94–5
SOS Racisme, 240–1
space of dominant positions, 194
space of positions, 170–1
space of possibilities, 15, 144, 209–10
space of standpoints, 125, 170–1

Index

spatiality
  possible spaces, 19–20, 22
  spatial unity, 19–21, 24, 50
  and trajectories, 54–7
specialisation, 2–3, 177–8, 181, 197
specific capital, 134, 201, 206
specificity, 182–3, 193, 197, 206
speech bubbles, 61–2
Spencer, Herbert, 131
Spinoza, Baruch, 116, 208
spiritual power, 131, 136
spokespersons, 100–1, 189, 224
spontaneism, 126, 147, 148
sport metaphors, 33, 64, 89, 123, 205
stability, 162–4
standpoints, 15, 104, 125, 147–8, 170–1, 176, 192
State, the, 26, 70, 154, 157–8, 160–4, 228, 234, 240–1
statistics, 22, 51, 176, 185
statues, 8, 137
status groups, 220
stigmatisation, 37–8, 40, 113
stimulus, 41, 59, 63, 69
stratification, 131, 158
structuralism, 60, 64, 125, 142, 146–50, 174, 197, 223, 226, 239
structure
  bodily structures, 12
  of capital, 163, 167, 217–18
  changes in structure, 151, 171, 174
  cognitive structures, 2, 11–12
  of the field, 2, 40–1, 128, 171, 201
  of the habitus, 68
  mental structures, 11–12, 94–6, 141
  narrative structure, 16–17
  objective structures, 11, 94–6, 118, 141, 146–8, 218
  practical mastery of, 150–2
  social structures, 8–9, 10–12, 95, 110, 146–7
struggles
  cognitive struggles, 154, 174–7
  everyday struggles, 197–8, 219
  field of, 1–2, 127, 170–1, 183, 225, 226

for legitimate vision of the world, 2, 154, 167, 171–2, 177–8, 226
logic of, 127
political struggles, 128, 167, 182
for power, 129–30, 134
practical struggles, 154, 177, 182, 197–202
of professional explicators, 198–202
scientific struggles, 127–8, 183, 219
symbolic struggles, 3, 174–5, 226, 234
theoretical, 182, 197–9, 202
subjectivism, 28–32, 38–9, 71, 89, 90, 93–4, 96, 98, 125, 127, 142, 172–3, 212
submission, 5, 12, 68, 72, 74, 85, 102, 107
succession, 23, 81, 130, 157, 161, 165, 166, 168, 185; *see also* inheritance
supporters, 32
symbolic action, 95
symbolic capital, 3–5, 7, 23, 28–9, 34–40, 43, 63–4, 87, 223, 226
symbolic effects, 4, 7–8, 36, 182
symbolic power, 4–8, 15, 28–9, 32–6, 39–42, 87, 90, 94–6, 107–13, 136, 223, 226
symbolic revolutions, 11
symbolic struggles, 3, 174–5, 226, 234
symbolic violence, 4
Syndicat de la magistrature, 159

taste, 7–8
taxation, 26, 161
television, 52, 101, 235
temporal power, 131, 136, 206
temporality
  calendars, 62
  chronological time, 44–5, 54
  future, 31, 64–7, 71, 72, 107, 220
  and habitus, 60–7, 71
  present, 60–7
  public and private time, 62
  subjective and objective time, 67
  temporal unity, 17, 18–19, 24, 50
  temporalisation, 65, 72
Temps Modernes, 55

294 *Index*

Thatcher, Margaret, 241
theodicy, 167, 169
theoretical constructions, 23–4, 124, 166, 177–8, 182
theoretical practice, 199
theoretical struggles, 182, 197–9, 202
threshold effects, 174, 175
Thuillier, Jacques, 235
To the Lighthouse (Woolf), 41, 54–5, 61–2, 66, 71, 74–82, 106–10, 112, 232, 234
totalisation, 24, 47, 49–50, 133
trade unions, 99, 159, 236
tradition, 14, 43
trajectories, 16, 47, 54–7, 195
transcendence, 34, 172
transcendentalism, 60, 88, 123, 137, 171–2, 210
traps, 74–6, 78–80, 103
Troeltsch, Ernst, 141
trust, 29–34
truth, 6, 38, 107–10, 112, 124, 128, 171–2, 183, 202, 204, 206–7, 210–12, 219

unconscious, 35, 42, 43–4, 60, 64, 67, 82, 176–7, 181, 196
unemployment, 152, 240
United States, 19, 25–6, 35, 73, 84, 148, 152, 158, 161–2, 238–9, 241
unity
  and habitus, 19, 20–1
  of the self, 17, 18–21, 24, 26–7, 50
  spatial unity, 19–21, 24, 50
  temporal unity, 17, 18–19, 24, 50
universality, 168, 202

universals, 215–16, 219
utopianism, 40, 205

validation, 204–5, 214–15
values, 98, 160, 162, 186
Van Gennep, Arnold, 81
verdict effect, 106–10, 112
viewpoints, 53, 152–4, 172
violence
  domestic violence, 74, 101
  inertia violence, 9
  monopoly of legitimate violence, 234
  physical violence, 3–4, 74
  symbolic violence, 4
virility, 81–2, 95–6, 107, 175
vis formae, 233
voluntarism, 38
voluntary servitude, 68, 72
vulnerability, 210–14, 232

war, 76, 77–9, 83, 85, 96, 105, 152; *see also* conflict
Weber, Max, 5, 32–5, 59, 100, 104–5, 132–3, 143, 167, 169, 178, 179, 203, 220, 233–4
welfare state, 241
Who's Who, 25, 35, 47
Wittgenstein, Ludwig, 58, 68–9, 70, 74, 105, 214
Woolf, Virginia, 17, 18, 41, 43, 47, 54–5, 61–3, 66, 71, 76–82, 106–10, 112, 232, 234
working classes, 179–80

Ziff, Paul, 22–3, 48, 69